Springer Series
FOCUS ON MEN

James Hennessy, Ph.D., Series Editor

Focus on Men provides a wide range of books on the major psychological, medical, and social issues confronting men today.

VOLUME 1
CIRCUMCISION
An American Health Fallacy
Edward Wallerstein

Edward Wallerstein is now retired after a 40-year career as a business executive, industrial engineer, and researcher in diverse fields—television, marketing, sociology, economics, education, and health. An innovator in the social application of technology, his cable television invention has been used since 1967. He designed and supervised the first New York City public school multimedia systems, the first bidirectional television system for pediatrics, and the first in-house television system for geriatrics. For five years he was Communications Coordinator in the Department of Community Medicine at the Mount Sinai School of Medicine, New York City, where his activities in the application of telecommunications ranged from patient education and self-help to postgraduate medical education. In each of his activities he has published, lectured, and traveled extensively. As a health consumer activist, this book reflects his conviction that the recipients of health care can and should question medical opinion.

CIRCUMCISION:
An American Health Fallacy

Edward Wallerstein

Springer Publishing Company
New York

Copyright © 1980 by Edward Wallerstein

All rights reserved

No part of this publication may be reproduced, stored in a retrieval system, or transmitted in any form or by any means, electronic, mechanical, photocopying, recording, or otherwise, without the prior permission of the copyright holder.

Springer Publishing Company, Inc.
200 Park Avenue South
New York, New York 10003

80 81 82 83 84 / 10 9 8 7 6 5 4 3 2 1

Library of Congress Cataloging in Publication Data

Wallerstein, Edward.
   Circumcision: an American health fallacy.

  (Springer series, focus on men ; 1)
  Includes bibliographical references and index.
  1. Circumcision. 2. Circumcision—Social aspects.
I. Title. II. Series. [DNLM: 1. Circumcision.
W1 SP685K v. 1 / WJ790 W198c]
RD 590.W34 617'.463 80-13878
ISBN 0-8261-3240-5
ISBN 0-8261-3241-3 (pbk.)

Printed in the United States of America

This book is dedicated to:

• those health providers who have already disavowed the necessity of routine newborn circumcision; and to

• the health providers who still encourage or accept the practice of routine circumcision, in the hope that they will reexamine their approach; and

• most important, to the health consumers who always have an obligation to question their health providers, never hesitating to question their answers.

Contents

Foreword 1 by Aubre de L. Maynard, M.D., F.A.C.S.   *ix*
Foreword 2 by Nicholas Cunningham, M.D., D.T.P.H., Dr. P.H.   *xiii*
Preface   *xvii*
Acknowledgments   *xix*

1. Questions to Answer; Answers to Question   *1*
2. The Circumcision Mystique   *6*
3. The Medical Mystique   *15*
4. Why Only in the United States?   *26*
5. The Circumcision Decision: Is It Informed Consent?   *41*
6. The Ill-fated Foreskin: Is It All Bad?   *52*
7. Therapeutic Circumcision: The Tight Foreskin   *62*
8. Penile Hygiene   *67*
9. Circumcision and Venereal Disease   *80*

10 Circumcision and Cancer   88
11 Circumcision and Premature Ejaculation   115
12 Circumcision and Masturbation   122
13 If Later, Why Not Now?   127
14 Pain and Psychological Trauma   135
15 Circumcision Risk   145
16 Jews and Circumcision   154
17 Female Circumcision   164
18 An Appeal to Reason   191
Appendix A   What Is Circumcision?   198
Appendix B   The Circumcision Frequency Rate   214
Appendix C   The American College of Obstetricians and Gynecologists (ACOG) Position on Circumcision   218
Notes to Chapters   219
Glossary   261
Indexes   265

Foreword / 1

By Dr. Aubre de L. Maynard

This book should achieve recognition as the most comprehensive and informative document that has as yet surfaced on the controversial subject of circumcision. The author, a layman, has researched the problem with thoroughness and distinction, and for those who have an interest in this ancient and almost ubiquitous practice, extensive notes giving sources both pro and con, have been appended. Mr. Wallerstein admits to bias against a practice which, in this country, has been carried to the point of abuse, as seen in current statistics, which show an inordinately high incidence of neonatal circumcisions in the United States as compared with the extremely low incidence in England and the Scandinavian countries. The revelation that about 85% of all American newborn males are circumcised is indeed startling, and certainly promotes the impression that the practice is routine, nonselective, and something of a salable service. More than all else, it is the almost total and indiscriminate use of circumcision that Mr. Wallerstein deplores. It soon becomes evident that his arguments are credible and suggest we reconsider the prolific use of circumcision in the United States.

Circumcision has been with us from time immemorial. Carried out in crude fashion and not without danger by primitive man, it has endured to the present, with techniques appropriate to our surgical progress and sophistication. It has remained obligatory ritual for Moslems and Jews as dictated by their religion, but it long ago invaded Christian precincts, becoming pervasive for other and sundry reasons.

In the last decade of the 19th century, it loomed importantly as a panacea for certain psychologic disturbances and nervous ailments allegedly linked to sexuality. Circumcision was conceived as a deterrent to masturbation, which was at the time considered a vitiating and physically harmful practice. Even female circumcision came into vogue. Involving removal of the hood of the labia minora covering the clitoris and excision of the clitoris itself, it was performed on prostitutes and "nymphomaniacs" to save them from the abyss of sexual promiscuity and degradation. These ridiculous indications for circumcision did not survive for long. Male circumcision, however, continued triumphantly as a valid therapeutic procedure for phimosis, and as a prophylactic against venereal disease and other infections that might cause balanitis (infection of the glans penis). Last and not least it was espoused as an hygienic measure.

From what has been now stated, it can be appreciated that in its course throughout the years, indications for circumcision have originated both in reality and in fantasy. If we assume that ours is an age of reason and enlightenment, it is time that the rationale for circumcision be clearly established and adhered to, exclusive of its acceptance as religious ritual.

As a physician, I recognize certain legitimate reasons for circumcisions:

1. When the preputial opening is so small that obstruction to urination occurs. Incident to this the preputial sac, the space between the prepuce (or foreskin) and the glans, distended with urine, may become enlarged. The valid treatment is circumcision.
2. Phimosis. This most common congenital anomaly of the penis is characterized by an inability to retract the prepuce over the glans. This leads to the collection of smegma, a cheesy, slightly malodorous material, the secretion of sebaceous glands, which collects between the glans and the prepuce in the male (and between the clitoris and labia minora in the female). In the male, if the foreskin can be drawn back over the glans only partially and remains so without change over a prolonged period of observation, circumcision is not only prudent, but becomes an obligatory measure. However, a study made by Gairdner in England of 100 newborn males found that only 4% had a fully retractable foreskin at birth.* At the age of 3 years, only 10% of them still had a nonretractable foreskin. Evidently, the foreskin in the vast majority of infants becomes fully retractable with time, and certainly in the majority does not require elective circumcision as a routine after birth.

The Gairdner study permitted the National Health Service of England to prohibit elective circumcisions on the newborn until it was clear that full retractability of the prepuce, in due time as the child got older, had not and would probably not occur, interfering with penile hygiene and offering the possibility of complications due to retained smegma. From Gairdner's findings, which later were confirmed by Øster,** one may conclude that there is no need for precipitate haste in circumcising the newborn. And also, can anyone preclude adverse effects on the infant's psyche from this initial traumatic painful experience?

---

*Douglas Gairdner, "The Fate of the Foreskin," *British Medical Journal*, vol. 2, Dec. 24, 1949, pp. 1433-1437.

**Jacob Øster, "Further Fate of the Foreskin," *Archives of Diseases of Childhood*, vol. 43, no. 228, April, 1968, pp. 200-203.

Since smegma has been alleged but not proven to contain material which is carcinogenic for animals, it is presumed that phimosis of any degree, with retention of smegma, has the potential for initiating penile carcinoma. Anent this, it has been claimed that circumcised males never develop penile carcinoma; and that carcinoma develops only in the uncircumcised male. Even if this were true, the answer to that is simple, namely, the maintenance of penile hygiene with soap and water as the cleansing agents. It is quite likely that the foreskin has a function in relation to the glans, probably as to sexual sensitivity, and should be retained as long as it can be fully retracted.

I congratulate Edward Wallerstein for a magnificent effort on a subject of importance that few people give serious thought to and merely accept as a matter of course on their doctor's advice. The pendulum is now swinging back to the reexamination of a procedure imposed on a vast number of Americans who had no choice in the matter. I therefore recommend this book highly because of the excellence of its substance and because it makes for facile reading on a medical topic for the layman.

—Aubre de L. Maynard, M.D., F.A.C.S.
March, 1979

Note: Dr. Maynard received his M.D. degree from New York University and was associated with Harlem Hospital throughout his professional career—a span of 41 years. He started as an intern in 1926 and became Director of Surgery in 1952, a post he held until his retirement in 1967. From 1962–67 he was Clinical Professor of Surgery, College of Physicians and Surgeons, Columbia University; he is now Clinical Professor of Surgery Emeritus.

He is a diplomate of the American Board of Surgery and a Fellow of the American College of Surgeons. In addition to being a Trustee of the New York Academy of Medicine, he is a Membre Titulaire of the Societe International de Chirurgie, and an Affiliate Fellow of the Royal Society of Medicine (London). He has lectured in over a dozen foreign countries and was the recipient of many honors for his innovative work in surgery.

He is author or co-author of 52 articles, and author or co-author of chapters on operative techniques in five books. In 1978 Appleton-Century-Crofts published his book, *Surgeons to the Poor—The Harlem Hospital Study*.

Foreword 2

By Dr. Nicholas Cunningham

Circumcision is probably an idea whose time has gone. Ritualistically, it means something; medically, it doesn't seem to make much sense. Thus, as a pediatrician, I say bravo to Ed Wallerstein, a layman who has finally focused a bright light on the hoary traditions, unfounded fears, and silly science that has left the United States as the only developed country where newborns are routinely circumcised for nonreligious reasons. What amazes Mr. Wallerstein is that American physicians, supposedly trained in the scientific method, have been so reluctant to assess the rationale for this unique example of surgical prophylaxis. In fact, most readers will be amazed by the contents of this book, but they will also be impressed.

There are three reasons why this book is important:

1. The timing is right. Circumcision is presently the most frequently performed operation in this country, and almost everyone except surgeons would like to cut down on unnecessary surgery. Eliminating routine newborn circumcisions would preserve an apparently useful part of the human body, improve the quality of the newborns' first days of life, cut hospital costs by about $50 million a year* and save the intern (or medical student or nurse) the nuisance of performing a tedious ritual for which the only interesting outcome is a complication. In fact, the main reason more infant boys don't get circumcisions today is that everyone in the hospital is tired of doing them!
2. The arguments are convincing. Mr. Wallerstein uses such a judicious mix of overwhelming evidence, intelligent reasoning, common sense, and *reductio ad absurdum* that the book is bound to impress a society always interested in both sex and self-criticism.

3. The book speaks for children. While Mr. Wallerstein doesn't stress it, the children's rights movement is just coming of age and what we are doing to our infant sons (consent or no consent) is little short of child abuse. Can you imagine what one good law suit on behalf of a lost foreskin would do today?

The book should have a major impact, and the fact that it was written by a nonmedical person and a Jew is all to the good.

But besides being topical and convincing, this study is fascinating to read. Mr. Wallerstein's review of Victorian theories about the conservation of sexual energy, his remarks on syphilophobia and racism, and his descriptions of the variety of diagnostic dogs this particular tail has wagged are amazing and revealing. He wields a sharp knife himself in dissecting the data presented by epidemiologists and showing how, by ignoring secular trends and socioeconomic factors, they have attributed cause and effect to all sorts of associations between foreskins and sexual prowess, cancer, and V.D.

Nevertheless, in defense of pediatrics, we did finally wake up. Yes, the eminent Emmett Holt, author of the first (1897) edition of *Pediatrics* and professor at Babies Hospital in New York, did subscribe to the same nonsense about phimosis, chorea, convulsions, epilepsy, strabismus, etc. as did his contemporaries. Not only that, but he and the great Jacobi both recommended not only circumcision but also corporal punishment and tying children's arms and legs as cures for masturbation. Since then, his successors at Babies and as editors of *Pediatrics* have moved slowly but steadily toward a more objective approach. Dr. Herbert Wilcox, head of Babies in the 1920s scolded my mother for letting her first son be routinely circumcised at another hospital in 1921. By 1933, *Pediatrics* recommended restraints but no punishment for masturbation, which was now seen as the result and not the cause of "nervous" conditions. By 1940 restraints were out, masturbation was no longer harmful, and was seen as unrelated to phimosis; circumcision was only recommended for a "very long" foreskin. By 1962, despite the controversy concerning penile and cervical cancer, the only indication for circumcision was difficulty in passing urine. Yet despite the pediatricians' reservations, culminating in the 1975 Academy of Pediatrics position ("no valid medical indication for circumcision in the neonatal period"), the operation continues to be performed regularly in most hospitals including Babies.

Perhaps the best we pediatricians can do now is to follow Mr. Wallerstein's recommendations about informed consent. Surely once the subject is out in the open (which it will be after this book is published), and parents are adequately informed about the potential problems, they will think twice before signing consent. Mr. Wallerstein mentioned a number of problems, but Dr. George W. Kaplan, a pediatric urologist who has had to repair a number of the disasters resulting from circumcision, has recently listed the dangers and complications.* These include bleeding (even the Talmud warns about this and suggests postponing the operation if previous sons have bled), phimosis (from the surgery), concealed penis (from taking off too much in a fat child), chordee (and other distortions of the penis), meatitis and glans ulcers (estimated to occur after 8% of circumcisions), and meatal stenosis (common in circumcised adults, rare in the uncircumcised). Infection has been found to occur in 8% of babies in one study, and circumcision is an important, avoidable cause of neonatal septicaemia, which can be fatal. Loss of the glans (or the entire penis from an electrocautery touching a Gomco clamp) is fortunately rare.

In sum, Mr. Wallerstein has done us and our children a great service in spelling out loudly and clearly what a wise pediatrician, Sir James Spence,** pointed out in *The Lancet* in 1964: that when it comes to the sexual organs, we should leave nature alone.

—Nicholas Cunningham, M.D., D.T.P.H., Dr. P.H.

*George W. Kaplan, *Current Problems in Pediatrics*, vol. 7, no. 5, March 1977, pp. 3-31.

**J. Spence, *Lancet*, vol. 2, 1964, p. 902.

Note: Dr. Cunningham received his M.D. degree in 1955 from Johns Hopkins University Medical School and became a Diplomate in Tropical Public Health (D.T.P.H.) in 1965 at the London School of Hygiene and Tropical Medicine. He received his Doctorate in Public Health (Dr.P.H.) from the Johns Hopkins School of Hygiene in 1977.

After pediatric residencies in Los Angeles and New York City, he was a National Institutes of Health Post-Doctoral Fellow in Neonatal Physiology at the Sloane Hospital, Columbia Presbyterian Medical Center. Later, at the Johns Hopkins School of Hygiene and Public Health, he was a special fellow in international health, a resident in preventive medicine, research associate, and lecturer.

He served with the United States Public Health Service Indian Health Centers in Arizona, and as a medical consultant to the U.S. Peace Corps. He has worked in Togo, West Africa and in Ilesha and Lagos, Nigeria.

From 1969-1977 he was Assistant Professor, Departments of Community Medicine and Pediatrics at the Mount Sinai School of Medicine and Assistant Attending Pediatrician at the Mount Sinai Hospital. Since 1977, he is Associate Professor, Departments of Pediatrics and Public Health, Columbia College of Physicians and Surgeons.

Preface

A book on circumcision seems unnecessary. Everyone knows that the surgery is good for the child; that is why it is practiced by enlightened people all over the world. I thought so too.

In the predominantly Jewish community in which I was raised, circumcision was accepted as the normal, natural thing to do. There was also pride in the knowledge that many Christians followed the example of Jews. Obviously circumcision was the wise course to follow.

When our son was born in the mid-1940s, my wife and I—"informed" health consumers—queried our obstetrician about circumcision. He was highly experienced; a chief of obstetrics at one hospital and an attending physician at two others; a Fellow of the American College of Surgeons; above all, our friend. He was taken aback by the question and rattled off a list of reasons for the surgery. We were convinced.

For many years thereafter, when the question arose in discussion, we would rattle off the same answers, with much assurance. After all, we were "authorities," taught by a master. Moreover, when anyone doubted us, we almost always felt that there might be an element of anti-Semitism in the very questioning of circumcision. We were so wrong.

The subject remained dormant for some 20 years until a young couple we know described their anxiety when they had to make a circumcision decision for their son the previous year. They had attended a birth class taught by 3 obstetricians; one was strongly pro-circumcision; one was equally vehement in opposition, and the third said it made no difference, therefore, the parents should decide.

This was incredible to us. Why would physicians either oppose circumcision or say it made no difference when "everyone" knew it was good for the child? My interest piqued, I sought answers at the local branch of the

New York Public Library. There I found one book on the subject, written in 1891. The historical material was interesting but the medical information was obviously outdated. Nevertheless the book was reprinted in 1974. The main reference and research branch libraries provided little additional information. Two other books by Americans were located—one by a free-thinker, the other by a physician. Both were passionately anti-circumcision, but were written with such bias and obvious error as to be totally without merit. The thought occurred to me that since the subject was medical, the books I sought might be found only in medical libraries. A search of such libraries revealed hundreds of articles on the subject, but not one additional book.

Was it possible that there was no up-to-date, carefully reasoned book on circumcision for either the medical profession or for prospective parents? In 1973 a well-qualified urologist published a book on circumcision. Here, perhaps, was the answer I was seeking. Upon reading it, however, I found that it, too, was so cluttered with factual errors, distortions, and statistical blunders that it could not be taken seriously.

After a dozen years of research, I found that no book on circumcision clearly defined the issues and presented substantiating data in an objective manner. I therefore became convinced that there was a need for a book which detailed the background and the rationale for and against circumcision.

It might be argued that the subject of circumcision is so simple that it is not necessary to devote a whole book to it; all pertinent information could be contained in one article. To explore this possibility, a review of the medical literature was undertaken, first the articles written from 1950 on, and then back to the early 19th century. No article was found which even began to cover all of the issues completely or convincingly. Instead, there was often intense subjective debate. A similar search of popular magazines from 1900 on revealed a reflection of the medical confusion; there was little independent thinking and much uncertainty. The subject matter is neither difficult nor complex. In my book, statistical data have been kept to a minimum. They will largely be found in the Notes sections, not the text.

Before researching this book, I considered myself reasonably well informed on the subject of circumcision. Actually, my knowledge was minuscule. Moreover, during the past 10 years I have discussed circumcision with hundreds of individuals—from well-trained medical specialists to unschooled lay persons. I was appalled not only at the lack of information, but also the plethora of misinformation and myths that are prevalent. The need for knowledge is obvious. It is my hope that this book will begin to fill this information gap.

Acknowledgments

Many individuals contributed to this book, and sincere thanks are due to them. Several graduate students helped to gather research material. Millicentrae Yates read the numerous drafts; her eagle eye and phenomenal memory were invaluable.

Various physicians including a surgeon, a pediatrician, an internist, psychiatrists, a urologist, and a neonatologist, who is also a member of the Milah Board, and other health professionals, among them a nurse, midwife, dentists, psychotherapists, and medical and psychiatric social workers read the manuscript. Each of the readers made valuable criticisms and suggestions that were incorporated into the final draft. Opinions, attitudes, and knowledge were sought from parents, parents-to-be, feminists, friends, and friends of friends—too numerous to list.

Two other individuals deserve special thanks—Judy Norsigian, one of the authors of *Our Bodies Ourselves*, and Doris Haire, president of the American Foundation for Maternal and Child Health. They helped to convince me of the need for such a book and encouraged my efforts.

Above all, thanks are due to my family who endured seemingly endless discussions of circumcision. Les and Anne, my son and daughter-in-law, read and reread the many manuscript drafts. Flo, my wife of 40 years, a professional social worker, bore the tensions that accompany the years of labor that went into the writing of this book. Her evenness of keel helped me to retain a steady balance and, more importantly, her sharp wit and wisdom made it possible for her to serve as a sounding board for ideas. Her objectivity, from great praise to sharp criticism, was always creative and helpful. The knowledge and skills she brought to this book were based upon decades of varied work experience, most relevant of which were the years spent in hospital social work, including pediatric, psychiatric, and surgical specialties.

1

Questions to Answer; Answers to Question

During the past year, more than 1¼ million American males underwent surgery—without anesthesia—within the first few days after birth. The operation was circumcision, the cutting off of the foreskin, the sleeve of flesh which covers the head or glans of the penis. (See Appendix A for descriptions and illustrations of the surgery.) This volume of surgery makes it not only the most frequently performed elective operation, but also the only one done on an almost routine basis. It is performed on about 9 out of every 10 newborn males.

This surgery to the newborn is a uniquely American medical phenomenon. No other country follows this practice, except where the operation is a religious ritual or puberty rite.

Early in the 20th century, all English-speaking countries began to practice newborn circumcision, although none did it to the same degree as the United States did. Since the 1950s, the incidence of its performance in Canada and Australia has diminished and in England it has been almost totally abandoned.

Scientists have expressed wonder at the acceptance of newborn circumcision by English-speaking countries and the continuation of the practice only in the United States. No one has attempted to explain this strange state of affairs.

This American practice would make sense if it could be demonstrated that this country's newborns have a genetic foreskin defect necessitating its immediate removal. But this is a ridiculous notion; a penis is a penis, regardless of country of origin. Why then are American newborns singled out as candidates for penile surgery?

It was not always so. American circumcision practice did not come over on the Mayflower. First introduced a century ago, circumcision was the "wonder drug" of American medicine. Physicians advocated the surgery to prevent or cure a laundry list of physical or emotional ailments—from asthma to epilepsy to tuberculosis and a hundred other diseases in between. Given such "facts," how could physicians not recommend and parents not agree to the surgery?

It took many decades for medical science to demonstrate the true origins of the many problems allegedly caused by foreskin retention. Despite the diminution of the long list of claimed benefits, the frequency of circumcision increased unabated. Today the operation is actively endorsed or passively accepted by most Americans, physicians as well as lay people, and is more popular now than ever before.

There are many reasons why most American parents want their sons circumcised. Some reasons are clearly erroneous, e.g., the mistaken belief that it is hospital policy or mandated by law. Other reasons fall into two basic categories: personal and health reasons. Among the personal reasons are the social pressures—"everybody does it"; also the desire for the boy to be similar in appearance to his father, siblings, and peers. For some the reason may be cosmetic: "It looks better." For others the reason may be religious. These parental reasons are both private and personal. Within the context of our culture, no physician would dissuade parents from such practice unless the surgery is life-threatening. In such cases, it can be postponed until the child is well enough to sustain the operation. Many American parents would deny that their opting for circumcision is based upon "personal" reasons. Most parents and physicians accept the health reasons, such as:

1. *A tight or very long foreskin.* In the newborn it may not be possible to pull the foreskin back to expose the glans. This condition is said to be pathological, and if not promptly corrected by circumcision, is believed to lead to dire consequences. This is therapeutic circumcision to correct a "defect." All other reasons are prophylactic, to prevent a future problem.
2. *Penile hygiene.* The penis in its natural state is said to be difficult to keep clean. Circumcision eliminates the problem of penile hygiene.
3. *Venereal disease.* A circumcised male is believed to be less likely to contract venereal disease.
4. *Cancer.* It is claimed that circumcision prevents prostatic and penile cancer in males and cervical cancer in their sexual partners.
5. *Improved sexuality.* Circumcision is said to prevent or reduce premature ejaculation.
6. *Masturbation.* Circumcision is believed to reduce the incidence of masturbation.

Parents are told that the operation is simple, relatively painless, and without risk, and that foregoing the surgery may simply be postponing it until later in life.

Most surgery to any part of the body is performed for therapeutic purposes—to correct a structural or functional defect. American physicians maintain that in many instances the newborn foreskin is too tight (or too long), therefore, it is necessary to remove it immediately. Isn't it strange that such newborn penile "defects" are virtually never found in other countries?

Although "therapeutic" factors account for much of the newborn circumcision surgery, the major reason is prophylactic. That is, admittedly there is nothing wrong with the foreskin, but the operation is recommended to prevent future health problems.

Circumcision is the only surgery performed for prophylactic purposes. It would be unthinkable and unpardonable to remove any body tissue or organ on the grounds that it *may* be a source of problem in the future. Nevertheless, these are formidable circumcision claims. They cannot be ignored or taken lightly, since their wide dissemination and acceptance account for the high circumcision rate in this country. Isn't it strange that foreign physicians are not equally concerned about correcting defective foreskins or preventing a host of health problems?

Although the majority of American physicians steadfastly hold to the correctness of therapeutic or prophylactic circumcision, an increasing number of physicians now question the practice. Not only are the claimed benefits said to be unsubstantiated, but they are also based upon false and sometimes fabricated data. The so-called tight or overly long foreskin theory is scoffed at; these conditions are natural and normal, rarely pathological. Moreover, it is accepted medical knowledge that there is an element of danger in any surgery—including circumcision. Life-threatening infection, hemorrhage, and injury are not rare; mutilations do occur, even an occasional death. The surgery may be physically or emotionally traumatic and removing erogenous tissue may actually inhibit, not enhance, sexual functioning. Most American physicians, while acknowledging occasional mishaps, reject the anti-circumcision claims as specious and unsubstantiated.

The pro- and anti-circumcision arguments are not new; the issue has been debated in the American medical press for at least 20 years. Because of the confusion, the American Academy of Pediatrics established a Task Force on Circumcision, which recommended in 1975 that newborn circumcision should *not* be performed routinely. The Pediatric Urologists Association also came to the same conclusion. Dr. Benjamin Spock, probably the best-known American pediatrician, supported routine circumcision in 1946 but strongly opposed it in 1976.

None of these (and other) pronouncements evoked a full discussion in either the medical or lay press. A few popular publications provided one-shot, brief reports, often too brief and sometimes distorted. Follow-up discussion was rarely encouraged; when discussion was encouraged, there was an outpouring of reader comments, attesting to interest and the desire for information.

Anti-circumcision articles in medical journals evoked hostile reactions sometimes bordering on hysteria. It is this hysterical reaction that accounts, in part, for the fact that rational critiques of the practice have not changed the attitude of wide acceptance in the United States. The American attitude is best described by the old wisecrack: "My mind is already made up. Do not confuse me with the facts."

But what are the facts? Is it possible that after thousands of years and hundreds of millions of operations, the facts are not known? No other surgery has such a track record; thus data gathering and analysis should not be difficult. There should not be confusion and doubt.

Both the pro and anti-circumcision claims cannot be valid. It is also illogical that other countries have not adopted the practice, if the arguments in favor of circumcision are correct. And why should the practice prevail in the United States if the claims are not valid?

If physicians are at odds about circumcision benefits, how can there be clarity among parents-to-be? Parents want to do what is best for their child, but what is the best course to follow?

In essence the problem resolves itself to this: If circumcision is good for the child, it should be done. If it is not good for the child, it should not be done. If it really makes no difference, why subject the child to unnecessary surgery? To subject a newborn to painful surgery requires a strong conviction on the part of physicians that this is the correct course to follow. Parents, conditioned by the attitude that "the doctor knows best," will usually accept their physician's judgment. Since almost 90% of all American newborn males are circumcised, this is ample evidence of the intensity of physician attitude and parental acquiescence.

However, regardless of the reasons given, several studies have shown that many Americans do not know what circumcision actually involves or why it is done. Other studies have revealed that a large percentage of women did not know whether or not their marital partners were circumcised. Even more startling was the finding that a high percentage of men were found to be in error about their own circumcision status. This ignorance has been acknowledged and decried, but not corrected; witness the absence of a comprehensive study by a physician or nonphysician, either for the health professional or health consumer. Given such lack of knowledge, many parents cannot make a rational decision for their child. They may give consent, but is it "informed" consent?

Not surprisingly, the present popularity of male circumcision has begun to carry over to females—only in the United States. After all, if the male operation improves sexual functioning, why shouldn't the female operation accomplish similar goals? This line of reasoning has led some physicians to endorse removal of the clitoral foreskin, not routinely, nor in infancy, but in adulthood to enhance orgasmic response. The rationale is unclear and the supporting "research" has not been carefully scrutinized. Yet the surgery marches on.

There appears to be a dilemma between medical theory and practice in regard to circumcision. Twenty-five years ago, it was rare to find an anti-circumcision article in the medical press. Since then, editors of medical journals have made impassioned pleas for objectivity and research. In the past decade, articles on the subject are more likely than not to be critical of one or all aspects of the practice; most express doubt and caution; few defend it outright. Yet the surgery continues with undiminished zeal. When tonsillectomy was questioned as often unnecessary, the incidence of its performance diminished; not so with circumcision. The reason for this dilemma will not be found in scientific rationale, but in the unique nature of circumcision. Unlike any other surgery, circumcision, in addition to being employed therapeutically and prophylactically, is heavily laden with sexual, religious, cultural, and social overtones. It is therefore difficult to obtain an objective analysis of the value of the practice.

The claimed advantages and disadvantages are clearly stated. The problem is to examine the evidence offered to prove or disprove the claims; that is the overall objective of this book. The concern is with therapeutic and prophylactic circumcision; religious and cosmetic aspects are not within the purview of this volume. Moreover, a discussion of the claims and counterclaims is not sufficient. It is also necessary to understand the history of circumcision to appreciate just how Americans have arrived at the present stage of acceptance. The origins of circumcision are relatively unimportant to this discussion. What is important is the intense mystique about this surgery, which developed in many parts of the world. When circumcision was introduced into the United States, the mystique as well as the surgery were accepted. Ordinarily this would simply make interesting history; unfortunately this mystique invaded American medicine and persists to this day.

2
The Circumcision Mystique

Long before recorded history, human beings were altering their body structures, and presenting altered representations of the body in their art. European sculptures from the Ice Age, 30,000 years ago, portrayed the human figure in grotesque proportions.[1] In real life, the elongation of lips, necks, earlobes, breasts, and labia as well as the binding of women's feet have been practiced for hundreds, if not thousands, of years. Other modifications involved invasion of body tissue, such as ear- and nose-piercing, scarification, tattooing, knocking out incisor teeth, and trepanning (skull puncturing). Trepanning is believed to have had a medical benefit, relieving internal skull pressure. The other procedures are believed to have been cosmetic; no one knows for sure. Surgery was also employed as punishment—ears, noses, hands, feet, penises, and testicles were amputated. Beheading was the ultimate surgery. Some of these methods of punishment are still in use in parts of the world.

Body modifications are widely practiced in the United States and in many other countries. The simple ones are ear- and nose-piercing and tattooing; the more complex are face-lifting, nose-bobbing, breast augmentation and reduction, fat removal, hair transplants, etc. The rationale for most current body modifications is simple and straightforward. Such changes are believed to enhance appearance. There is neither myth nor mystery about them. However, when male or female genital modification is involved, a very different rationale emerges; the issue becomes clouded with myth and mystery.

Genital modification takes many forms; the most common is circumcision, performed in a variety of ways on both sexes. Although theories abound, no one knows when, where, how, or why male circumcision began.

According to the 1973 *Encyclopedia Britannica*, "the origins of the practice are as dark as the Egyptian night."[2] Egyptian artifacts provide evidence that the procedure was well established there at least 6,000 years ago, long before its adoption by the ancient Hebrews. This is confirmed by the *Encyclopedia Judaica*, which comments: "It seems that Abraham did not start the practice of circumcision."[3]

Regardless of its precise origins, male circumcision is still practiced by about one quarter of the world's population, including Moslems and Jews worldwide, many black Africans, Oceanians, nonwhite Australians, and some peoples of North and South America. Essentially, male circumcision involves the removal of all or part of the foreskin. However, two other, more strenuous procedures, are also employed: subincision and *salkh*. Subincision is practiced by primitive peoples, mainly in Australia. It is performed after circumcision and involves slitting the penis lengthwise through the urethra. The wound is not permitted to close so that the urethra remains exposed throughout adulthood.[4] Some of the early anthropologists denied that this operation is very painful.[5]

Salkh (or *selkh*) is practiced by some Bedouin Arabs and consists of flaying the skin from below the navel to the upper thigh.[6] Although subincision and *salkh* have been known to the Western world for over a century, there has been no satisfactory explanation of their origin or purpose. These practices have not been adopted by other cultures; they are simply anthropological curiosities.

One unusual aspect of subincision (and other rituals) is the blood mystique. During the surgery, blood is dropped on others attending the rite, and older men—previously subincised—reopen their scars in order to bleed.[7] This use of penile blood is not limited to nonwhite Australians; Mayan high priests cut open their penises so that their blood would flow onto warriors.[8]

In the Jewish circumcision ritual (still observed by the Orthodox) some blood must be shed. If not, the glans is intentionally pierced. This applies also to modern-day converts who must shed a symbolic drop of blood. Moreover, in the Orthodox ritual, until a century ago, the bleeding penis was taken into the mouth to suck the blood.[9] This symbolic use of blood is also part of current Christian ritual, the Eucharist. In taking Holy Communion, wine, representing the blood of Christ, is sipped.

Other surgeries with religious overtones should be mentioned in passing. Young boys were castrated to become church-choir sopranos. Some surgery was self-inflicted in moments of religious frenzy—the Skopts of Tsarist Russia cut off breasts and genitalia; the Dervishes and Tamils punctured their cheeks with a metal pin. These practices simply illustrate the wide variation and acceptance of body modifications.

As previously indicated, circumcision is not limited to males. However, the term "female circumcision" is a misnomer, since a variety of procedures go under the rubric of circumcision. These include removing the clitoral foreskin, or removing part or all of the clitoris and/or labia. In addition, the vagina may be forcibly penetrated or the labia sewn together, a practice called infibulation. For further discussion of female genital surgery, see Chapter 17.

Female "circumcision" is still practiced by many Islamic peoples; in several parts of Africa, including Ethiopia and Egypt; in New Guinea; nonwhite Australia; Malaysia; as well as in parts of South America. There are theories which contend that it is possible that female circumcision antedates male circumcision. However, these are purely conjecture.

Since the origin and spread of circumcision are obscure, it is necessary to rely upon ancient religious and historical writings, which, of course, cannot be taken as absolute truth. The Old Testament discusses circumcision in many contexts, and Orthodox Jews maintain that the ritual was ordained by God to Abraham.[10] The New Testament also contains many references including the fact that Jesus, born a Jew, was circumcised. Although Christians did not adopt the practice,[11] Paul circumcised Timothy in order that he would be a more effective proselytizer among Jews.[12]

Although the word "circumcision" does not appear in the Koran, Moslems consider it an obligatory ritual, according to custom. It is believed to have been practiced by Moslems prior to the birth of Mohammed.[13] Among different Moslem sects the rite is performed at different ages: at birth, in early childhood, during adolescence, or prior to marriage.

One of the earliest historical references to circumcision mentions that Pythagorus had to submit to the operation (circa 530 B.C.) in order to study in Egyptian temples.[14] Herodotus (circa 484 to 425 B.C.) spoke of circumcision in relation to cleanliness.[15] Philo (circa 20 B.C. to 50 A.D.) was the first Jewish writer to advance hygienic reasons for circumcision.[16] However, according to the *Encyclopedia Judaica* "These [Philo's hygienic reasons] have never been claimed for it as a rite in the Jewish religion.... Originally a ritual procedure, it was undertaken for medical reasons only later."[17] It is noteworthy that hygienic reasons for circumcision were accepted by physicians for Jews and Egyptians, but not accepted for Arabs, Mayas, Incas, Aztecs, American Indians, and nonwhite Australians.[18] Could there be an element of racism here?

Because in ancient times little was known about circumcision, it became fair game for any and all kinds of postulations. According to anthropologist Robert Briffault: "The Virgin Mary was said to have been circumcised [based] on the principle that every incident in the biography of Christ had to have its exact counterpart in that of the Virgin."[19] Strabo, the first century B.C. Greek geographer, stated on two different occasions (without providing substantiating evidence) that Jews also circumcised girls.[20] Strabo would have been correct had he referred only to the Fellashas, or black Jews of Ethiopia,[21] but Strabo was writing about all Jews.

Some writings of the early Christian Era have been subjected to careful scrutiny and found to be unworthy of belief. For example, it has recently been claimed that the works of Ptolemy, the most illustrious astronomer of ancient times, are actually a fraud. Other academics have come to Ptolemy's defense; the debate continues. For a variety of unknown reasons (best left to the speculation of theologians, anthropologists, and psychiatrists) circumcision acquired a mystique of its own. This was certainly true for the Jews, who went beyond religion and hygiene and endowed circumcision with mystical qualities. In addition to the article on circumcision, the *Encyclopedia Judaica* has a subsection entitled "Folklore."[22] Some of the items mentioned include the protection of the infant from "evil spirits" by lighting candles, burning incense, or not allowing the child to be alone during the night prior to the circumcision ritual. In some communities, the knife used in the operation was kept under the mother's pillow and in Salonika the ablated foreskin was taken to the cemetery for burial. These practices were not adopted by all Jews, nor have these customs become an integral part of the religious circumcision ritual.

Equally strange was the mystique that developed among some Christians. Although abjuring the ritual, to this day many Christians celebrate the day of Jesus' circumcision, January first, as a Holy Day, the Feast of the Circumcision. Moreover, great controversy and commotion arose concerning the fate of Jesus' foreskin, which fostered scholastic debate that endured for centuries. Many legends developed and were widely believed; among them:

- Mary carried the foreskin on her person.
- The foreskin was entrusted to St. John or Mary Magdalen.
- It was left to the Apostles.
- It was brought to Charlemagne.
- It was stolen by Charles V in 1527.
- The relic emitted a wonderful odor which had a strange effect upon women.
- After many travels and conquests, the relic emerged in 12 abbeys simultaneously including Paris, Bologna, Metz, Nancy, and Antwerp. It was used to cure impotence, infertility, and to ease labor pains.
- A Queen of Sicily was cured of an "incurable" disease by the relic.
- Some nuns (in an unnamed monastery) were said to have committed "insolent conduct" with the foreskin.
- Lengthy debates ensued over the necessity of possessing a foreskin in heaven on Judgment Day.

- Saint Birgitta proclaimed a vision of the Mother of God holding Jesus' foreskin in her hand.[23]
- Saint Agnes of Blannbekin agonized over Jesus' circumcision every January 1, and had repeated visions of swallowing His foreskin.[24]

Veneration of the foreskin was practiced until 1870 and Honoré Guy de Balzac used this subject as a humorous theme in one of his *Droll Stories*. Such veneration extended to other parts of the body of Jesus and the Virgin Mary.

The mystique surrounding circumcision and the foreskin is to be found in many cultures. Elaborate ceremonies and precise rules as to when, where, how, and by whom it should be performed, who may attend the ritual, etc., universally govern male and female genital rituals. The method of disposal of the ablated part is also of major concern and ranges from burying, to burning, to eating.[25] When the foreskin is eaten, it is usually served to a younger brother to give him strength.[26] Before eating, the foreskin is often roasted, and the shriveling of the tissue is used to foretell the sexual fortune of its former owner.[27]

Another role that circumcision has played is as a major differentiating factor among peoples. There are, according to the *Encyclopedia of Religion and Ethics* "repeated contemptuous references [by Jews] to the [uncircumcised] Philistines." And not only to the Philistines: "The Jews alone, with their rigid adherence to circumcision and their haughty attitude to all others than themselves, have had to bear the brunt of opposition and ridicule . . . ."[28] Those who were uncircumcised used circumcision as a term of opprobrium and vice versa. For circumcised Arabs and Turks, calling someone "the son of an uncircumcised dog" was a favorite curse. Shakespeare reflected this attitude to circumcision in *Othello*, where the hero recounts how a Turk attacked a Venetian, and how he, in turn, attacked the Turk: "I took by the throat the circumcised dog and smote him, thus."[29]

Although major emphasis is placed on circumcision, the issue is much broader. Circumcision is but one aspect of the massive sexual mystique that has developed over the millennia. Phallic worship has been copiously discussed in the literature. Sexuality was, and still is, little understood and many myths have proliferated. Such myths were reinforced by anthropological writings from the 16th century on. The effects achieved by male and female genital surgery were stressed. These writings were also heavily imbued with racist overtones, which still exist in some contemporary anthropological writings.

One of the most prolific 19th-century writers on the sexuality of primitive peoples was Dr. Jacobus Sutor.[30] Although his writings were recognized as highly unreliable, he was copiously quoted in early 20th-century anthropological material and his writings were republished in 1935.

Astonishingly, he is still used as a source in present-day writings on sexual customs. For example, the authors of the *Cradle of Erotica* (published in 1963) commented that Dr. Sutor showed ". . . little capacity for distinguishing between native fact and fiction." The authors of *Cradle of Erotica,* nevertheless quote him extensively and add that the reader should approach what he has to say cautiously, though not with undue skepticism or presumption of error."[31] According to Sutor,

> The Hindu . . . is as lascivious as the monkey.[32]

> The Hindu has a thin short penis and a long tapering prepuce averaging 3½ inches in erection.[33]

In contrast to Sutor, Sir Richard Burton is considered a noted explorer, linguist, and ethnologist whose writings gained wide readership and acceptance. Yet Burton's racism and exaggerations are no less blatant than Sutor's:

> The Chinese are omnivorous and *omnifutentes* [all fornicating]; they are the chosen people of debauchery . . . their systematic bestiality . . . is equalled only by their pederasty. . . .[34]

> The Arabian Arab . . . has a very small member . . . the African Arab . . . is long, thick and flabby . . . [the African Arab] has the membrum virile [penis] of the African Negro.[35]

The theme of the black man's enormous penile size was echoed by Dr. Jacobus Sutor: "The Sudanese Negro possesses the largest genital organ of all the races of mankind . . . The Negro is a real 'stallion man.'"[36] Dr. Sutor attributed huge penile size to circumcision; he claimed the foreskin restricted the penis from growing to its normal length.[37] This circumcision myth is still believed by some people, and such references are to be found in the literature.[38] Moreover, Dr. Sutor reported, circumcision also provides enormous sexual prowess: "A well-fed circumcised Negro can perform on a woman nearly the whole night and only spend [ejaculate] five or six times."[39]

An almost identical statement was made about a black man in the United States in 1973 by an American urologist. In this case, however, sexual prowess was attributed to being uncircumcised.[40]

The myth about the black penis still persists in the United States and elsewhere. In *Eros Denied* (1964), Wayland Young wrote:

> Above all, of course, *They* have enormous pricks. This is something we simply can't get over. . . . In some circles, where Negroes are unfamiliar, it may be the

first thing we mention to them. . . . An American Negro in Rome said about some society women at a party "They ask you . . . the length . . . of your prick."[41]

Wayland Young added:

The . . . official ethnological view about this is that it is probably not so. [Gunnar] Myrdal says it is common belief. . . .[42]

A Brazilian sociologist, A. de Silva Mello (1953), claimed that the myth was true and that German girls preferred blacks to German men for that reason. Mello claimed that German girls came in droves to the Berlin Anatomical Institute to admire the collection of African penises held in permanent erection by means of the preservative injected into them.[43] Wayland Young commented:

As far as I know, an anthropometric study to settle this vexed question has still not been made. It would be excessively simple, and one can only suppose that it is the general fuzz surrounding sex in our culture, and particularly the fear of seeming ridiculous, which has prevented it.[44]

In writing about circumcision, anthropologists added a medical component. In addition to the mythology of greater sexual prowess resulting from circumcision, anthropologists also suggested medical benefits. Felix Bryk, quoting Dr. N. B. Risa (1906), stated:

[Foreskin retention] leads to erection and release through ejaculation, to enuresis, to onanism and pederasty with their psycho-pathological reactions and finally to moral crimes.[45]

Bryk also wrote:

The Jews owe their superiority over the Christians to the removal of the prepuce. . . .

. . . the fruitfulness of the circumcised lies in their specialization of the sexual technique and the regulation of the sexual instinct.[46]

The idea that Jews had acquired mystical powers and medical protection via circumcision was believed for centuries. As plague after plague swept through Europe, Jews appeared to succumb in fewer numbers than Christians.[47] The alleged reason: Jews were circumcised. No one understood that confining Jews to a ghetto was, in effect, a crude quarantine. The prevalence of this attitude helped make it possible for physicians to accept what was probably the first epidemiological study of venereal disease. Conducted in 1855 at the Metropolitan Free Hospital in London, the study showed that of all religious groups Jews had the lowest venereal disease rate. The reason, they concluded: circumcision.[48] This myth about circumcision and venereal disease is still being peddled today.

This is not the only myth regarding circumcision; others are prevalent. For example, in 1966 Masters and Johnson reported that virtually all of their male study subjects believed that foreskin retention provided better ejaculatory control, and many believed that circumcised males had a greater tendency to impotence.[49]

The extensive anthropological writings of the 19th century were widely publicized and became popular reading for many physicians, who were intrigued by the reports of genital surgery in general and male and female circumcision in particular. Male circumcision was said to improve sexuality, prevent masturbation, and provide a host of other benefits, while clitoridectomy (removal of the clitoris) was said to eliminate female masturbation and hypersexuality. Because of their lack of knowledge of sexuality, and the dread fear of masturbation, the physicians' minds were receptive to these studies and they became a major factor in the acceptance of clitoridectomy and male circumcision.

The concept that modern circumcision practices were derived from primitive peoples is startling, but true; the evidence is clear and admitted in the case of clitoridectomy. In 1891, Dr. P. C. Remondino wrote:

> . . . It is safe to assert that a strict adherence to the Mosaic law for the males and to some of the African customs for the females would most assuredly relieve all these cases that might come under the caption of reflex neuroses.[50]

In mid 19th-century Western medicine, clitoral surgery was virtually unknown. Clitoridectomy on a relatively large scale was first introduced into England in 1858 and into the United States in the late 1860s; the only precedent for this drastic operation was anthropological. (See Chapter 17 for more detailed information regarding clitoridectomy.)

Male circumcision was known to Western medicine, but rarely was performed on non-Jews in the United States prior to 1870. It was only after the introduction of clitoridectomy that male circumcision was introduced. The "logic" was simple. Fears of excessive sexuality were not limited to women, and if clitoridectomy was advisable for females, why not an equivalent operation for males? However, the equivalent male operation would involve penile amputation, which was unacceptable on a large scale for obvious reasons, although such amputations were performed in extreme cases to stop masturbation.

Infibulation (sewing up the foreskin or labia) was similarly employed.[51]

This procedure had no medical precedent. It was and is performed in some African societies, but only on women. When infibulation was introduced in the United States, it was applied to both sexes to stop masturbation. No primitive society used infibulation for that purpose.

Male circumcision became the surgery of choice, not only to reduce sexuality but also to stop bed-wetting and to prevent venereal infection. The operation soon emerged as a long-sought panacea for almost every imaginable disease. Thus the introduction of clitoridectomy and male circumcision was not based upon sound medical research, but misinformation, which, in turn was based upon concepts derived from primitive practices. The circumcision mystique, propagated by early anthropological writings, was therefore incorporated into medical thinking a century ago. Today, in the United States, clitoridectomy is no longer performed to reduce sexuality, and almost all of the claimed benefits of male circumcision have passed into the realm of medical history. Nevertheless, the circumcision mystique continues to influence medical thinking in the United States, exemplified by the unscientific discussions of the subject found almost exclusively in American medical literature.

3

The Medical Mystique

It is not difficult to accept the fact that a century ago American medicine could be influenced by the circumcision mystique of primitive peoples. The profession had relatively little knowledge of the cause of most ailments and less knowledge of their cures. It was convenient therefore to latch on to a circumcision solution to many problems. It is quite another matter to suggest that the circumcision mystique still exists in American medicine. This is a serious charge and is not made lightly. The mystique takes many forms:

1. The present-day acceptance of the surgery is largely based upon prior acceptance, not on new information.
2. There is an appalling lack of objective research. Doctors will tell why they perform the surgery, but have little or no substantive data to support it.
3. The operation is so popular that physicians who do question the surgery fear taking a firm stand in opposition; others have given up trying to understand or to do anything about the problem.
4. Most of the literature—past and present—is rife with errors, as well as sexist and racist biases.
5. Serious studies have been conducted both here and abroad that take sharp issue with the American practice. The reaction to anti-circumcision pronouncements is either passivity (ignoring them) or anger—not reasoned debate.
6. What is most important is that the surgery continues with almost a fanatic zeal. There is perhaps a gnawing fear that in not circumcising, some mysterious calamity may befall the child, saying in effect: "We really don't know, but play it safe and do it." In the

absence of empirical evidence to substantiate circumcision claims, the continued practice is based on mysticism, not medicine.

In 1977, Dr. George W. Kaplan, presenting an overview of circumcision, wrote:

> There has been an inordinate amount of rhetoric and emotion engendered by previous discussions of the merits or lack of thereof of routine newborn circumcision, perhaps because there is so little irrefutable data.[1]

The health consumer has the right to assume that any surgical procedure is based upon the maximum irrefutable data available. How, then, is it possible for a pediatrician to claim in 1977 that "there is so little irrefutable [circumcision] data"? On what basis is the surgery performed? Is it "rhetoric and emotion"?

There is no lack of circumcision "data"; there are mountains of it. The problem is quality, not quantity. The "data" are not based on scientific research methodology; they are refutable and sometimes fraudulent.

"Fraud in Research is a Rising Problem in Science" was the title of a front-page article in the *New York Times* (1977). The author wrote that in addition to deliberate bias, there is sloppiness in conducting experiments and carelessness in interpreting results.[2] If this is true in the basic sciences, it should not be surprising that it is at least as, or more true, in an emotionally charged subject as circumcision. An examination of the circumcision literature substantiates this point.

An interesting reference to circumcision, which may provide a clue to the problem, came from a religious encyclopedia: "The literature is enormous, but most of it must be dismissed as 'freakish,' the subject being one which has naturally proved attractive to erratic minds. . . . [3]" Presumably, this comment referred to religious writings. Whether the term "freakish" applies to the medical literature is debatable; perhaps a more precise term would be "unscientific." However, calling the subject of circumcision "one which has naturally proved attractive to erratic minds" would tend to limit discussion and research. This may account for the paucity of objective material; no one wants to be accused of having an "erratic mind."

There have been numerous efforts by physicians and nonphysicians to evaluate circumcision. These have mostly taken the form of articles in the medical and lay press, which, due to space limitations, have largely been confined to one or another aspect of the subject—rarely a full discussion.

Four books on the medical and health aspects of circumcision have been published in the United States and two in England.[4] Although the books do not suffer from space limitations, the contents are biased beyond belief. The British books (really booklets) are worthy of passing note. The first (1890) was a scathing denunciation of the practice under the title *The Barbarity of Circumcision.*[5] The second book (1893), *Circumcision: Its Advantages and How to Perform It*,[6] took a diametrically opposite view. Both books are obviously outdated and have long been out of print; they are only of historical interest. Perhaps the most amazing book on circumcision was written in 1891 by a physician, Peter Charles Remondino, with the title: *History Of Circumcision From The Earliest Times To The Present.* This book is a compendium of interesting history but unimaginable medical errors. Remondino claims that circumcision will cure or prevent about 100 diseases or conditions including: alcoholism, asthma, epilepsy, hernia, syphilis, cholera, plague, gonorrhea, masturbation, eneuresis, paralysis, chorea, rectal prolapse, gout, feeble-mindedness, rheumatism, kidney disease, lunacy, and tuberculosis. In addition, Remondino suggested that males born with short or no foreskins are more intelligent than males with normal or long foreskins.

Remondino's statements go far beyond the province of medicine. He makes the definitive claim that the origin of circumcision predates the Old Testament:

> In the far-off land of Ur . . . [Kurdistan] . . . something over 6,000 years ago, the fathers of the Hebrew race, inspired by a wisdom that could be nothing less than of divine origin, forestalled the process of evolution by establishing the rite of circumcision.[7]

No proof is offered.

Dr. Remondino was supposedly writing a book on circumcision for physicians. Yet he commented on subjects that have nothing remotely to do with circumcision. For example:

> . . . the physique of the Netherland maids, who are cold and impassive, with a layer of adipose tissue that answers the same purpose as that of the blubber in the whale. . . .[8]

> . . . the willowy, swaying gait produced in the Chinese beauty by the lack of a sufficiency of foot.[9]

Remondino predated Hitler's master race theory:

> The ancient Germans lived a life of chastity until their marriage [and to this] can be attributed the superior physical development of the race. . . .[10]

Such statements cannot be condoned simply because they were written in 1891, when medicine was relatively primitive. The fact is that this book went through many printings, the last of which was in 1974. Moreover,

Remondino's book is the only one on circumcision in New York City Public Libraries.[11] Thus, such material is still being disseminated and presumably believed. In the medical press, dozens of articles used Remondino as a source. Recently (1974), one physician called Remondino's reasoning "pertinent and carefully thought out," and endorsed his claim that circumcision would prevent a wide variety of ailments.[12] A search of the medical literature since Remondino was first published reveals no serious challenge to his statements.

From reading Remondino and his latter-day disciples, the only conclusion to be drawn by both physicians and lay persons is that every male should run, not walk, to the nearest surgeon to be circumcised. With such proclaimed benefits, it is no wonder that Remondino influenced the wide acceptance of circumcision in the United States.

A lack of objectivity is also to be found among writers who are unalterably opposed to circumcision. It is almost like Newton's Third Law of Motion, "For every action, there is a corresponding reaction, equal in magnitude and opposite in direction." An examination of the claims made by two anti-circumcision writers will illustrate this point. Joseph Lewis, in his book *In The Name Of Humanity* (1956), claimed that, " . . . there are more deaths as a result of circumcision than cancer of the prepuce." But a few pages later he admitted " . . . There are no medical statistics available as to how many children have died as a result of circumcision."[13] Lewis claimed that the shock of circumcision can cause allergies, skin conditions, stammering, rheumatic fever, and heart disease. He wondered " . . . how many become mental misfits, how many go into the insane asylum . . . become criminals. . . . " He stated categorically that circumcision " . . . is a definite . . . cause of masturbation," and that " . . . the intensity of sexual sensation is impaired by circumcision. . . . "[14]

Intemperate and unsubstantiated statements are not limited only to lay writers; some medical writers are equally culpable. John M. Foley, M.D., stated in his book, *The Practice of Circumcision: A Reevaluation* (1966):

> Circumcision provides a convenient and socially acceptable outlet for the perverted component of the circumciser's libido.
>
> [The popularity of circumcision in the United States] . . . stems from the sadism of the crypto-pervert.
>
> [Another explanation is] . . . latent female antagonism towards the penis . . . among the biggest boosters of circumcision are neurotic females whose unhappy sex lives prompt them to injure a man where he feels it most.[15]

The sexist theme of blaming women for circumcision will be noted later in other contexts.

The most current book on circumcision was written by Dr. Abraham Ravich in 1973. Dr. Ravich received his M.D. degree from Columbia University College of Physicians and Surgeons. He specialized in and practiced urology for some 50 years. Considering his credentials, Dr. Ravich was presumably well trained and highly experienced and, therefore, should have been qualified to write a scientific work on circumcision. However, nothing written in the field better illustrates the pervasive circumcision mystique than does this book. The very title of the book, *Preventing V.D. and Cancer by Circumcision*,[16] bespeaks its questionable contents. "Preventing V.D. . . . " indeed! When this book was published (1973), venereal disease had already reached epidemic proportions in the United States, especially among young people, of whom perhaps 75% of the males were circumcised. Linking circumcision to venereal disease is bad enough, but when discussing the dangers of possessing a foreskin, Ravich claimed that irritation under the foreskin caused promiscuity, masturbation, and disease as well as unbridled sexual desire in both men and women. (The only case history given of these conditions resulting from foreskin retention is that of unbridled sexual desire on the part of one black male.) Like Remondino, Dr. Ravich discussed a broad range of topics; for example, he provided his own interpretations of the Bible, paraphrased biblical quotations, giving his own medical interpretations of them, and attributed prehistoric epidemics to sexual immorality, and later epidemics to retention of the foreskin.[17] Dr. Ravich also moralized at length:

> With the widespread sexual promiscuity, venereal diseases, homosexuality and constantly increasingly mixture of races and ethnic groups, the smegma from the 20% of the young males who remain uncircumcised, plus that from the 50% of the rest who are more or less incompletely circumcised, may be a source of viral infections and urogenital cancers in the future.[18]
>
> Smokers use more alcohol, change jobs and spouses more, move and enter hospitals more. They have multiple sex partners, and early sex is generally associated with early smoking.[19]

In discussing medical questions, Dr. Ravich made major blunders. For example, he mentions the Pap smear, which is a diagnostic test for cervical cancer. The cost of such a test in the early 1970s was less than $30, yet he inflated the cost tenfold, to about $300 per person.[20]

More serious is his attack upon the Pap test as a *cure* for cancer. Probably nowhere in medical literature has anyone ever considered the Pap test as a cancer cure.

> The famous Pap test which has been widely trumpeted at tremendous cost as a *cure* and preventive of cancer of the cervix may actually be less responsible than the increasing popularity of early routine circumcision [emphasis added].[21]

The Orthodox Jewish ritual involves tearing the inner foreskin lining with the fingernails. Dr. Ravich defended this procedure on the grounds that it "produces less hemorrhage than cutting".[22]

Dr. Ravich suggested that circumcision be compulsory:

> ...Just as more or less universal compulsory vaccination has been so successfully instituted against smallpox, so ... they may also ultimately move to make early complete circumcision compulsory at no greater danger than vaccination.[23]

These are but a few of the errors and distortions in the Ravich book; more will be mentioned in other contexts. Although some of Dr. Ravich's statements have been criticized by a few physicians, no general critique has appeared in the medical or lay press. Physicians use the book as reference. Given the blatant blunders in the books on circumcision, it should come as no surprise that many serious medical journal writers also succumb to the same mystique. They draw erroneous and extraneous conclusions and refuse to come to grips with their own thinking, which would logically lead them to take a firm stand on a controversial issue.

In 1947, Dr. Eugene A. Hand delivered a paper at the American Medical Association Convention that purported to show the relationship of circumcision to venereal disease among soldiers in World War II. Essentially the findings were that Jews and circumcised Christians had a lower venereal disease rate than uncircumcised Christians and Negroes. *Newsweek* reported the paper at length and characterized it as "sensational and heavily documented." Among the *Newsweek* quotes from Dr. Hand's paper were:

> ... the sex education of the Negro is meager. His sex habits promiscuous, and his acceptance of venereal disease without fear of social taboo has increased the infection rate for his race to almost 100%. For the widely educated Jew, circumcised at birth, the venereal disease rate has remained the same or decreased.

> Certain forms of cancer were less common in Jews and circumcised gentiles. These include cancer of the tongue because with syphilis rarer in these groups, there was less precancerous irritation of the mouth.[24]

To what degree this kind of racism toward blacks or reverse anti-Semitism—"Jews are smart, follow their practice"—has affected the acceptance of circumcision in the United States is anything but clear. But from a purely medical point of view, relating circumcision to cancer of the tongue is, to say the least, implausible. No physician before or since Dr. Hand has made such a statement. Tongue cancer is not common in any group, circumcised or not. The disease is more frequently found in older people; Dr. Hand's study subjects, United States Army men, were primarily young men. With the sharp decline in syphilis and the increase in circumcision, there has been *no* decline in tongue cancer, whose primary causes are believed to be related to heavy smoking and heavy drinking, rather than the possession or lack of a foreskin.

Examining Dr. Hand's study in detail reveals an absence of both scientific sampling technique and statistical analysis, as well as a lack of attention to a variety of important demographic characteristics. Utilizing such an unscientific approach, in addition to his biased racial attitude, led Dr. Hand to fallacious conclusions.

In 1969, an article appeared in *The New England Journal of Medicine* titled, "Ritualistic Surgery; Circumcision and Tonsillectomy." The author stated:

> In our own civilization, two procedures are widely performed on a non-scientific basis. One is circumcision and the other is tonsillectomy.
>
> There is . . . the tacit understanding between parents and physician that circumcision is the most appropriate course of action. . . .
>
> As Morgan so succinctly stated: "it is encouraged by Scripture, the beliefs of the medical profession, the intuition of women, folklore, and the health insurance agencies."[25]

But then Bolande, who opposed routine tonsillectomy, concluded the circumcision portion of the article with this statement:

> Little serious objection can actually be raised against neonatal circumcision, since its adverse effects seem miniscule.[26]

Not surprisingly, this conclusion was challenged by another pediatrician, Dr. R. S. Ganelin, in a subsequent issue of the same journal. Dr. Ganelin characterized circumcision as "primitive, meaningless, and potentially dangerous" and protested the reason given for not objecting to the surgery, namely that it " . . . usually causes no harm."[27]

Many medical textbooks are quite clear and succinct in their opposition to routine circumcision, as the following quotes illustrate:

> Although circumcision is the most common surgery performed on male infants, the medical indications for this procedure are not established.[28]

> Neither the American Pediatric Society nor the American College of Surgeons offers a definite opinion as to when and why circumcision should be performed.[29]

> ... it is hard to justify the common practice of circumcising the newborn infant.[30]

Despite these current medical textbook statements, many physicians literally throw up their hands in despair about the subject:

> The question of circumcision is age-old and will never be settled.[31]

> The advantages and disadvantages of this operation are controversial and not conclusive.[32]

> [There is] ... reasonable doubt ... that the decision pro or con is reached in any scientific manner.[33]

> Circumcision sparks hot debate and fence sitters are scarce.[34]

Some physicians are less hesitant about taking a firm stand, even accusing the American medical profession of performing the operation because it is a lucrative practice. One physician referred to circumcision as "chronic remunerative balanitis"[35] (inflammation of the penis). The charge of performing unnecessary surgery has been leveled at American physicians not only in regard to circumcision, but also regarding brain surgery, mastectomies, and hysterectomies.[36] It will be noted that when the British National Health Service no longer covered routine circumcision, the circumcision rate precipitously dropped.

One aspect alluded to but rarely explored is the possible harm the operation may cause. As one pediatrician wrote:

> Most practicing pediatricians have seen unfortunate consequences from the operation of circumcision, and seen or personally heard of a death resulting from it.[37]

The existence of a circumcision controversy is clear, yet the practice continues unabated. The medical profession, aware of the intense differences of opinion, has urged that clarity be established through objective research. A 1963 editorial in the *Journal of the American Medical Association* entitled "Routine Circumcision" was, in effect, a plea for objectivity and further research, and an admission that the facts about circumcision are still unknown:

> To most physicians this challenge is particularly attractive; to a few it may prove paralyzing. ... every physician must be wary of ignoring or failing to collect data which might provide him with conclusive evidence.

> So be it with circumcision! . . . circumcision today continues to serve symbolic purposes. At the same time it is purported to . . . "relieve" phimosis, to "prevent" infection, to be "prophylaxis" against carcinoma . . . Yet it can hardly be said that circumcision commands attention from hordes of investigators trying to support or refute these contentions.
>
> Consequently, the conflicting professional opinions and the confused lay opinions . . . are understandable . . . the present situation regarding circumcision does little for the professional or the public . . . The paradox is obvious; the ubiquity of the procedure makes it all the more blatant. The cost and complications alone should encourage resolution of the issue.[38]

Unfortunately, the editors of the *Journal* did *not* achieve their goal of an objective appraisal by the medical profession. In 1965, Dr. W. K. C. Morgan wrote a blistering attack on circumcision, "The Rape of the Phallus,"[39] which was published in the *Journal of the American Medical Association*. The reader response was overwhelming. More than 1,000 requests for reprints were received, until then, probably the largest number of requests for an article printed in the *Journal*, thereby attesting to physician interest in the subject. Moreover, dozens of letters concerning the article were received. While some praised it, most condemned it. The contents of the negative responses were largely scurrilous; some physicians refused publication of their letters; others insisted on anonymity. Very few attempted a reasoned debate. So intemperate was the attack on the article that when Dr. Morgan had the opportunity to reply to a severe critic, he thanked him profusely for the opportunity to do so, noting that another critic had suggested that he be brought before the House Un-American Activities Committee.[40]

The *Journal of the American Medical Association* carried no subsequent article in defense of circumcision, which would have been expected, if the editors had believed Morgan to be in error. Five years later, in 1970, when Dr. E. Noel Preston wrote a critique of circumcision, it was published as the lead article in the *Journal of the American Medical Association*.[41] Physicians again reacted intemperately. This was followed not by a defense of circumcision, but by a humorous spoof, "The Foreskin Saga."[42] In contrast, Dr. G. W. Kaplan made a special point of the fact that he had not included humor in his 1977 article on circumcision because "Both humor and emotion tend greatly to cloud the real underlying issues."[43]

Objectivity was provided by the American Academy of Pediatrics Task Force on Circumcision, which reviewed the circumcision argumentation and concluded in 1975 that:

> There is no absolute medical indication for routine circumcision of the newborn.[44]

The Pediatric Urologist Association also stated its opposition to routine infant circumcision.[45] Others also spoke out. One of the most forceful statements in opposition to circumcision was made in 1976 by Dr. Benjamin Spock:

> I am in favor of leaving the penis alone. Pediatric opinion is swinging away from routine circumcision as unnecessary and at least mildly dangerous. I also believe that there is a potential danger of emotional harm resulting from the operation. Parents should insist on convincing reasons for circumcision—and there are no convincing reasons that I know of.[46]

The opposition to routine circumcision in the United States is formidable, and yet the debate, as well as the surgery, persist. Considering the fact that approximately 85% of American newborn males are routinely circumcised, the pro-circumcision forces have obviously won the debate. It is difficult, if not impossible, to explain this phenomenon on a scientific basis.

Some people maintain that circumcision is a very private, personal decision similar to ear- and nose-piercing, tattooing, or cosmetic surgery and, therefore, no one has the right to interfere with such a decision. There can be no disputing such individual preferences. However, the medical profession does not recommend circumcision for its cosmetic effect, nor does it attempt to influence or alter patients' personal or religious attitudes. Supposedly, the recommendation is made solely for reasons of health.

Because of the intense cultural and social pressures, and the almost unanimous acceptance of circumcision 20 years ago, it would be understandable if, as a result of the growing opposition, there had been a gradual rather than a sharp decline in the circumcision rate. But this decline did not occur; the rate increased during the period of the opposition.

At the present time defense of circumcision is to be found almost exclusively in the United States. This is so despite the fact that all of the arguments presented in support of routine circumcision can be sharply rebutted by empirical evidence. The pro-circumcision advocates are vehement in their attacks on the opposition, often stooping to arguments that can hardly be called objective. For example, in 1973, three physicians, R. Dagher, M. L. Selzer, and J. Lapides of the Departments of Urology and Psychiatry at the University of Michigan Medical Center, wrote a strong defense of circumcision, which appeared in the *Journal of Urology*.[47] The article is entitled "Carcinoma of the Penis and the Anti-Circumcision Crusade." The essence of the article is that circumcision prevents penile cancer, an opinion that is widely challenged. Much of the article is devoted to an attack upon those opposed to the practice. The writers claimed that opposition was based, in part, on the anxiety and fears of castration, but also admitted that in the past the claimed benefits of circumcision were unscientific and exaggerated.

The authors of the article blamed the opposition to circumcision on the protest movement:

> ... the catalytic element for the anti-circumcision swell lies in the current aura of protest. Various minority and deprived groups now speak up and demonstrate with unaccustomed vigor. Movements abound to save wild horses, polar bears, islands and lakes. The establishment is seen as a universally bad guy.

In other words, ecology "freaks," who insist on protecting the environment, now want to protect the prepuce! It is doubtful that such a statement by physicians could appear anywhere in the world except the United States. Dagher et al. see themselves as defending the medical establishment. Yet, in the previously noted 1963 editorial in the *Journal of the American Medical Association,* the profession's attitude to circumcision was shown to be paradoxical and confused.[48] Since 1963, voluminous empirical data have been published that present cogent arguments either in direct opposition to routine circumcision or that raise serious doubts about the efficacy or advisability of the procedure. Unfortunately, editorials, research findings, and pronouncements by the medical establishment have had no appreciable effect upon the frequency of its performance.

In 1978 Dr. Karen E. Paige wrote an article titled, "The Ritual of Circumcision." She noted:

> Once established, circumcision survived on its own momentum.
>
> When a custom persists after its original functions have died, it may be accorded the status of ritual. ... When the same operation is variously reputed to accomplish antithetical goals—in the case of circumcision, to repress sexuality and to liberate it, to make the penis or clitoris less sensitive and more sensitive—we can be sure we are dealing with a ritual, not rational thinking.[49]

The only logical explanation is that the circumcision mystique is so deeply imbedded in American medical history that it still pervades modern-day medicine and accounts for the continuation of the practice.

4

Why Only in the United States?

It is indeed strange that most American male infants are routinely provided with the many "benefits" of nonreligious circumcision, while the infants of other medically advanced nations are denied such "benefits."

The biologist Desmond Morris noted this enigma in 1973 and called upon the medical profession to explore the origin of "this . . . form of adult aggression."[1] Calling for a study is valid, but to refer to infant circumcision as "adult aggression" is a conclusion drawn before the facts are in and sheds little light on the situation. No such study has been undertaken.

To understand the reasons for the current American practice, it is necessary to pose three questions:

1. Why did routine nonreligious circumcision originate in the United States?
2. Why, after the practice spread to other English-speaking countries, did the frequency of performance rise relatively slowly in these countries and relatively rapidly in the United States?
3. Why has the high rate continued in the United States, while the rate has diminished in the other countries?

These are not simple questions and there are no simple answers. It is necessary to first understand what occurred and then to seek clues to answer why it occurred.

Nonreligious circumcision is a relatively recent phenomenon whose precise emergence is obscure. A British physician observed: "It is not clear when [circumcision] changed from a religious rite to a widespread surgical procedure."[2] One reason for this obscurity is that a century ago no nation kept records of circumcision. Prior to the turn of the century, almost all babies were delivered at home and, therefore, most circumcisions were performed at home or in doctors' offices. No nationwide data were maintained. This absence of data was and is true particularly in the United States, where even today some hospitals do not record circumcision in the medical chart.

Since national data haven't been available, estimated frequencies were and are often based upon educated guesses, unrepresentative hospital records, or studies of nonrandom samples. I have made an attempt to review statements in the medical and lay literature concerning circumcision frequency in the United States. A table showing the estimated frequency rates from 1870-1979 and their derivation will be found in Appendix B.

Although I was working with admittedly crude data, several trends do emerge. The United States was apparently the first country to introduce nonreligious circumcision, in the early 1870s. At that time, the rate was estimated to be about 8%; after 1910 the rate had reportedly risen to 56%.[3] No one has offered a satisfactory explanation for this phenomenal increase! According to Dr. Roscoe L. Wall, Jr. (1968), the phenomenal rise in the American circumcision rate was not based upon clinical evidence of a need for circumcision. Dr. Wall commented:

> At the turn of the present century a few authors began to champion the cause of non-ceremonial circumcision. In spite of their growing numbers, however, there was a surprising scarcity of significant medical data, even in textbooks, until two decades ago[4] [i.e., circa 1948].

Dr. Wall also claimed that after 1948 most of the medical articles written were critical of the practice, but nevertheless the rate continued to climb. It is indeed true that the circumcision rate continued to climb; however, Dr. Wall is imprecise as to timing. In the 15-year period—1948 to 1963—most medical articles favored circumcision, including those which called attention to infection, hemorrhage, and injury; their conclusions were not to end the practice but to urge greater caution in its performance. After 1963, the articles began to shift in the direction of outright opposition.

Routine infant "health" circumcision was adopted early in this century by England, Canada, Australia, and New Zealand, but by no other country. A 1950 British study of merchant seamen[5] showed the circumcision rate (by year of birth to be: 1914, 19%; 1924, 22%; 1930, 30%. Granting that the frequency rate for merchant seamen is not projectible to the entire British population, the comparison between the two countries (19% in Britain in 1914 to 56% in the United States after 1910) strongly suggests the United States' higher rate.

During the 1930s and 1940s, the circumcision rate increased in all

English-speaking countries, but not to the same degree as in the United States. By the 1950s a change began to occur in England—the rate declined. This was noted in 1964 by an American physician, Dr. Charles Weiss,[6] and in 1966 by a Canadian physician, Dr. Hawa Patel.[7] Statistical substantiation of the precipitous drop in the British rate was provided by a study by M. P. M. Richards, J. F. Bernal, and Yvonne Brackbill in 1976.[8] In exploring the possible traumatic effects of circumcision, Richards et al. sought data on circumcision frequency in both the United States and Britain. While they were able to obtain nationwide data from Britain, no equivalent data were available in the United States. The British Department of Health and Social Security reported that a census of 400,000 boys born in Britain in 1972 showed that fewer than one-half of 1% were circumcised (0.41%). These figures are reliable since they represent close to 100% of all males born that year in Britain.

Since no comparable figures were available for the United States, the researchers queried 18 American teaching hospitals and found the rate to be 83%. The American figures, however, are not very reliable since these 18 teaching hospitals are not representative of the 7,000 teaching and non-teaching hospitals. Moreover, only 14,000 males, less than 1% of the total American male births in 1973, were born in these hospitals.

Regardless of the preciseness of the British data, and the lack thereof of American data, one fact stands out—the circumcision rate in Britain is very low, while the American rate is quite high. A brief exploration of some of the factors that have influenced British medical opinion can help provide an understanding of the vast difference in approaches between the two countries. Dr. Charles Weiss stated that the climate of opinion in Britain changed "as a result of studies" and also commented: "It is not possible to have elective circumcision performed within the National Health Service without payment."[9] Thus, two elements are suggested for the decline in the British rate: Health Service coverage and knowledge. As to the "studies" that affected the British rate, the most influential was probably that of Dr. Douglas Gairdner, who challenged the time-honored assumptions upon which the surgery was based. Richards et al. specifically credited Dr. Gairdner for the decline in British circumcision practice.[10] (We will discuss Dr. Gairdner's research in Chapter 7 of this book.) Gairdner's study was published in 1949, about a year after the introduction of the British National Health Service. While Gairdner may have influenced some British physicians, it is unlikely that all or most British physicians read the article and suddenly changed their views on circumcision. The key factor was probably the study's influence on the leaders of the National Health Service, which led to the decision not to cover elective circumcision. Thus, concomitant with the termination of Health Service coverage, the operation quickly changed from an almost essential surgery to one of less or no importance.

Gairdner's research was widely disseminated and frequently quoted in medical journals in all English-speaking countries. Although his findings caused a dramatic reversal of the practice in England, the effect upon the United States' practice was almost nil.

In Canada and Australia the change in approach to circumcision was different from that of the United States or of England. In 1967 the *Medical Journal of Australia* printed a sharp attack entitled "Penile Plunder."[11] Four years later the Australian Pediatric Association recommended "that newborn male infants should not as a routine be circumcised."[12]

The editor of the *Medical Journal of Australia* commented upon this recommendation (1971):

> The resolution of the Australian Pediatric Association of course conforms with the weight of informed pediatric opinion of British medicine today—that routine neonatal circumcision is founded partly on tradition and partly on a misunderstanding of normal anatomy, that it is hardly ever necessary in infancy and seldom in later life, and that as neonatal circumcision incurs an appreciable morbidity and occasional mortality, its use as a routine measure cannot be justified.[13]

In 1966 the *Canadian Medical Journal* published the Patel article, which was critical of routine circumcision.[14]

The effect of these pronouncements was a reduction in the circumcision rate in Canada and Australia, but not to the same degree as in England, as shown in the following tables:[15]

Year	Australian Circumcision Rate %
1973-1974	49.6
1974-1975	48.6
1975-1976	43.7

Year	Canadian Circumcision Rate %
1972	46.3
1973	44.8
1974	44.3

The rates are declining slowly in Australia and Canada; they are only half that of the United States, but are still much higher than the circumcision rate in England. The reason for the difference in circumcision rates in

England vs. Canada and Australia is simple! The British National Health Service does not cover newborn circumcision, whereas both the Canadian and Australian Health Services do cover the surgery. This means that British parents who insist on elective circumcision must pay for it. Canadian and Australian parents can obtain this service free of charge. Thus if physicians are paid to circumcise, they tend to perform the surgery. If their salary does not cover this "service" (as in Britain), they tend to shy away from it. It is difficult to prove that venality was *the* factor, but it certainly was *a* factor in the reduction of the British circumcision rate.

In this regard, the situation in the United States is especially interesting to note. Although Blue Shield does not pay for newborn circumcision, Medicaid (MediCal) does pay, and many health insurance policies (e.g., Major Medical) also cover this procedure. There is no question but that there is monetary gain from circumcision in the United States both for the physician and the hospital.

Charges of venality have been made in American medical literature. Moreover, in 1974, a quarter of a century after the British National Health Service refused to cover elective circumcision, American urologists Guthrie and Burger were urging American insurance carriers to pay for this operation.[16] Therefore, from a monetary standpoint, the American attitude is quite different from that of the other English-speaking countries.

There are no definitive findings to explain why routine circumcision took hold only in English-speaking countries. The possible influence of mid-Victorian values will be discussed later in the chapter. Of course, the obverse question is: Why didn't other countries adopt the practice a century ago? However, putting the past aside, it is relevant to determine why other medically advanced countries still continue to reject a practice which the American medical profession finds so beneficial. Is it possible that physicians in these countries are unaware of American medical attitudes or that these countries are less concerned about the health of their children? Are the rejecting countries so blinded by anti-Semitism that they will not seriously consider a practice so intimately associated with the Jews? After examining the facts, the answer to these questions is: No! Foreign medical establishments are familiar with American medical thinking; American medical literature is widely distributed abroad.[17] As to greater concern for its children, even a cursory examination of child health and care in the United States reveals a sorry state on many criteria:

- Infant mortality: The United States in 1973 ranked 14th; it had a higher infant death rate than most industrialized countries.[18]
- Child abuse: Although precise data are not available, various estimates put the figure of abused children between 500,000 and 1,000,000 with "30,000 to 40,000 instances of 'truly battered children' each year," of

whom approximately 700 die.[19] It is estimated that 1 child in 7 is abused or neglected.[20]
- Malnutrition: In 1970, 25% of American children were living below the poverty level and were malnourished.[21]
- Immunization: About 40% of the 1- to 4-year-olds in 1973 were unprotected against one or more of the diseases for which vaccines are available (polio, measles, diphtheria, pertussis, and tetanus).[22]
- Runaway youth: An estimated one million youths run away from home each year; they are often considered "throwaways."[23]

Although comparable data from other countries might reveal better, similar, or worse situations, it would be difficult to conclude that the United States practices circumcision because of greater concern for its children.

Although anti-Semitism does exist to varying degrees in many countries, it is not a major factor in the rejection of circumcision. If the benefits were demonstrably true, the procedure would be accepted in spite of anti-Semitism. For example, the two names associated with polio vaccine—Salk and Sabin—are both Jewish, and even anti-Semitic countries use the vaccine. More importantly, countries that are less anti-Semitic than the United States, e.g. the Scandinavian countries (Denmark, Norway, Sweden, and Finland) have not adopted circumcision. The simple fact is that the world medical profession rejects American circumcision thinking and practices as unsound. This point was made very sharply to me in personal visits and correspondence with health authorities in the Scandinavian countries.

In Norway, in 1973, I asked Dr. Valdemar Kirkland, an official of the National Ministry of Health why circumcision was not practiced in his country.[24] Dr. Kirkland, who had received some of his medical training in the U.S., replied by saying he had never understood why it was done in the U.S. In the discussion that followed, Dr. Kirkland stated that Norway has never found it necessary to circumcise routinely. When pressed for details, he stated that his field was primarily public health and suggested a conference with the pediatrician who has been the director of a well-baby clinic in Oslo for 26 years. The pediatrician, Dr. Dag Riis, reiterated what Dr. Kirkland had mentioned and also stated that newborn circumcision was a rarity in Norway.[25] Asked whether foreskin problems were ever presented to his clinic, he replied in the affirmative; there were foreskin problems, just as there were problems with all body parts, but they were treated medically, not surgically. When I asked whether they found it necessary to circumcise children at the clinic, the answer was yes, but very rarely. The clinic staff saw an average of 700 new baby boys each year and, over the past 26 years, about 20,000 baby boys had been cared for. Of this number, Dr. Riis recalled 3 circumcisions. This represents a circumcision frequency of about 0.02%. Compare this approach to the typical American rush to surgery: "To cure phimosis, either a dorsal slit or a complete circumcision would be required."[26] Note the word "required," not "considered" or "suggested" or even "possibly necessary." In contrast, Norwegian medical authorities would first treat the condition medically, including hospitalization if necessary, before even considering surgery. Norwegian medical authorities reject routine newborn circumcision as unnecessary and I found the same attitude in all Scandinavian countries. For example, an official of the Finnish National Board of Health estimated that males with foreskin problems were hospitalized from 5 to 8 days to *avoid* circumcision.[27] It should be noted that in Finland, as well as the other Scandinavian countries, health care, including hospitalization, is free. There is no monetary gain for physician or hospital. Thus the attitude to routine infant circumcision in Scandinavia is a clear and unequivocal "no."

However, the rejection of circumcision by other countries does not explain its prior or current acceptance in the United States. Was there anything unique about American medicine and health attitudes a century ago that facilitated acceptance of nonreligious circumcision?

Since nonreligious circumcision began in the early 1870s, it is necessary to seek clues in the prevailing medical knowledge and attitudes from 1800 on. There is no evidence that nonreligious circumcision (circumcision for health reasons) began at any specific moment in time or was based upon any singular event. Rather, the rationale for acceptance developed during almost a century of stress on the dangers of sexuality in general, and masturbation in particular.

At the beginning of the 19th century, medicine the world over was primitive. The causes, contagions, and cures for most diseases were unknown and epidemics were common occurrences. Centuries-old herbal medicine and bloodletting were the mainstays of American medicine; surgery was a horror in terms of pain, infection, and mortality. Furthermore, there was little that was indigenous to American medicine; Britain, more specifically, Scotland, was the source of most American knowledge, and one of the prevailing British theories was that: "All disease could be reduced to one basic causal model, either the diminution or increase of nervous energy."[28] Based upon his medical studies in Edinburgh, this theory was espoused and articulated by the famous American physician, Dr. Benjamin Rush. If nervous energy was the basis of all disease, one of the most obvious expenditures of such energy was in orgasm. In 1812, Dr. Rush wrote that overindulgence in sex resulted in:

> seminal weakness, impotence, dysury, tabes dorsalis, pulmonary consumptions, dyspepsia, dimness of sight, vertigo, epilepsy, hypochondriasis, loss of memory, malangia, fatuity and death.[29]

However, Dr. Rush balanced this view by claiming that abnormal restraint in sexual matters was also dangerous, causing:

> tremors, flushing of the face, sighing, nocturnal pollution, hysteria, hypochondriasis, and in women the furor uterinus [nymphomania].[30]

Crude as these ideas may seem in the light of present-day knowledge, Dr. Rush's statements were amplified manyfold and persisted, in one form or another, well into the 20th century. Among the leading American exponents of the theory of sexuality and disease was Sylvester Graham, the developer of Graham flour and crackers, who also wrote a book on the subject[31] in which he added dozens of diseases to Dr. Rush's list. According to Graham, sexual abuse or misuse could disturb the stomach, heart, lungs, skin, and brain. Sexually-induced ills were not only caused by overt acts but also by lascivious thought and imagination. According to Vern Bullough, author of a history of sexual variance: "Graham concluded that one result of excessive sexual desire was insanity, and insanity itself incited excessive sexual desire."[32]

Graham's book, first published in Boston in 1834, went through 10 editions, the last one in 1848. It is important to note that no one had any serious clues to the causes of most physical and/or mental diseases at that time, and the publication of such "facts" could be done without fear of rebuttal. Bullough notes that all sexual activity was considered debilitating—one ejaculation was believed to be equivalent to the loss of 4 ounces of blood. In fact, hypersexual behavior could even result in death.[33]

Of all harmful sexual behavior, nothing compared to masturbation, which, in addition to being harmful, was also considered a sin. And if male masturbation was considered a sin, female masturbation was considered an abomination. There were many "facts" put forward to "prove" the dangers of masturbation. For example, masturbation caused lunacy and lunacy, in turn, caused masturbation. Even if the practice ended prior to adulthood, the damage resulting from childhood masturbation was irrevocable. Moreover, Dr. Joseph Jones claimed (1889) that masturbation was inheritable.[34] Later, the term became the catchword for all forms of "unnatural" sex, from homosexuality to the use of contraception.[35]

One of the most prominent opponents of masturbation was John Harvey Kellogg, whose Battle Creek Sanitarium and breakfast foods are still well known. In 1882 he wrote that masturbation was a sin against nature, equal to sodomy, but far more dangerous because it was the one most extensively practiced and there were no bounds to its indulgence.[36] According to Kellogg, masturbation caused: "urethral irritation, inflammation of the urethra, enlarged prostate, bladder and kidney infection, priapism, piles and prolapse of the rectum, atrophy of the testes, varicocele, nocturnal emissions and general exhaustion."[37] But Kellogg made an additional "discovery." A masturbator could be detected by a variety of 38 suspicious signs, including: changes in disposition, sleeplessness, bashfulness, round shoulders, lack of breast development (in females), use of tobacco, acne, biting the fingernails, and the use of obscene words.[38] Since there could hardly have been a child alive at that time (1882) who did not manifest one or more of these tell-tale signs, it is understandable that such ideas evoked enormous fears among parents. Concerned parents did not want their children to suffer from the horrible "consequences" of masturbation.

The beliefs that hypersexuality was dangerous to physical and emotional well-being, and that masturbation had devastating effects were accepted by all Western medical establishments. However, the reaction to these concepts was greater in England and the United States, because they tended to conform with the dominant economic, social, and cultural development of the time. The United States was an expanding industrial and mercantile power; England was at the heyday of imperialist expansion.

In some ways medicine clearly reflected social and economic thinking. Sexually related diseases were not the only ones to which the medical profession paid attention. One incredible example of the politicizing of American medicine was the disease "Drapetomania." This "disease" only afflicted blacks—to be more specific, black slaves. There was only one symptom, the mania for running away. This "disease" was first diagnosed by Dr. Samuel Cartwright in 1851 in *The New Orleans Medical and Surgical Journal*.[39] Not surprisingly, the "disease" disappeared after the Civil War.

Although the origins of sexual attitudes date back to early human history, the second half of the 19th century saw the emergence of a unique mental and behavioral approach known as Victorianism, which affected not only England but all English-speaking countries. During the reign of Queen Victoria (1837-1901), England was the world's most powerful nation. England not only ruled the seas, but was the leading manufacturing and mercantile nation. Colonial rule over black, brown, and yellow peoples expanded and the concepts of upper class and racial superiority were accepted principles. In the United States, although there were no comparable colonial conquests, attitudes of racial superiority toward blacks and American Indians were rampant. White native-born Americans openly expressed attitudes of upper-class superiority over the millions of immigrants from Europe and Asia.

The theory that sexual activity was debilitating was connected with these attitudes, and concern over the loss of sexual energy was mainly directed to the upper classes. It is worth speculating that the powers that be believed that greater self-control was important for upper-class whites in order to maintain their domination over the poor and "inferior" peoples. Just such a theory was widely popularized in the United States by the physician George M. Beard who, over a period of 15 years (1869–1884), wrote expressing concern that:

> the growing complexities of modern civilization . . . had put such increased . . . [stress in working] that larger and larger numbers of people were suffering from nervous exhaustion . . . Such exhaustion was particularly great among the educated, brainy workers in society, who represented a higher stage on the evolutionary scale than the less advanced social classes, and thus as man advanced, it became more and more necessary to save his nervous energy.[40]

Thus, concern was limited to the upper classes, the "superior" ones who, of necessity, had to preserve their nervous (sexual) energy. Dr. Beard reflected the thinking of the Victorian period.

The precursors of Victorianism and Victorianism itself are well described by Vern L. Bullough in his book *Sexual Variance in Society and History*. Although Bullough does not specifically relate this to circumcision, his descriptions of the period lay the bases for understanding the prevalent attitudes toward disease and sex. According to Bullough:

> [Victorianism was] much more than prudery . . . it set the tone in many matters of morals, manners and even taste.[41]

> The Victorian hostility to sex . . . [was] influenced by the medical concepts . . . of masturbation.[42]

It was within this context that sexual conduct was carefully defined. Some urged that sexual intercourse between married couples be limited to "one indulgence . . . each lunar month." Others urged sex only for procreation. Children "begotten in the moments of intoxication remained stupid and idiots during their whole life." A pregnant woman who enjoyed sex was sure to miscarry.[43]

The remedy for sexual overindulgence could be found, according to Graham, in the use of Graham flour and crackers. Kellogg advocated the use of his breakfast cereals. Others recommended concentration on religious thoughts and good works. For those unable to control their sexual impulses, medical and surgical solutions were employed. Bullough described some of these "therapeutic" measures:

> Some doctors perforated the foreskin of the penis and inserted a ring or cut the foreskin with jagged scissors. Others applied ointments that would make the genitals tender to touch, and others applied hot irons to girls' thighs. In some cases clitoridectomies were performed and in a few cases actual amputation of

the penis was attempted to prevent masturbation. Castration was not unusual.[44]

The United States Patent Office issued about 20 patents for medical appliances to prevent masturbation. The earliest was recorded in 1861; the latest 1932. Similar devices were used in Britain and on the continent.[45] The brutality employed to prevent or to stop masturbation may be shocking, but in view of the medical knowledge of the period, it is somewhat understandable. For example, in 1876 Dr. Abraham Jacobi, one of the founders of pediatrics in the United States, blamed polio on masturbation.[46] In 1881, Dr. M. Landesburg maintained that masturbation caused "chronic catarrhal conjuctivitis."[47] Two years later, a physician writing in a French medical journal blamed chronic ear infection on masturbation.[48] In 1894, Dr. A. J. Block referred to female masturbation as "moral leprosy."[49]

Little change occurred in the attitude toward masturbation between 1850 and 1900. An 1855 editorial in the *New Orleans Medical Journal* stated:

> ... Neither the plague, nor war, nor small pox, nor a crowd of similar evils have resulted more disastrously for humanity, than the habit of masturbation: it is the destroying element of civilized society.[50]

Before paresis was discovered to be caused by syphilis, it was thought to be the result of masturbation.[51] (The syphilis organism was not identified until 1905.) Concerned parents were willing to use almost any means available to prevent childhood polio, adult paresis, and a hundred other physical and mental diseases allegedly caused by masturbation. It should also be recalled that not only was United States' medical knowledge limited, but medical training was considered inferior in comparison to European standards. Major improvement in medical education did not occur until after the Flexner report of 1910, which resulted in the closing of dozens of second- and third-rate medical schools. Moreover, any medical nostrum, regardless of content, purity, or effectiveness could be sold, since the Pure Food and Drug Act was not passed until 1906.

As a result of the introduction of anesthesia, around 1850, the pain of surgery was largely overcome and surgical solutions were sought for many medical problems. With the development of the germ theory of disease and aseptic surgery, around 1875, surgical morbidity and mortality were sharply reduced. The introduction of anesthesia and antisepsis resulted in an enormous increase in the use of surgery.

Another factor that began to influence American medicine in the latter half of the 19th century was Jewish immigration. Although there had been Jews in America since the 17th century, the number was small. Immigration increased somewhat between 1800–1850, but from 1850–1900 the numbers swelled greatly. Jews settled in large and small cities; several Jewish hospitals were established and many Jews entered the medical profession. Contact between Jews and non-Jews increased, and with such contact, there was a growing awareness of Jewish circumcision practices.

It is within this context that nonreligious circumcision began to be practiced in the United States in the early 1870s. Initially, the surgery was performed much more frequently on upper-class rather than lower-class infants, to prevent masturbation and hypersexuality. Considering that masturbation and hypersexuality were treated by such horrible means as penile amputation and castration, circumcision was a relatively mild form of therapy.

By the 1880s, other elements appeared that further encouraged secular circumcision. An 1855 British study had revealed that Jews had a relatively low rate of venereal disease, purportedly due to circumcision. An American replication study in 1884 showed identical results. Moreover, by the 1880s, a syphilophobia had developed in the United States.[52] Syphilis was viewed as God's punishment for evildoers, and a few physicians even refused to treat such patients.[53] But now there was a syphilis "preventative"—circumcision.

With the popularization of the germ theory of disease and the knowledge that germs can cause odors through foul-smelling putrification, attention was focused on body odors and how to eliminate them. In 1973 Dr. George T. Klauber wrote: "The practice of circumcision lends itself well to the North American preoccupation with hygiene and the banishment of all body odor."[54] Evidence of this preoccupation may be noted from the introduction of deodorants. As Nora Ephron noted: "The underarm deodorant, which was the first product to capitalize on the American mania for odor suppression, was introduced over a hundred years ago, in 1870."[55]

Concomitant with the continued fear of masturbation was the emphasis on mental disorders. With the development of the germ theory of disease, many organisms were identified as the causes of physical ailments, but mental diseases remained a mystery. No germs could be found to cause hysteria, epilepsy, nervousness, depression, chorea, or insanity, for example. Although the causes of mental diseases were not understood, cures were sought through surgery. This was particularly true for women, who were believed to suffer from mental disorders more frequently than men. A popular "cure" for the female "mental disorders" such as masturbation, hysteria, and nervousness was clitoridectomy. The psychiatrist Dr. René Spitz (1952), commenting on the use of surgery to prevent or stop masturbation, noted:

> One of our most widely known psychiatrists, the late Dr. Bernard Sachs, recommended cautery of the spine and genitals in the different editions of his handbook up to 1905. Infibulation of the prepuce and labia majora was equally recommended. Circumcision in boys was a prevalent practice up to a very recent

date. A leading textbook on pediatrics advised the use of a double splint. . . . The same book, as do most other pediatric textbooks, recommends circumcision in boys and is not averse to circumcision in girls, or cauterization of the clitoris. Indeed after 1925, ten percent of the therapeutic measures [against masturbation] advocated in the United States were surgical interventions, while in the other countries, such measures were no longer recommended.[56]

Thus, until approximately 1940, long after physicians in other countries had abandoned surgical solutions for masturbation, leading American pediatric and child psychiatry textbooks still recommended infibulation and circumcision of both sexes. Castration and penile amputation were no longer being employed, but the clitoris was still being cauterized or cut off. The removal of the clitoris represents one of the ugliest aspects of American medicine—and only of American medicine. The precise reason for the difference in the American and European approach has not been explained. It may be hypothesized that the enormous reservoir of experimental "material" in the United States among black and immigrant women made such surgery relatively easy to perform without criticism.

This was noted by Dr. Aubre de L. Maynard (1978) in his book *Surgeons to the Poor*:

> . . . Moribund or . . . "refuse" slaves . . . were . . . sold for as little as a dollar, usually purchased as speculation or by "surgeons." . . . The Negro has always been appropriated as choice "clinical material" by the medical profession. . . . The Negro was always next in line beyond the experimental animal.[57]

Another unique American phenomenon was the Orificial Surgical Society, founded in 1890 by E. H. Pratt, a surgeon at the Cook County Hospital in Chicago. The Society was without doubt the most bizarre medical group in the United States. The organization was largely concerned with orifices below the waist, and provided training for surgery of the prepuce, clitoris, and rectum, the latter organ being given special emphasis. Dr. Pratt published his first book[58] on the subject in 1890, and the Society published a journal from 1892 to 1923. A textbook by Dr. Pratt appeared in 1912 and a revised edition[59] was issued in 1925. The 1912 textbook states:

> I have been astonished at the multitude of sins concealed within the rectum.
>
> Circumcision of the girl or woman of any age is as necessary as for the boy or man.[60]

Dr. René Spitz noted that the Society members "seem to be the last followers to spring from the original invention of the excision of the clitoris."[61] The Society was not an insignificant group, as they had hundreds of members and supporters nationally, some of whom operated on thousands of patients.[62]

A cursory examination of articles in the *Journal of the Orificial Surgical Society* reveals some startling therapeutic practices. For example:

- Dr. Cora Smith Eaton circumcised two women to treat headaches.[63]
- Dr. M. K. Kreider circumcised a boy to cure spinal curvature.[64]
- Dr. C. B. Walls used circumcision to treat "hip joint disease," and commented that Jews rarely suffered from this ailment. He further stated that "60 percent of the insane are so because of some abnormal condition of their sexual organs."[65]
- Dr. T. E. Costain recommended circumcision as treatment for hydrocephaly.[66]

Originally the Society only allowed physicians into membership, but later it admitted osteopaths and chiropractors. By the 1920s, many of the member physicians had their licenses revoked. Since no history of the Society has been written, it is unclear whether the license revocation was due to the Society's theories and practices, or because of association with osteopaths and chiropractors.

The essence of much American medical thinking from 1870 to 1920 was that surgery was a quick solution and/or preventative for a host of physical and emotional problems. Circumcision, male and female, is an important case in point. Given the paucity of medical and psychiatric knowledge through the first quarter of the 20th century, wild statements about sexuality and circumcision were made with impunity. For example, in 1904, G. Stanley Hall, one of the fathers of child psychology, warned of the dangers of oral sex, noting that cunnilingus and fellatio caused cancer of the tongue and anyone engaging in such "perversions" would have offspring with "perverted instincts."[67]

The practice of circumcision as a panacea for numerous ills was reflected in the *Journal of the American Medical Association* which, in 1910, published an article introducing a new circumcision clamp. The physician-author claimed that this device was so simple to use that men and women could now perform circumcision upon themselves.[68]

So intense was the circumcision propaganda that almost no one dared challenge the accepted "facts." In fact, no real challenge was made in the American medical press until the 1950s—80 years after the introduction of nonreligious circumcision in the United States. And, judging from the continued high frequency of circumcision, an adequately serious challenge has yet to be made. Instead the literature is rife with speculation rather than fact. For example, as recently as 1977, one physician continued to blame women for the high circumcision frequency rate in the United States, stating that it: " . . . largely seems to be a function of the mothers' wishes, and may be an indirect indication of their attitude toward the future sexual activities of their sons."[69]

The above brief historical review of 19th-century medicine reveals intense attitudes toward sexuality in general and masturbation in particular. The remedy for sexual "problems" was often surgical. Despite the ample evidence of what took place, there are few reliable answers to why the American approach was so different from that of the rest of the world and why this approach persisted only in the United States.

5

The Circumcision Decision: Is It Informed Consent?

Current medical opinion holds that permission for any and all surgical procedures should be based upon the informed consent of patients. Of course, in the case of infant circumcision, informed consent must be given by the parents. But some physicians maintain that they, in the final analysis, should make the decision:

> [Circumcision] is a decision to be made by the medical profession rather than by the dictates of social demand.[1]

Others take a contrary view:

> The decision to circumcise or not to circumcise belongs to the parents and circumcision should be performed only with their informed consent.[2]

One pediatrician recently claimed that informing parents about circumcision is burdensome and time-consuming, and noted: "Parents are irritated by any discussion of the subject because their minds are already made up."[3]

Many parents consider themselves well-informed and therefore favor circumcision. But how can parents be truly knowledgeable when the medical profession itself is in the midst of intense debate on the subject? The fact is that most parents are not really informed about circumcision. They give consent, but is it informed consent?

Several in-hospital studies were conducted with women who had recently given birth to boys to determine their knowledge of, and attitudes toward circumcision. In one such study, 72% of the mothers claimed that their physicians had never discussed the matter with them.[4] When asked why they permitted the procedure to be done, the replies ranged from the belief that circumcision was mandatory or was the law to the idea that all males were supposed to be circumcised, or that it was done in response to the strong desire of a family member.

In another study,[5] Dr. Hawa Patel, a physician, claimed that most parents did not discuss the matter with their physicians. The decision to circumcise was based on cultural and social factors rather than upon medical advice. Dr. Patel commented that parents are "anxious, confused and misinformed"; he added that this is understandable because of the paucity of objective information about the subject.

A typical hospital decision-making situation was described by one pediatrician.[6] Immediately following delivery, a time of tension and fatigue, the nurse asks the mother to sign the circumcision authorization. Not having been told anything to the contrary, the mother thinks: "It must be the thing to do, or our doctor would have told us about it."

In 1977, a surgeon criticized the current decision-making process as not leading to informed consent, commenting:

> Whether or not circumcision is indicated as a routine procedure is, at best, moot.... Circumcision should be treated no differently from any other surgical procedure.... It should be treated with respect.... The parents of the child should have the opportunity of *informed* consent. Unfortunately, all too often the consent to circumcise is included in a sheaf of papers that the mother signs hurriedly on her way to the delivery room. No discussion has been held regarding the merits of the procedure or of the inherent risks. As a surgeon, I find this inexcusable.[7]

A more rational process, as described by another physician, would leave the final decision to the parents, based upon informed consent:

> There are pros and cons about this procedure, which was once done almost routinely in hospital nurseries. After they have been given a full explanation of the advantages and risks of circumcision, the parents will be able to make their own decision about it.[8]

To avoid forcing a hasty decision, one group of physicians has suggested waiting at least 12 hours after birth in order to (among other things) provide an opportunity to discuss the procedure's advantages and disadvantages with the parents.[9]

In considering informed consent, it should be borne in mind that an estimated 23 million Americans cannot read. Thus, even the few lay press articles on the subject of circumcision are unavailable to this population segment. While informed consent is not based solely upon the ability to read, such capability would be helpful in obtaining a broader view of the subject. Moreover, an increasing number of pregnancies are occurring among teenagers—1 million a year. The largest rise is in the youngest group, ages 11 to 13. These children, inadequately parented and inadequately parenting, are hardly in a position to give informed consent for themselves let alone their offspring.

An added problem of informed consent is that many people haven't the faintest idea what the term circumcision means. This fact has been extensively verified in medical literature during the past 25 years. The information was largely derived from studies attempting to verify the purported link between circumcision and cervical cancer. Since the hypothesis was that women were less likely to get cervical cancer if their sex partners were circumcised, women so diagnosed and control groups were asked about the circumcision status of their marital partners. The large number of erroneous responses was startling.

A study by Drs. M. Terris, F. Wilson, and J. H. Nelson[10] not only discussed their own findings but also summarized the findings of similar studies. When clinic patients were studied, as many as 50% of the women stated that they simply *did not know* whether their husbands were or were not circumcised. In another study, the percentage of "did-not-knows" ranged from 10%-35% among various subgroups in the sample. Studies of private patients, presumably a higher education and income group, revealed lower figures—between 5% and 10% among different subgroups.

The above figures represent women who said they did not know their husbands' circumcision status. Having found such a high percentage admitting ignorance, there was concern as to whether the responses of women who claimed positive knowledge were, indeed, accurate. Verification was therefore undertaken via actual physicial examinations of the men. In one study, verification revealed that women who professed to know their mates' status were in error in 38% of the cases. This led to the hypothesis that men might also be ignorant of their own status. In one study, 213 men admitted to a cancer hospital were asked to describe their own circumcision status. This was followed by actual physical verification by physicians. The researchers found that over 34% of the men were in error.[11] Other studies of middle-class men also revealed ignorance, although at lower percentages. The problem was further complicated by the frequent finding of partial circumcision, in which only a fraction of the foreskin was removed, and of some uncircumcised men who possessed unusually short foreskins. These findings led researchers to conclude that they could not rely on questionnaires to determine circumcision status; physical examination was necessary.

Confusion about circumcision is not limited to the illiterate nor to those not knowledgeable about surgery. Dr. Mary Howell, a pediatrician and former

Dean of students at the Harvard Medical School, stated that of her 4 male children, the 2 youngest were uncircumcised. However, the 2 older boys (born in the early 1960s) were circumcised because: "In those days we thought it was practically against the law not to do it."[12] Dr. Howell was bold enough to buck the trend. However, she is the exception, not the rule.

Parents who want to be well-informed about circumcision will find accurate information difficult to obtain. Professionals at least have access to the medical literature, but the nonprofessional must rely on information imparted by physicians either in person or via popular publications. A review of this literature reveals the disarray within the profession on this question.

Although "health" circumcision has been practiced in the United States since the early 1870s, the *Readers Guide to Periodical Literature*, which indexes all articles in major lay periodicals, does not list one article on circumcision in the 70-year period from 1870 to 1940. (In 1906 there were 2 articles related to theology. Such articles are not included in this survey.) Apparently physicians either felt no need to write about the subject for lay publications, or the publications felt no need to publish such articles. The concept that "the doctor knows best" prevailed during the first 70 years of the surgery's practice, so that there was acceptance, not debate or even discussion.

The first article to appear in a popular journal was written in 1941 by Dr. Alan F. Guttmacher for *Parents Magazine*.[13] Dr. Guttmacher provided both historical background and a brief description of the surgical techniques. He was ardently pro-circumcision; he called attention to the need for drawing the foreskin back daily for proper cleaning if the child was uncircumcised, and mentioned the problems that can arise if the foreskin is "tight." Dr. Guttmacher also warned that not circumcising could lead to impotence. He provided 5 major reasons in support of circumcision:

- Care of infants' genitals is easier for the mother
- Focusing on the penis may lead to masturbation
- Venereal disease is less easily contracted
- Penile cancer, though extremely rare, is less frequent in the circumcised
- Circumcision may be necessary later in life.

Ostensibly to provide a balanced view, Dr. Guttmacher listed 3 reasons why some doctors opposed routine circumcision:

- It is an unnecessary operation and, as with any surgery, there is risk
- A circumcised boy will feel self-conscious in the presence of uncircumcised boys
- There is some blunting of male sexual sensitivity.

Dr. Guttmacher made short shrift of the anti-circumcision arguments, stating that the risk is negligible if proper care is used; blunting sexual sensitivity was considered an advantage, not a disadvantage; possible embarrassment was not discussed further.

During the following 6 years, 1941 to 1947, there were no additional articles on the subject in the popular press. Then, in July 1947, *Newsweek* reported that new medical evidence showed that circumcision prevented venereal disease.[14] Also, in a brief reply to a query, *Hygeia Magazine*, stated that circumcision was "medically justified," and gave venereal disease and penile cancer prevention as the reasons.[15]

There was another 7-year hiatus before *Time* magazine carried an article in 1954 stating that new data provided evidence that circumcision prevented cervical cancer in women.[16] Later that same year, Dr. L. E. Holt, Jr., wrote the first tentatively critical article for *Good Housekeeping* magazine.[17] Dr. Holt listed 4 reasons that circumcision is recommended:

- It relieves any obstruction to the passage of urine
- It facilitates cleanliness
- It protects against venereal infections; and
- It reduces the incidence of penile cancer.

While Dr. Holt gave some credence to the latter two reasons, he challenged the first two. The problem of a tiny foreskin opening, he noted, is exceedingly rare and therefore not a valid reason for accepting routine circumcision. As to cleanliness, Dr. Holt stated that there is serious question as to whether washing the area in the newborn is important. Nor, Dr. Holt said, was there evidence of the necessity of forced retraction of the foreskin. If the organ is left alone, retraction will be achieved during normal growth. Forced retraction and overzealous cleaning might cause injury and infection.[18] Dr. Holt maintained that since venereal disease can be treated and penile cancer is a rare occurrence, these considerations should be balanced against the risks involved in circumcision. He concluded: "The welfare of the child must be considered, not the prejudices of the grownups, for it is he who suffers the pain and discomfort—and consequences, if any."[19]

Although Dr. Holt did not refer to Dr. Gairdner's research (1949) he paraphrased his opinions. In other words, it was not until 5 years after Dr. Gairdner's article was published in Britain that the first indications of opposition to routine circumcision appeared in the American lay press.

A 5-year gap occurred before the next article appeared (1959) in *Parents' Magazine*. The writer stated that, " . . . almost all doctors find many parents know little or nothing, actually, about the operation."[20] Although the article raised some questions, its conclusions were pro-circumcision.

In 1964, *Science Newsletter* reported that a link had been found between circumcision and cancer; circumcision was urged to prevent cancer.[21]

The first article taking cognizance of the medical controversy over circumcision, appeared in 1968 in *Good Housekeeping* magazine. It was an editorial that pointed out that although circumcision is one of the most frequently performed operations, it is seldom discussed. The topic is avoided and therefore many parents lack reliable information upon which to base a decision.[22] Although attempting a balanced discussion and recognizing the medical controversy, the article recommended circumcision in order to promote "hygiene and in helping to prevent disease."

Starting in 1970, anti-circumcision articles began to appear in medical journals. The reaction of the lay press is interesting to observe. When Dr. Preston's 1970 article, "Whither the Foreskin?"[23] appeared in the *Journal of the American Medical Association*, the *New York Times* carried a one-column summary. However, the writer, Jane E. Brody, added some refutation. She quoted a Texas urologist who held that circumcision made men "less prone to venereal infections." She noted the observation by an obstetrician that an examination of United States Army recruits revealed poor penile hygiene practices.[24] *Scientific American* made a brief editorial comment and *Time* magazine simply reported the Preston article. None of these publications carried any follow-up stories—the matter was simply dropped.

In 1975, the findings of the Task Force on Circumcision of the American Academy of Pediatrics were published in *Pediatrics*. The task force concluded: "There is no absolute medical indication for routine circumcision of the newborn."[25] Although several women's magazines did report the findings, the Academy's statements were largely ignored and distorted. *Good Housekeeping* provided a 2-inch, one-column brief statement stressing the need in the uncircumcised of "lifelong careful penile hygiene."[26] *Woman's Day* printed a 1½-page objective summary by Barbara Seaman.[27] *McCall's* provided a ⅓-page article that contained a serious distortion. The author admitted that circumcision is probably not necessary " . . . if the male is super scrupulous about keeping clean."[28] The words "super scrupulous" do not appear in the Task Force Report—they represent the thinking of the article's writer and would appear to be a distortion reflecting personal bias. Everyone would agree that the penis should be kept clean, but so then should the entire body. One might go further and say the penis and the entire body should be kept scrupulously clean—no argument there. But how do you keep the penis "super scrupulously" clean? How can a mother give such a guarantee? Since she obviously cannot, the implication is clear—it is better to circumcise.

Moneysworth reported a summary of the Task Force Report.[29] They also requested readers' views on the subject, which were published two months later.[30] The editors stated that never, in their 5-year history, were they "so inundated with such articulate and passionate responses." The letters ranged from serious and conflicting statements by physicians and health educators to the wildest subjective myths, thus reflecting the confusion that exists among professionals and lay people.

In 1979, Jane E. Brody wrote an article in the *New York Times*, in which many of the doubts about circumcision were expressed.[31] Although in her article 9 years earlier Ms. Brody refuted Dr. Preston's conclusions, in her 1979 article she accepted most of Dr. Preston's thinking.

In summary, although circumcision had been practiced for a century in the U.S., general press articles on the subject were nonexistent during the first 70 years of that century and quite rare during the last 30 years. In fact, during the entire century (1870-1970) and even up to the present time, no article has appeared that thoroughly covers the subject. Although many have decried the ignorance of the general public, few have attempted serious elucidation.

One might hypothesize that medical journal articles might be too brief to provide full and reasoned debate, but that physician-written books could cover the subject of circumcision more thoroughly, since space limitations in books aren't as stringent. I found, however, that such medical books were much less objective and scientific than many of the journal articles (see Chapter 3). The same situation exists in respect to books written for the general public—they are often even less accurate than the articles. In contrast to the paucity of articles in the popular press published during the past 25 years, there has been no shortage of child care books in which circumcision is discussed. Hundreds of such books have been written by physicians, nurses, health educators, midwives, lay persons, and others.

The first important modern child care book was written by Dr. Benjamin Spock in 1946. *Baby and Child Care* sold tens of millions of copies and virtually became the Bible on the subject of child care for millions of Americans. Dr. Spock's view on circumcision reflected the uncertainties within the medical profession, in that he gave parents 3 alternatives: (1) circumcise; (2) if circumcision is not elected, push the foreskin back daily; or (3) leave the foreskin alone. There is some suggestion that Dr. Spock questioned the advisability of routine circumcision, since he wrote that leaving the foreskin alone is "the simplest way and the one used throughout a great part of the world."[32] While Dr. Spock specifically stated that circumcision "is not necessary," he preceded that remark with the statement: "I think circumcision is a good idea, especially if most of the boys in the neighborhood are circumcised—then a boy feels 'regular.'"[33] (The social acceptance factor was also mentioned by Dr. Guttmacher in 1941, but Dr. Guttmacher argued that a circumcised boy might feel embarrassed in the presence of his uncircumcised peers.)

Baby and Child Care has gone through many printings and editions and in the 1976 edition, probably written a year or two earlier, Dr. Spock altered his views and stated:

> If the foreskin has been removed, the smegma does not collect and there is no place for infection to occur. This is the main justification for circumcision—to my mind. . . . [34]

In other words, penile hygiene now became the main justification for the the procedure. Shortly thereafter, Dr. Spock further updated his views and made one of the most forceful statements in opposition to circumcision: "There are no convincing reasons that I know of."[35]

Although Dr. Spock abandoned his earlier belief in the importance of peer and paternal identification, i.e., that a boy should feel "regular," this view is still found in guidebooks.[36] Although many "authorities" present penile identification as *one* of the reasons for recommending circumcision, a recent guidebook (1976) stated: "The baby should . . . match his father and this should be your main rationale for choosing circumcision."[37]

Since this specious argument is still prevalent, it deserves comment. Generally speaking, a boy wants to feel "regular" and identify with his father and his peers. However, such identification must be within the bounds of reason. For example, if a boy's father is tattooed or has an appendectomy scar, or wears eyeglasses, should the child be similarly provided? In discussing the penis though, identification seems to acquire some special arcane meaning in that a boy's penis, different in appearance from his father's or his peers', is considered potentially traumatic. The speciousness of this argument can be seen when the consequences are reduced to an absurdity.

- Suppose a boy's peers are circumcised but his father is not, with whom should the boy identify?
- Suppose the father is partially circumcised, should the surgeon use the father as a model for surgery in order to achieve maximum penile identification? If not, how will the parents explain the difference between father and son?
- Suppose the father dies, or the parents separate, should the mother use circumcision status as a criterion for choosing a stepfather?
- Suppose the son and his natural father were not circumcised, but the stepfather is circumcised. Should the son undergo surgery to match the stepfather? If so, will there now be a conflict between the son and his natural father, if he is living, or with the boy's memory of his father, if he is dead?
- Suppose the boy was circumcised and the family moves to a place where circumcision is not practiced. What should be done to make

the boy feel "regular"? Should he be fitted with a prosthetic prepuce or a foreskin falsie to avoid embarrassment?

What has happened to the millions of American boys who were circumcised during the past century whose fathers were not? The difference was very likely noticed and when questioned parents probably stated, with much ease and assurance, that it was better to be circumcised. There is no evidence that a national psychiatric trauma has occurred during the period of change.

Or take the case of Britain, where millions of boys were circumcised up to 1950, before the rate precipitously declined. That is, from about 1900 to 1950, many boys were circumcised while their fathers were not, and since 1950 the reverse is generally true. Again, there is nothing in British medical or psychiatric literature indicating any trauma resulting from lack of paternal penile identification. Thus, if the parents understand circumcision and are at ease with their decision, penile identification can be handled simply and without undo concern. This question was succinctly dealt with by three physicians in *Taking Care of Your Child* (1977): "We feel medical procedures should be for medical reasons and not to make a baby look like someone else."[38]

The vast majority of parents who need and seek information on circumcision are largely relegated to the so-called guidebooks. After reviewing a hundred or so of such books, my general conclusion is that they are confused and contradictory. While no useful purpose would be served in reviewing each book individually, some salient comments have been selected to illustrate the confusion and error.

The approach to the question of circumcision in such books ranges across a broad spectrum from "Your doctor will decide," to "The parents will decide," to "The parents should ask the doctor and decide jointly." According to some books, hospitals assume that parents insist on circumcision; other books state that parents assume that hospitals insist on it. Therefore, since there is no apparent need for discussion, the operation is usually routinely performed.

Peer and paternal penile identification is still one of the most frequently mentioned reasons for recommending circumcision, as is the ease of hygiene.[39]

Some books urge that circumcision be performed only if the foreskin is redundant (i.e., excessively long). However, no one realistically defines "redundant"; redundancy, therefore, becomes a subjective judgment, resulting almost invariably in circumcision.[40]

Most guidebooks discount the factors of pain and trauma; a few consider it important and urge topical anesthesia.

Prevention of masturbation is still occasionally mentioned, sometimes using the euphemism "nervousness" instead of "masturbation."

What is striking about the majority of guidebooks is the fact that they do state that there are few or no medical indications for circumcision, and that it is mainly done for social, cultural, or traditional purposes. However after making the disclaimer of medical necessity, most go on subtly, or not so subtly, to suggest circumcision. Although there is a diminishing tendency to ascribe medical reasons for circumcision, one or more such reasons are also frequently presented. These include improved hygiene; prevention of penile, prostatic, and cervical cancer; reduction in the incidence of venereal disease; and reduction of premature ejaculation.

A few books present both sides of the debate and then attempt to demolish the anti-circumcision argument.

Some books with serious errors go through many editions with little change in their approach. Others, however, do update their information. For example, the popular woman's guidebook, *Our Bodies Ourselves*, stated with respect to cervical cancer (1973): "Women whose husbands were circumcised in childhood get it less often than other women."[41] This statement was in error and the second edition, published 3 years later, correctly stated that cervical cancer is related to early intercourse, frequency, promiscuity, Herpes II Virus, being poor, practicing poor hygiene, etc.[42] Circumcision is not mentioned at all.

Earlier in this chapter, evidence was presented to show that many people do not know what the term circumcision means. It is not an obscure word as its frequent appearance in both the Old and New Testaments has created familiarity for many. The proliferation of health information has also increased awareness of the term. Most general and medical dictionaries simply define circumcision as the removal of all or part of the foreskin or prepuce (the words are interchangeable). While the definition is correct, it contains the implicit assumption that the reader has knowledge of the meaning of "penis" and of "foreskin." Lack of such knowledge can result in serious misconceptions about the procedure. Thus, knowing the word and being familiar with its dictionary definition are no guarantee that the full meaning of circumcision is really understood.

With the more open attitude toward sex and the wide dissemination of sexually explicit materials in recent decades, it can be assumed that most men and women have at least some basic knowledge of the penis. The foreskin is quite another matter. Due to the high circumcision rate during the past 50 years, the majority of males below the age of 50 do not possess a foreskin, and male knowledge tends to be limited to locker-room observations. The majority of women in this age group have probably never seen a foreskin at close range. Therefore, many adults have a limited idea of the meaning of circumcision. It is not that the procedure is difficult to understand; the problem is that it is seldom clearly explained. However, such an understanding is essential if an *informed* consent decision is to be made. If clarification is to be obtained, an understanding of the penis and foreskin is necessary, and circumcision procedures must also be discussed. Some readers may feel well informed about the penis, foreskin, and circumcision procedures or may feel that this information is unnecessary; other readers may feel squeamish about surgical descriptions and illustrations. However, this is the operation that a majority of parents elect or agree to for their sons. It is important, therefore, that parents be familiar with the surgery they impose upon the infant—without anesthesia. For this reason, I have included a description of penile and foreskin structures as well as various circumcision techniques, which will be found in Appendix A. However, in order to understand and appreciate what is involved in this surgery, it is first necessary to understand both the nature and function of the foreskin—the most maligned body tissue.

6

The Ill-Fated Foreskin: Is It All Bad?

To discuss circumcision intelligently it is necessary to have some knowledge of the structure and function of the foreskin. Structural knowledge involves gross anatomy, cell composition, blood and nerve systems, etc.; functional knowledge involves relating the structural aspects to penile function.

Unfortunately, knowledge of penile function itself is still in a relatively early stage of development. The first pioneering study of human sexual physiology was published in 1966 by Masters and Johnson.[1] In spite of the impetus that this work gave to dozens of other studies, in 1975 the World Health Organization deplored the lack of medical study of human sexuality.[2]

Although much has been learned about human sexuality in general, serious scientists readily admit that they know relatively little about the orgasm process, particularly the nerve cell and blood flow mechanisms of erection and detumescence.[3] (Detumescence, the opposite of erection, is the reduction of penile or clitoral erectile tissue.)

If little is known about the relationship of penile structure to penile function, even less is known about the relationship of foreskin structure to penile function. Although there is some knowledge of foreskin structure, there is an almost total lack of information regarding its function, particularly in coitus. The assumption was made that this tissue served no useful function, and therefore could be removed with almost as much impunity as hair is cut or nails are trimmed. Thus, the subject has commanded little research attention. The prevailing attitude has been that it is unnecessary to study tissue that will be cut off at birth. Moreover, for over a century foreskin reten-

52

tion has been assumed to be potentially dangerous, while its removal has been considered beneficial.

Circumcision opponents, on the other hand, maintain that study of the foreskin's development and structure reveals that this tissue is indeed useful. As a covering, it protects the glans from irritation. The copiousness and sensitivity of the foreskin's nerve structure indicate that it is erotogenic tissue with a useful if not important role in coitus. Opponents of circumcision also maintain that the supposed benefits that the glans is said to derive from the operation are myths and that, in fact, removal diminishes sexual sensation. After millennia of experience with circumcision, it is rather surprising to find that such contradictory views are still held. But since no large-scale or definitive research has been undertaken, the subject is open to speculation and to diametrically opposite claims.

Many physicians have commented on the lack of knowledge of the foreskin. In 1949, Dr. Douglas Gairdner urged that before the foreskin is removed it be understood, but no one has gathered the necessary data.[4] In 1951, Dr. Deron Hovsepian called attention to the lack of information about the anatomy and development of both the penis and foreskin.[5] In 1967, Dr. J. E. Wright decried the total absence of knowledge of the foreskin by the public at large, pointing also to the low level of knowledge of the "anatomy, physiology, and protective function" of the foreskin on the part of recently graduated physicians.[6] In 1972, Dr. R. S. Illingworth wrote that "the anatomists have never studied the form and evolution of this [preputial] orifice."[7]

Although this lack of knowledge is deplored by some physicians, the prevailing medical view was and is that the foreskin is useless tissue. As far back as 1891, Dr. Peter Charles Remondino claimed that the foreskin "cannot . . . be compared to any other useful part of the body . . . it serves no intelligent purpose."[8] He believed the foreskin had afforded early man protection: when man was living unclothed amid heavy brush, the foreskin protected the penis, he said, but it was useless in the modern era. This is an unprovable hypothesis. Many primitive peoples still live among heavy brush. Some practice circumcision, others do not. Almost all wear protective genital coverings and many did so prior to the advent of missionary prudery. Also, this hypothesis can be examined from another aspect by considering female circumcision. Many primitive groups that circumcise males also circumcise females; almost all groups that circumcise females also circumcise males. If the male foreskin was useful in early times, but is useless now, can the same be said for the female foreskin? And if female foreskin was cut off, why was it also necessary to cut off the clitoris and the labia? Are these useless appendages? No one has made such a claim.

Remondino's century-old opinion was repeated verbatim in 1974 by a physician who embraced Remondino's writing almost as gospel. Quoting Remondino, he stated:

> This appendage to civilized man has been termed "a useless bit of flesh." Times were . . . when man, living in a wild state, found locomotion on all fours handier. . . . With the improvement in man's condition . . . the prepuce became a superfluity. . . . [9]

However, the concept of uselessness has been only one aspect of the total perception of the foreskin that has permeated American medicine; actually, the foreskin has been considered dangerous. At the turn of the century, it was implicated in over 100 diseases. It is now known that no such relationship exists. Yet even today, for a variety of other reasons, foreskin retention is still considered potentially dangerous. Of course, this does not mean that the foreskin is ideal, perfect tissue. It can present problems in infancy or later life. But then again, what body tissue, organ, or system is immune to problems throughout life? The question must, therefore, be viewed in perspective.

More than a billion men the world over retain their foreskins and, while exercising minimal penile hygiene, live out their lives with no significant foreskin problems. For those men who, out of ignorance or carelessness, practice no penile hygiene, problems can occur. A lack of hygiene can result in irritations, infections, odors, swelling, etc., and such malfunctions can cause an unretractable foreskin, thereby interfering with sexual function. If gross neglect persists for years, tiny stones (calculi) can form under the foreskin; if such neglect persists for decades, some physicians maintain that it can cause penile cancer. These problems should not be taken lightly. However, it should be noted that the issue is one of almost total lack of hygiene for years or decades. Patients who present problems of advanced foreskin deterioration are likely to be poor, with limited access to hygienic and health care facilities and whose general body neglect is reflected in many other serious physical ailments and in conscious avoidance of medical treatment. Moreover, lack of attention to or abuse of any body tissue, organ, or system, over time, will result in problems. Inadequate nutrition, excessive use of alcohol or tobacco, and inattention to disease symptoms can be serious and even fatal. If the skin, anus, hair, vulva, ears, mouth, etc. are not kept clean for a period of years, severe problems will result. In that regard, the foreskin is little different from any body part. Given minimal care, there should be no problem; neglected, there will be problems.

It should be noted in passing that the pathologic conditions exhibited as a result of male foreskin neglect also occur in females. Actually, problems involving the external female genitalia occur more frequently and are often more serious than those of the male's.

If the foreskin is not to be viewed as vestigial, useless, and potentially harmful tissue, then it is necessary to understand its presumed role: protection of the glans, and sexual function as erogenous tissue. An infant's glans is very delicate and can be seriously irritated by urine. The foreskin acts as a cover for the glans and produces smegma for a protective coating. Dr. George W. Kaplan emphasized that the foreskin protects the meatus (urinary opening). When the foreskin is removed, the meatus becomes susceptible to inflammation (meatitis) and ulceration, conditions virtually never found among uncircumcised boys. Meatal stenosis (closing of the urinary opening) is found much more frequently in circumcised boys.[10] The foreskin also protects the glans against trauma. If diapers are not changed frequently enough, the bacterial decomposition of urine can be a serious irritant to the entire genital area, especially the glans. This is particularly true for circumcised infants: " . . . deprived of this protection [foreskin] the glans become susceptible to injury from sodden clothes. . . . "[11] When the foreskin is retained, diaper irritation can of course affect the foreskin. The point is that it is better to have the irritation on the outer foreskin than on the glans. Moreover, evidence of the protective role of smegma can be noted by the body's reaction to an increased need for protection—the production of more smegma. An excessive collection of urine under the foreskin or the decomposition of such urine stimulates increased smegma production.[12] As to protecting the glans from traumatic injuries, the role of the foreskin is obvious. Unlike the female vulva, which is largely hidden, the male genitalia are exposed and vulnerable to all kinds of trauma. Four specific types of injuries are noted in the medical literature: zipper injuries, burns, toilet seat syndrome, and hair or thread injury.

The entrapment of penile skin by zippers is a common phenomenon.[13] Burns from fire or chemicals can affect any part of the body, and without a foreskin the glans would be injured.[14] Toilet seat syndrome is a term coined by physicians to describe a particular type of penile trauma. When little boys are old enough to urinate from a standing position, their height is often just sufficient for their penises to reach over the rim of the toilet bowl when the seat is raised. If the seat accidentally falls, it can cause painful, if not serious, injury to the penis. This occurs more frequently than is generally believed. In 1973, the American Medical Association published an editorial on the subject in its *Journal*[15] and later carried physician comments.[16]

Another injury that an uncircumcised boy is better protected from than is a circumcised one is hair or thread injury. There have been many cases reported in which human hair or thread is caught in the coronal groove of circumcised boys. Dr. A. J. Thomas called it "penile strangulation."[17] Drs. Mofenson and Greensher referred to it as the "penis tourniquet syndrome."[18] Such injuries may be serious. In uncircumcised boys, the groove is covered by the foreskin.

Any of the above injuries can occur regardless of circumcision status, but there is less chance of injury to the glans itself when the foreskin is present. If necessary, a seriously damaged foreskin can be removed. The same does not hold true for the glans, since its removal would have a major effect upon sexual functioning. Thus the foreskin serves a very definite protective function, which is not denied by the medical literature. Yet pro-circumcision forces reject this protective capacity, claiming that it is better to remove the foreskin and allow the glans to become toughened and protect itself. Their rationale is that after circumcision the epithelial (skin) layer of the glans becomes toughened (cornified) and this is purported to have several advantages: reducing or eliminating premature ejaculation and masturbation and providing protection against venereal disease. As will be shown in subsequent chapters, these claims are simply untrue.

The second function of the foreskin is its role in coitus. If the foreskin is vestigial tissue, having no useful purpose, the assumption can be made that the foreskin has no sexual function. It is certainly true that millions of men survive and function sexually without this tissue. Moreover, if the foreskin develops a pathologic condition it can interfere with sexual function and, in such cases, circumcision improves capability. Obversely, millions of men with foreskins are also able to function sexually. This means that the penis can function with or without this tissue.

There is no substantive evidence that circumcised men perform well and uncircumcised men perform poorly or vice versa. Nor is there any evidence that uncircumcised men and their partners enjoy sex more or less than their circumcised counterparts. Sexual satisfaction and problems occur in both groups. The issue, therefore, is to provide substantive evidence of the foreskin's sexual function. There is absolutely no controversy that the foreskin, particularly the inner layer, contains erogenous tissue. This is true for the penile as well as the clitoral foreskins.

During early fetal development, the genital structures form in exactly the same manner in both sexes. The blood supply and nerve systems are identical; in fact, the gross and microscopic anatomy are also identical. Only after several months of gestation does sex differentiation begin. The penis and its foreskin become larger than the clitoris and its foreskin. The genitalia of each sex are supplied by almost exactly the same number of blood vessels and nerve cells. Since the surface area of the clitoris and its foreskin is far smaller than the male counterparts, the concentration of nerve cells per area is greater in the female genitalia than in the male.[19]

Knowledge of the erogenous qualities of the male foreskin was indirectly confirmed by Masters and Johnson in their chapter entitled, "Orgasm, Anatomy of the Female," written for *The Encyclopedia of Sexual Behavior*. They noted:

The Ill-Fated Foreskin: Is It All Bad?

> The prepuce protects the clitoris in the same manner that the foreskin protects the glans or head of the male penis. The clitoris and prepuce form the most sensitively erotogenic area of the female body.[20]

Since the male and female prepuces (foreskins) are identical in their embryological development, cell structure, and nerve and blood supply systems, it is logical to assume that the male foreskin is also "sensitively erotogenic." This is precisely the view taken by Scandinavian physicians in opposing circumcision, i.e., they maintain that circumcision is sexually harmful. According to Dr. William Robertson (1974): "It is their [the Scandinavian physicians'] thesis that the foreskin with its exquisite nerve endings can't be spared."[21] A similar view was taken in 1970 by another physician in the *Journal of the American Medical Association*:

> Sensory pleasure of foreskin is . . . lost from circumcision. The surface of the exposed glans, as we know, has no capacity to receive or transmit any fine sensations of heat or touch.[22]

In coitus, the penis thrusts into the vagina. The foreskin, as an integral part of the penis, must obviously play a role in the coital process; this is simple to demonstrate. As the penis becomes erect, its internal structures elongate, causing the glans to protrude through the foreskin opening. The outer foreskin layer shifts away from the glans to cover the elongated penile shaft. The key to the foreskin's role in coitus is the position of the "sensitively erotogenic" inner layer. As the erection becomes stronger, the inner layer first folds upon itself like the lining of a sleeve extending beyond the sleeve. The inner foreskin layer continues to shift away from the glans toward the shaft. (See Appendix A.) At maximum erection, the inner layer is fully exposed and covers the upper part of the shaft. Upon thrusting, this erotogenic tissue comes into direct contact with the vaginal wall.

Circumcision proponents acknowledge the foreskin's role in coitus but claim that the tissue is *too* erotogenic, thereby triggering premature ejaculation. This view is not based upon fact; orgasm is induced by a variety of physical and emotional factors. Moreover, if the foreskin is a contributing or a major factor in inducing premature ejaculation, then its removal should reduce the incidence of this problem. As will be shown, no data exist to substantiate this claim.

In addition, if physical stimulation of the uncircumcised glans and the foreskin were the only or even the prime factor triggering orgasm, women should have orgasms more quickly than men, because the concentration of approximately the same number of nerve cells in a smaller area is much greater in women than in men. Actually, female orgasm timing shows just the reverse. It is rare for a woman to have an orgasm after a few seconds of direct clitoral stimulation, but such a rapid response is often common in men, regardless of circumcision status. Furthermore, although it is claimed that removal of the male foreskin will retard ejaculation, it is also claimed that removal of the female foreskin will speed orgasm. Such diametrically opposite theories cannot both be true; actually both are false.

In fact, the complete function and functioning of nerve cells are still little understood. Recent technology—the electron microscope and radioisotopes—have revealed a totally new picture of nerve function, causing neuroanatomists and neurophysiologists to revise their understanding of the nervous system. Preliminary investigations of the optic (sight), olfactory (smell), and trigeminal (facial) nerves have provided startling results.[23] Even the manner in which nerve cells function is just beginning to be elucidated.[24]

No neurological experiments have been reported for the foreskin and, therefore, the role that this erogenous tissue plays in coitus is unknown. In addition, although it is unanimously agreed that the foreskin tissue is erogenous, the effects of its removal have not been investigated. Empirical evidence of the foreskin's role in coitus is difficult to obtain. Uncircumcised men who have had foreskin problems that interfered with their sexual performance frequently report an improvement after being circumcised. Uncircumcised men with no sexual problems who undergo circumcision often report sexual problems afterwards. This may be due to emotional factors as much as to physical factors.

It is physically and ethically impossible to conduct objective research on the role of the foreskin in coitus and the effects of its removal. Foreskins can hardly be removed and replaced at will to conduct before-and-after studies. No man with an intact, well-functioning foreskin would or should agree to its removal for experimental purposes. Moreover, a replacement foreskin could never function in a manner identical to the original, since it would be impossible to reconnect the thousands of capillaries and nerve endings. Thus, although it is highly erotogenic, the precise sexual role of the foreskin can only be assumed.

In the absence of concrete knowledge, the area is a fertile one for the development of myths. Much has been written about the sexual role of the foreskin, but most of it is mythological.

Eight hundred years ago, Rabbi Moses Maimonides (1135-1204), the famous physician and philosopher, thought that circumcision weakened the penis and made Jewish men more temperate sexually. He also accepted the idea that the uncircumcised penis was so sexually superior that if a Jewish woman had intercourse with an uncircumcised man she would not want to separate from him.[25]

This view was contradicted by Dr. H. Speert in 1953. He claimed that among certain unidentified African tribes, women demanded that their husbands be circumcised to prolong coitus.[26]

In 1974, the Maimonides view was upheld. Dr. Lester Persky, a supporter of circumcision, stated that among several unidentified African tribes, when both circumcised and uncircumcised males were available as bedmates, it was the uncircumcised males who were sought after rather than those who were circumcised.[27] Ejaculatory control, a problem for many men, has become highly mythologized. The myth takes two forms: that circumcision provides better ejaculatory control; and that such control is better when the foreskin is retained. For example, a physician, writing of his own circumcision experience, stated: "I can now [after circumcision] ejaculate almost at will. . . ."[28] This statement is contrary to the more popular notion that it is the uncircumcised man who can exercise ejaculatory control.

Masters and Johnson found that the fallacy of greater ejaculatory control by men with intact foreskins was almost universally accepted by their male study subjects, whether they themselves were circumcised or not. Moreover, the study subjects also believed that circumcised men had a greater tendency to impotence.[29] To explore the idea of greater ejaculatory control, the researchers tested 35 circumcised and 35 uncircumcised men for penile sensitivity. No clinically significant difference could be established between the two groups and they concluded that " . . . from a physiologic point of view, a retained foreskin contributes little if anything to the individual male's ejaculatory control."[30] This was the first published research concerning relative penile sensitivity; there is much that can be faulted in this experiment. The sample was small and the sensitivity test did not relate to sexual gratification or even ejaculation in coitus. There is a need for replication using larger samples and refined techniques to measure sensitivity before the Masters and Johnson findings can be accepted as definitive.

Thus, the conclusion is inescapable—knowledge of the foreskin is too limited to fully understand its sexual function. The statements characterized above as mythology may not necessarily be false, but it will take more than hearsay or speculation to prove them true. Sexual gratification is a complex and highly subjective matter. To date, no sexual gratification scale has been established, and there is little likelihood of this occurring in the foreseeable future.

Another factor causing the negative view taken of the foreskin is its secretion of smegma, which, as noted before, serves a useful function. For that matter, so do many other sources of body secretions, which are variously described in positive, neutral, or negative terms. Salivary glands are viewed positively when tasty food is called mouth-watering, neutrally the secretion becomes saliva, and negatively if it is spit. Regarding the sweat glands, a person "labors by the sweat of his brow." If frightened, he may break out in a "cold sweat." There was an old saying: "Horses sweat, men perspire, but women glow." The odor of sweat may have the positive connotation of physical exertion or the negative connotation of lack of hygiene. There are thousands of ecstatic literary references to a woman's readiness for intromission as measured by the extent of her vaginal (and other) secretions. Nasal secretions are called snot and there are few who wax poetic over cerumen (earwax). Tears can denote a variety of emotions: usually sadness, but sometimes happiness, e.g., weeping for joy, or laughing hard enough to cry. Regardless of how body secretions are described, they are handled routinely without a second thought. Tears and noses are wiped; napkins absorb saliva; sweat and vaginal secretions are removed by bathing. It is also true that any gland can go haywire. Excessive earwax accumulation can require removal by medical personnel. Salivary and sweat glands can become infected. But these aberrations are seldom cause for alarm or surgical intervention. Contrast this, however, with the attitude toward smegma. It is rare to find any word or phrase in either lay or medical literature that is remotely positive or even neutral when applied to smegma. The most frequently used adjectives include slimy, filthy, foul-smelling, disease-producing, and carcinogenic.

Recent animal studies have shown that scent plays an important role in sexual attraction. In some species, scent gland secretions have been found in the females and identified as pheremones.[31] Even more recently, pheremones have been discovered in human females.[32] Dr. Alex Comfort has hypothesized that the foreskin may be a scent-diffusing organ for dispensing pheremones in both men and women.[33] Although this is only a hypothesis, it poses an interesting dilemma. Fastidious hygiene disposes of such scents; perhaps they should be retained. Contrarily, one scent is removed by bathing and then others are applied after bathing, including musk oil, which is used by men as a supposed sexual attractant.

Not to be completely negative about circumcision, mention should be made of the usefulness of the ablated foreskins in plastic surgery and experimental biology. When deformities of the penis occur that require repair by plastic surgery, the foreskin conveniently provides the needed grafting tissue. This is a real advantage. The other case is the use of discarded foreskins for the preparation of culture media in which to grow viruses such as polio. To the degree that foreskins may have contributed to the development of the polio vaccine, circumcision should be saluted. However, such applause is questionable since other body tissue can be substituted.[34]

One final thought: if the foreskin is so heinous a tissue that it warrants surgical removal in infancy, what about routine circumcision for animals, since all mammals possess a foreskin? According to Dr. H. Speert (1953): "Large amounts of smegma are produced by the horse, and the penis is one of the common sites of cancer in this species."[35] Veterinarians who were queried rejected the idea of routine animal circumcision as ludicrous. Apparently "dumb" animals can take care of their genitalia; "smart" animals (humans) cannot. The very thought of animal circumcision would arouse humane societies and animal lovers to protest such brutality. Yet it is acceptable for humans.

7

Therapeutic Circumcision: The Tight Foreskin

Circumcision for health reasons falls into two categories: therapeutic and prophylactic; therapeutic to cure a defect, prophylactic to prevent a future problem. Prophylactic circumcision will be discussed in the chapters that follow; this chapter is devoted to the issue of therapeutic circumcision in newborns. Circumcision after the newborn period is discussed in Chapter 13.

Therapy implies a curative process; something is wrong with the foreskin, requiring its removal. What, precisely, is defective in the newborn foreskin necessitating surgery? The main reason is phimosis. Loosely defined, phimosis is a tight foreskin. That means that it is not possible to retract the foreskin to expose the glans. Such tightness in the newborn may be due to two factors: (1) The preputial opening may be too small or too firm to permit the glans to protrude; (2) The glans may adhere to the inner foreskin lining, making separation difficult.

One of the major differences between these two causes of phimosis is the frequency with which they occur. Problems with the newborn preputial orifice (opening) are rare, and such anomalies are not of major concern to this discussion. If the preputial orifice is so small as to prevent passage of urine, corrective measures are required. This may take the form of stretching the tissue, surgical enlargement, or, most likely, circumcision. The latter is truly therapeutic circumcision, for which there can be little or no objection. But it should be stressed that this is a rare condition.

Phimosis, caused by an adherent glans, as will be shown, is not rare. It may occur in perhaps 90% of all newborns. At that age, this condition is normal—not pathological—and it is this supposed "defect" that makes American newborns prime candidates for circumcision.

The first really critical study of therapeutic newborn circumcision was published in the *British Medical Journal* by Dr. Douglas Gairdner in late 1949.[1] The singularity of this study is that it is based upon actual observations of the foreskins of 300 boys of various ages. Foreskin observation is so simple a procedure—and so obvious—yet this had never been done previously. As a result of his findings, Gairdner took strong exception to the then-current attitude toward circumcision and provided substantial data to back up his claims. This study is so unusual in its approach that it is worthy of detailed comment.

First, Gairdner deplored the lack of knowledge of the normal anatomy and function of the foreskin. He then discussed the embryological development of the foreskin and demonstrated (based upon fetal and newborn autopsies) that the foreskin and glans develop as one structure. Gairdner noted that separation may begin during the final months of pregnancy, but the full separation of the foreskin and glans rarely occurs before birth, and thus the incomplete separation of the foreskin and glans renders the normal prepuce of the newborn nonretractable.

Dr. Gairdner examined the foreskin retractability of 100 newborns. Only 4 were fully retractable, 54 were partially so, and 42 were totally unretractable. This was a startling discovery. Circumcision had been and still is recommended both in the medical and lay literature in the United States because the foreskin is "tight" and cannot be pulled back to expose the glans. This is defined as a pathological condition called phimosis. But Gairdner showed that such tightness in most newborns is normal and therefore is not a pathological condition requiring surgery. In the normal course of development the foreskin separates from the glans by itself. Studying an additional 200 boys up to 5 years of age, Gairdner found that at 6 months of age, the foreskins of 80% of the infants were not fully retractable, but by 3 years only 10% were not retractable.

Dr. Gairdner noted that in almost every case the foreskin could be retracted forcibly. This actually involved tearing the foreskin from the glans, precipitating some bleeding and thus possible infection. Such infections have been frequently reported in medical literature. Moreover, stripped of its foreskin cover, the meatus (urinary opening) becomes susceptible to ulceration, called Brenneman's ulcers. Such meatal ulcers are virtually never found in uncircumcised boys. Although both infections and Brenneman's ulcers are usually amenable to simple treatment, they occasionally can be serious.

Gairdner also commented that any child below 5 years of age with an unretractable foreskin "should be accepted with equanimity as normal," and noted that for a child over the age of 5, separation can easily be accomplished without surgery.

As to smegma, the normal secretion produced under the foreskin, Gairdner claimed that this substance protects the glans. This is particularly important if wet diapers are left on too long, since decomposition of the urine can cause irritation of the glans if it is not coated with smegma.

Reviewing all the claims made for circumcision, Gairdner rejected them as unconvincing and concluded that the prepuce of the young infant should be left in its natural state.

Gairdner's study received wide exposure in medical journals of all English-speaking countries and his work has been quoted in dozens of articles. Although ardently pro-circumcision writers in the United States have attacked Gairdner's conclusion that routine infant circumcision is unwise, none has bothered to replicate his study. This is indeed strange; if Gairdner is wrong, why not redo the study to prove him wrong? If Gairdner is correct, why do American physicians still recommend therapeutic newborn circumcision to cure phimosis?

Gairdner's study was replicated in Denmark in 1968 by Dr. Jacob Øster.[2] Øster hypothesized that Gairdner's data might be unreliable on 3 counts; first that he had relied on single, not continual (longitudinal) observations; second, the sample had been limited to newborns and children up to age 5; third, the sample of uncircumcised children had been selected in a country that did practice circumcision and sample selection might possibly have been biased. Dr. Øster was the school health officer of a Danish town where all the 1,968 male school children between the ages 6-17 were uncircumcised. A total of 9,545 observations were made; one subsample was examined annually for 7 years and another subsample for 8 years. Dr. Øster's data in many ways paralleled that of Dr. Gairdner. Preputial adhesions were found in 63% of the boys aged 6-7, but in only 3% of the boys aged 16-17. Among the 95 boys who were 17 years old, there were no adhesions.[3] Smegma was found in 1% of the 6-7-year-olds and in 8% of those aged 16-17. Dr. Øster believed that smegma production increased at puberty. Out of a total of 1,968 boys, 4 required preputial dilation, after which they developed normally; 3 required circumcision, giving a circumcision rate of 0.15%. In retrospect, Dr. Øster hypothesized that the 3 circumcisions might have been avoided and suggested the possibility that the surgery was iatrogenic (caused by medical treatment), resulting from too strenuous attempts at retraction. He concluded—as did Gairdner—that the foreskin should be left to develop normally. If patience is exercised, adhesions will almost always resolve as the child matures.[4]

The fact that the Gairdner and Øster studies are not challenged, but are accepted, is reinforced by the report of the American Academy of Pediatrics' Ad Hoc Task Force on Circumcision (1975), which noted:

> A diagnosis of phimosis cannot be made with assurance in the newborn period because the cleavage plane between the glans and the . . . preputial layer . . . is not developed at birth. . . . It therefore follows that "phimosis of the newborn" is not a valid medical indication for a circumcision.[5]

Thus, the accepted theory expounded in both medical and lay literature for treating phimosis of the newborn by circumcision is totally in error. A nonretractable foreskin is normal. The reaffirmation of the findings of the two studies attests to their soundness. It is no wonder that Dr. Gairdner is credited with having helped influence British medical opinion against routine circumcision.[6]

During the 14 years following the publication of Dr. Gairdner's findings, there were occasional articles critical of American circumcision practices. Most, however, continued to support the procedure and offer "proof" of its advantages, including the "treatment" of phimosis. Even current medical dictionaries, published long after the Gairdner and Øster studies, do not take their findings into account. One such dictionary states that phimosis is: "Narrowness of the opening of the prepuce, preventing its being drawn back over the glans."[7] Another medical dictionary defines it as: "Tightness of the foreskin so that it cannot be drawn back over the glans."[8] Neither definition is accurate. Phimosis may be due to narrowness of the opening at the tip of the foreskin, or it may be due to the foreskin's adhering to the glans, which is not even mentioned. Moreover, both definitions imply that phimosis is a problem or abnormality. This would be the case in adulthood; however, phimosis caused by an adherent glans is a normal condition in infancy.

Although a normal infant foreskin may not retract easily, in many books this is given as the precise reason for electing circumcision:

> Circumcision is medically obligatory if the foreskin is so tight that it cannot easily be retracted over the glans.[9]

> Basically there is no need for circumcision if the foreskin is easily retracted over the head of the penis.[10]

> There are two distinct medical points of view: that which favors its [circumcision's] routine use on male infants, and that which would reserve it for babes in whom the foreskin cannot be drawn back readily.[11]

Regardless of how the above statements are qualified, they mean one thing—circumcise. Others take a more rational view:

> Unless the prepuce is so tight that it obstructs the passage of urine [an exceedingly rare occurrence] there is no medical indication for circumcision.[12]

Antithetical views may also be noted in the opinions of two physicians addressing their fellow pediatricians. Dr. Charles Schlosberg wrote (1971):

> ... it is important to consider phimotic predisposition.... To determine... predisposition [to phimosis] one grasps the prepuce ... and pushes it ... Mild bleeding will occur.[13]

For bleeding to occur, the foreskin must literally be torn from the glans. The opposing view was stated by Dr. George W. Kaplan (1977):

> ... freeing adhesions ... is tantamount to cruel and unusual punishment and is unfounded physiologically and medically.[14]

Views contrary to medical evidence are still being offered in the popular press: Jane E. Brody, writing in the *New York Times* (1979), quoted a pediatrician who urged that preputial adhesions be broken by the physician at 3 or 4 weeks of age.[15] Thus, despite the definitive research of Øster and Gairdner, accepted by the American Academy of Pediatrics, many American physicians persist in holding to the outdated view that phimosis in the newborn is a pathological condition requiring immediate surgical remedy.

8
Penile Hygiene

Probably the most widely acclaimed circumcision benefit is that it simplifies penile hygiene. This is the key to all its other alleged advantages. The reasoning is a follows:

- The penis in its natural state is difficult to keep clean.
- Such lack of cleanliness provides a convenient place for smegma and dirt to accumulate and for germs to hide.
- Among these germs are those that cause venereal disease.
- The accumulated smegma, deposited on the cervix in coitus, causes cervical cancer, and the smegma infiltrating the urethra causes prostatic cancer.
- The subpreputial accumulations irritate (stimulate) the erogenous foreskin lining, causing masturbation.
- The very presence of the foreskin makes the glans excessively sensitive. This results in premature ejaculation.
- Over long periods, smegma can cause penile cancer.

The problem with the above statements is that, although they seem reasonable and logical, they are either patently false or at best unsubstantiated.
  According to many American physicians, the uncircumcised penis is a difficult organ to keep clean; in fact, so difficult that preventive surgery is urged for the sake of cleanliness. No other body organ is dealt with so summarily for supposed hygienic purposes. If the penis is actually such an unhygienic organ, then it should follow that about 75% of the world's male population, i.e., those who remain uncircumcised throughout life, must be paying a dreadful price in pain and disease as a result. There is no evidence that

this is true. If the world's uncircumcised male population had severe foreskin problems, physicians in other countries would have adopted either newborn or adult circumcision practices. They have done neither. Moreover, Britain, which largely abandoned newborn circumcision a quarter-century ago, has found no need to reinstate the surgery because of penile hygiene problems or for any other reason. In fact, some primitive peoples, who previously practiced both male and female circumcision, although retaining the female practice, abandoned the male procedure more than 50 years ago with no apparent ill effects to the males.[1]

Two hypotheses have been presented to explain the initial acceptance of circumcision for penile hygiene: climate and superior culture. Neither hypothesis has much validity. There is some logic in the climate hypothesis in that people in tropical areas are more prone to certain skin diseases. An examination of a map showing the distribution of countries practicing circumcision reveals a preponderance within 20° north or south of the equator.[2] However, there are many exceptions. For example, in southern Asia, the Moslem countries (Pakistan, Bangladesh, etc.) practice circumcision, but India, Thailand, Vietnam, Laos, and Cambodia do not. Similarly, in Africa, many groups practice male circumcision, while other groups living but a few miles away do not.[3] In South America, very few groups follow the practice, generally most do not. Another exception is the Athabascan Indians of the Yukon, who do circumcise, although they live in a cold climate. Thus, it is certainly possible that a long time ago climate may have played a role in the introduction of circumcision in some areas. However, at this point it is an unproven hypothesis. The distribution of countries practicing clitoridectomy and infibulation follows similar climatic lines. No one has claimed that the female surgery is practiced for hygienic purposes, however.

Some circumcising peoples practiced cultural chauvinism in that they considered themselves superior to other groups who did not adopt the practice. The ancient Hebrews scorned the Philistines for many reasons, including their not practicing circumcision. However, it would be a serious error to view noncircumcising peoples as having had lower cultural levels. The culture of the Hindus was not lower than that of the Moslems; nor were ancient Greek and Roman cultures lower than those of ancient Egypt or Israel. Actually, the noncircumcising Greeks considered themselves superior to the Jews and were successful in having many young Jews obliterate evidence of their circumcision. (See Chapter 16, "Jews and Circumcision.") But ancient cultural and climatic factors have nothing to do with the present-day acceptance of newborn circumcision for hygienic reasons in the United States.

In the United States, hygienic reasons have most often been cited as the justification for circumcision. We must discover, therefore, if the penis in its natural state really is so difficult to keep clean. Would teaching penile hygiene and providing the wherewithal for its practice solve the problem?

There is no question that some men do not practice proper penile hygiene. This statement, in one form or another, appears dozens of times in the medical literature. It is based largely upon the experience during World War II, when millions of men were examined prior to induction. This was one of the points made in 1970 by Jane E. Brody in refuting Dr. E. Noel Preston's article.[4] Ms. Brody quoted a Tennessee obstetrician to the effect that observation of military recruits revealed a high percentage who did not practice proper penile hygiene.[5] This statement is undeniably true. Unfortunately, no attempt has been made to clarify the picture presented. It is necessary to realize that:

1. To be of draft age in World War II and to be uncircumcised was to some extent tantamount to being poor. Therefore, the statement could be made that the poor did not follow proper penile hygiene practices to the same extent as did the well-to-do.
2. The total health of recruits who were poor was nothing less than scandalous. This was reflected in all criteria, including penile hygiene.

No nationwide circumcision study in the United States has been conducted. Thus, it is impossible to compare the demographic characteristics of circumcised to uncircumcised males. This is as true today as it was 100 or 50 years ago. However all studies of small, nonrandom, and unrepresentative samples suggest that the poor, rural, and minority member males were less likely to be circumcised than middle-class, urban, and white males. For example, the unrepresentative sample of military men in World War II studied by Dr. Eugene A. Hand (1947) showed that almost 100% of the Jews were circumcised; among non-Jews the rate was 30% for whites and 17% for blacks. (The sample was unrepresentative because it was taken from one military hospital near New York City. Jews and blacks, who comprised about 3% and 10% of the national population, respectively, constituted 22% and 25%, respectively, of the sample.)

Virtually all men recruited in World War II were born in the 20-year period 1907-1927. Dr. Hand's sample revealed a circumcision rate among white Christians at almost twice that of blacks.[6]

In a 1966 study in one Canadian hospital, where the overall circumcision rate was estimated to be 50%, private patients were more likely to be circumcised than were ward patients. This situation was also found to exist in England.[7] A similar picture was also reported for the United States by Dr. H. Speert (1953) who, in a study at the Sloane Hospital in New York City, showed that the 1937 circumcision frequency was 3 times greater for private patients than for ward patients (72% vs. 23%). However, by 1951, the circumcision rates were equal (73%).[8]

Thus, the well-to-do were more likely to be circumcised than the poor. This fact appears to contradict the basic argument for penile hygiene, since the poor have less access to hygienic living conditions and health care than do their wealthier counterparts. Therefore, from the standpoint of purported hygienic benefits, the poor would have benefited more from circumcision than the rich, and yet they were less likely to be circumcised.

It is interesting to note that in the decade following the introduction of the National Health Service in England, the drop in the circumcision rate was initially *less* among manual workers than nonmanual workers.[9] In other words, among the "upper" strata of society, there was a "first in-first out" phenomenon.

Poor penile hygiene among army inductees could therefore have been as much a matter of social class as circumcision status. In fact, had a study been undertaken of uncircumcised officers, the incidence of poor penile hygiene would very likely have been different from that of enlisted men.

But what was the total health status of draftees in World War II? Examinations revealed an appalling health picture of adult American males; about half of all men called up for military service were rejected for physical, emotional, and educational reasons. Many serious ailments were discovered in these examinations, reflecting an almost total absence of health care and health education, particularly among the poor, minority, and rural populations.

For example, dental studies among these population segments showed that few, if any, had ever visited a dentist on a periodic basis. Tooth decay, gum disease, and orthodontic problems were rampant. One study of the 2 million men called up for the draft in 1942 revealed that 10% were rejected because they did not have 12 sound teeth out of a possible 32.[10] The dental condition of draftees remained unchanged in the later war years, and as the war continued, the need for additional manpower increased but the reserve pool of available men diminished. This made it necessary to reduce dental standards for acceptance to such an extent that by the end of the war dentists quipped: "All a draftee needed was two jaws, preferably one upper and one lower."

Poor health and poor hygiene are often reflected in many parts of the body. In fact, a correlation could likely have been established between poor oral hygiene and poor penile hygiene. Should it have been hypothesized therefore that foreskin retention was related to poor oral hygiene and vice versa?

There is ample evidence that dental hygiene has not improved markedly since World War II for large segments of the American population.[11] Yet no one has suggested that teeth be routinely extracted to prevent cavities or other dental problems. On the other hand, the circumcision rate in the

United States has increased since World War II, but the "gains" anticipated from this massive application of surgery have not materialized.

Health problems a generation ago and today are by no means limited to penile or oral hygiene. There was a great hue and cry during and after the war to improve health care; however, relatively little has been accomplished, despite astronomical expenditures of $140 billion in 1976[12] and an anticipated $228 billion in 1981.[13] The lion's share of such sums goes for treatment of episodic and chronic ills; a small portion goes to research, less to preventive medicine, and a paltry sum to health education. The net effect of this approach to health care expenditure priorities has been noted frequently.[14]

Whether the issue is preventive innoculations or health examinations, the spread of carcinogens, lice infestation, or the availability of health care, one fact stands out—the poor are underserved in health care delivery, preventive services, and health education. This was dramatically revealed in a front-page story (1977), in the *New York Times*:

> [The dimensions] of the problem were suggested . . . by Senator Ernest F. Hollings [of South Carolina] . . . he and a doctor visited one aging shack that housed 16 people, living without heat, electricity, running water, bath or toilet. The doctor diagnosed one case of pellagra. Among the family, a child had rickets, another scurvy.
>
> Across the region there were skin diseases, rotting teeth, uncorrected vision problems, sores, infections, scarlet fever, strep throat—all untreated. Two-thirds of the children had parasites in the digestive tract; some regularly vomited up or defecated foot-long round worms.[15]

The list of health problems in the United States is almost infinite: alcoholism, drug abuse, venereal disease, occupational hazards, undiagnosed ailments such as diabetes and hypertension, impurities in the water, food, and air, to name but a few. Thus, despite the outpouring of tens of billions of dollars for health care, millions of Americans live in conditions of dire neglect of health and hygiene. Preventive medicine and health education are relegated to secondary importance and this is reflected in the total health picture in the United States.

The massive American health problems cannot be solved by physicians or surgeons alone. In fact, no real dent will be made until the root causes of poverty, poor housing, malnutrition, unemployment, inadequate education, discrimination, etc. are addressed. This is true for all aspects of health and hygiene; it is certainly true for penile hygiene.

In fact, the problem is not simply penile hygiene, but genital hygiene affecting both sexes. Actually, genital hygiene is even more important for women than for men. *New York Times* writer Jane E. Brody stated in 1977: "The problem of urinary tract infections (U.T.I.) is known only too well to millions of American women and a lesser number of men."[16] Ms. Brody explained that women are more susceptible to U.T.I. than are men because their urethras are shorter, which allows easy germ migration to the bladder, and because the female urethral opening is nearer the anal and vaginal orifices, which are sources of infectious organisms. In fact, hygienic problems of the female external genitalia occur with greater frequency and often with greater severity than in the male counterparts. Putting aside venereal diseases, which affect both sexes, infections of the bladder, tumors of the urethra, and external genital cancers occur much more often among women than among either circumcised or uncircumcised men.

Female genital hygiene vis-à-vis circumcision can be considered by reversing the sex roles. Consider the following statements:

1. The clitoris is covered by a foreskin;
2. The inner lining of the foreskin secretes smegma;
3. Some, perhaps many, women do not keep the clitoral area clean;
4. As a result smegma, dirt, germs, and other body materials can accumulate under the foreskin;
5. Such accumulation can be malodorous, irritating, and cause infections and adhesions;
6. Foreskin problems can interfere with coitus;
7. Some physicians believe that over extended periods of time such constant irritations can cause cancer of the clitoris.

Each of the above statements is true. Therefore, the simple conclusion that could be drawn is that if the clitoral foreskin can pose such problems, it should also be cut off in infancy! A startling conclusion? Not really, because if you substitute "men" for "women" and "penis" for "clitoris" in the previous statements, you derive the rationale for male hygienic circumcision. Yet no one in recent years has suggested routine female circumcision to improve genital hygiene. However, should some enterprising surgeon develop a simple nonanesthesia procedure for female newborns to facilitate female hygiene, it would be rejected out of hand as unnecessary and cruel. Yet an analogous procedure is routinely visited on American males!

Why is male hygienic circumcision readily accepted in the United States, while the female counterpart is considered abhorrent? One of the answers lies in crude sexism. Women are blamed for male circumcision! Before discussing this bizarre concept, the question of penile hygiene must be examined both by itself and, more importantly, within the framework of total body hygiene.

Probably all Americans accept the advisability of keeping the body clean. They are constantly bombarded by messages to do so by the media, whose objective is to sell products relating to body hygiene from head to foot and all parts in between. Body hygiene is recognized as a lifetime activity, from the cradle to the grave. Infants must be bathed; so too must the infirm and the aged. In many cultures (Japanese, Jewish), even the dead are washed before burial. Body hygiene is also recognized as a prerequisite for good health. The neglect of any aspect of bodily hygiene can have untoward consequences.

In addition to the concept of total body hygiene, certain organs are singled out for special attention. For example, lack of hair care can result in matting, odors, and eventually skin problems. Excess earwax must be cleaned out to avoid discomfort and hearing difficulties. The folds of the outer ear must also be cleaned carefully to avoid infections.

Some organs, such as the mouth, require skill for proper hygiene and tend to receive special attention. Toothpaste, powders, brushes (manual and electric), pressurized water cleaners, toothpicks, dental floss, mouth washes, plaque identifiers, and gum massagers are but some of the products used in dental hygiene. Yet, despite the use of such products, dentists recommend periodic prophylactic visits in order to clean the teeth and care for the gums. This is accepted standard practice going back at least 50 years.

One possible remedy for lack of hair and dental hygiene would be the removal of these parts, since people can and do get along without them. However, such a drastic course of action has *not* been proposed as a general panacea for a lack of hygiene. Yet this is precisely what is being recommended when circumcision is rationalized as a panacea for male genital hygiene.

At the opposite end of the digestive tract is the anus, where fecal material is discharged. Children are taught to wipe themselves after each bowel movement. If fecal material remains in the anal area or soils the hands, it is easily removed by hand-washing or bathing. Lack of anal hygiene can lead to irritation and infection.

Attitudes toward body hygiene often have social, cultural, and economic derivations. For example, the sauna, snow bathing, and birch stick skin beating are associated with the Finns. Orthodox Jewish women are provided with a ritual bath (mikvah) for use after menstruation. The bidet was introduced some 300 years ago for female hygiene and is still popular in France and other European and Latin American countries. At the opposite end of the cleanliness spectrum, some people do not bathe for years and live to be 100 years old (without the benefit of circumcision).[17]

Nowadays, in the United States the daily bath or shower is more the rule than the exception. However, this was not always so. A century ago, the suggestion by one physician that women bathe once a month was considered a radical idea.[18] At the turn of the century, inside plumbing was rare, especially among the poor. As previously noted, this is still true in several parts of the country.[19] Without inside plumbing, daily bathing was a rarity; the commonplace was the Saturday-night bath. There are many references to children being sewn into their underwear for the winter. Thus, attention to body hygiene was, and to a degree still is, a reflection of economic status.

This is also true in other parts of the world. The Moslems and Hindus of the Asian subcontinent are often compared in order to show that the former have fewer penile problems because of circumcision. However, the noncircumcising Parsis of India have fewer problems than the Moslems, but then again the Parsis are a well-to-do group in contrast to the impoverished Hindus and Moslems.

In the United States, the enormous attention to body hygiene is attested to by the proliferation of soaps, shampoos, dentifrices, deodorants, etc., which can be found in any drugstore or supermarket. Special products are provided for the eyes, nose, skin, lips, hair, ears, feet, nails, teeth, etc. The genitalia of the female are singled out for special attention by such items as menstrual products, douches, sprays, deodorants, towelettes, etc. Some of these products are not only superfluous, but useless or even harmful. The notable exception is the male genitalia, for which not one hygienic product is offered. (Cruex and other brands of powder are sold for "jock itch." However these relate to the crotch, not the penis. The Revlon Company introduced a penile spray in 1970-1971, but the product was short-lived.) In view of the prevalence of circumcision, perhaps such products are thought to be unnecessary.

Without passing judgment on the proliferation of hygienic products or the advantages and disadvantages of their use, we must note that advertising has served the purpose of calling attention to the need for body hygiene. Most Americans now accept hygienic practices as a matter of routine.

Of course there are people who neglect body hygiene. In any city, a visit to "Skid Row" reveals many men and some women literally lying in the gutters. Among such people there is an almost total lack of hygiene, and they almost invariably suffer from a wide variety of ailments.

The obvious solution for a lack of specific body part hygiene is to provide proper knowledge and the necessary concomitant sanitary facilities. Surgery is an unacceptable solution.

In order to understand why circumcision has become the preeminent solution for the "problem" of male genital hygiene, it is necessary to review a number of societal attitudes toward sexuality, primarily female sexuality. A century ago, masturbation was viewed not only as evil but harmful, particularly for women. This fear of masturbation still lingers on and creates a dilemma, inasmuch as proper hygiene requires touching the genitalia, but such touching is also frowned upon by many parents as a possible source of stimulation. Moreover, according to one physician (1976), since the female sex organs are more hidden than their male counterparts, this confers an aura of mystery, resulting in avoidance by girls of even touching themselves.[20] To overcome this mysteriousness, some women's groups have urged women to explore their own bodies and those of other women.[21] Anatomically correct dolls—female and male, circumcised and uncircumcised—are now being merchandised.[22] In spite of these endeavors and other sex education efforts, Dr. Doris E. Fiedler stated in 1975 that many myths and misconceptions still exist and that most women are misinformed about correct genital cleansing techniques.[23]

Although a discussion of female genital hygiene may appear to be a digression from the subject matter, it is highly pertinent, since this is where the American medical profession's sexist attitudes come into play. Male circumcision is urged precisely because it is claimed that since women are hesitant and misinformed about their own genitals they are, therefore, deficient in genital hygiene. Ergo, they cannot teach proper hygiene to their daughters; and, more to the point, they cannot teach proper genital hygiene to their sons. This so-called "inability" to practice and teach penile hygiene becomes a significant although specious factor in the high circumcision rate. Almost a century ago, Dr. P. C. Remondino wrote: "It is all very well to instruct the mothers . . . to keep the parts within the prepuce clean, but they can not or will not do it."[24] In 1946, prior to his reconsideration of circumcision, Dr. Spock echoed Remondino, noting: "The mother shrinks [from retracting the foreskin]."[25] A nurse, describing the daily need to cleanse the foreskin, wrote (1959): "To some mothers this means a frightening ordeal."[26] And Dr. Patel (1966) claimed that mothers gave approval for circumcision because they were uncertain about their ability to teach genital cleanliness to the child and were, furthermore, doubtful of his cooperation.[27]

Although it is unfortunately true that mothers have the major, if not sole responsibility, for their sons' penile hygiene, it does not necessarily follow that women are stupid, unwilling to learn, or incapable of practicing and teaching good hygiene. Physicians have propounded this myth to the point where it has become accepted by many women. Such an attitude is clearly sexist and as long as such sexism exists in the United States, circumcision will be practiced to ostensibly promote penile hygiene and the blame will continue to be placed upon women.

Thus, the standard line of reasoning is as follows:

- The uncircumcised penis is difficult to keep clean;
- Lack of penile hygiene can lead to dire consequences;
- Mothers are incapable of assuming responsibility for penile hygiene;
- Therefore, to compensate for the mothers' shortcomings, cut off the offending part.

Some medical writers go far afield from the question of penile hygiene in their attacks on women's attitudes. It is claimed that mothers desire circumcision as a means of harming or dominating the child. In Chapter 3, we mentioned Dr. John Foley's blatantly sexist claim (1966) that: " . . . among the biggest boosters of circumcision are neurotic females, whose unhappy sex lives prompt them to injure a man where he feels it most."[28] Other writers, though more subtle, are just as sexist. In 1975, two pediatricians wrote:

> The enthusiasm of American mothers in endorsing this operation has been explained by one author as "an intensely matriarchal society permanently influencing the physical characteristics of its males."[29]

That these attitudes have been adopted and internalized by women can be noted from a 1966 study in which a physician interviewed the mothers of 100 recently circumcised Canadian infants and reported that:

> In 74 cases the mother made the decision for operation. Mothers frequently have very firm views on the subject; in 33 cases they would have insisted on the operation. Twenty-six mothers had not discussed the subject with their husbands, complaining that the latter were indifferent or insisting that it was a woman's business. They frequently discussed the subject with friends, relatives and neighbors and sought information from baby books and women's magazines.[30]

Another alleged penile hygiene advantage of circumcision with sexist overtones is mentioned by "Dr. Valentine" (1974) in relation to coitus: "Semen, vaginal secretions and any lubricants that have been used are 'trapped' under the skin, there to remain for several hours or overnight. . . . "[31] This statement must be challenged on two counts: No one has even attempted to demonstrate that allowing such substances to remain overnight is in any way harmful. Moreover, if it is harmful to the male, how detrimental is it to the female to bear this "trapped" material overnight?

In the absence of logical and medical reasons to support circumcision, penile hygiene is inflated to preposterous proportions and, in turn, the mother becomes the villain. That is, she is either hostile to her son and wants to hurt him or she is incapable of practicing good penile hygiene without circumcision.

Although there are many references in medical literature to women not practicing proper genital hygiene in regard to their own bodies, there are few, if any, references to the mothers being unable to clean or teach cleanliness to their daughters regarding their daughters' genitalia. One may therefore ask whether girls are simply considered less important than boys, especially since female anatomy may make cleanliness even more difficult than it is for males. If, for the sake of discussion, these sexist arguments are accepted as correct, why is this attitude limited to American and Canadian women? Such charges are not leveled against women in any other country. This type of reasoning is cultural in nature and is supported by many American medical practitioners.

Bear in mind that three-quarters of the world's males are uncircumcised; also little serious emphasis is placed on penile hygiene and only a tiny proportion have foreskin problems. Uncircumcised men have been known to survive in the jungle without the benefit of modern sanitation for 30 years and have suffered no skin or foreskin problems.[32] In contrast, physicians report poor penile hygiene among "intelligent private patients."[33]

The stereotypic view that the poor are dirty and the well-to-do clean, or that blacks are dirty and whites are clean is challenged from several sources. For example, a 1978 study in West Germany revealed that 43% of the Germans believed they are cleaner than the rest of the world and 77% considered themselves immaculate as individuals. However, the study showed that about 75% of German men did not wash themselves daily from head to foot.[34]

On the other hand, some black Africans consider themselves to be cleaner than the English. A Nigerian professor, in a 1979 pamphlet for his countrymen who were planning to go to England, advised them to bring a sponge with them because the British do not take baths regularly.[35]

There is no question that prolonged lack of hygiene can cause serious problems and people often seek assistance for such problems when it is too late to be of help. Whether this attitude stems from ignorance, fear, or false modesty is hard to state. This is a real problem and appears to be world-wide in scope. Physicians often relate cases of patients seeking help with foreskin problems only after prolonged suffering.[36] But the problem is not limited to males. There are thousands of examples of women who identify lumps in their breasts or are aware of unusual vaginal bleeding and refuse to seek medical advice because they are fearful that the consequence may be a mastectomy or a hysterectomy.

The problem of penile hygiene must be dealt with on an educational, not a surgical level. To perform millions of prophylactic circumcisions in anticipation of potential future problems is the wrong approach which, in the long run, can cause more harm than good. The authors of a health science textbook wrote (1969):

> Although this practice [circumcision] makes cleanliness easier, it is not a requisite for good hygiene. Improperly performed circumcisions may cause more problems than they are purported to prevent.[37]

Even physicians who are strongly against circumcision are influenced by the penile hygiene rhetoric. The American Academy of Pediatrics Task Force

Report on Circumcision, which categorically opposed routine newborn circumcision stated:

> A program of education to continuing good personal hygiene would offer all the advantages of routine circumcision without the attendant surgical risk. Therefore, circumcision of the male neonate cannot be considered an essential component of adequate total health care.[38]

This is a clearly stated and reasoned summary. However, even with this sound approach, the following statement is found in the body of the Task Force Report: "If circumcision is not elected, the necessity for lifelong penile hygiene should be discussed. . . . "[39] This statement is not incorrect. It can be faulted only because it relates exclusively to *penile* hygiene. That is, every aspect of personal hygiene is a lifelong necessity. There is no body part for which hygiene should be practiced for only a limited period, i.e., at what age should one stop bathing, shampooing hair, washing the anus, or brushing teeth? Even when all one's teeth are extracted, the dentures must be brushed or cleaned and oral hygiene continued. To single out penile hygiene creates the impression that hygiene for this organ alone is exceedingly complex and difficult. That little is known about the foreskin and relatively little attention is paid to its care derives from the fact that it is felt that there is little need to study or care for it since it will be lopped off at birth. Therefore, in order to promote circumcision, the impression generated by the medical profession is that caring for an uncircumcised penis is an arduous task.

Quite to the contrary though, hygiene for an uncircumcised penis is simple. In regard to newborns, care should be exercised since the foreskin may still be physically attached to the glans and pushing the foreskin back too soon can tear the connecting tissue, which, in itself, is not too serious a matter except that it will make the glans very tender for a few days. In such cases, a protective ointment may be applied and care should be taken to make sure that diapers are changed frequently in order to avoid retention and decomposition of urine. The foreskin of a newborn can be left alone for a few days, weeks, months, or longer. Dr. E. N. Preston states that special attention need not be paid to it for 3 years.[40] Dr. D. Gairdner[41] extends this period to 5 years; Dr. J. Øster suggests an even longer period.[42] If this seems difficult to accept, remember that a baby's mouth is similarly left alone until the first teeth emerge. No guidebook suggests brushing an infant's gums. There is no need for it, since at that age the normal mouth flora and saliva take care of mouth hygiene. Similarly, the smegma is there to protect the glans and no harm will come from doing nothing about the infant's foreskin for months or years. At this age, the body takes care of itself.

The foreskin can be pushed back when it is ready. But, again, the body takes care of itself. The penis is capable of erection from birth on, usually as a response to local irritation or stimulation. When such an erection occurs, the glans will protrude from the foreskin and normal separation will occur. In addition, within the first year of life, all children discover their genitals and, in the course of such normal play, often pull the foreskin back.

When the foreskin and glans have separated, pushing the foreskin back is very simple and can be done while bathing the child. If there are any doubts or questions, an experienced nurse or physician can be asked to demonstrate proper techniques. Caring for the folds of the female genitalia is just as simple—or as complicated. In fact, there may be special problems with the labia, which on occasion, may fuse. Parents are often concerned about this problem and ask their physician to break the adhesions. Dr. T. G. Shiller had this advice (1973) for that condition: " . . . So long as the baby is able to urinate comfortably the situation is best left alone. . . . "[43]

By the time the child is several months old, the daily bath will have become associated with shampooing the hair, washing the ears, anus, between the toes, and the glans. Since such routine will continue until the child is old enough to bathe himself, it will become a well-established habit and good body hygiene practices will be followed as a matter of course.

The question of penile hygiene is as much attitudinal and cultural as it is medical. The threats of dire consequences resulting from neglect of penile hygiene because it is too difficult a task constitute nothing less than coercive scare tactics to frighten parents into accepting circumcision. The medical profession of no other country adopts this view.

Some American physicians (1978) carry the question of penile hygiene in uncircumcised males to extremes, claiming that older boys as well as men may need to wash the penis more than once a day, because the secretions accumulate rapidly.[44] No mention is made of the need for the equivalent practice in females.

In most countries where routine circumcision is not followed and a modicum of hygiene is maintained, there are few foreskin problems. And when such occur, they are usually handled medically, rarely surgically. Where abysmal hygiene exists, more of *all* types of health problems will occur. However, it is the United States that is under discussion, and here there is no excuse for poor sanitation or lack of health information.

The American medical establishment must overcome its own sexual hang-ups and sexist attitudes. The myth that American women are either male-haters or ignoramuses, which causes them to be unwilling or unable to properly care for their sons, must be challenged. If mothers the world over are capable of teaching their sons proper body hygiene from mouth to anus, then so are American mothers. The need is for the American medical establishment to reform its attitudes and encourage health education as much as they now do circumcision.

9

Circumcision and Venereal Disease

For well over 100 years, medical and lay journals in England, and even more so in the United States, have claimed that one of the benefits of circumcision is the prevention of venereal disease. These claims were based upon the results of two studies, one conducted in London by Dr. Jonathan Hutchinson in 1854-1855, and the other at Metropolitan Hospital in New York City in 1882-1883.[1] In each study a demographic analysis of venereal disease patients showed that of all religious groups, Jews had the lowest incidence of venereal disease. In seeking a rationale for this phenomenon, the distinct physical difference—that Jews were circumcised and non-Jews were not—appeared to be the obvious reason. Such factors as the closeness of Jewish family life, Orthodox religious practices, and the isolation of Jews, just recently emerged from ghetto existence, were not considered. There also was the fact that many Christian prostitutes refused to consort with Jews, a carryover from the Middle Ages, when the death penalty was the punishment meted out both to Jews who visited a Christian prostitute and the prostitute herself.[2] (This was also true in Nazi Germany under Hitler's Nuremburg Laws; it was known as *Rassenschande*.)

The conclusions drawn from these early investigations might be excused because of the lack of knowledge of both venereal disease and epidemiology. Epidemiology had not yet been developed as a medical specialty, nor had the organisms that cause venereal diseases been identified. Instead, these findings were considered both logical and spectacular and viewed as absolute "evidence" of the efficacy of circumcision. Once such studies have been published in medical journals, they are rarely challenged and, in this case, not only were they not challenged but they were perpetuated and embellished. This led to the development of a medical rationale to explain why circumcision protects against venereal disease:

1. The foreskin and its attendant smegma provide a convenient place for organisms to hide;
2. When the foreskin is removed, the glans toughens making it more difficult for organisms to penetrate it.

While both statements appear logical, they are not true. They were and still are, however, believed to be true by many physicians. For example, Dr. Alan F. Guttmacher, a well-known gynecologist and obstetrician, wrote an article for *Parents' Magazine* in 1941 encouraging circumcision for many reasons, one of which was: "Venereal disease is less easily contracted by the circumcised male. . . ."[3] A few years later (1947), an editorial in the lay health magazine *Hygeia* carried an almost identical statement.[4] In that same year *Newsweek* reported the "sensational and heavily documented" findings of Dr. Eugene A. Hand. The magazine article began with the statement that little information has been published in the medical literature to prove or disprove the widespread contention that circumcised men are "not likely" to contract venereal disease.[5] The study by Dr. Hand, according to *Newsweek,* provided definite proof of the link between lack of circumcision and venereal disease. Moreover, although the research paper mentioned syphilis and chancroid, the entire study sample was devoted to gonorrhea. In other words, by inference, circumcision provides protection against gonorrhea.

Because the study employed sizable test and control samples (1,082 and 1,391, respectively), the report had an aura of authenticity. However even a cursory examination of the demographic breakdown of the samples illustrates skewing. Among the patients who had gonorrhea (the test sample), 1.5% were Jews and 50.0% were blacks. The control sample—with no venereal disease—included 37.5% Jews and 5.5% blacks. Since blacks were represented in the United States population at least 3 times as heavily as Jews, a control sample weighted with more than 6 times the proportion of Jews to blacks is unacceptable. Moreover, even taking Dr. Hand's skewed data, of the 103 circumcised blacks, 69% had gonorrhea; of the 392 circumcised white Gentiles, 31% had the disease. Thus, circumcision could hardly have been considered protection against gonorrhea. The major problem with the study was that the approach was based upon a preconceived notion of Jewish superiority and black inferiority (see p. 20). It could be argued that this study by Dr. Hand and the other statements quoted above are more than 30 years old and, therefore, no longer believed. As will be shown, this is not the case.

Before examining more recent statements linking circumcision and venereal disease, it is important to understand the epidemiology of the diseases since World War II. Simply defined, a venereal disease is one which is transmitted sexually. Although some 18 diseases have been so defined,[6] 30 years ago the two most common were syphilis and gonorrhea, which accounted for over 99% of all identified venereal infections.

This was the situation until the late 1960s, when a third venereal disease—Herpes II—was identified as a serious public health problem. Unlike syphilis and gonorrhea, which are caused by bacteria, Herpes II is caused by a virus. Nowadays Herpes II viral infections have probably become the second most common venereal disease. In 1975 the incidence of Herpes II infections was estimated at between 250,000 and 1,000,000 new cases.[7] Although this type of infection was almost never identified prior to 1965,[8] it is now believed to be more prevalent than syphilis.[9]

Currently, gonorrhea still accounts for a major proportion of reported venereal disease cases. An examination of reported new cases of gonorrhea since World War II is shown in Table 9-1. New cases reported are far from accurate. Many physicians do not report cases of venereal disease from "good" families, to save them from embarrassment; therefore, the figures are understated, but they do demonstrate a trend.

In 1972, Earl Ubell wrote in the *New York Times* that "The infection is out of control."[10] Moreover, in 1975 the number of cases was 50% higher than 1970, and in that year one epidemiologist claimed that, in addition to the one

Table 9-1   Gonorrhea: New Cases Reported, By Year

Year	Cases*
1945	313,000
1950	287,000
1955	236,000
1960	259,000
1965	325,000
1970	600,000**
1971	670,000
1972	767,000
1973	843,000
1974	899,000
1975	1,000,000
1976	1,002,000
1977	1,000,000

Sources: U.S. Department of the Census, *Statistical Abstract of the United States,* Washington, D.C., 88th ed., 1967, p. 86, for the years 1945-1965; the 97th ed., 1976, p. 91, for the years 1970-1974; for 1975, 1976, 1977 see *Sexually Transmitted Diseases,* Statistical Letter, U.S.D.H.E.W., issue no. 127, May 1978, p. 9.
*Figures are rounded to nearest thousand.
**The huge increase from 1965-1970 reflects the high incidence of venereal disease in Vietnam and the emergence of an antibiotic-resistant strain of gonorrhea.

million reported cases, there were an estimated 1½ million unreported cases.[11] In 1976, it was shown that the increase in gonorrhea was 4 times as great as the population growth in the past 10 years.[12] In 1977, Dr. Stanley Falkin wrote that gonorrhea is the most common bacterial disease in humans and that there are probably as many as 2 million cases in the United States.[13]

There appears to be a tapering off of the gonorrhea epidemic. The 1976 figure represented an increase of only 2/10 of 1% (0.2%) over 1975, whereas the usual annual increase was 10%,[14] and in 1977 there was a small drop in reported cases.

Syphilis is the one major venereal disease where the rate has dropped. Although most physicians accept the data showing the decline in syphilis, others challenge that view, claiming that the decline "lowered clinicians' index of suspicion."[15] In other words, if physicians do not expect to find it, they do not test for it; moreover, syphilis has often been found to coexist with gonorrhea and Herpes II. The syphilis data are given in Table 9-2.

The sharp decline in the syphilis rate in recent years may also be noted from the report that in New York City there was a drop of 35% in the first 9 months of 1977 compared to 1976.[16]

There is no evidence to support the hypothesis that a correlation exists between the increase in the circumcision rate and the drop in the incidence of syphilis. The decline in syphilis cases between 1945 and 1950 was 38%, and from 1950 to 1955 was 44%. If this hypothesis were true, then reductions in

Table 9-2 Syphilis: New Cases Reported, By Year

Year	Cases*
1945	352,000
1950	218,000
1955	122,000
1960	122,000
1965	113,000
1970	91,000
1971	96,000
1972	91,000
1973	88,000
1974	84,000
1975	26,000
1976	24,000
1977	20,000

Sources: U.S. Department of the Census, *Statistical Abstract of the United States*, Washington, D.C., 88th ed., 1967, p. 86 for the years 1945-1965; the 97th ed., 1976, p. 91 for the years 1970-1974; for 1975, 1976, 1977 see *Sexually Transmitted Diseases*, Statistical Letter, U.S.D.H.E.W., issue no. 127, May 1978, p. 9.
*Figures are rounded to nearest thousand.

the syphilis rate of this order of magnitude over two 5-year periods should be reflected in a commensurate increase in the circumcision rate in the past. No such evidence exists. Thus, the glans-toughening theory of syphilis prevention is not supported by the evidence.

The major decline in reported syphilis cases (230,000) occurred in the decade following World War II (1945-1955) because:

1. Although a specific test for syphilis was devised by Wasserman in 1906, it did not gain wide usage until the 1920s and 1930s, when many hospitals began using it as a routine admission test. The effect of the Wasserman test was similar to that of the Pap test for cervical cancer. Early identification made treatment more effective.
2. In the 1930s several cities instituted a compulsory Wasserman test as a condition for obtaining a marriage license. This practice spread during the 1940s.
3. During World War II, tens of millions of American men and women were tested for syphilis by military and/or by civilian employers.
4. After World War II (1945), antibiotics—particularly penicillin—came into general use, and certain antibiotics are a specific cure for syphilis and gonorrhea. (There is no known cure for Herpes II.) Although gonorrhea bacteria have become resistant to some antibiotics, syphilis bacteria have not.

The net effect was identification of many syphilis cases and mandatory treatment with penicillin, which was readily available. Treating so many cases reduced the number of carriers, thereby lessening the danger of both sexual and congenital infection and precipitating the drop in the syphilis rate.

The claimed link between circumcision and venereal disease must be examined in relation to the above epidemiological trends, which were well known by 1970. On the one hand is the fact that gonorrhea and Herpes II have been rapidly increasing, although syphilis has been declining since World War II. On the other hand, by 1970 the circumcision rate was very high and had been so for many years. While the current rate is estimated at 85%, over the past 50 years the minimum average annual rate was at least 50%. Therefore it stands to reason that a minimum of 50% of the most sexually active males (ages 15-45) have been circumcised. If there were a direct relationship between circumcision and venereal disease, there should have been a maximum drop of 50% in the venereal disease rate. However, allowing for the increase in sexual freedom over the past 20 years, a conservative drop of 25% or even 10% might be expected. In other words, the venereal disease rate should drop in a direct proportion to the rise in the circumcision rate. The data not only shows that this has not occurred, but that the opposite has happened in the case of gonorrhea and Herpes II. As noted, the drop in the syphilis rate is unrelated to circumcision, not only epidemiologically, but also, as will be shown, by the very nature of the syphilis organism. And yet the claimed link between circumcision and venereal disease persisted unabated into the 1970s. The epidemiological data are largely ignored.

In 1966, two urologists, Drs. Garvin and Persky, although supporting circumcision as prophylaxis against venereal disease, raised some doubt about its efficacy against gonorrhea: "Most urologists will agree that circumcision is not a 100% prophylactic against all venereal disease especially gonococcal infection."[17]

Later comments by other physicians disregarded such caution and claimed that circumcision offers protection against venereal disease in general. Writing for the *New York Times* in 1970, Jane E. Brody quoted urologist Dr. Vincent Vermooten: "Circumcised men are less prone to venereal infection."[18] Dr. Marvin Eiger stated in a 1972 issue of *Today's Health,* a publication of the American Medical Association: "Certain types of venereal disease are rarer among the circumcised possibly because their penises are less subject to slight breaks in the skin that might admit disease germs."[19] Urologist Abraham Ravich was not so selective in the title of his recent book on the subject (1973): *Preventing V.D. and Cancer by Circumcision.*[20]

In 1974, Dr. David Reuben wrote in his popular book, *How To Get More Out of Sex:* "... military doctors discovered that circumcised men were less susceptible to Venereal Disease ... (No one knows exactly why—maybe the foreskin simply gives germs a place to hide.)"[21] Dr. John Secondi (1975) asked rhetorically: "Do men who are uncircumcised run a greater risk of getting venereal disease than circumcised men? Yes, especially if their hygiene is poor."[22]

Although these statements appear to be reasonable, they have no basis in fact. This is true not only because of the epidemiological data, but because of other known medical facts.

1. Venereal disease germs, particularly gonorrhea and Herpes II, which together today account for probably 95% of all venereal disease, can enter the male via the mouth, rectum, and eyes. Syphilis germs usually enter through breaks in the skin. However the *main* point of entry is through the meatus (urinary opening) of the penis. This has been confirmed by many medical writers.[23] Thus, if venereal disease germs enter the urethra via the meatus, circumcision can neither aid nor deter their transmission.
2. As for venereal disease germs hiding under the foreskin, this theory, particularly in relation to syphilis, is based upon incorrect scientific information. Little basic research has been done on the syphilis germ since it was discovered in 1905. The germ was long thought to be anaerobic (i.e., requiring the absence of oxygen to survive). This mistaken theory could have given credence to the idea that the syphilis germ would thrive in the relatively closed environment under the foreskin; therefore, circumcision would reduce the incidence of syphilis by exposing the germ to oxygen. However, in

1974, Drs. Cox and Barber of the University of Massachusetts demonstrated that the syphilis germ is aerobic (requiring the presence of oxygen to survive).[24] Should it now be argued that the foreskin should be retained to prevent syphilis?

3. It has been claimed that there is a higher incidence of venereal disease complications in uncircumcised men and that 75% of all chancres, sores that are usually the first sign of syphilis, appear on the foreskin.[25] This is a questionable claim. Chancres do appear on the foreskin, but they can also appear on the glans, shaft, and anus, or on any other part of the body.[26] In the absence of a foreskin, the chancres would appear on the glans. Thus, while the foreskin can certainly be a site of infection, its absence will not eliminate venereal infections; the symptoms will simply appear on other genital sites.

The claim that greater complications occur in uncircumcised men has little meaning. Venereal disease complications result from neglect of the infection, whether the man is circumcised or not. On the other hand, prompt treatment usually mitigates complications, regardless of the presence or absence of a foreskin. Although no nationwide study has been made of the differences in demographic characteristics between circumcised and uncircumcised men, it is possible that uncircumcised males tend to be poorer and concomitantly less educated, and they may have less access to health care than circumcised men. If so, then these social factors would be more relevant to the incidence of venereal disease complications than circumcision status would be.

It should be stressed that the overwhelming proportion of male venereal disease cases occurs in the age group of 15- to 30-year-olds, and at least 75% of them are circumcised. Thus circumcision offers *no* protection against venereal disease.

Dr. Persky, one of the urologists quoted above, questioned the efficacy of circumcision in preventing gonorrhea in 1966. He updated his earlier view in 1979 to include *all* venereal diseases, stating that the man who retains his foreskin is "not more susceptible" to venereal infection than the man who is circumcised.[27]

The experience among the noncircumcising Scandinavian countries is worthy of note. A study showed that there was a marked decline in the incidence of gonorrhea in Sweden, which was attributed to the purchase of condoms. Other Scandinavian countries—Denmark, Finland, and Norway—did not promote condom usage and did not report a decrease in gonorrhea rates.[28] In other words, condoms—not circumcision—provide one answer to the drop in the gonorrhea rate.

Although the evidence is abundantly clear that venereal infections are unrelated to circumcision, a current spate of articles continues to stress the contrary. Two British physicians (1975) claim that there is evidence of a relationship between Herpes Simplex Virus and the absence of circumcision.[29] An American pediatrician noted in 1977 that Herpes II Virus was found twice as frequently in uncircumcised males.[30] The only published reply to the critique of circumcision in *Human Nature* (1978)[31] stressed infections in the subpreputial sac, where heat, darkness, and moisture prevail.[32]

It is hardly necessary to refute these statements in great detail. If circumcision were the remedy, because of the high circumcision rate in the United States, all venereal diseases, including Herpes II should have largely disappeared. They have not. Venereal disease germs can be harbored under the foreskin and also in the prostate[33] and seminal fluid.[34] In fact, there is a growing concern over the rise of venereal infections in nongenital sites.[35] Hygiene, prevention of infection spread, and a therapeutic regimen are indicated—not surgery. Heat, darkness, and moisture under the foreskin may encourage bacterial and viral growth. But such conditions are not only found in the subpreputial space. They exist in the labia, anus, mouth, underarms, and between the toes; and a variety of infections do occur in those places. Prevention and treatment are indicated—not surgery.

The overemphasis of the relationship of circumcision to venereal disease tends to delimit the problem to males. However, in some ways venereal infections are more serious in women. In men, venereal disease is usually symptomatic (i.e., physical symptoms appear—sores, pus, pain, etc.). Moreover, the male genitalia are more easily inspected. In contrast, the female external genitalia are more hidden, and the infections are often asymptomatic (i.e., physical symptoms do not appear). Although there may be no noticeable symptoms, the woman can infect her sexual partner. Furthermore, venereal infections can affect all the external as well as internal genitalia of women as well as men.[36] Shall the external genitalia of women be removed simply because they can be the sites of venereal infections? It makes as much sense to do this as it does to remove the male foreskin to prevent venereal disease.

Despite what medical authorities have repeatedly written, the increased circumcision rate in the United States has not caused concomitant decreases in venereal disease rates, especially for gonorrhea or Herpes II. On the contrary, the rates for these two diseases have skyrocketed. The drop in syphilis seems unrelated to circumcision. These epidemiological facts put the burden of proof on anyone who claims that there is any relationship between circumcision and venereal disease. The epidemic character of gonorrhea and Herpes II does not represent a new development, only an increase in the severity of an ongoing trend that has been repeatedly documented over the past 10 years. Blaming the foreskin for the high incidence and complications of venereal disease obscures the real issues. The major problem of venereal disease is to prevent it and, failing that, to treat it promptly. The surgical removal of a possible infection site is not a solution.

10

Circumcision and Cancer

The American Cancer Society estimated that in 1978 there would be about 700,000 new cancer cases reported in the United States, and that approximately 390,000 Americans would die of the disease.[1] Cancer is the second leading cause of death,[2] and its frequency is growing at an alarming rate.[3]

Probably no other disease evokes as much fear and anxiety as does cancer and for good reason. There is no universal cure, nor are its causes even certain. Treatment often involves major surgery, radiation, and chemotherapy. Although excellent results are obtained in some cases, the disease is quite often fatal.

Cancer is even difficult to define. According to the American Cancer Society (1977): "Cancer is a large group of diseases characterized by uncontrolled growth and spread of abnormal cells."[4] This definition is descriptive and does not address the primary question: What causes cancer at any site? The basic answer is that for the most part the causes of cancer are simply not known.

Although fundamental knowledge of cancer is scanty, epidemiological studies have provided much information. As far back as 1775, an English physician, Dr. Percival Pott, noted the relatively high incidence of scrotal cancer among chimney sweeps.[5] Soot was correctly implicated as a cause of this type of cancer. From the 19th century on, further discoveries have led to the isolation and identification of hundreds of cancer-producing substances, called carcinogens, including tars in cigarette smoke, diethylstilbesterol (DES), polychlorobiphenyls (PCBs), asbestos fibers, and red dye #2. Carcinogens have been found in the air, water, soil, food, pesticides, and medications. In fact, the World Health Organization's International Agency for Research on Cancer estimates that up to 90% of all cancers are triggered by environmental agents.[6] Recent study in the United States has revealed a wide geographical variation in cancer distribution, which also tends to implicate environmental factors.[7] In addition, there are firm theories that excessive exposure to sunlight can cause skin cancer. Large doses of X-rays can shrink or cure some cancer, while excessive doses can, in themselves, cause cancer.

Worldwide cancer data show that some nations have a high incidence of one or more specific types of cancer and a low incidence of other types. Genetic factors appear to provide a predisposition, or an immunity, to certain types of cancer. For example, Jewish women have a lower cervical cancer incidence, but a higher breast cancer incidence than non-Jewish women.[8] Nutritional, hygienic, and social class factors also appear to be involved in the etiology of cancer.[9]

With the foregoing as brief background, we will examine the allegation that circumcision is related to cancer prevention. Specifically, it is claimed that circumcision prevents prostatic and penile cancer in men and cervical cancer in their sexual partners. Typical of the subject's presentation in the professional literature is a 1975 statement in *Nursing Care*:

> ... The incidence of cancer of the penis is much higher in uncircumcised males, and cancer of the cervix is higher in women married to men who are not circumcised.... Cancer of the prostate was also less common in circumcised males.[10]

The alleged benefits of circumcision are based upon two hypotheses:

1. Jews have low rates of cancer of the cervix, prostate, and penis because of the practice of infant circumcision. (The assumption is made that non-Jews circumcised in infancy also derive the same benefits.)
2. Smegma is a carcinogen—and an extraordinarily powerful one at that—causing cancer via even minimal contact.

The manner in which smegma allegedly causes cancer at specific sites is as follows:

> *Cervical Cancer.* Smegma is deposited on the cervix during coitus, thus "causing" cancer at that site. However, smegma can only reach the cervix during coitus, which may occur once a day, once a week, or less often, depending upon sexual habits. The duration of such contact is usually a few seconds or minutes. Moreover, the smegma-cervix contact does not take place until a woman becomes sexually active, i.e., in the teen years or later.

Prostatic Cancer. Droplets of smegma work their way back through the penile opening (meatus) into the penile tube (urethra), reaching the prostate. However, some of these droplets would, in turn, be flushed out when urinating and therefore only very small quantities of smegma could reach the prostate and "cause" cancer of that organ.

Penile Cancer. In a normal uncircumcised penis, smegma is produced from the day of birth. If not washed off, the foreskin keeps smegma in constant contact with the glans. In addition, many medical authorities maintain that circumcision toughens the glans. Thus an uncircumcised penis runs a double risk in that it would have a less toughened or more delicate glans, which supposedly would be more susceptible to smegma's constant carcinogenic attack.

Penile contact with smegma is much greater than that of either the cervix or prostate; it is constant rather than periodic and in relatively large quantity. Thus, if the smegma-carcinogen theory is valid, the incidence of penile cancer among uncircumcised men should at least approximate the incidence of cancer of the prostate or cervix, and this should be relatively simple to demonstrate via an examination of epidemiological data.

The smegma-carcinogen link, if it is true, would be a very important discovery. First, cancers of the cervix, prostate, and penis could be eliminated or at least reduced by circumcision. Second, such a discovery would greatly advance medical knowledge, since it would be the first body substance found to cause cancer, and this could lead to the possibility of discovering other body-produced carcinogens.

One aspect of the smegma-carcinogen theory that is generally not discussed in medical or popular journals is that of female smegma. Just as smegma is produced under the male foreskin, it is also produced under the clitoral foreskin and may come in contact with the female's urethra, vagina, cervix, and rectum. For that matter, since the penis may come in contact with female smegma during coitus, female smegma could be blamed for causing prostatic and penile cancer. If the smegma-carcinogen theory is accepted as fact, then it would seem quite logical to routinely circumcise infant girls to prevent cancer.

This matter could even be carried one step further. All mammals produce smegma; this is particularly true of the horse, as we mentioned in Chapter 6. Therefore, this animal's secretion should also be investigated as a carcinogen. Then mammals known to be susceptible to cancer from this source could also be circumcised! As yet, no one has suggested carrying the circumcision craze to this extreme.

Many Americans have strong feelings about circumcision, and nowhere is this more evident than in the alleged claim that circumcision prevents cancer. Many of the religious, sexual, and cultural biases are potentiated by the fear of cancer. So intense is the wish that a circumcision-cancer link can be proved that the data are often falsified, exaggerated, erroneously presented, or misinterpreted, thereby leading to false conclusions. The fact is that there is no relationship whatsoever between circumcision and cancer at any site. Moreover, there is not a shred of evidence to support the theory that smegma is carcinogenic. Although this may be difficult to believe, detailed evidence proves it to be so. In the three sections that follow, each cancer site allegedly linked to circumcision is examined separately. The claims made, the evidence upon which they are based, and epidemiological data are explored in detail.

Cervical Cancer

First, some anatomical definition is necessary. The uterus, of which the cervix is a part, is a pear-shaped organ whose larger, rounded end, called the body or corpus, is located in the abdominal cavity; the narrower neck portion, or cervix, protrudes into the vagina. There have been no claims made that circumcision is related to cancer of the body of the uterus; the claim is that smegma from an uncircumcised penis causes cancer of the cervix. It is important, therefore, that in examining data for uterine cancer a clear distinction is made between cancer of the uterine corpus and cancer of the cervix.

Furthermore, it is important to understand how cervical cancer develops. Cancer cells first appear on the surface of the cervix. This is known as cancer in situ. Cancer in situ is not fatal, but, if not identified and treated, the in situ cancer may invade deeper cervical tissues. When deeper tissues are invaded, the cancer is called invasive carcinoma, which can be fatal, if untreated.

Cancer of the uterus (both the corpus and cervix) is the fourth highest cause of female cancer deaths, following breast, colon and rectum, and lung cancers.[11] The American Cancer Society estimates of deaths and new cases of uterine cancer for 1978, compared to total female cancer rates, are shown in Table 10-1.

According to Table 10-1, invasive carcinoma of the cervix accounted for less than 5% of all female cancer deaths and less than 6% of new cases. No one could possibly deny the seriousness of cervical cancer to the individual patient and her family, or to society. Certainly no exaggeration is needed. However, in discussing cervical cancer, bias often supersedes facts. In 1970. Dr. S. I. McMillen claimed that: "Cancer of the cervix . . . comprises

Table 10-1   1978 Cancer Estimates for Women

	Deaths		New Cases	
	Number	%	Number	%
All cancers	176,500	100.0	348,000	100.0
Uterine body (corpus)	3,300	1.9	28,000	8.0
Cervix (invasive)	7,400	4.2	20,000	5.8
Total Uterus (Corpus and cervix)	10,700	6.1	48,000	13.8

Source: American Cancer Society, *1978 Cancer Facts and Figures* (New York, 1977), p. 10.

twenty-five percent of all cancers in women."[12] In 1973, Dr. Abraham Ravich wrote: " . . . the incidence of cervical cancer is . . . about thirty-five percent of all female cancers."[13]

What can possibly be gained by physicians inflating the incidence of cervical cancer? Such presentations may be scare tactics to encourage circumcision, distortions of data to substantiate opinions, or simple ignorance. In contrast, when referring to the lower incidence of cervical cancer among Jewish women, pro-circumcision physicians deflate the figures to almost zero. For example, Dr. Marvin Eiger, in a 1972 issue of *Today's Health*, stated: "Cervical cancer . . . is practically non-existent among Jewish women."[14] Dr. Eiger is wrong in claiming that cervical cancer is "practically non-existent among Jewish women," since studies among Jewish women with cervical cancer have been conducted, e.g., with 200 patients at the Johns Hopkins Medical Center[15] and in Israel with several hundred women.[16]

The important point is *not* whether Jewish women get cervical cancer; they do and the numbers are not minuscule. What is important is the epidemiological fact that Jewish women have a relatively low rate of cervical cancer when compared to non-Jewish women. The question is, why is this so? Is it because of some genetic factor that provides immunity to cervical cancer; or is it because Jewish males are circumcised, or is it a combination of various other factors? Early studies of the low incidence of cervical cancer among Jewish women (1900–1910) did not attribute this fact to circumcision, but to the use of the ritual bath (mikvah) after menstruation, which was and is obligatory for Orthodox Jewish women.[17] Later, this hypothesis was discarded because most Jewish women stopped using the ritual bath but their cervical cancer rate remained low.

Thereafter, the hypothesis that circumcision was the reason for the low cervical cancer rate among Jewish women developed. If this hypothesis is true, then routine circumcision of non-Jewish male infants should, over time, sharply reduce the incidence of cervical cancer among non-Jewish women. The idea of protecting non-Jewish women from cervical cancer was alluded to in the pro-circumcision literature of the 1930s and 1940s, but there was little clinical evidence to prove or disprove it.[18]

It was not until the 1950s that proponents of the circumcision-cervical cancer theory sought epidemiological evidence to demonstrate that non-Jewish women received the same protection as did Jewish women, provided their husbands were circumcised in infancy. The general methods employed were comparison studies of women with cervical cancer and control women who did not have the disease. The control groups were matched to the test groups by age, ethnicity, social class, etc., and all the women in both test and control groups were asked about the circumcision status of their husbands.

One such study was reported in 1954 by Dr. E. L. Wynder, et al.[19] According to their report, the study results proved the link between circumcision and cervical cancer. This was an important "discovery" and, not surprisingly, it was picked by *Time* magazine and therefore received a relatively wide readership.[20] The public reaction to this "news" was described by Dr. David Reuben, whose popular sex books have sold millions of copies. Dr. Reuben was ardently pro-circumcision, encouraging the surgery to prevent cervical cancer. His style may be flippant, but his intent is serious. He noted: "When the news came out that smegma might contain a substance that provokes cancer of the cervix, there was a run on circumcisions."[21] Dr. Reuben described a scene in which the wife grabbed her husband's foreskin between her thumb and index finger and said: "Either it goes, or I go,"[22] (The next day "it" went.)

Unfortunately, both the popular and medical press limited their reporting of the Wynder study to the circumcision factor alone. However, the researchers came to other important conclusions: "Epidermoid cancer of the cervix has been noted in women exposed only to circumcised males and in virgins. Other etiological factors must therefore exist."[23] Many physicians pounced upon the study as proof of the value of circumcision; other researchers subjected it to closer scrutiny and questioned the findings. One important but almost overlooked aspect of this study was the fact that a significant portion of the women in the sample (10% of the whites and between 20% and 30% of the blacks) were unable to state their husbands' circumcision status. Therefore, some researchers expressed concern about the responses of the women who did claim to know their husbands' status: Could they have been in error?

The clue to such questioning came from Dr. Wynder and his colleagues, who stated that they studied factors that can be evaluated by an interview study.[24] They also stated that they had anticipated problems concerning knowledge of circumcision status and therefore asked the questions carefully.[25] This is quite an important point since, in the final analysis, the women's statements about circumcision status were the underpinning of Dr. Wynder's research.

Researchers suggested replication studies in which the husbands' circumcision status would be verified by actual physical examination, rather than verbal questioning of wives. Several such studies were conducted, with startling results. As previously noted, Terris and colleagues summarized the findings of a number of such studies.[26] In one study, 50% of the women's statements as to the circumcision status of their husbands were found to be in error. Perhaps the most startling study, conducted by Drs. A. M. Lilienfeld and S. Graham (1958), showed 34% of the *men* to be in error in respect to their own status.[27] Lilienfeld and Graham therefore challenged the validity of any study purporting to show a circumcision-cervical cancer link that was not based upon actual physical examination of males.

Additional studies of cervical cancer, based upon physical examination of male partners to determine circumcision status were then conducted. An American study by Terris et al. (1973) also explored the factor of degree of circumcision, theorizing that the more complete the circumcision, the lower the chance of cervical cancer. The results were that: "No differences were found in circumcision status of husbands of cervical dysplasia patients and controls."[28] (Dysplasia means cellular deviations from the normal.) These findings were consistent with those of a 1965 British study conducted in a similar fashion, which reported: "These results do not support the theory that women whose husbands are circumcised will be less likely to develop cervical cancer than those whose husbands are uncircumcised."[29]

One of the factors *not* taken into account in the Terris study was the mode of contraception employed, if any. The condom would provide a barrier between the penis and cervix, and thus provide immunity from cervical cancer, should smegma be a factor. The diaphragm would eliminate penis-cervix contact but not penis-vagina contact. Theoretically, smegma in the vagina could affect the cervix when the diaphragm was removed. Birth control pills and intrauterine devices would provide no protection against either type of contact. The 1965 British study mentioned above did take into account contraceptive methodology employed and found no relationship between circumcision and cervical cancer.

Both the American and British investigators reported conflicting and unsubstantiated data from other parts of the world. For example, Jewish women have a relatively low rate of cervical cancer, but Moslem women, whose husbands are circumcised in infancy, have a much higher rate. The Parsis of India, who do not circumcise, have a lower cervical cancer rate than their Moslem neighbors, who do circumcise.

Terris et al. faulted their own work inasmuch as no physical examinations were performed to determine the circumcision status of extramarital partners, if any. They urged worldwide replication studies. However, the World Health Organization as early as 1964 took an unequivocal position: "At the present time there is no clear evidence that circumcision has a definite value as a prophylactic measure in the prevention of carcinoma of the uterine cervix."[30] This statement was based upon the total available data. There is *no* evidence of a circumcision-cervical cancer link and much evidence that such a link does *not* exist. This is so despite the fact that complete worldwide cancer or circumcision data do not exist.

Of some 150 nations in the world, fewer than one-third publish national cancer data. Among those nations not publishing such material are the 3 with the largest populations—the People's Republic of China, India, and the U.S.S.R. Moreover, none of these countries practices circumcision. Of the 44 countries that do publish national cancer data, many do not list cervical cancer separately from uterine body cancer. Thus for these countries a circumcision-cervical cancer relationship cannot be explored. Most countries do not practice circumcision; where it is practiced (except for the United States), it is a religious rite and may be performed in infancy, at age 4-6, 8-10, or at puberty. Different groups in a given country circumcise at different ages. Moreover, no country practicing circumcision for religious reasons, other than Israel, publishes cervical cancer data. However, some countries do publish cervical cancer data that are as accurate, if not more so, than those of the United States. Many countries, e.g., Norway, Sweden, and France, maintain National Cancer Registries. Physicians are mandated to report all cancer cases to assure appropriate follow-up. Such registries provide accurate cancer data. The United States does not maintain such a registry.

Some countries publish cancer data by deaths, others by new cases. A comparison of the rates of new cases of cervical cancer in Norway and Sweden (both noncircumcising) with the United States' rate (circumcising), and also a comparison of the United States' death rate with France's (noncircumcising) is shown in Table 10-2.

Table 10-2 Cervical Cancer per 100,000 Population

Deaths			New Cases		
Country	Year	Rate	Country	Year	Rate
United States	1972	9.0	United States	1972	32.0
France	1966	4.6	Sweden	1968	25.0
			Norway	1967	20.2

Sources: *Cancer Registries* for Sweden, Norway, and France for the years shown. For the United States data, *1972 Cancer Facts and Figures* (New York: American Cancer Society, 1970).

If the theory linking circumcision to cervical cancer is correct, then the United States should have a lower incidence of new cases and/or deaths than do France, Sweden, and Norway. An examination of the data in Table 10-2 shows that the theory is *not* substantiated.

Another study (1955) also helps to disprove the circumcision-cervical cancer theory. Examining the average number of cervical cancer cases in 3 countries over a 19-year period, the research revealed that the rate per 100,000 women for Israel was 2.2; for Sweden it was 17.0; and for the United States, where 10 cities were studied, the rate was found to be 44.0.[31] The study does indicate that Israeli women have a low rate of cervical cancer. The question is whether this is related to the prevalence of the practice of male circumcision. Closer scrutiny of the total study reveals a rather different conclusion. Despite the obvious weakness of the United States' data, in Sweden, in the 1940s, fewer than 1% of the total male population was circumcised, whereas, in the United States the figure for men married to women with cervical cancer very likely approximated 25%. The American cervical cancer rate, therefore, should have been below that of Sweden, if the circumcision-cervical cancer theory was true. Actually the American rate was 2½ times higher than Sweden's, and thus circumcision could not have served as a preventative factor.

In addition, the two studies of Jewish women with cervical cancer mentioned earlier (one done at Johns Hopkins Medical Center and one done in Israel) reported that no link was found between this cancer site and the circumcision status of the marital partners.

It should be borne in mind that the supposed culprit in the circumcision-cervical cancer link is smegma: smegma is believed to be carcinogenic. This theory was explored in animal experimentation (human experimentation would be impermissible) and the results were negative, with one exception. One researcher inserted human smegma into the vaginas of monkeys 1 or 2 times weekly for 3 years and was unable to produce any cancers of the cervix or vagina. Another researcher inserted human smegma into the vaginas of mice 2 to 3 times weekly for 12 months and was unable to stimulate the production of genital cancers, although insertion of a known carcinogen regularly produced vaginal cancers.[32]

The one study that claimed to demonstrate the carcinogenic action of smegma was conducted in 1947 at the Columbia University College of Physicians and Surgeons and the Beth Israel Hospital in New York City. The researchers concluded: "Provided our results can be duplicated and improved, this may be the first experimental production of cancer by external application of an external product of the animal body."[33] Although this conclusion might well have been a milestone in cancer research, the study was never duplicated; the reasons will be noted upon detailed examination of the study.

The study employed horse smegma as the test substance and cerumen (earwax) for control. A buried skin tunnel was made midline in the back of mice, and the test or control substance was inserted into the tunnel. Of the 800 experimental animals, 250 died before the experiment was concluded and were not included in the test results. No cause was given for the premature death of 31% of the sample. The skin tunnel broke down in "approximately 40%" of the remaining animals. In such cases the test or control substance was injected under the skin. At the conclusion of the experiment, 53% of the test and 53% of the control animals were "available" for examination for evidence of cancer. No reason was given to explain why 47% of the sample (test and control) were *unavailable* for examination. The researchers found a variety of tumors—lung, lymphoid, mammary, and others in 30% of the test and 15% of the control animals examined. Longevity was carefully monitored. The results were as shown in Table 10-3.

Some comment on this experiment is called for:

1. The study is invalid in its conceptualization and research design. No animal deposits smegma in coitus via an artificially created midback skin tunnel.
2. Even assuming total study validity, what would happen if other body substances—feces, urine, hair particles, menstrual fluid, enzymes, etc.—were so inserted? Would they be carcinogenic? If so, of what significance would that be? If hydrochloric acid, a normal stomach secretion, were to be sprayed into the eye, pain, irritation, and blindness would result. Does that mean that this acid is harmful to the stomach?
3. What serious conclusions can be drawn from an experiment in which: 31% of the animals died before the experiment was concluded; 40% of the skin tunnels broke down; 47% of the test or control animals were *not* investigated for tumors?
4. Strangely, the survival rate for smegma-treated animals was much

Table 10-3 Percent Survival Rate

Days	Test Sample N = 400	Control Sample N = 150
200	85	88
300	74	80
400	65	57
500	47	30
600	26	6
700 or longer	12	1½

higher than for the control group. No conjecture was made to explain this phenomenon; perhaps it can now be claimed that smegma injections increase longevity!

With such shortcomings, it is no wonder that the experiment was not replicated. Nevertheless, the study was often cited as reference to prove that smegma is a carcinogen. In recent years the "research" has largely been ignored.

One highly researched theory is that viruses cause many types of cancer, including cervical cancer. Dr. Abraham Ravich claims to have been the first (1941) to suggest the viral theory of cervical cancer, stating that the virus is "presumably present in the slimy smegma under the foreskin."[34] No explanation of how the virus found its way into the smegma is given. Obviously it must come from somewhere, unless one accepts the obsolete theory of spontaneous generation.

Over the past decade, dozens of studies have attempted to link a virus, specifically the Herpes II Virus, to cervical cancer.[35] Some reports concerning the Herpes II Virus do not even discuss circumcision as a possible factor.[36] However, Dr. W. A. Knaus claimed that there was a link between viruses as a cause of cervical cancer and circumcision, because the virus can hide under the foreskin; however, he admitted that animal experimentation (similar to that done with smegma) was negative. Dr. Knaus reported on an experiment conducted over a 4-year period with 400 monkeys. Repeated injections of Herpes II Virus were made into the cervix of each animal. No malignant changes occurred.[37]

Other researchers have differing views. While they accept the virus-cervical cancer link, they do not specify any relationship to circumcision. For example, the Herpes II Virus has been found in the male ejaculate and prostate, as well as the vas deferens (the tube that carries sperm from the testes) and on the penis.[38] Sexual contact could therefore spread the virus regardless of circumcision status.

It is obvious that the main transmission of a venereal infection (bacterial or viral) from female to male is via the penile opening (meatus) through the urethra and into the other organs of the genitourinary system. Conversely, a venereal infection of the male genitourinary system could be transmitted to the female via the infected ejaculate or via germs on the surface of the penis. In the case of syphilis, breaks in the skin can serve as another mode of transmission. In no way would these modes of transmission be affected by circumcision status. The enormous increase in venereal disease, despite the high circumcision rate in the United States, substantiates this.

Dr. S. I. McMillen (a supporter of circumcision) claimed that there was a bacterium in smegma that was carcinogenic and identified it as "the cancer-producing Smegma bacillus."[39] This, in itself, would be a noteworthy discovery; unfortunately, there is no evidence to support this claim. Moreover, no bacterium has been found to be a direct cause of cancer, although some are thought to provide predisposing conditions. For example, a physician writing about a venereal disease (granuloma inguinale caused by the germ *calymmato bacterium granuloma*), which may provide a predisposing environment for cervical cancer, found the bacterium on the penile shaft, foreskin, and labia.[40] This is undoubtedly true; however, if the foreskin had not been present, the bacterium would presumably have also been found on the glans. Circumcision status would have no bearing on germs found on the shaft or labia.

As stated earlier, if there is a link between circumcision and cervical cancer, it should be apparent in American cancer data because of the consistent rise in the circumcision rate. Cervical cancer in situ should be in sharp decline. This has not occurred. The American Cancer Society estimated that there would be 40,000 new cases of cervical cancer in situ in 1978, twice the rate of invasive cervical cancer.[41] This means that if the cancer in situ is neither identified nor treated, a sharp increase can be anticipated in invasive cervical cancer. What is more startling is that cancer in situ is appearing in ever younger women. According to the American Cancer Society: "Women susceptible to cervical cancer include those over 20 years of age, and those younger who have begun to make sex a part of their lives."[42] If the circumcision-cervical cancer theory were valid, this could not be possible. Women in their teens are more likely to have sex with men their own age or in their 20's, of whom at least 75% are circumcised. Thus cancer in situ among teenagers would be in sharp decline or would have all but disappeared.

Fortunately, there has been a 65% decline in uterine corpus and cervical cancer deaths during the last 40 years.[43] This is attributed to improved health care and early diagnosis, largely as a result of the Pap Test. Although the causes(s) of cervical cancer are still unknown, all attempts to correlate this disease with circumcision status have failed. During the course of many studies, other positive correlations were found; many are clearly sex-related. In 1968, Dr. A. Lilienfeld of the Johns Hopkins School of Hygiene was quoted as claiming that the number of sexual contacts may be the critical factor in cervical cancer—not circumcision status.[44] Nuns rarely develop the disease, while prostitutes usually have a very high incidence rate. Those who practice moderation in sexual activity—Orthodox Jews and the Amish—also have a low rate. Correlations exist between cervical cancer and poor state of health, poor nutrition, poor hygiene, poverty, early onset of sexual activity, promiscuity, number and spacing of children, etc., *but not circumcision*.[45]

Prostatic Cancer

Like cervical cancer, prostatic cancer poses a serious health problem. The American Cancer Society estimated that in the United States there would be 57,000 new cases diagnosed and 20,600 deaths attributed to cancer at this site in 1978. It also estimated that prostatic cancer would be the third leading cause of American male cancer deaths.[46]

As with most cancers, the cause of prostatic cancer is unknown, although the presence of smegma has long been suspected as a causative factor. Typical of the presentations of the alleged link between circumcision and prostatic cancer was the statement made by Dr. Marvin Eiger in *Today's Health* (1972). The prostate, he claimed, is the most common male cancer site in Sweden. He reported that a Swedish physician, who compared Israeli and Swedish Jews with noncircumcised Swedes, determined that: "The uncircumcised man is more than twice as likely to develop this form of cancer."[47] This is a clear and unequivocal statement—if a man is not circumcised, he runs more than twice the risk of getting cancer of the prostate than a man who is circumcised. If this is true, it should not be difficult to demonstrate.

The American Cancer Society publishes cancer death rates for selected sites for 44 countries that keep such records. If indeed there is a link between circumcision and prostatic cancer, Israel (with a circumcision rate of close to 100%) should have a low, if not the lowest death rate; the United States (where about 50% of men over the age of 50 are circumcised) should be somewhat higher than Israel but among the countries with the lowest rates; noncircumcising countries should have the highest rates. (Moslem countries that do circumcise do not publish such data and therefore are not included.) Data for selected countries are shown in Table 10-4.

Table 10-4 Prostatic Cancer in 1972-1973—
Death Rates Per 100,000 Population

Rank Order	Country	Rate
1	Netherlands	22.9
2	Sweden	21.1
3	Switzerland	19.3
11	United States	14.4
32	Israel	7.5
42	El Salvador	1.2
43	Honduras	0.8
44	Thailand	0.2

Source: American Cancer Society, *1978 Cancer Facts and Figures* (New York, 1977), p. 15.

Looking at the data in Table 10-4, we see that the 3 countries with the highest death rates—the Netherlands, Sweden, and Switzerland—do not circumcise. This would appear to bear out Dr. Eiger's theory. However, the 3 countries with the lowest death rates—El Salvador, Honduras, and Thailand—also do not circumcise. The United States ranks eleventh among the 44 countries listed. This means that 10 countries have higher death rates, but 33 countries have lower rates than the United States. Instead of ranking among the lowest, the United States ranks within the top quartile, with a relatively high rate. Most interesting is the position of Israel with a rank order of 32. This means that, instead of being low if not the lowest on the list, there are 12 countries that have lower prostatic cancer death rates and *none* of these 12 countries practices routine infant circumcision.[48] The Israeli prostatic cancer death rate is more than 10 times higher than the average of the 3 countries with the lowest rates. These data therefore provide no substantiation for the theory linking circumcision to prostatic cancer.

However, the above data are crude in that they show the death rate based upon total population, which includes all age groups. This poses a special problem in regard to understanding prostatic cancer, as this disease is clearly age-related. There are few deaths from this disease among men under 40; the greatest prevalence is found among men over the age of 55 or 60. It is precisely this factor of age-relatedness that distorts Dr. Eiger's previous statement. Dr. Eiger was reporting on a study conducted by Dr. A. Apt, who, comparing prostatic cancer rates between Sweden and Israel, found that Sweden had an incidence 4.7 times that of Israel's.[49] Although the figures were accurate, his conclusion, that Israeli circumcision was the cause of this vast difference, was inaccurate.

1. He selected Sweden—a country with one of the highest rates of prostatic cancer—as a basis for comparison with Israel, which was bound to bias the results. Had another noncircumcising country with a very low rate been chosen, completely opposite results would have been obtained.
2. Dr. Apt did not take into consideration the age factor.

Dr. E. Noel Preston analyzed Dr. Apt's data, taking into account the proportion of the population in both Sweden and Israel aged 60 and over, the age of greatest risk for prostatic cancer. Dr. Preston found that Sweden had 7.2 times as many men in the older age group as did Israel. Therefore, it could be expected that Sweden would have had a prostatic cancer frequency 7.2 times that of Israel's. But the data showed a difference of only 4.7 times that of Israel's. Dr. Preston asked: "Would this mean that non-circumcision protects against prostatic cancer?"[50]

Another study compared the incidence of prostatic tumors between Jews and non-Jews and found the incidence to be 3 times greater among the latter (Jews 8.8%, non-Jews 23.9%). This would seem to give credence to Dr. Apt's thesis. However when the data for non-Jews were examined by circumcision status, the researchers found that there was no significant difference between circumcised and uncircumcised men in the incidence of benign tumors (76% vs. 73%) or malignant tumors (24% vs. 27%). They concluded that there was no evidence to link circumcision to prostatic cancer. They further remarked that if anyone supports routine circumcision, the prevention of prostatic cancer should not be one of the reasons.[51]

There is a large body of epidemiological data on prostatic cancer, but none of it shows any relationship to circumcision. These data were summarized by Dr. L. M. Franks at a conference of the American Cancer Society in 1973. Among the findings were that:

- Regional differences in the United States varied from 17.1 per 100,000 for non-Latin Texans to 37.8 in urban Iowa;
- In Canada regional differences varied from 17.0 in Newfoundland to 39.0 in Saskatchewan;
- Japan had a very low rate, 3.2 to 4.3 for different parts of the country;
- Israel showed a rate of 3.1 for non-Jews and from 10.8 to 13.2 for Jews (depending upon country of origin).[52]

Thus, wide differences in prostatic cancer rates exist within a given country based upon geography, ethnicity, etc. Although Dr. Franks was unable to account for these differences, nowhere in his analysis does the word circumcision appear.

To further explore the possible relationship between circumcision and prostatic cancer, detailed data from two countries—Norway and the United States—were examined. Norway was chosen because that country does not practice circumcision and, therefore, Norway's relatively high prostatic cancer rate should remain stable. The United States, on the other hand, has had an increase in the circumcision rate over the past 100 years. Assuming that a link does exist between circumcision and that cancer site, this should be reflected in some decline in prostatic cancer. Norway, where a National Cancer Registry is maintained, showed an increase in prostatic cancer of 19% between 1955 and 1967, an average annual increase of 1.5%.[53] Whatever may have caused the increase, circumcision status could not have been a factor, since Norwegian males are not circumcised. In the United States, in spite of the rising circumcision rate, the rate of prostatic cancer has not declined in the past few decades. According to the American Cancer Society, the incidence of this disease has increased "by more than 20% in the past 25 years."[54] In the absence of facts, rumors run rampant. Dr. Mark A. Silvert recounted the theories claiming that prostatic cancer is caused by *over*indulgence in sex and equally "authoritative" theories claiming that the disease is caused by *under*indulgence in sex.[55]

Although there simply are no sound epidemiological or other data linking circumcision to prostatic cancer, the myth persists in current medical literature. Totally unscientific data are still presented and defended in a manner that reveals the low level of medical research and the persistence of holding on to a theory that has no basis in fact.

In 1942, Dr. Abraham Ravich postulated a link between circumcision and prostatic cancer.[56] A quarter of a century later (1966) Dr. Fred Rosner wrote in support of routine circumcision: "Less well-recognized and appreciated is the diminished incidence of carcinoma of the prostate among Jewish males. . . . "[57] Dr. Rosner's source was Dr. Ravich. However, that same year (1966) two physicians specifically challenged Ravich's hypothesis of smegma migrating up the urethra as the etiology of prostatic cancer, noting that this cancer usually arises in the posterior lobe of the prostate. They therefore considered the Ravich hypothesis "untenable."[58] Yet Dr. Ravich repeated his earlier hypothesis in his 1973 book and added the bladder and rectum (via anal intercourse) as cancer sites caused by foreskin retention.[59] To support his claim that the link exists between circumcision and prostatic cancer, he presented a table showing 1,407 prostatectomy cases in which cancer was found. He compared the incidence among Jews and non-Jews and showed that for the years 1930-1941, the cancer rates were 1.7% for Jews and 20.0% for non-Jews. For the years 1942-1948 the differences were similar—2.0% for Jews and 18.0% for non-Jews. The 1930-1941 sample consisted of 768 Jews and 75 non-Jews; the 1942-1948 sample had 507 Jews and 57 non-Jews.[60]

Faulting such data is not difficult. The figures were derived from the doctor's private practice and are not a random or even a remotely representative sample and therefore are not projectible. Of the two sample groups, Jewish patients outnumbered non-Jews by about 10 to 1, an unacceptable research technique. The sample was drawn exclusively from patients who underwent prostatectomies, and no account was taken of those who did not have or did not need the surgery. One physician, commenting on Dr. Ravich's table, doubted that any scientist would take these data seriously.[61] Nevertheless, some urologists continue to take Dr. Ravich seriously and use his data to support their own views.

Drs. Robert Burger and Thomas Guthrie, in an article entitled "Why Circumcision?" (1974) made only one reference to prostatic cancer: "In 1942 Ravich postulated that circumcision decreased the incidence of cervical and prostatic carcinoma."[62] Not surprisingly, many physicians criticized the authors for making such a statement.[63]

In reply to these criticisms, Dr. Burger wrote:

> Dr. Sorrells [one of Dr. Burger's critics] states that we imply that circumcision is related to prostatic carcinoma. I have reread our article and cannot find this statement.[64]

Dr. Burger is less than candid. Although it is true that he did not categorically state that circumcision is linked to prostatic cancer, he certainly did imply it by mentioning Dr. Ravich's 1942 postulate without comment or question. Having done so, he left the reader with the impression of at least tacit support of Dr. Ravich's theory. In his reply to his critics, Dr. Burger implied that he was disassociating himself from Dr. Ravich's theories; however, in the very next sentence of his rebuttal, he stated:

> I would like, however, to refer him and others to a recent text which reviews much of the literature on circumcision and analyzes these arguments. The book by Dr. Abraham Ravich has its primary impact between pages 80 and 160 and covers the subject thoroughly.[65]

Such equivocation! After apparently disassociating himself from Dr. Ravich, Dr. Burger then refers his readers to Dr. Ravich's 1973 book, which, he stated, "covers the subject thoroughly." However, the recommended pages contain many erroneous statements (see Chapter 3 for further discussion).

To summarize, we see that the overwhelming epidemiological data demonstrate that the cause of prostatic cancer remains a mystery. Its etiology has nothing to do with circumcision, yet the myth persists in current medical literature.

Penile Cancer

Cancer of the penis is a rare disease and yet, by default or design, it remains one of the most potent arguments for circumcision in the United States. Parents are told that cancer of the penis is rare in this country precisely because circumcision is so widely practiced. But this is simply not true. Penile cancer is an age-related disease, seldom occurring below the age of 50. The majority of American men below age 50 are circumcised and the rate of penile cancer among them is very low. However, the majority of American males age 50 and older are *not* circumcised, and the rate of penile cancer in this group is also very low.

The tendency to exaggerate genital cancer incidence was noted in the prior sections. However, in the case of penile cancer, which involves the prime male sex organ and all its attendant emotional ramifications, the tendency to exaggerate is much greater.

If there were any relationship between circumcision and genital cancer, it would be reflected in penile cancer incidence to a greater degree than in the cervical or prostatic rates. The reason was discussed earlier: the glans of the uncircumcised penis is in constant, extensive contact with the alleged carcinogen smegma, whereas smegma contacts the cervix and prostate less extensively and less frequently. Penile cancer, if the smegma-carcinogen theory is valid, should be a major public health problem among uncircumcised males, far exceeding that of cervical or prostatic cancer. The very opposite is true. This can be simply demonstrated by examining Table 10-5, which gives the cancer incidence at the 3 sites in question.

Prostatic cancer deaths are almost 100 times as frequent as those from cancer of the penis; new cases of prostatic cancer are 57 times more frequent than those of penile cancer. Cervical cancer deaths are about 33 times higher than those resulting from cancer of the penis; and new cases 20 times higher. Thus, penile cancer in the United States is nowhere near the public health problem of cervical or prostatic cancer.

The above statistics, showing the relatively low incidence of penile cancer in comparison to the cervix or prostate, are based on the assumption that exposure to greater amounts of a "carcinogen" would increase the cancer frequency. Is it possible that this assumption is incorrect, and that cancer incidence is based less upon carcinogen quantity, but more upon tissue susceptibility? In other words, are the tissues of the cervix and prostate more susceptible to the alleged carcinogenic action of smegma than is the glans of the penis?

A careful examination of the facts reveals that the tissue susceptibility theory is not correct with respect to smegma. The logic for the tissue susceptibility concept comes from the fact that certain carcinogens have a specific affinity to specific tissues; for example, asbestos particles affect the lungs and DES affects the reproductive system. But asbestos and DES are known carcin-

Table 10-5   Selected Cancer Rates (1977)

Site	Estimated Deaths	Estimated New Cases
Prostate	20,100	57,000
Cervix (Invasive)	7,600	20,000
Penis	225	1,000

Sources: American Cancer Society, 1977 *Cancer Facts and Figures* (New York, 1976), p. 11, for prostate and cervical cancer; personal communication, American Cancer Society, July 27, 1977, for penile cancer information.

ogens; smegma is not. Known carcinogens are exogenous (arising outside the body), whereas smegma is endogenous (arising from within the body).

Carcinogens are substances foreign to the body. Could it be that smegma is a substance natural to the penis but foreign to the cervix and prostate? If this were true then the penis would have a relative immunity to smegma but the tissues of the cervix and prostate would not carry such an immunity.

The tissue susceptibility theory would suggest that the prostate is about 3 times more susceptible to smegma's carcinogenic attack than is the cervix, since the frequency of prostatic cancer is almost 3 times that of the cervix. But we have shown in prior sections of this chapter that, at most, only minute particles of smegma could possibly reach the anterior lobe of the prostate, whereas virtually all prostatic cancers originate in the posterior lobe of the prostate. If smegma were the cause of prostatic cancer, smegma would have to be one of the most potent carcinogens known. All evidence points in the opposite direction.

Putting aside the question of prostatic cancer, is it possible that smegma is a substance foreign to the cervix and therefore dangerous to this "susceptible" tissue? All evidence discussed earlier in this chapter showed no relationship between circumcision, and by inference smegma, and cervical cancer.

But this question may be viewed from another perspective. All mammals produce smegma, and none is circumcised. When mammals reproduce, smegma is deposited. If smegma contained a carcinogen or even an irritant, then the propagation of the species would be jeopardized. No such phenomenon exists.

It could be argued that the relatively low American penile cancer rate reflects the high circumcision rate. If countries that do not practice circumcision have rates far higher than does the U.S., this might be possible evidence of a circumcision status-penile cancer relationship. To explore this question, penile cancer data for selected foreign countries were examined (see Table 10-6). The countries were chosen for two reasons: first, they do not practice circumcision and second, they maintain National Cancer Registries.

Table 10-6 Penile Cancer per 100,000 Male Population

Deaths			New Cases		
Country	*Year*	*Rate*	*Country*	*Year*	*Rate*
United States	1972	0.3	United States	1972	0.8
France	1966	0.3	Sweden	1968	1.1
			Norway	1967	1.1
			Finland	1968	0.5
			Denmark	1972	0.9

Sources: The National Cancer registries of the respective countries; for the United States, private communication, American Cancer Society, May 26, 1972.

Looking at Table 10-6, we see that the outstanding facts are:

1. There is no difference in death rates between the United States and France, and no significant differences in new cases between the United States and the 4 Scandinavian countries.
2. New case rates in the other countries vary from the United States by −0.3 per 100,000 for Finland to +0.3 for Norway and Sweden: an insignificant figure of 3 cases per million male population.
3. Penile cancer is a rare disease in the United States, where circumcision *is* practiced, and it is equally rare in France, Sweden, Norway, Finland, and Denmark, where circumcision is *not* practiced.

Another way to test the circumcision status-penile cancer theory is to examine that portion of the United States population supposedly at greatest risk, i.e., those who are *not* circumcised and who are also age 50 and older.

The total male population of each of the older age groups was listed and the estimated percentage of those uncircumcised (see Appendix B) was used to derive the approximate total number of men 50 years and over who are uncircumcised. About 14 million men are estimated to be both age 50, or older, and uncircumcised.[66] Assuming that no men below age 50 and no circumcised men will get penile cancer (both assumptions are false), then the 1,000 new annual cases would come from this pool of 14 million men. This means that 0.008% (8/1,000 of 1%) of the men in this pool would get penile cancer each year. To put it another way, 99.992% of the men in this pool will *not* get penile cancer, in spite of the fact that they retained their foreskins for 50 or more years. Among this pool of 14 million men, the odds of getting penile cancer are 8 chances in 100,000, very low odds indeed.

The question under discussion is whether foreskin retention in and of itself is a direct cause of penile cancer. If retention and the concomitant presence of smegma, supposedly so intensely carcinogenic, had anything whatever to do with penile cancer, then the incidence within this pool would be hundreds or even thousands of times higher.

The American figure of 8/100,000 uncircumcised males age 50 and over is a crude estimate, because penile cancer occurs so infrequently as compared to major sites (lung, breast, colon, etc.) that the penile data are usually grouped under the category "other male genital." It is useful, therefore, to examine data from a country like Norway, which keeps accurate records of penile cancer and where the circumcision rate is less than 1%.

In Norway, the incidence of new cases of penile cancer per 100,000 male population age 50 or over is as follows:

Year	Incidence
1955	3.1
1958	2.7
1961	3.8
1963	4.0
1967	3.8

Source: "Trends in Cancer Incidence in Norway 1955-1967," *The Cancer Registry of Norway* (Oslo, Norway: Universitetsforlager, 1972), pp. 59, 66.

Thus, Norway's uncircumcised males aged 50 and over have a penile cancer incidence of approximately 3 or 4 per 100,000. As previously shown, the United States rate for the equivalent group is about 8 per 100,000, or roughly twice that of Norway. Since both groups retained their foreskins for 50 or more years, circumcision status cannot account for this difference.

Where did the idea that foreskin retention causes penile cancer come from? The same "logic" that concluded that Jews had low rates of venereal disease and cervical cancer because of circumcision also concluded that since Jews had a low rate of penile cancer it was due to infant circumcision. Dr. A. L. Wolbarst (1932) wrote: ". . . Cancer of the penis does not occur in Jews circumcised in infancy. There is no case on record."[67] This statement has been made repeatedly in the medical literature. For example Dr. D. Hovsepian wrote in 1951: ". . . Yet not a single case [of penile cancer] has ever been recorded in a Jew ritually circumcised in infancy."[68] His source was Dr. Wolbarst's 1932 article.

It is true that penile cancer is exceedingly rare among Jews; however, since 1932 at least 6 articles reporting individual cases of penile cancer among Jews circumcised in infancy have been published in American medical literature.[69] In these 6 cases, reasonably good body and genital hygiene was practiced. Most cases of penile cancer are found in uncircumcised men; nevertheless, the disease may occur in men circumcised in infancy. Therefore, as was noted in a textbook on pediatric surgery: "The argument that carcinoma of the penis will be prevented by circumcision is hardly valid, for there are cases of this disease in circumcised males."[70]

In spite of this publicized knowledge, it is ignored or distorted in the medical literature. Drs. Robert Burger and Thomas H. Guthrie, writing in 1974, stated: "Carcinoma of the penis has only been reported once when neonatal circumcision was performed."[71] No source was given for this statement.

Unfortunately, familiarity with some of the medical literature may cause more confusion than clarification. In 1953, Dr. H. Speert made the definitive statement: "Smegma has long been assumed to be the tangible agent responsible for carcinogenesis in the penis."[72]

In 1961, Dr. Samuel Licklider reported on the 131 cases of penile cancer treated at the Memorial Hospital for Cancer and Allied Diseases in New York City in the 40-year period from 1919 to 1959. The distribution of these 131 cases by religion revealed that 4 were Jews. According to Dr. Licklider, this table demonstrated the low incidence of penile cancer among Jews. The reason given was circumcision. However, the doctor made special note of the fact that the circumcision status of the 4 Jews was not known. Moreover, and much more serious, is the fact that circumcision status was not determined for any of the 131 cases. Nevertheless, Dr. Licklider concluded his article with the statement: "These data confirm the clinical impression that cancer of the penis is rare among Jews and support the hypothesis that accumulated smegma is an etiological factor in this disease."[73] How such a conclusion can be drawn without determining circumcision status defies explanation. Furthermore, not only was circumcision status not investigated, but neither was the sample examined as to age, social class, general body health and hygiene, or venereal disease.

Even if the assumption is made that circumcision in infancy will prevent all penile cancer, Dr. V. F. Marshall calculated (1954) that in order to prevent one case of penile cancer, hundreds of thousands of newborn circumcisions would have to be performed.[74]

In 1976, Drs. W. F. Gee and J. S. Ansell made an analysis from a different point of view. Since, according to these doctors, no significant difference exists between the incidence of penile carcinoma in circumcised Americans and uncircumcised Scandinavians (1/100,000), they used tropical countries, with the least optimal conditions, as a basis for comparison. When calculated, the difference in incidence was found to be 9/100,000. Drs. Gee and Ansell stated that since circumcision complications occur at a rate of 1/500, the known risks (1/500) outweigh the presumed benefits (9/100,000).[75]

Cancer of the penis should be viewed objectively and in perspective. Cancer can occur at almost any site and the frequency of penile cancer is on a par with that of the male eye and male breast:

Selected Cancer Occurrence, 1977

Site	Deaths	New Cases
Penis	225	1,000
Male eye	200	800
Male breast	300	700

Sources: American Cancer Society, *1977 Cancer Facts and Figures* (New York, 1976), p. 10 for male eye and male breast data. For penile cancer, private communication, American Cancer Society, July 27, 1977.

Perhaps more meaningful is a comparison of cancer of the external genitalia of men with that of women.

External Genital Cancer, 1977

Site	Deaths	New Cases
Penis	225	1,000
Vulva (labia and clitoris)	540	2,500

Source: Personal communication, American Cancer Society, July 27, 1977.

Cancer deaths and new cases involving the external genitalia occur about 2½ times more frequently in women than in men.[76] As previously noted, the figures for the penis (and vulva) may be imprecise because the numbers are relatively small, and this may be misleading. It is possible to turn to another Scandinavian country, Sweden, for precise data for genital sites.

Incidence of Genital Cancer in Sweden

Time Period	Site	New Cases
1959–1965	Vulva	720
	Penis	346
1968	Vulva	121
	Penis	43

Sources: *Cancer Incidence in Sweden 1959-1965*, pp. 35, 36 and *Cancer Incidence in Sweden 1968*, p. 20. Both published by the National Board of Health and Welfare, The Cancer Registry, Stockholm, Sweden, 1971.

We see from the Swedish data that external genital cancer occurs between 2 and 3 times more frequently in females than males. Therefore, anyone who would hasten to circumcise male infants to prevent penile cancer should, by the same token, consider circumcising female infants as well.

The infrequency of the incidence of penile cancer can be noted from the Licklider study (see above), in which a total of 131 cases were reported in a New York City cancer hospital over a 40-year span, an average of 3.3 cases per year. The rarity of penile cancer can also be noted from the records of the 3 teaching hospitals of Case Western Reserve School of Medicine in Cleveland, Ohio. In a 15-year period (1954-1969) 48 cases were treated: an average of 3.2 cases per year or about one case per teaching hospital per year. This was reported by Dr. J. R. deKernion et al. at a National Conference on Urologic

Cancer in 1973.[77] However, when the same doctors discussed underdeveloped countries, exaggerated penile cancer data were presented that have no foundation in fact. Drs. deKernion et al. stated: "While less than 1% of male malignancies in the United States are carcinoma of the penis, the disease accounts for 12% of all malignancies among the Hindus of India, and is common in China and Africa."[78] This type of evidence is presented to "prove" the circumcision status-penile cancer link. It is in error in many respects.

The incidence of penile cancer for the United States is given as "less than 1%." The percentage is imprecise for a country that publishes national cancer data. A more accurate listing would be less than 3/10 of 1%.

The incidence for India is given as "12% of all malignancies"—a precise percentage for a country that does not publish national cancer data. What does "all malignancies" mean? Does it mean those of men *and* women? To minimize these figures, the assumption was made that the doctors meant to include only male malignancies. Then, if the 12% figure is accurate, India would have an annual penile cancer death rate of approximately 75,000 and a new case incidence of about 125,000 per year.[79]

Although 12% is a fantastically high figure, we might think perhaps it is accurate, since the authors did provide a source—not an Indian journal, but a 1971 Australian and New Zealand medical journal. Tracing the reference given reveals that the *12% figure is really 2%*! The report cited was a follow-up study of 153 penile cancer patients in *one* hospital in Vellore, India. The authors of the study stated in their opening sentence: "Carcinoma of the penis accounts for 2% of all malignant tumors seen at this South Indian Hospital."[80] Drs. deKernion et al. not only committed the error of transcribing 2% as 12%, but compounded the blunder by extrapolating the experience of one Indian hospital to all of India, unacceptable statistical legerdemain.

Drs. deKernion et al. also stated that penile cancer "is common in China and Africa." The source for that statement is the *East African Medical Journal*, published in Uganda in 1966. Neither China nor most African countries publish national cancer data. Visitors to the People's Republic of China (including the writer and his family in 1974, 1975 and 1976) were told that a system of nationwide health data gathering had not as yet been established. The reference article from Uganda was a study of one Kampala hospital during a 7-year period (1956-1963). Of the 153 cases believed to be penile cancer (an average of 22 per year), diagnosis was fully confirmed in 105 of these cases. (There are few hospitals in Uganda and cases are brought to Kampala from rural areas.) The author stated: "In Western countries, carcinoma of the penis is a rare condition whereas in many Asian and African countries this tumour is a major problem."[81] Again, deKernion et al. broadly extrapolate from one Ugandan hospital to all of Africa. As for China, the country is not even mentioned.

In fact, some of the medical literature concerning Africa points to differences in penile cancer frequency among peoples of a given country who do circumcise, and also among peoples of a given country who do not, "suggesting that factors other than retention of smegma may operate in the genesis of this tumour."[82]

The presentation of precise statistics where they don't exist is not uncommon in the medical literature on circumcision. In an editorial in *Science Newsletter* (1964), penile cancer, as a proportion of all male cancers, was given at 20% for China and 10% for India.[83] No source was given.

Dr. George W. Kaplan (1977) stated: "In China, penile carcinoma accounts for 18% of all carcinomata."[84] Again, no clarification was given to indicate whether "all carcinomata" refers to men and women or only to men. The figure of 18% is based upon a medical source, not from the People's Republic, but from a 1971 Australian pediatric journal.

There is absolutely nothing wrong in saying that reliable data are not available when such is the case. In *Proceedings of the National Conference on Urologic Cancer, 1973*, one author, L. M. Franks, in writing about prostatic cancer in China, said precisely that.

The obvious question concerning cancer of the penis as well as any other genital cancer site is: What causes the cancer? The answer is not known. There are ample data deomonstrating that foreskin retention, by itself, does not cause penile cancer. In addition, there is no evidence that smegma is carcinogenic. Nevertheless, new theories are put forward. Dr. John Cairns, writing in *Scientific American* in 1975, claimed:

> One particularly good but rare example of a long incubation period is provided by cancer of the penis. This cancer is seen only in old men but it is certainly caused by factors operating in youth because it is prevented by circumcision in the first few days of life but not if circumcision is postponed for a few years.[85]

There are two obvious errors in this statement. First, penile cancer is not "seen only in old men." Although the disease occurs most frequently in men over 50, it also occurs in men in their 30's. In the Case Western Reserve report (cited above), the 48 cases fell within the age range of 31 to 85; the average age was 63. Second, the disease is not "prevented by circumcision in the first few days of life." There have been many cases of penile cancer reported in men who were fully circumcised within a few days after birth.

In actuality, Dr. Cairns is expounding an incubation theory: something unidentified, but of extraordinary potency exists in, on, or under the foreskin, which must be removed within the first year of life in order to avoid incubation and the development of penile cancer 50 or more years later. Based upon this theory, Dr. Cairns recommended very early circumcision.

There are examples of long-term incubation periods in medicine. For example, primary syphilis, if untreated, may affect the brain (a condition called paresis) 40 years later. Diethylstilbesterol (DES), prescribed for many pregnant women in the 1950s to prevent miscarriage, has resulted in vaginal and other cancers in offspring 20 years later. Large doses of X-rays applied to the thyroid area produced thyroid cancers decades later. Exposure to asbestos dust in the 1940s has resulted in the development of a specific type of lung cancer in the 1970s. However, in each of the above examples, the ill effects—paresis, vaginal, thyroid, and lung cancer—occur in a relatively high percentage of those exposed. The link is clear. However, the very opposite is true vis-à-vis circumcision and penile cancer.

It is one thing to propose a new theory; it is another to test it. As Dr. Carl Sagan observed: "In my view, the human condition would be greatly improved if such confrontations [testing hypotheses against scientific observations] and willingness to reject hypotheses were a regular part of our social, political, economic, religious and cultural lives."[86] Dr. Denis P. Burkitt suggested (1978) the manner in which hypothesis testing is likely to be fruitful: "Experimental work is likely to be most fruitful when it tests a hypothesis that is consistent with epidemiological evidence."[87]

Dr. Cairns's theory is negated by all available epidemiological evidence. Assuming that "something" will incubate in an uncircumcised penis during the first years of life and cause penile cancer later on, what will happen if this incubation is permitted for 5, 10, or 20 years? The risk should be greater. However, the data showed that for every 100,000 men who retained their foreskins for 50 or more years, only 8 developed penile cancer annually—an exceedingly low percentage. If Dr. Cairns's hypothesis was correct, thousands of men, not 8, would develop the disease.

Is it possible that something else causes penile cancer in the 8 out of 100,000 men who contract the disease? Physicians put forward a variety of factors. Dr. David Grimes (1978) observed: "Studies from diverse cultures indicate that carcinoma of the penis is rare among men with good hygiene, regardless of circumcision status. Among men with poor hygiene, circumcision offers little protection."[88] Thus, not surprisingly, penile cancer is associated with poor hygiene. It is often associated with repeated, untreated, venereal disease and chronic infection.[89] The frequency of occurrence is at least 2:1 among indigents versus non-indigents: "The association of penile cancer with filth and smegma is well established."[90]

In other words, penile cancer victims are usually described as very poor minority members whose total hygiene and health care picture is abysmal, and who suffer from repeated, often untreated, venereal infections. Moreover, such patients almost invariably present many other pathologic symptoms as well. Under such conditions, penile cancer can develop regardless of circumcision status.

Penile cancer may be more prevalent in poor countries whether or not circumcision is practiced. Then again, in poor countries, problems of nutrition, hygiene, and the lack of medical care may also be much worse and these factors may be far more important in penile cancer than the practice of circumcision. Many studies of poor countries that do practice circumcision show a significant number of penile cancers.[91] In Jamaica, where circumcision is not practiced, Dr. E. Noel Preston reported that the majority of penile cancer patients also had multiple untreated venereal infections.[92]

In almost all cancer studies, wide differences have been noted in geographic distribution, national origin, ethnicity, social class, etc.; this may well be true of cancer of the penis. It is also possible that there may be a genetic immunity or predisposition to the disease. However, the incidence of penile cancer is one of the lowest for any bodily site, and it can be readily diagnosed.

The penis is actually an unusual organ for the development of cancer. Almost all organs require screening by X-ray, internal examination, etc., to identify cancer—but the penis is completely external. It is handled daily in urination, washing, or sex. It is one of the easiest organs for the individual or his physician to examine, and any aberration can easily be spotted and early signs of malignancy treated.

One of the major problems of penile cancer is the delay in seeking medical assistance. Men presenting symptoms of this malignancy will often admit to suffering severe pain and discomfort for years or decades.[93] They are aware that something is wrong, but too embarrassed to submit to examination. The problem therefore, is to raise the living standards of members of the poorest strata of society, improve their nutritional and hygienic conditions, provide adequate health care, etc. The problem is socioeconomic, not surgical.

The American attitude toward penile cancer reflects both the fear of cancer in general and cancer of the male sex organ in particular. The feeling seems to be that if there is the remotest chance of penile cancer, it would be better to prevent it by routine infant circumcision. The Ad Hoc Task Force on Circumcision considered this question and recommended against circumcision. Pediatricians who have seen the adverse effects of circumcision are generally opposed to the practice. Conversely, urologists, who usually deal with foreskin problems, are often the ones who recommend circumcision. However, the Pediatric Urologists Association has recommended that routine circumcision of infants not be done. This question has also been considered in Britain and rejected; there was a similar decision in Scandinavia. That the United States is the only country in the world to continue the practice is a reflection of attitudes toward surgery and sex, rather than a reflection of medical rationale. Dr. Alex Comfort summed up the situation: "Unless you are Jewish, don't cut it off. Penile cancer is a rare hazard. Wash, don't amputate."[94]

11
Circumcision and Premature Ejaculation

Another popular circumcision fallacy is that, performed either in infancy or adulthood, circumcision prevents or cures premature ejaculation. Such a discovery would appear to be of spectacular importance since, according to Dr. Helen S. Kaplan (1974), this sexual dysfunction is the most common presenting male symptom in clinical practice: "The combination of dysfunctions encountered most frequently in clinical practice is premature ejaculation in the husband and some degree of sexual dysfunction in the wife."[1]

The rationale linking circumcision with premature ejaculation is both ingenuous and ingenious. First, there is absolute acceptance of the fact that both foreskin layers (particularly the inner layer) have exquisitely sensitive nerve endings, which trigger early and intense arousal—too early and too intense—thus provoking premature ejaculation. Therefore, according to this line of thought, eliminate the foreskin and the problem will also be eliminated. Moreover, after circumcision the glans is exposed and, over time, is said to become toughened. (The medical terms used to describe the toughening process are "cornification" and "keratinization.") The toughened glans now purportedly requires greater stimulation for arousal, which, in turn, leads to a longer time interval between intromission (insertion) and orgasm. Dr. David Reuben described the process in the following manner:

> How can circumcision prolong erection?
>
> Like this:
>
> The foreskin fits over the end of the penis like a glove on a finger—and like a glove it protects the head of the organ from rubbing against clothing and other objects.

When the glove is removed by circumcision, the head of the penis is toughened—even calloused—which takes away its hair-trigger sensitivity and allows more prolonged friction with the super smooth lining of the vagina.[2]

Other medical writers take a somewhat more tentative view. Campbell, et al. (1971) wrote that the toughening of the glans "most likely decreases sensitivity," and stated that proponents of circumcision agreed that: "This may not be a disadvantage since it may be conducive to prolonged erection."[3] In a similar vein, urologists R. Burger and T. H. Guthrie (1974) took issue with physicians who opposed circumcision on the grounds that it diminished penile sensitivity. They theorized: "... such diminished sensation might reduce the incidence of premature ejaculations."[4]

Nurse L. J. Carbary (1975) erroneously embellished this concept: "... circumcision makes sexual intercourse more enjoyable because ... without the foreskin the glans penis comes in direct contact with the vagina."[5] However, she failed to note that the foreskin draws back in erection and thus the glans comes in direct contact with the vagina regardless of circumcision status.

Self-help health books, which have become increasingly popular, often deal with premature ejaculation. In one such book (1976), the author suggested 5 ways to reduce or prevent premature ejaculation. First on the list is circumcision.[6] (On the next page of that book the author claimed that breast cancer is caused by abortions.)

Thus, whether the statements are made in absolute or qualified terms, the conclusion is clear; circumcision may/might/will reduce the incidence of premature ejaculation and/or improve sexual enjoyment. If this were true, it would be a powerful argument for circumcision, since it is generally agreed that prolonged lovemaking is a desired goal and anything that interferes with it should be avoided.

Unfortunately, statements are easy to make but much more difficult to prove. In the first place, sex therapists have found that even defining premature ejaculation is not a simple task. Among the factors to be considered are the questions of "when," "where," and "with whom." Premature ejaculation clearly exists if the male has an orgasm prior to intromission. If orgasm occurs within a few seconds after intromission, it is also usually considered premature. Beyond that, definition becomes considerably more complex. For example, if the partners have orgasms with equal rapidity, then it would not necessarily be a case of premature ejaculation. The question then becomes: premature for whom, or with whom? If a firm erection can be maintained for 5 minutes, but the partner requires an even longer period in order to have an orgasm, the male could be considered a premature ejaculator—with that particular partner. However, the same man, having intercourse with a woman who has an orgasm within 2 or 3 minutes after intromission, cannot be considered a premature ejaculator. Therefore, the question is relative and also relates to the attitudes of the sex partner.

Sex researchers use many different definitions of premature ejaculation. Masters and Johnson do not consider it a problem unless it occurs 50% or more of the times coitus is attempted.[7] Dr. Jon Meyer of Johns Hopkins claims that a man who ejaculates before 15 thrusts after intromission is a premature ejaculator.[8] Dr. Helen S. Kaplan maintains that a man should be able to exert voluntary control over his ejaculatory reflex.[9] Drs. J. R. David and E. M. Blight, Jr. propose a different definition, based " . . . not in terms of length of time in intromission but whether the sexual partner is satisfied with the length of the coital thrusting."[10] The American Psychiatric Association Task Force on Nomenclature provides yet another definition: " . . . ejaculation occurring before the individual wishes it, because of persistent and recurrent absence of reasonable voluntary control during sexual activity."[11]

Definition is still further complicated by the point of view of the writer; for example, in 1948, Dr. Alfred C. Kinsey et al. stated: "For perhaps three-quarters of all males, orgasm is reached within two minutes . . . and for a not inconsiderable number . . . the climax may be reached within less than a minute or even within ten or twenty seconds after coital entrance."[12] In other words, Kinsey estimated that for about 75% of American males the time lapse between insertion and orgasm ranged from 10 seconds to 2 minutes. Kinsey also found that although this pattern was more acceptable among men with lower educational levels, better educated men tried to delay orgasm as long as possible.[13]

Trained as a zoologist, Kinsey noted that most mammals, including primates, ejaculate almost instantly upon intromission. He therefore saw this as a problem for humans, since some women require 10-15 minutes or longer of intense stimulation in order to orgasm.[14] Kinsey noted, regarding the longer time period of stimulation needed by some women: "It is, of course, demanding that the male be quite abnormal in his ability to prolong sexual activity without ejaculation if he is required to match the female partner."[15]

Attitudes concerning premature ejaculation are not only conditioned by educational levels; religious attitudes also are a factor. For example, Rabbi Samuel Glasner noted that among Orthodox Jews: "Although some rabbinical authorities at various times recommended that coitus should be performed rapidly, and with a minimum of byplay, others were more liberal . . . in this regard."[16]

Dick Gregory, although well known as a comedian, also delivers serious lectures to college students. A reporter touring with him noted that Gregory tells students that maintaining an erection for more than 45 seconds leads to cancer of the prostate.[17] Ergo, providing a rationale for rapid ejaculation eliminates the problem!

Unfortunately, not only is premature ejaculation difficult to define, but the precise cause is not known. As recently as 1976, one physician noted that the blood flow dynamics of erection and detumescence are delicate and little understood.[18] That same year, another physician claimed that the precise mechanism of detumescence has not been elucidated.[19]

Most psychiatrists who treat the malady stress emotional, not physical factors: Dr. M. R. Lansky wrote (1976) that many factors are involved in premature ejaculation, but the one most frequently encountered in clinical practice is anxiety.[20] This was confirmed by Drs. David and Blight (1978), who stated that there was no organic cause in 90% of the cases of erectile dysfunction.[21] Dr. Helen S. Kaplan reported to the 1977 convention of the American Psychiatric Association, that uncomplicated cases of premature ejaculation (that is, those not involving emotional factors) were so rare that she had difficulty identifying 20 cases for study.[22] In two review articles on the subject (Jonas and Jonas, 1974, and Fink and Fink, 1976), many possible causes are discussed; none is physical and circumcision is not even mentioned.[23] And, more important, treatment of premature ejaculation as an anxiety syndrome has been reported successful in about 90% of the cases.[24]

Thus, despite the lack of clear definition and causal agents, there are two conflicting theses: (1) circumcision does affect premature ejaculation; and (2) premature ejaculation is an anxiety syndrome totally unrelated to physical factors such as circumcision. Given these opposing viewpoints, wherein does the truth lie?

As in any scientific endeavor, the burden of proof must remain with those who present an hypothesis. To this day, and for at least 50 years, statements have been made repeatedly in the medical and popular press, in one form or another, that foreskin removal is related to premature ejaculation. Yet not a scintilla of evidence has been presented in support of this hypothesis. The only exception is that of personal testimonials from adults who underwent the surgery.

For example, Dr. Valentine (a pseudonym), extolled the effects of his circumcision in 1974 in a journal published by the American Medical Association. He claimed that his sexual gratification was improved by circumcision, so much so that he concluded that improved sexual response was more important than any other medical reason for recommending the surgery. He commented:

> The overpowering erotic sensation has been dulled . . . The presence of a foreskin hastens ejaculation. . . . Does circumcision tend to retard ejaculation? In my case it definitely has. The diminished sensation allows greater ejaculatory control. . . . I can now ejaculate almost at will.[25]

It would be difficult to find a more glowing tribute to circumcision as an ameliorative or cure for premature ejaculation. This enthusiasm was so extreme that a urologist, an ardent supporter of circumcision, reminded Dr. Valentine that " . . . the greatest sex organ lies between the ears!"[26]

Other physicians have cautioned against giving credence to personal testimonials about adult circumcision and sexuality, noting that men who are circumcised as adults cannot be considered "reliable judges" because the operation may have been performed to alleviate a problem that hindered their sexual activity and that "there are no objective data."[27]

Although Dr. Valentine's statement is purely subjective, it nevertheless fosters the myth of the relationship between circumcision and premature ejaculation, which Masters and Johnson found to be prevalent among their study sample. However, as previously discussed, Masters and Johnson conducted tests to verify or disprove this hypothesis and found that no significant differences exist between the sensitivity of circumcised and uncircumcised penises.[28]

Dr. Morton Freidman (1978) took issue with the purported link between circumcision and premature ejaculation, claiming that he had never seen evidence of such benefits and that men who are circumcised are no less likely to ejaculate prematurely than uncircumcised men.[29]

In fact, one physician reported that premature ejaculation can occur following adult circumcision. This is probably an emotional reaction to the surgery, since the problem usually subsides in a few weeks or months.[30]

Counterposing one physician's statement with another, or using the limited Masters and Johnson research, provides no definitive or conclusive proof or disproof of the hypothesis; however, working on the assumption that circumcision does have the effect of reducing or preventing premature ejaculation, epidemiological data could be explored to verify the assumption. However, this is a difficult, if not impossible task, because no accurate worldwide data exist.

If circumcision reduces premature ejaculation incidence, men in noncircumcising countries should frequently have problems with premature ejaculation; the opposite should be the case in circumcising countries. A line graph of the frequency of this syndrome in Britain should resemble a roller-coaster, reflecting the on-again, off-again circumcision practice in that country. No such studies have been undertaken, and no statements have been presented in medical or psychiatric literature attesting to frequency differentials based on circumcision.

However, at issue is the problem in the United States. Thirty years ago, when Kinsey reported his findings on male sexuality, perhaps 50% of the most sexually active males (ages 15–45) were circumcised; today the figure is closer to 75%. Therefore, assuming circumcision is a factor, there should have been a corresponding or at least a modest drop in the frequency of the premature ejaculation syndrome. In fact, the drop should be even greater, as premature ejaculation is more common among younger men, the very ones who are more likely to be circumcised. (For reasons that are not fully understood the aging process retards ejaculation.) However, there is absolutely no evidence to demonstrate any drop in the frequency of premature ejaculation.[31] On the contrary, the dysfunction appears to have increased—or at least it is more frequently reported. Fink and Fink noted: "It has become a more frequent complaint in the last quarter century...."[32] Some authors attributed the increase to "women's rising expectations of sexual satisfaction."[33] Another author stated that: "Premature ejaculation is one of the most common disorders of sexual functioning in the male."[34] In a recent study (1978) of 100 white Christian couples whose average age was 37, 36% of the men reported problems with premature ejaculation. It was the most frequently reported sexual dysfunction.[35]

Of course, these statements cannot be taken as evidence of an absolute increase in premature ejaculation, because no reliable nationwide statistical data are available now, nor were they available 10, 20, or 30 years ago. Nor can Kinsey's study be used as nationally projectible data. However, the above statements clearly indicate that the dysfunction has certainly *not* passed from the scene as a result of the increase in circumcision. Changes in mores and the sexual attitudes of women and men must also be taken into account. As yet, there is no valid way to quantify these factors. Still, it is clear that circumcision has not resolved the problem of penile "oversensitivity."

Since most young American men do not possess a foreskin, the problem of premature ejaculation can no longer be attributed to its retention. Now it is claimed that the problem is that the exposed glans is *too sensitive*. This can be attested to by the promotion in sex-oriented publications of topical anesthetics for the glans, as well as the recommendation by physicians that condoms be used to reduce sensitivity.[36] Both have failed to have an appreciable effect on the problem.[37]

One interesting feature of the presentation of the hypothesis linking circumcision with premature ejaculation is the total absence of discussion of Jewish men. The reported low incidence of venereal disease and genital cancer among Jewish men was a major factor in the acceptance of circumcision as a disease preventative. However, as practically all Jewish males have been circumcised since time immemorial, Jews should be almost totally free of the problem of premature ejaculation. But no one writing on the subject has ever suggested that Jewish men never or rarely ejaculate prematurely. Sex clinic attendance has its full complement of Jewish male patients.

To summarize the evidence regarding premature ejaculation:

1. Medical data indicate that organic factors may account for about 10% of the causes of this syndrome.
2. This is in keeping with psychiatric findings that premature ejaculation has an emotional basis in about 90% of the cases.

3. The emotional basis of premature ejaculation in many cases is further demonstrated by the more than 90% success rate in treating the syndrome in psychiatric therapy.
4. The use of condoms or topical anesthetics by circumcised or uncircumcised males has little or no effect in reducing premature ejaculation.
5. Although Jewish males are circumcised in infancy, this population is certainly not free of people suffering from premature ejaculation.
6. All evidence suggests that in spite of the increased circumcision rate, there has been no decrease in the frequency of premature ejaculation. In fact, the evidence suggests that the problem is increasing in sex clinics. At present, it is the most frequently presented male problem.

The only conclusion that can be drawn is that there is no evidence to link circumcision with premature ejaculation.

12
Circumcision and Masturbation

Some historical background of the uniquely American attitudes toward masturbation was discussed in Chapter 4. A century ago, masturbation was believed to be not only sinful, but also the cause of many male and female physical and emotional problems. The physical ills attributed to it ranged from polio to turberculosis and the emotional ills were said to culminate in insanity and death. Masturbation was considered so serious an affliction that every effort was made to prevent or stop the practice; circumcision was one of the milder solutions. Lacking scientific knowledge of the etiology of most diseases, it was apparently easy to accept the "fact" that masturbation was the culprit. Then, as medical knowledge advanced (1875–1910), pathogenic microorganisms were isolated and identified as the causes of many of the physical ailments previously attributed to masturbation.

Yet, even with these discoveries, circumcision continued to be practiced to prevent or cure masturbation, since it was still believed to be the source of many emotional ills. Germs had not been found to cause most mental illness and so, with the baffling array of still unexplainable emotional disorders, masturbation seemed as good an explanation as any for such illnesses; at that period in history no one had any better explanations.

In 1891, Dr. Peter C. Remondino made positive claims about circumcision and masturbation:

> It is only of late years that circumcision, in its true relations to onanism [masturbation] has received full consideration.
>
> . . . The practice of [onanism] can be asserted as being very rare among the children of circumcised races. . . .[1]

Dr. Remondino was reflecting on circumcision, the recently developed surgical approach to masturbation. However, the antagonism to masturbation has very deep roots—going back thousands of years in Jewish and other religious writings. For example, some Jewish theologians considered masturbation a "reprehensible sin," others a "capital crime." So extreme were the views on "self-abuse" that:

> As a precaution against masturbation, it was forbidden for a man to hold his penis even while urinating, except in the case of a married man whose wife was readily available for intercourse.[2]

Several writers have undertaken the task of tracing the social history of masturbation. Dr. Karen E. Paige wrote (1978): "This odd Western obsession accompanied the transition from an agrarian to an industrial economy in Europe and the United States between 1700–1914. Masturbation was always a middle-class worry."[3] Although there is much evidence to support Dr. Paige's first statement, the second is open to question. All religious groups in Europe and the United States (Protestant, Catholic, and Jewish) severely condemned masturbation and they influenced all classes of society; however, the middle and upper classes were the ones that had greater access to the new medical "cures."

Dr. René Spitz, a psychiatrist, viewed the history of masturbation from a medical viewpoint. He noted that physicians in the 18th century tried to cure masturbation, whereas in the 19th century they attempted to suppress it. Up to 1849 diet and hydrotherapy were prime therapeutic modalities; from 1850 to 1879, the most frequently recommended treatment was surgery. Dr. Spitz added: "It is only in the second half of the nineteenth century that sadism becomes the foremost characteristic of the campaign against masturbation."[4]

When surgical intervention to stop masturbation was in vogue, dozens of methods were employed in addition to circumcision (see Chapter 4) including vasectomy.[5]

Perhaps the most comprehensive and typical American medical outlook concerning childhood masturbation in the early part of the 20th century is to be found in the pediatric textbook *Diseases of Infancy and Childhood*, by Dr. L. E. Holt, a standard medical text for almost half a century.[6] It was first published in 1897; the eleventh revised edition was published in 1936. The early editions stated that masturbation was to be treated by mechanical restraint, corporal punishment, and circumcision even if phimosis did not exist "because of the moral effect of the operation." For girls, the approach was even more severe and included complete circumcision, cauterization of the clitoris, blistering the inner thighs, the vulva, or the prepuce.[7]

The 1936 edition finally admitted that such measures failed to cure masturbation. However male circumcision was still recommended even if there was no pathological condition because, "it has proved of benefit by suggestion."[8] In other words, the boy was taught in painful surgical terms that he must stop masturbating. It is no wonder that Dr. Gordon D. Jensen (1978) wrote about masturbation's "florid mythology" and "heinous history."[9]

Although many deeply religious people still look upon masturbation as sinful, the medical profession has largely, but not completely, changed its views on the subject. A more up-to-date view may be gleaned from the psychoanalytically oriented *Psychiatric Dictionary* (1960), which stated:

> It is recognized that all children masturbate during the infantile period, most do during adolescence, and some do, during the latency period. Masturbation, then, can be considered psychologically normal during childhood, and is a major avenue for the discharge of instinctual tension. Under present cultural conditions, masturbation can also be considered psychologically normal during adolescence, and to some extent even in adulthood. . . . [10]

According to most authorities, the really important consequences of masturbation are the guilt feelings about the practice itself and the fantasies that typically accompany it. Such guilt feelings may last for years. Despite repeated assurances to the contrary, in the 1960s many adolescents still attributed almost every conceivable ill to masturbation, including: "pimples, insanity, stooped shoulders, weakness, loss of manly vigor, weak eyes, ulcers, impotence, feeblemindedness, cancer, to name only a few."[11]

Thus, many of the 19th-century views toward masturbation persist to the present day. This is not surprising, because such ideas have been disseminated to the public for decades. *The Boy Scout Handbook* warned of the dangers of masturbation from 1911–1945.[12] A study conducted in 1937 revealed that "82% of male adolescents thought its effects were noxious and as many as 16% thought insanity could be the direct result."[13] In 1942, a study showed that 75% of the parents at a child guidance clinic "had threatened their children with the danger of masturbation."[14] Not only were such attitudes prevalent in the 1940s among lay people, but a 1959 survey taken among medical students and faculty of 5 eastern medical schools revealed that 50% of the medical students and 20% of the faculty believed that excessive masturbation produced insanity.[15] A diametrically opposite view was expressed by Wilhelm Stekel, a disciple of Freud's. He maintained that under certain circumstances *not* masturbating could cause insanity.[16]

Dr. Lester W. Dearborn, discussing masturbation in 1973, noted that there is a dichotomy of views: the well-informed accept masturbation as not only normal, but also desirable and beneficial. Others hold to outmoded dogmas of the past and believe that the practice is harmful.[17] This dichotomy of views is reflected in the approach to circumcision either as a cure or preventative for masturbation.

Dr. Alan F. Guttmacher noted (1962) that up until the 1940s girls were often circumcised to cure masturbation, but that this is no longer done.[18] In 1942, Dr. Benjamin Spock, discussing the use of circumcision for both boys and girls to treat masturbation, concluded that: "circumcision or other operative procedures should . . . be avoided at almost all costs in the treatment of masturbation."[19]

Note that both Drs. Guttmacher and Spock were addressing the topic of childhood circumcision as a therapeutic measure to treat masturbation, not newborn circumcision as a prophylactic measure to prevent masturbation. Medical opinion then changed and became unanimous in agreeing with Dr. Spock's 1942 view that circumcision should never be performed to treat masturbation. Yet, despite this rejection, the concept that newborn circumcision will prevent masturbation and its ill consequences was still found in many statements of the 1940s and 1950s. For example, in 1941 Dr. Alan F. Guttmacher wrote that circumcision makes it easier for the mother to care for her son's genitals because:

> It does not necessitate handling of the penis by the infant's mother, or the child himself in later years, and therefore does not focus the male's attention on his own genitals. Masturbation is considered less likely.[20]

It might be argued that when this statement was made (1941), the old attitudes toward masturbation prevailed. However, some 15 years later, Dr. Guttmacher was still professing the same point of view in his book *Pregnancy and Birth*. He noted that: "They [believers in circumcision] fear that this necessary handling of the genitalia encourages masturbation."[21]

Dr. Guttmacher was not alone in presenting such views in the late 1950s. Writing in a lay health publication in 1959, nurse Gloria Whorton encouraged parents to have their sons circumcised, claiming that irritation under the foreskin "may call undue attention to the area and may indirectly contribute to masturbation."[22]

In *The Modern Family Health Guide* (1959), edited by Dr. Morris Fishbein, who for many years was the editor of the *Journal of the American Medical Association*, the identical view was expressed. However, this time the word masturbation was avoided by substituting a euphemism: "Inflammations under the foreskin are also associated with various nervous manifestations."[23]

Later medical writings mentioned the possible link between circumcision and masturbation, but questioned or discounted the concept. Dr. Fred Rosner wrote (1966):

> Enuresis and masturbation are said to be less frequent in the circumcised male, but the causes for these conditions are obscure and are probably unrelated to the presence or absence of the prepuce.[24]

Two years later, Dr. Roscoe L. Wall, Jr., repeated this conclusion almost word for word.[25]

Within the past 10 years, the prevailing medical view toward masturbation has become more relaxed. This approach was taken by Dr. Robert E. Gould (1977), who commented: "Today it would be hard to find a sexual behavior expert who does not consider autoerotic activity within the realm of 'normal' and 'healthy'. . . . ."[26]

With the emergence and growing acceptance of such views, routine infant circumcision to prevent masturbation is no longer recommended. References to the circumcision-masturbation link have practically ceased to appear in the literature. Yet the doubts linger on in subtle ways. A nurse in 1975, advising mothers on the care of an uncircumcised infant, stated that the foreskin should be pulled back but that: "This procedure should be done quickly so as not to overstimulate the baby."[27] She urged circumcision for fear of the danger of encouraging masturbation.

The "problem" of masturbation has undoubtedly not ceased. Feelings of guilt still exist and, having been fostered for centuries, the lingering fear of the possible ill effects of the practice also still exist among some physicians and many lay people who continue to warn children not to do "it."

In this climate of fear, it is very possible that some parents still hold the view that somehow circumcision will reduce the problem of masturbation and, therefore, accept the surgery for their infants. Three physicians, writing in 1978, stated that although parents often do not verbalize popular myths, they often believe them, noting: "These include the belief that circumcision prevents adolescent masturbation and genital fixation."[28] The extent to which circumcision may be used for this purpose is impossible to measure. It cannot be assumed to be nonexistent. Hopefully, with the passing of time, masturbation fears will pass into medical history and with them the "prophylaxis" for the nonexistent problem.

13
If Later, Why Not Now?

In addition to all of circumcision's supposed health benefits, parents are warned that if they reject infant surgery, they may only be postponing the procedure to a time when the operation would be more troublesome and serious; ergo, it is better to "get it over with now." This seems like a logical position. That is, if the chances of needing this surgery are high later on in life, then it would be better to have it done in infancy. The fallacy, however, is that the risk of adult circumcision is small; and often, especially in the United States, the procedure is medically unnecessary.

Before examining the limited American data, we can look at information from other countries to find clues to the infrequency of circumcision surgery performed at any time after the child is a few days or a few weeks old.

In Oslo, Norway, over a 26-year period in which 20,000 male babies were cared for, 3 circumcisions were performed—a frequency rate of 0.02%.[1] In Denmark, 1,968 children up to the age of 17 were examined over a period of several years. In this group, 3 circumcisions were performed—a frequency rate of 0.15%. In this study, in retrospect, the physician believed all 3 operations might have been avoided.[2] Both of the above studies related to the infrequency of circumcision in infancy and puberty; they did not deal with the issue in adulthood.

Health officials of each Scandinavian country were queried about adult circumcision, i.e., those performed on males aged 15 and over. (The standard international code for recording *all* surgical procedures by age starts at "below 15," followed by older age groups.) None of the health officials could provide precise data, because the numbers were so small that they were not worth compiling. Each official stressed that foreskin problems were presented but said they were largely treated medically—surgical solutions were extremely rare.

The Finnish National Board of Health had compiled national case records for the year 1970 on phimosis and paraphimosis.[3] (Phimosis means that the foreskin is tight and cannot easily be retracted to expose the glans. Paraphimosis is a condition in which the foreskin is forcibly retracted and will not easily return to its normal position.) They showed a total of 409 such cases (aged 15 and over), which represented slightly more than 2/100 of 1% (0.023%) of the total male population in that age category.[4] This means that 99.977% of the males in that age group did *not* present foreskin problems. The Finnish authorities noted that only a tiny fraction of this number required surgery—too small a number to provide an accurate statistic. They were reluctant even to make a *guesstimate*. When pressed, they claimed that the figure was probably not higher than 10%, or 41 circumcisions. If, for the sake of discussion, the circumcision rate is taken to be 25%—not 10%—that would mean 102 operations or an adult circumcision rate of less than 0.006%; conversely 99.994% of the Finnish male population aged 15 and over did *not* require circumcision. This means an adult circumcision rate of 6 per 100,000. Finnish authorities declared that surgery for the below age 15 group was even rarer than for age 15 and over.

Since the approach taken to phimosis and paraphimosis by other Scandinavian countries is almost identical to that of Finland, the assumption can be made that if data were available from Norway, Sweden, and Denmark, they would approximate that of Finland.

With the situation in the Scandinavian countries as background, the picture in the United States can be explored. As was found in respect to so many other facets of circumcision, there has been no definitive research on the question of postnewborn surgery. This was admitted by Dr. David Grimes (1978), who wrote that the risk of the necessity of circumcision after infancy is "unknown."[5]

What makes the subject more complex is the need to differentiate between those who *actually undergo* the operation later in life and those who *actually need* the surgery for medical reasons. These two questions are very different, and difficult to separate. Unlike newborn circumcision, for which there are no nationwide data, there are some nationwide data for postnewborn operations; the data, however, are deficient for a variety of reasons, which will be discussed. Nevertheless, the data are useful in providing some understanding of the scope of the problem.

The question can be simply posed: If an American infant is not circumcised at birth, what are the risks that the surgery will be required later? Is it one chance in 10, 100, 1,000, 10,000 etc.? Such a crude estimate can be made. The National Center for Health Statistics showed that for the years 1965 to 1977 there were approximately 100,000 postnewborn circumcisions each year.[6] (The range was from a low of 89,000 in 1965 to a high of 111,000 in

1975.) These figures cannot be taken as precise data on such postnewborn operations for two reasons:

1. They do not represent a nationwide count of such operations; none was conducted. The figures are based upon a representative sample of hospitals. Therefore the figures could be in error by plus or minus several percentage points.
2. The figures only take into account circumcisions performed in hospitals, even if the stay is not overnight. They do not (and cannot) include the many operations performed in physicians' offices. Therefore the government figures understate the true rate.

Statistical deficiencies notwithstanding, the government figures are the only data available, and they can be helpful in exploring the problem. When the reported surgical rate is examined by age, comparing those under 15 years and those age 15 and over, an interesting pattern emerges:

Nonnewborn Circumcisions in the United States[7]

Year	Circumcisions	% Under 15	% 15 and Over
1965	89,000	54	46
1968	102,000	65	35
1973	99,000	54	46
1975	111,000	47	53

Although there are differences between one year and another, the deficiency of the data makes it impossible to discern a clear trend or to explore the precise reasons for the differences. Nevertheless, it is apparent that approximately one-half of the operations are performed on "adults" (age 15 and over), and one-half on "nonadults" (under age 15).

The statistical break at age 15 creates a problem in interpretation. Clearly, the operation performed on a male age 15 or older should be classified as an adult circumcision; but what does "under 15" mean? It could refer to males ages 10 to 14, in which case the procedure could also be classified as an "adult" operation. Or the category could refer to males aged one week, one month, one year, or older, which would put the surgery in a different light.

In response to my request for a more detailed age breakdown, the National Center for Health Statistics indicated that although precise data were not available, it was their impression that the "overwhelming majority" of the "under 15" age group was below the age of one year. Essentially, this means that the lower age group represented *delayed* newborn operations and not, in the main, "adult" surgeries. This is confirmed by other data, which will be examined.

For a variety of reasons, such as illness, prematurity, low birthweight, and penile structural problems,[8] newborn circumcision is (or should be) automatically delayed. If a newborn develops a fever (usually indicative of infection), is severely jaundiced, manifests breathing problems, or shows any other signs of illness or malfunction, physicians recommend postponing circumcision until the problem has cleared. This may take a week or a month or even longer. In premature or low birthweight babies (especially those under 5 pounds), there will almost always be a delay in circumcision until the baby has gained sufficient weight and strength to sustain the operation.

In addition, babies delivered at home are rarely circumcised at birth. If the child is to undergo the surgery, the parents usually wait until they can take the child to a physician's office or to a hospital. Using these 3 categories —illness, prematurity or low birthweight, and home delivery—it is possible to estimate the number of delayed circumcisions that may be counted in the "under 15" age category of nonnewborn operations as follows:

Delayed Newborn Circumcisions

Reason	Estimated Number of Males[9]
Illness	20,000
Low birthweight or prematurity	144,000
Home births	11,000
Total	175,000

In each instance, the estimate is conservative. For these 175,000 infants, circumcision will likely be postponed for a week or more and, therefore, the case will be included in the government data, provided the surgery is performed in a hospital.

Given an estimated national circumcision rate of 85%, the assumption can be made that the circumcision rate for the above 175,000 infants will likely be lower because parents might be more conservative about subjecting a not-so-well infant to surgery. Mothers who deliver at home by choice frequently do so to avoid excessive surgical intervention and might well oppose routine circumcision. Mothers who deliver at home because no hospital facilities are available might be unable to have circumcision performed because of the unavailability of a physician or hospital; e.g., they might live in poor rural areas.

The circumcision rate for this group of 175,000 might therefore be about 60%, or approximately 100,000 operations. If half of these operations are performed in doctors' offices (a high estimate), this would mean 50,000 hospital circumcisions. According to the government figures, the average number of hospital circumcisions performed in the under 15 age category was 54,000 for the years 1965, 1968, 1973, and 1975. Thus, the estimate of 50,000 possibly delayed newborn circumcisions performed in hospitals would represent 93% (or almost all) of the younger age category circumcisions reported in the government statistics.

With this analysis, it is now possible to examine the number of non-newborn and adult circumcisions annually performed in the United States, as differentiated from the delayed newborn circumcisions. Again taking the figures for the years 1965, 1968, 1973, and 1975, the average number of "over age 15" operations was approximately 47,000. Assuming an error in the under 15 age group of 10,000 (a gross exaggeration), this would mean that the adult rate might be 57,000. Moreover, assuming that an additional 50%—or 29,000 operations—are performed in doctors' offices (a high estimate, as adult circumcisions are more likely to be performed in hospitals), the maximum number of adult circumcisions would possibly be 86,000 annually.

To put these 86,000 operations in perspective, it should be understood that the procedure can only be performed on the population at risk, i.e., those males who possess a foreskin. There are approximately 38,000,000 uncircumcised males in the United States.[10] This means that out of every 1,000 uncircumcised males, each year fewer than 3 (2.3) will undergo the surgery after infancy and 997 will not. This figure is identical with a United States Army estimate of 3 out of every 1,000 men.[11] (In the army, the men are under constant medical surveillance and surgical care is readily available and free. Moreover, army surgeons want patients returned to duty quickly and would tend to choose surgical rather than more time-consuming medical approaches. Thus, the army rate may be higher than the civilian rate.) In Canada, the adult circumcision rate is 1.7/1,000.[12]

Commenting on adult circumcision in the United States, Drs. L. King, et al. wrote (1978) that very few civilian adults undergo circumcision. Most adult operations are performed by the military to offer a degree of protection against certain diseases common to the tropics.[13] According to these physicians, one of the popular myths about circumcision is that it is a requirement for admission to the armed forces.[14]

Whether the true figure is 2, 3, or even 6 per 1,000 men, it is obvious that only a tiny fraction of potential patients undergo circumcision after infancy; more than 99% do not. Thus, the figure for noninfant circumcision is quite low. However, when this figure is compared to those of the Scandinavian countries, the United States' figure is inordinately high.

Greater perspective can be gained by exploring the approach taken by all the Scandinavian countries, where newborn circumcision is not practiced. Theoretically, the degree to which foreskin problems prevail should be much greater than in the United States, where more than one-half the males do not possess foreskins.

Earlier in this chapter, the Finnish adult circumcision rate was calculated to be approximately 6/100,000. The United States' rate was crudely calculated to be about 3/1,000 or 300/100,000. Thus the United States' rate is about 50 times higher than that of Finland.

What is of equal or even greater interest in regard to these Finnish statistics is the mode of treatment of phimosis and paraphimosis. The 409 cases in Finland were hospitalized for a total of 1,975 days or approximately 5 days per case—5 days without hospitalization or medical care costs to the patient, during which time full wages were received. It is no wonder that it was unnecessary to resort to surgery in most cases and, if surgery was required, an extended hospital stay was allowed. In contrast, in the United States, no reference was found in the medical literature suggesting hospitalization to avoid circumcision. Moreover, hospitalization, particularly if uninsured, is costly, and the fear of pay and/or job loss may present serious problems.

A United States noninfant circumcision rate so much higher than Finland's cannot be accounted for only on the basis of the preference of Finnish physicians for medical rather than surgical solutions to foreskin problems. Nor can this difference be attributed to the colder Finnish climate or better penile hygiene among Finns. These factors might account for some of the difference, but not a difference of this magnitude.

Earlier in the chapter it was pointed out that it is necessary to distinguish between those who undergo the surgery and those who actually require the surgery from a medical standpoint. Most people assume that if an adult undergoes circumcision, there must have been a serious foreskin problem. That is simply untrue. Certainly some males have the procedure done for medical reasons, but others have the operation for nonmedical reasons including: cosmetic effect; religious conversion to the Jewish or Moslem faiths; and the urging of wives, based upon the false fear of cancer.

There are numerous references in the medical and lay literature to men desiring the operation because they or their wives believe the penis will look better. Dr. A. G. M. Campbell et al. noted (1971): "urologists are surprised at the number of men who want to be circumcised for cosmetic effect."[15] In this regard, Drs. King et al. commented that circumcision should be con-

If Later, Why Not Now?

sidered not only for medical conditions but also for "social and cosmetic reasons."[16] Unfortunately, there are no data in regard to the number of men who elect circumcision for these reasons. The United States is the only country to follow the practice of cosmetic circumcision.

Among Jews, the intermarriage rate has been estimated to be as high as 40%.[17] Jewish women marrying uncircumcised non-Jewish men may create a situation in which the male undergoes the surgery either for purely religious reasons or simply to please his wife. Among blacks, there have been numerous conversions to the Moslem faith and men not circumcised in infancy undergo the surgery because of religious convictions.

As we discussed in Chapter 10, some women have urged their uncircumcised husbands to undergo circumcision, erroneously believing that such surgery would protect them from cervical cancer.

There is no way to estimate the number of adult circumcisions performed for cosmetic purposes, religious reasons, or due to wifely pressure. It would not be surprising if the figures were in the thousands or possibly the tens of thousands. Regardless of how high or how low these figures are, the major reason given for noninfant circumcision is "medical." Whether the medical reason is valid, or whether other modalities besides surgery could have been utilized, as they are in Finland, is impossible to state.

One thing is certain, the American medical profession has a reputation for being knife-happy not only for minor surgery, but for major surgery as well. A few facts are pertinent here:

1. There are 60,000 board-certified surgeons in the United States, twice as many as 10 years ago. There are an additional 25,000 non-board certified physicians who perform surgery.[18]
2. On a per-capita basis, there is twice as much surgery performed in the United States as in England. Moreover, most surgery in England is free, so there is no personal financial gain for the surgeon.[19]
3. A congressional committee reported (September 1977) that Americans eligible for government medical benefits undergo surgery twice as often as do the general population.[20]
4. It was estimated that 2.4 million unnecessary operations were performed in 1974 at a cost of $3.9 billion, and 11,900 people may have died as a result of these operations.[21]
5. When second opinions were sought, one-third of the patients were found to not require surgery. Of 4,700 patients who were judged not in need of surgery, 37% required some medical (not surgical) treatment after a one year follow-up and 58% required no treatment at all.[22]

6. So serious and costly have the problems become that the federal government has embarked on a campaign to urge second opinions before undergoing surgery.[23]

If unnecessary surgery is performed in large numbers for major procedures, including hysterectomy, gall bladder removal, tonsillectomy, and appendectomy, it takes no stretch of the imagination to assume that this would also apply to circumcision. It is no wonder that the American noninfant circumcision rate is so much higher than Finland's. The relatively high American noninfant circumcision rate reflects not only the difference in approaches between United States and Finnish physicians, but also the difference in approaches among American physicians themselves. Some general practitioners with 30–40 years of experience with a large proportion of uncircumcised patients reported that they did not have one case of foreskin problems that required circumcision. On the other hand, urologists who were queried almost routinely suggested circumcision for patients with foreskin problems. Thus, the bugaboo about the high likelihood of requiring circumcision later in life can be put to rest. No high likelihood exists. Taking into account both the nonmedical circumcisions and those performed because many American physicians refuse to consider less drastic modalities, only 3 men per 1,000 undergo circumcision annually. If proper penile hygiene were taught and exercised, and if the Scandinavian medical approach were followed, the United States' rate would be as low as Finland's: 6 per 100,000.

14

Pain and Psychological Trauma

When newborn circumcision began to be routinely practiced, the positive aspects were considered to be of such a magnitude that they completely outweighed any possible negative aspects. To a large degree this view is still held. There has not been one article in a medical or lay journal specifically devoted to a total overview and analysis of the potentially negative psychological aspects of circumcision. The question is usually scoffed at as nonsense. Even the approach to newborn circumcision pain is simplistic and contradictory.

Some writers declare that there simply is no pain. For example, the authors of *The Mothers' Medical Encyclopedia* (1972), stated: "Circumcision of a newborn boy is not painful for the child."[1]

Dr. Marvin Eiger (1972) was critical of those who claimed that the surgery is painful. He called such views: "Poppycock!" The doctor explained that when the surgery is done in the first two or three days after birth ". . . discomfort is minimal, since the fairly subdued infant is relatively insensitive to pain."[2]

Lorraine J. Carbary (1975) stated that no anesthesia is necessary because there is no pain. The absence of pain was said to be related to the squeeze technique which: ". . . causes numbness in a few minutes, making the procedure practically painless."[3]

Others have taken a somewhat different view. Dr. E. T. Wilkes (1959) said the procedure was "not very painful"; Dr. F. W. Rutherford (1971) stated that "circumcision is momentarily painful." Dr. Charles Schlosberg claimed (1971) that there was no more pain than an injection.[4] In 1972 the Boston Children's Medical Center staff claimed that it was painful but not traumatic:

The baby cries when the actual cutting is being done. .

Nothing in the baby's behavior would suggest that the operation has been a trauma.[5]

According to the textbook *Maternity Nursing* (1976), mothers are often anxious about the baby at this time, and therefore the nurse is advised to reassure her " . . . that the procedure has not been very painful for her child. The infant will cry during the operation, but this is due as much to the necessary restraints as to the discomfort."[6] The myth that circumcision pain is due as much to the restraint employed as to the surgery itself was repeated by Drs. Isenberg and Elting (1976). In fact, they went even further and claimed that the pain is more of a reaction to the restraint than to the surgery:

> As for anesthesia, none is needed. Although the baby may scream and kick during the procedure, this seems to be more a reaction to being bundled to the circumcision board than actual pain. Many babies fall asleep during the process. Since a good portion of the baby's nervous system is not yet formed, especially that part that localizes pain, circumcision done at this age the first few days after birth is probably the best time.[7]

The claim that newborn circumcision is relatively painless is extended to the postnewborn period. A South African physician, Joseph Katz, wrote (1977): "No anesthetic is necessary during the first 2½ to 3 months after birth."[8]

The concept that circumcision is painless or moderately and only momentarily painful, or that the child reacts as much or more to the restraint as to the surgery has been challenged by others. For example Dr. Charles Weiss noted in the *Journal of the American Medical Association* (1970) that the newborn is intelligent and has a rapidly increasing sensitivity to pain. Therefore, circumcision without anesthesia for some infants is severely traumatic, and local anesthesia is recommended by many anesthesiologists and psychiatrists.[9]

Others expressed similar views. Dr. R. S. Illingworth wrote (1968): "Circumcision without anesthesia is a cruel practice."[10] A British physician, Dr. J. M. Howat, argued (1976) that "General anesthesia is required in all cases."[11] (Recommending general anesthesia, however, raises the question of the risk from the anesthesia itself.)

In 1978, two pediatricians, Drs. Kirya and Werthmann, noted that little attention has been paid to the fact that there is circumcision pain, and therefore few efforts have been made to eliminate it. They provided a vivid description of a newborn undergoing circumcision:

The infant cries vigorously, trembles, and tries to wriggle out of the restraint. He may eventually become plethoric, dusky, and mildly cyanotic because of prolonged crying. Occasionally, this results in respiratory pauses and regurgitation of feedings.[12]

Dr. David A. Grimes provided a similar description, noting "flushing" and "the propensity . . . to vomit."[13] Because of the possibility of vomiting, several physicians have urged that surgeons keep a portable suction unit nearby "to clear possible regurgitation" during the surgery.[14]

The main point of the article by Drs. Kirya and Werthmann was to introduce a local anesthetic injection technique to eliminate pain. Physicians are not the only ones concerned about circumcision pain. Dr. George Wald, Emeritus Professor of Biology at Harvard and Nobel Laureate, wrote:

> . . . Why does anyone think that circumcision does not hurt them? Well they can't say it hurts and they don't seem to remember it later.
>
> It is a barbarous thing to meet a newly born infant with the knife with a deliberate mutilation.[15]

And yet in 1978, three British physicians wrote: "Circumcision is usually performed at an age when there seems little need to bother about the pain inflicted."[16] They went further and discounted long-term effects:

> There is . . . no reason to believe that the early pain of circumcision has long term developmental effect even if there is evidence which suggests that circumcision may be related to early disturbance of the relationship between mother and child.[17]

Compare this view with that of Drs. Kirya and Werthmann, who stated that one of the functions of normality is the ability to feel pain, and that every normal newborn can feel pain. They noted that the theory that infants do not feel pain or won't remember it anyway is unsubstantiated. Drs. Kirya and Werthmann further commented that the long-term effects of painful newborn experiences are unknown.[18]

Penelope Leach (1976) not only argued that there is pain, but also raised the possibility that it may be remembered. She commented:

> Babies feel pain from birth. Of course they do not anticipate pain, nor as far as we know, do they remember it. But at the time it is inflicted they feel and respond to it. Many authorities [believe] that circumcision without pain prevention is thoughtlessly cruel.
>
> In some centers techniques have been developed by which the skin which must be removed is frozen with a topical anesthetic spray.[19]

Barbara Seaman (1976) quoted psychiatrist René Spitz:

> Nobody who has witnessed the inhuman way in which these infants are tied down and then operated on without anesthesia—the infants screaming in manifest pain—can reasonably deny that such treatment is likely to leave traces of some kind on the personality.[20]

Another psychiatrist, R. D. Laing, recalling a scene from a film of a circumcision in which the screaming infant's face is grotesquely contorted with pain, declared that there is trauma:

> This ritual mutilation was done without local anesthetic and within 24 hours of birth. There is no scientific way of telling, but if you look at the baby, there's simply no doubt.[21]

How is it possible for so many writers to have such divergent views on so "simple" a question as pain in newborn circumcision? Do some writers believe there is pain, but want to conceal this fact because it might tend to discourage the acceptance of circumcision? Is it possible that the "authorities" simply do not know? Do some babies actually sleep through the procedure? These are complex questions and relate primarily to the individuality of the newborn.

All normal newborns are alike in that they have one head, two arms, two eyes, one nose, etc., etc.: all of the essential external parts. If there is no indication of improper body function, the assumption can be tentatively made that all internal systems are okay. But there the similarities among newborns cease.

There are probably a hundred or more criteria that may differentiate one newborn from another. Among these are genetic makeup, prenatal environment (mother's health, nutrition), ease and type of delivery, prematurity, body weight, and size.

It is well known that if the mother is addicted to heroin, the infant will likely be born addicted and manifest withdrawal symptoms. Similarly, most medications administered to the mother just prior to or during delivery will often be found in the body of the newborn. A heavily sedated mother will deliver a heavily sedated child; an anesthetized mother (e.g., in a Caesarian birth) may deliver an anesthetized child. According to pediatrician T. Berry Brazelton, it takes "at least a week" for the newborn body to excrete the various medications from its body.[22]

Two investigators, Oswald and Peltzman, reported a relationship between newborn cries and anesthesia, noting: " . . . investigators have shown that the early vocal behavior of newborn infants is affected by the kind of anesthetic drugs given the mother during labor . . . "[23] Thus it is possible that a baby sedated via his mother's system may sleep through a circumcision procedure. However, it is most unlikely that a normal unmedicated baby would react without pain to circumcision. It is a known fact that most babies do scream during the operation, yet the claim is made that the pain is of no consequence because the infant's nervous system is not fully developed at birth and therefore the pain is not localized. As will be noted, this statement is in error and, additionally, must be challenged on its face. What difference does it make if the pain is localized or generalized? Pain is pain. Circumcision enthusiasts discount all aspects of possible trauma. Therefore, claiming that the pain is not localized eases the burden of proof that circumcision may be traumatic.

Such statements regarding the immaturity of the infant's nervous system are easier to make than to prove. Actually there is no proof of their validity and, in fact, there is a growing body of empirical evidence to the contrary. During the past decade, medical technology has advanced sufficiently to allow intensive study of fetal brain development and neurology. Dr. Dominick P. Purpura, who heads the Neuroscience Department at the Albert Einstein Medical School in New York City, reported (1975) the results of studies correlating brainwave, visual, and other physiological tests with autopsy studies of premature infants. This study revealed that "brain life" begins during the seventh and eighth months of pregnancy.

> It is curious that a human infant's brain cortex is so well developed by the time it is a full term infant.
>
> Until we started to take similar looks into the human brain over the past four years, it wasn't clear to anyone as to when these same features of the mature brain circuitry make their appearance.
>
> Suddenly, new circuits develop. New types of connections appear during that period of time [between the seventh and eighth months] which are the kinds of connections that one sees in the normal full term infant.[24]

In other words, by the time a fetus reaches full term, its brain circuitry is far more advanced than previously believed. These neurological studies are confirmed by behavioral studies of the newborn.

The First International Conference on Child Studies was held in 1978 at Brown University, Providence, R.I., and was attended by 600 specialists. Among the questions posed were: When do infants first hear, see, and touch and when do they first begin to experience emotions? The conference reported that:

> Physicians and medical researchers are finding that babies can have all of these experiences much earlier in life than was previously believed.

The early detection of complex sensory and emotional development in infants as young as 1 or 2 days old was the focal point [of the conference].[25]

Many physicians reported the results of their studies to the conference. Dr. Michael Gilmore of Yale University stated:

> ... The research shows just how active the newborn is. He actually works on receiving information. He is trying to make order out of what he sees.[26]

Dr. T. Berry Brazelton reported on how early an infant's sensory capabilities develop:

> We know that taste and touch probably begin while the baby is still in the uterus. Smell comes shortly before birth. Vision and hearing—we know there is a response there.[27]

The 1978 conference received wide press coverage; however, many similar findings had been reported earlier.[28] The earlier findings, reported in 1971, based upon less sophisticated technology, were so radically different from what was then believed that they were "discounted out of hand."[29] Some examples from the 1971 report are given below. These earlier researchers noted an almost infinite variety in newborn reactions.[30] They reported that newborns see, hear, and are sensitive to touch.[31] In short, the newborn is a thinking and feeling human being. Although the brain is immature, the newborn remembers objects if they reappear in his line of sight within 2 or 3 seconds.[32]

Dr. Robert L. Fantz of Case Western Reserve University, Cleveland, Ohio, noted that the research has demolished the myth that the world of the newborn is one of total confusion, that his visual world is formless, and that his mind is blank.[33]

Dr. L. Joseph Stone of the Department of Child Study at Vassar, reported that ideas about the newborn are changing. The neonate is more aware and sensitive to the outside world and he also responds and is influenced by his interaction with it at an earlier age than previously had been believed.[34] Dr. Stone further commented that of all the newborn's powers, the most impressive are sensory. There are responses to temperature changes, tastes can be distinguished, and as early as the third or fourth day a preference for sweets and a dislike for bitter substances are shown. He noted that Dr. Lewis Lipsitt of Brown University has demonstrated that newborns can distinguish one odor from another and despise foul odors.[35]

If, according to the 1971 report, the newborn can see, hear, smell, taste, and respond to touch and heat in the first few days after birth, can the newborn also feel and localize pain? Dr. T. Berry Brazelton addressed this question at that time. He noted that a newborn may cry as a result of the discomfort caused by too tight a rubber band around his scalp from an electroencephalograph or the electrodes from an electrocardiograph.[36] When blood is taken from a neonate's heel, the response is to pull the foot away. When the foot to be punctured is firmly held, the infant will bring the other foot to push the doctor's hand away, Dr. Brazelton said.[37]

Other studies have demonstrated the differences between crying from pain and crying from other causes in newborns. Using sound spectrographs, P. F. Oswald and P. Peltzman observed:

> Our attention has been focused on the distress cry of infants. We have recorded numerous distress cries resulting from routine medical procedures such as taking blood samples and minor surgery such as circumcision. The distress cry is louder, longer, and noisier than the hunger cry. It also tends to be irregular, with more interruptions and gagging.[38]

Based upon the foregoing studies, it is difficult to accept statements that circumcision is not painful, or that the newborn brain is not sufficiently developed to feel or localize pain. Therefore, given the apparent conclusion that circumcision is painful (except for newborns sedated via the mother), the next question to be considered is whether the pain is momentary—i.e., only for the duration of the surgery—or whether the newborn responds to the pain in a traumatic fashion over longer periods of time. Until recently, the circumcision literature has totally ignored this question. The often-repeated assumption is that once the surgery is over, the newborn takes nourishment and/or falls asleep and the incident is forgotten. That might well be true; however, there are no empirical data to prove the point. While there is, as yet, no substantive evidence of long-term psychological trauma, the question has begun to be explored via recently developed techniques.

Before describing this research, it should be noted that circumcision pain often does not necessarily terminate with the surgery. The healing process—which takes about one week—may be painful. Care must be exercised in keeping the wound clean and in protecting the sensitive glans. An ointment is usually suggested to cover the penis during this period. As will be discussed in the next chapter, infections and hemorrhage are not uncommon occurrences, and both minor and major injuries happen more often than is reported in the literature. These mishaps may require medical and/or surgical intervention. For newborns exposed to such sequelae, the pain may well be more than momentary.

The theoretical framework surrounding concern about possible psychological trauma from circumcision is simple to follow. For at least 50 years the assumption has been made that infant and childhood trauma evokes negative responses later in childhood, adolescence, and/or adulthood. If trauma occurring at the age of one year can be reflected in negative behavior 5, 10, or 20 years later, can such trauma occurring at the age of 11 months evoke similar problems later? If it is true at 11 months, is it also true at 10, 9, 8, etc., or even at one month or earlier? Some pediatricians and psychiatrists maintain that even traumas occurring in the uterus will adversely affect the newborn later in life. To put it another way, at what age can trauma occur that will *not* have an effect at a later date?

More specifically, can newborn circumcision cause emotional trauma that will leave a permanent imprint? Although this question cannot definitively be answered based upon current knowledge of developmental psychology, some authorities do claim that such imprinting can occur. For example, in 1971, a medical encyclopedia carried the following statement: "Some psychiatrists believe that even at this early age the operation [circumcision] may leave scars on the mind as well as the body."[39]

That newborn circumcision is a psychologically traumatic experience is obvious. The infant, after living in the protected uterine environment for 9 months, goes through the birth trauma and usually is almost immediately separated from the mother, except for feeding. After 2 or 3 days of such separation, the infant is firmly restrained, placed under strong lights, and subjected to a surgical procedure without anesthesia. The only question is whether the trauma is short-lived, as is generally believed, or of longer, possibly permanent, duration, as is suggested by some research.

In recent years, both the theory and practice of natural childbirth have received much prominence and acceptance. Although the major emphasis in natural childbirth is the health and well-being of the mother, consideration is also given to the fact that natural childbirth is better for the child. One method of natural childbirth that places special emphasis on reducing birth trauma has been devised by Dr. Frederick LeBoyer.[40] According to the LeBoyer method, the delivery room is kept warm, with subdued lighting and a minimum of noise. There is no rush to cut the umbilical cord and the newborn is submerged in a warm bath; the mother is immediately given ample opportunity to fondle her child. Based upon Dr. LeBoyer's attending 10,000 births, 1,000 of which followed his method, the doctor concluded that babies born with minimal trauma developed into happier and emotionally healthier children than those born in the traditional manner. Although these findings appear to be logical, they have not been confirmed via rigid controls in longitudinal studies. They do represent a new approach to childbirth, with strong emphasis on minimum trauma to the child—including an avoidance of circumcision.

There is ample evidence that newborn experience can affect behavior throughout life. For example, a premature baby may be allowed to remain in the incubator, and may be largely untouched for days, or the baby may be handled and caressed frequently by either parents or nurses. Dr. T. Berry

Brazelton found that the babies who are handled "do nearly twice as well" as the untouched newborns, that they "gained weight, began to develop more quickly." These results showed up after one year.[41]

One animal research study with newborn rats (1960) revealed that stress either in the form of electric shock or removal from the nest caused deviations in behavior and physiology in adulthood, such as negative responses to new environments and earlier maturation. Objective and quantitative indices of stress are provided by the hormones of the endocrine system.[42] The researcher cautioned against extrapolating from animal experimentation to human biology and also reported that he had been unable to identify the critical element in the stimulation process that leads to such predictable and profound effects.[43]

In 1976, a joint British-American research team (Richards, Bernal, and Brackbill) reviewed the literature on newborn animal stress studies and their conclusions suggested that such studies might be relevant to similar stress in humans. One such stress—circumcision—was explored, leading to the hypothesis that: "The physical insult in the form of male circumcision has both behavioral and physiological consequences that may have been uniformly misinterpreted by developmental scientists."[44]

In exploring newborn gender behavioral differences, the research team was struck by the fact that British and Dutch studies showed no gender differences, while American studies did show differences. The gender differences in the behavior of American newborns were based upon skin, electrical, light, and taste stimuli. Male and female British and Dutch newborns showed little difference between sexes in response to a variety of stimuli. Female American newborns responded similarly to their European counterparts of either sex. On the other hand, American male newborns responded differently. In seeking an explanation for these differences, the researchers noted that, unlike European males, the American male study subjects were circumcised; this, they suggested, might account for the differences.

After reviewing prior studies, the researchers noted that most of the American studies were conducted somewhat differently from the British and Dutch studies, which may account for the differences in some test results. However the taste studies were conducted in identical fashion. Richards et al. described one such taste study conducted by other researchers in 1970. Female study subjects had a greater preference for sweet substances than did circumcised male subjects. No such gender differences were found where uncircumcised males were studied.[45]

Richards et al. reported on 2 studies comparing circumcised and uncircumcised male newborns using Non Rapid Eye Movement (NREM) in 1971 and sleep in 1974.[46] Both studies found significant differences between the groups.

In 1976, one member of the British-American team, Yvonne Brackbill, investigated the effects of circumcision on heart rate responses to continuous auditory stimulation in 30 male newborns. Comparison groups were females and uncircumcised males. No heart rate differences were noted between females and uncircumcised males during experimental or control periods. In comparing scores for females and uncircumcised males with those of circumcised males, 7 of the 16 comparisons showed significant differences, however.[47]

These three limited studies clearly demonstrate that circumcision may well affect newborn behavior and physiology. What is not clear is either the direction or the duration of these effects. Despite these limitations, the British-American research team concluded:

> In view of all the evidence showing long-term behavioral, physiological, anatomical and even neuropharmacological effects of "minor" events in early animal development, . . . we would be unwise to assume without empirical demonstration that the circumcision effects are short-lived.[48]

This area of study has begun to interest other investigators as well. There have been numerous studies of the effects of stress on newborns, which showed an important reaction by the adrenal cortex. One such study by a North Carolina research team (1976) used circumcision as the stress factor and demonstrated a marked increase in cortisol (a secretion of the adrenal gland) both 20 and 40 minutes after the surgery.[49] In another study of newborn gender differences, uncircumcised boys were intentionally selected on the assumption that circumcision would bias the results.[50]

Recognizing the potential problem of pain and trauma, Dr. Muriel Sugarman wrote in *The American Journal of Orthopsychiatry* (1977):

> This practice [circumcision] has long been considered benign and well tolerated by the neonate because of his assumed insensitivity to pain. Recently however . . . investigators have commented on the effect of circumcision on newborn behavioral states and on the establishment of biorhythms. In light of the increasing evidence we have of the extreme sensitivity of the newborn, it might be well to rethink the whole issue of routine circumcision and its possible long-term effects on infant behavior. . . .[51]

Two conclusions can be drawn from this chapter's discussion:

1. The statements, made repeatedly during the past 100 years, that circumcision pain is of minor significance and that circumcision trauma is of no consequence, are, to say the least, open to question.
2. With the increasing attention to and knowledge of neonatal development, evidence has emerged—tentative, to be sure—that both circumcision pain and trauma may well be matters of concern in later development.

15

Circumcision Risk

That circumcision entails risk is not a debatable question; it is a fact. Any surgical procedure, no matter how simple, carries with it some risk—minimal to be sure—but risk nevertheless. For the past 50 years the *Index Medicus* has included a subsection titled "Adverse Effects" under "Circumcision." Dozens of articles have been published delineating a wide variety of complications; all were related to one or several cases, or to experience in one community or one hospital over a specific period of time.

To explore circumcision risk it is necessary to know 3 things: the nature of the risk; the degree, mild, moderate, or severe; and the frequency of occurrence. The medical profession is unable to provide this information because:

- There has been no nationwide risk study.
- The term "risk" is difficult to define.
- Mishaps are not always entered in the patient's charts.
- All risk studies, with one exception, were not based upon follow-up after discharge.
- No long-range studies (over months and years) have been conducted to determine the long-term effects of circumcision.

Despite the absence of research, many physicians maintain that the risk is either nonexistent or too infrequent to be of concern and thus conclude that the benefit-risk ratio is very high. In 1966 and 1968, two physicians summarized various risk studies. Dr. Fred Rosner concluded that circumcision complications were "exceedingly rare," although he admitted that they do occur.[1] He presented the following data:

- A 1953 report from New York City by H. Speert,[2] noted that out of an estimated 500,000 circumcisions performed during a 13-year period there was one death. (That death resulted from a Jewish ritual circumcision performed in the home.)
- At Sloane Hospital in New York City between 1933 and 1951, 10,802 newborn circumcisions were performed with 1 infection, 4 cases of bleeding, and 1 injury. (Risk rate 0.06%.)
- In the Huntington Memorial Hospital, Pasadena, California, 1,844 circumcisions were performed in 1949 and 1950 with 3 cases of bleeding. (Risk rate 0.16%.)

Dr. R. L. Wall, Jr., essentially denied the existence of any risk. He cited as evidence the following studies:

- One physician, identified only as "distinguished," was quoted: "In many thousands [of circumcisions] performed at Johns Hopkins Hospital . . . I can recall no complication of any moment." No year was given. No records were examined.
- Two doctors (Miller and Snyder, 1953) reported no serious mishaps in 24,000 circumcisions.[3]

Dr. Wall did not define "of any moment" or "serious"; therefore, the only conclusion to be drawn is that circumcision risk is small, if not negligible. The risk figures of Drs. Rosner and Wall range from a low of 0 to a high 1.6 per thousand (0.16%).

In 1978, Dr. Karen E. Paige claimed (without substantiation): "Overall, the complication rate for routine circumcision stands at only 1 percent of all operations."[4] One percent means one in a hundred operations, or more than 6 times higher than the highest figure previously noted (1.6/1,000). The fact is that no one really knows the "overall" figure.

Dr. M. Eiger (1972) presented a different view of the risks involved:

> I myself have seen plenty of botched circumcisions—cases where babies bled after the operation, where more skin than necessary was removed from the penis, where infection developed at the site of the incision. No one would deny that some circumcisers do a better job than others.[5]

Although Dr. Eiger gives some examples of botching, his numbers are vague. How many is "plenty"? Is it 5, 50, or 500? No one seems to know or can definitively say. However, Dr. Eiger added a new dimension—the skill of the surgeon. This dimension is commented on repeatedly in the literature. Even Dr. Wall noted: "When routine circumcision is performed under the proper conditions and by well-trained personnel, risk of surgical complications of any consequence is small."[6] Dr. Wall is undoubtedly correct. As a surgical procedure, circumcision is relatively simple, if performed under "proper conditions" and by "well-trained personnel," the risk should be minimal. The problem is that neither of these two criteria is met in many places, including the allegedly best hospitals.

As to "proper conditions," this means an aseptic environment—sterile instruments, mask, gloves, etc. Yet, as will be noted later, infections are among the most common circumcision complications. This should not be surprising, since it has frequently been reported that between 1,500,000 and 2,000,000 patients acquire infections in American hospitals each year.[7]

There is unanimous agreement that circumcision should be performed by a skilled operator or, if he is unskilled, performed under the closest supervision. (In 1948, my attention was called to the fact that in one large New York City hospital the pediatric nurse regularly performed circumcisions; in 1977 it was reported in a private communication that a Jewish ritual circumcisor (mohel) was performing almost all the newborn circumcisions in a large New York City hospital.) However it is well known that major surgery, far more complex than circumcision, is often performed without supervision; the attending physician signs the surgical report later and often collects the fee. This practice, called "ghost surgery," has become so prevalent that it was the subject of a nationwide television program in 1977.[8]

The *New York Times* reported (1978) that "between 50% and 85% of the surgery at teaching hospitals was done by residents" and that often "residents are left without full-time supervision."[9] The report referred to major surgery; it is likely even more true for circumcisions, which are usually delegated to the lowest person in the medical hierarchy.

Drs. Levitt, Smith, and Ship of the Albert Einstein School of Medicine, New York City, cautioned (1976) that circumcision is frequently done by junior medical staff or unskilled personnel.[10] Drs. W. F. Gee and J. S. Ansell (1976) listed the personnel who performed circumcisions in a Seattle, Washington, hospital: "a medical student under supervision, an intern or resident, or ... an attending physician."[11] In other words, only the medical student is supervised. The interns and residents are not. Dr. David A. Grimes (1978) stated that the surgery is "not innocuous" and that surgical problems keep occurring, particularly when the surgeon is inexperienced.[12]

The problem of unskilled operators is not limited to the United States. A South African physician wrote (1977): "This procedure is done by many, some perhaps less skilled than they should be."[13]

The question of circumcision risk, therefore, cannot be dismissed with impunity. Although no nationwide data exist, enough information is available to glean some idea of the range of problems resulting from surgical ineptitude. It should be noted that surgical blunders are prevalent in all types of surgery to an alarming degree. Even nonphysicians do major surgical procedures.[14]

A key difficulty in studying circumcision risk is the problem of collecting data. In the first place, some hospitals do not record circumcision surgery—let alone complications—in the chart. This was noted by Dr. Wall in 1968:

> ... during the past five years ... no complications were coded in the hospital records. It was interesting to note that 30% of the circumcisions performed were not included on the discharge summary sheet for proper coding.[15]

A similar situation was noted in 1976 by Drs. Gee and Ansell, who conducted a 10-year study of circumcision risk in one hospital. They found that "most complications" were not entered in the patients' charts. The information required could only be "ferreted out" from the nurses' notes.[16]

Although risk information is not readily available, statements to the effect that morbidity is minuscule are made repeatedly in the literature. And if morbidity is considered negligible, mortality is said to be almost nonexistent. In 1941, Dr. Alan F. Guttmacher claimed that he never heard of a death in any of the hospitals with which he was affiliated. Dr. H. Speert (1953) wrote that there was one death in 500,000 circumcisions in New York City, but that death was not caused by a physician in a hospital setting. In other words, there were no deaths reported due to circumcisions performed by physicians. This information was quoted by Dr. Rosner in 1966, who counted the one non-physician death and derived a death rate of 1/500,000. This death rate figure was accepted almost as gospel by some pro-circumcision and anti-circumcision physicians in 1974 and 1975.[17]

On the other hand, Dr. R. S. Illingworth (1968) insisted that most practicing pediatricians had seen or heard of such a death.[18] The editors of *Family Health* commented (1972) that deaths due to circumcision may be attributed to other causes—pneumonia, blood poisoning, liver or kidney failure, etc.[19] They cited the *British Medical Journal*, which claimed an average of 15 deaths annually when circumcision was almost routinely performed. Since the United States' population in 1950 was almost 4 times greater than Britain, and the frequency of circumcision about twice as great in the U.S., it is possible that the American annual death rate could be at least 100. But most physicians here claim that there are *no* deaths resulting from circumcision.

A sharply contrary view was expressed in 1978 by Dr. Sydney S. Gellis, writing in the *American Journal Diseases of Children*. Dr. Gellis was vehement in declaring that: "... there are more deaths each year from complications of circumcision than from cancer of the penis."[20] Dr. Gellis did not provide a source for this claim. Since there were about 225 deaths from cancer of the penis in 1978, Dr. Gellis was claiming a circumcision mortality rate greater than that. Wherein does the truth lie; is the death rate from circumcision zero or more than 225, or somewhere in between?

If morbidity data are frequently not entered in the chart, presumably to avoid malpractice suits, then it is even less likely that a death will be attributed to circumcision, for the same reason.

There is general agreement that circumcision risk falls into 3 categories: hemorrhage, infection, and surgical injury. In each category the severity can range from mild to moderate to severe. No one would disagree that severe hemorrhage, infection, and surgical injury constitute definite circumcision risk. However, the problem becomes more complex when classifying mild or moderate "complications." For example, which of the following situations would constitute a "complication"?

- Some unexpected bleeding occurs during the surgery, which is easily controlled by medication, pressure, or sutures.
- An infection is noted soon after surgery and is treated by prompt administration of an antibiotic.
- The penile shaft or glans is nicked by a scalpel and heals readily with or without medication.

These are difficult questions to answer. The real risk factor arises if the above "complications" go unnoticed; serious problems may ensue. Moreover, in many cases the judgment of listing a "complication" in the chart is left to the intern, resident, or attending physician. With the wide prevalence of malpractice suits, it is not unreasonable to assume that minor incidents may not be noted in the chart.

The most common circumcision complication is hemorrhage. According to Dr. John Denton (1978) the "rate reported at times as being up to 2%."[21] No source was given for this statistic. In some cases, hemorrhage was so severe that heroic measures had to be taken, including blood transfusion.[22]

Drs. Gee and Ansell found it necessary to define hemorrhage, for the purpose of their study, as having occurred if the patient's chart entry showed that the physician made special efforts to stop bleeding from 4 to 72 hours after circumcision. This occurred in 59 of the 5,521 cases observed (1.1%).[23] This means that excessive bleeding may occur during surgery or several hours or days later. The question of whether hemorrhages occurred that may not have been entered in the chart was not addressed in this research paper.

Infections are not uncommon as a result of circumcision, but, if caught in time, are usually ameliorated with antibiotics. Nevertheless, in the above-mentioned study of 5,521 circumcisions (1976), an infection rate of 0.4% was reported, including a case where a spinal tap was necessary.[24] Drs. King et al. suggested (1978) that circumcision infections occur more frequently than reported, because most of those that are reported are "minor."[25]

There are hundreds of examples of circumcision injuries and comments reported in the medical literature. For example, in 1962, Drs. van Duyn and Warr reported that " . . . major losses of penile skin as a complication of circumcision are fairly common."[26] The consequences of excessive skin loss depend upon the extent and location of the loss. In some cases the body heals itself, but in some situations there can be discomfort in erection, scar tissue, and penile curvature.[27] Levitt et al. (1976) described the plastic surgery that they employ to correct circumcision mishaps. In one case, they stated that even after the surgery "the deformity of the glans and penis persists."[28] A 1968 study of 433 circumcisions with a plastic bell clamp showed 3 injuries, a problem rate of 0.70%.[29] In 1971, A. G. M. Campbell et al. reported a case where stitches were taken through the urethra; they stated that at a meeting of the American Academy of Pediatrics they were told that although this serious complication is not a common occurrence " . . . it is no longer rare."[30] Campbell et al. also stated:

> Surgical misadventures [circumcision injuries] are by no means isolated incidents.[31]
>
> Serious complications are not rare.[32]

They further commented that since urologists encounter adult foreskin problems in their practice, they often favor newborn circumcision. However, they noted: " . . . Most pediatric urologists argue against routine circumcision because of the poor results and complications they see."[33]

It is not necessary to provide a compendium of all reported cases of circumcision surgical trauma to prove that there is risk in this surgery.

There is also an additional circumcision risk problem not covered in the above statements—that of delayed complications. Prior to the late 1940s, women remained in the hospital for about a week after childbirth. This meant that a circumcised newborn was presumably under the watchful eye of the hospital nurse prior to discharge. Based upon World War II experience, the hospital stay has been reduced to about 2 or 3 days. Since circumcision is often done on the second or third day, the infant now leaves the hospital within a short time after surgery—with no medical follow-up unless a pediatrician sees the child from birth on. Among poorer families, health care may not be sought for at least a month; thus delayed problems may go unnoticed until they are serious.

There has been only one study of delayed circumcision complications. It was conducted in Canada by Dr. Hawa Patel in 1966.[34] In this unique study, Dr. Patel personally examined 100 circumcised Canadian infants about 6 months after discharge and interviewed one or both parents. He found this method to be superior to mail or telephone questionnaires or even outpatients' records. His findings showed that of the 100 cases: 3 bled 5-7 days postoperatively; 4 cases required sutures to stop the bleeding; and 7 infections were noted after hospital discharge. There was 1 severe meatal ulcer; 8 cases of meatal stenosis (narrowing of the urinary opening); and 1 case required a recircumcision. In other words, Dr. Patel found serious problems in 24 of the 100 cases.

The need for aftercare is obvious; this has been noted repeatedly in the literature. Dr. E. N. Preston (1970) also differentiated between immediate complications—hemorrhage, infection, and surgical trauma—and delayed complications several days later as a result of the wound coming into contact with feces and urine.[35]

This was also emphasized by A. G. M. Campbell et al. (1971), who called for special care of the glans and meatus for 10 days after the operation, since these parts are no longer protected by the foreskin. Moreover, they noted that pediatric urologists feel that the frequency of postcircumcision complications could be considerably reduced if proper aftercare information were given to parents.[36] Yet, in 1976, Drs. Levitt et al. wrote: "Little if any follow-up care is directed to this minor surgical procedure."[37]

Another physician noted that some injuries do not show up until 4 or 5 months after surgery.[38] In 1978 Dr. D. Grimes wrote that postcircumcision complications occur more frequently than are reported, and commented, "the incidence is unknown."[39]

It is indeed startling that the problem of delayed complications is recognized but not studied. As noted, only one study was conducted in Canada, not the United States, and that study was completed more than a decade ago.

Surgical injury is further complicated by two additional problems: cosmetic effect and improper patient selection. What constitutes adequate circumcision? This question was posed by Dr. D. Grimes in 1978. He commented that if you examine the amount of foreskin removed, there does not appear to be any consensus among physicians.[40] In other words, one physician or parent may judge that insufficient foreskin was removed during the circumcision and order a recircumcision, or the first operation may be judged unsightly and surgery reordered. Such situations are not rare, nor should they be surprising in view of the inexperience and the ineptitude of many people who perform the surgery. A recircumcision to remove additional foreskin is less complicated than the reverse—the use of plastic surgery to correct the removal of too much foreskin.

Rules for infant selection or rejection for surgery should be relatively simple to promulgate and to observe. The rules exist, but apparently they are not always followed. There is unanimity among physicians that two groups of newborns should *not* be circumcised: those who are not well and those with structural penile defects. Among the former are premature or low birth-weight infants or those with infections or respiratory problems. Chief among the latter are infants with hypospadias, in whom the meatus is positioned on the underside of the penis, instead of its usual position at the tip of the glans; they will require plastic surgery to repair the problem. In such cases the foreskin may be used as a skin graft. Yet recent reports in the medical literature indicate that both premature and hypospadic infants continue to be circumcised routinely.

Drs. Kirkpatric and Eitzman (1974) discussed the problems encountered when two premature infants were circumcised. Heroic measures, including spinal taps and blood transfusions, were necessary. They commented: "Both of these small immature infants had life-threatening infections from which they almost died . . . early circumcision . . . is contraindicated in a baby who is ill or otherwise at risk."[41]

It should not be necessary for physicians writing in a medical journal in 1974 to reiterate that an ill child or one who is at risk should not be circumcised. Even more important is the use of the words "life-threatening" and "they almost died." These physicians were successful in saving the lives of the two infants. Had they not been successful, the infants would have died.

Circumcisions of hypospadic infants were noted in 1976 by Drs. Gee and Ansell, who studied 5,521 circumcisions. There were 22 newborns with hypospadias. Of these 22 cases: 13 were recognized and not circumcised; 6 were *not* recognized and were circumcised; 2 were recognized but circumcised anyway; 1 was not recognized until after the first circumcision incision was made, after which the tissues were sewn together.[42] In other words, of 22 hypospadic newborns, 9 (41%) underwent the surgery. This is not a proud example of patient selection for a teaching hospital.

When a circumcision injury results in mutilation, it often receives publicity due to a large malpractice suit award. Within the past few years the *New York Times* has reported on damages awarded for infant circumcision injuries:

May, 1974 (Baltimore, Md.) $733,000 Damage Awarded Boy in Faulty Circumcision.

Nov. 2, 1975 (Seattle, Wash.) Family Awarded $850,000 for Circumcision Accident.[43]

Within the past decade there have also been several cases recorded of an infant's penis being severely burned by electrocautery. In one case the entire penis sloughed off and the child was raised as a girl.[44] These are clearly the extreme cases; they simply demonstrate that very serious injuries do occur, which can involve total penile loss or lifelong loss of penile function. It is not possible, based upon the few press reports, to know the extent of such incidents. There are no national malpractice records involving infant circumcision;[45] however, it should be obvious that these isolated malpractice awards do not tell the whole story.

Moreover, circumcision problems may appear much later in life. Masters and Johnson noted a case of painful glans sensitivity to vaginal acidity and concluded: " . . . There is room for presumption that if he had not been circumcised routinely, he might not have been so handicapped."[46]

The problem as noted by Dr. A. G. M. Campbell et al., is that it is not possible to estimate the true frequency of "undesirable results," since there have been no long-range studies.[47] If the true incidence of undesirable results is unknown, what information should physicians impart to parents who may raise questions about circumcision risks? Campbell et al. addressed this problem. They suggested: "While it is not necessary to scare parents by telling them about every obscure risk, you should outline the general risks."[48] But what are the "general risks"? Many types of problems are well known, yet their frequency remains a mystery. Physicians would like to tell patients about risks in numerical terms—a probability of 1 in 100 or 1 in a million—but there are no sound data upon which to base such numbers.

Two physicians, Drs. Gee and Ansell (1976), attempted to generalize from the experience of 5,521 circumcisions in one hospital. After discounting many mishaps as minor, they concluded:

Only 14 complications [0.2% or 1/500] are considered really significant. . . .

Before undertaking that ritual in the neonate, the physician should be aware that significant complications may occur as a result of circumcision in one of 500 newborns so treated.[49]

This is the only risk rate based upon a large sample that carefully delineated the specific types of risks. It is not projectible nationally because it was conducted in only one city. On the other hand, this risk rate of 0.2% should not be ignored. it is higher than Rosner's (0.16%) and lower than Paige's (1.0%), noted earlier in this chapter. If the figure of 1:500 proves to be reasonably accurate, this would mean that there would be about 2,500 cases of *significant* complications estimated from the 1 ¼ million newborn circumcisions performed annually. If the true figure is really half that rate or 1:1,000, then there would be 1,250 significant complications annually. On the other hand, if the true figure is closer to the one suggested by Dr. Paige, then there would be 12,500 significant complications. Whether the precise figure is 1,250, 2,500, or 12,500, the essential question is whether the alleged benefits of routine circumcision outweigh the risks. There is no evidence that they do.

That it is necessary to speculate wildly about the frequency of significant complications is nothing less than scandalous. Risk estimates range from 0 to 1 in 100; deaths from 0 to more than 225 annually. A nationwide study of this question is obviously in order. If the risk is very low, this should be proved. If the risk is high, it should be exposed. That such a study has not been conducted suggests that the issue may be too hot to handle.

16

Jews and Circumcision

No group has been as intimately associated with circumcision as have the Jewish people. Many people—Jews and non-Jews—have assumed that Jewish ritual circumcision is as much a health measure as it is a religious rite. Therefore, since the Jews have the longest continuous history of circumcision, including an oral and written tradition, the Jewish experience should provide time-tested evidence of the alleged health benefits of the practice.

It should be emphasized that the intent of this chapter is *not* to debate any religious aspects of circumcision, but solely to examine the health aspects that have been attributed to Jewish ritual circumcision and their influence upon current acceptance of the practice. Was circumcision introduced as a health measure? Was the methodology, perfected over millennia, the optimum in health procedures? What health benefits can be demonstrated?

In antiquity there were several references to the health aspects of the Jewish ritual. Philo of Alexandria (1st century A.D.) maintained that it prevented disease and promoted fertility.[1] Herodotus (circa 484–425 B.C.) spoke of circumcision for reasons of cleanliness.[2] However, such statements should be accepted cautiously, since they represent opinions, not necessarily facts. For example, Strabo, the 1st century B.C. Greek geographer, stated on two different occasions that Jews circumcised girls as well as boys.[3] Strabo may have gotten this idea from the Ethiopian Fellashas—the so-called black Jews—who did and still do circumcise girls.[4] Most of Strabo's writings no longer exist, and even some of his "facts" about geography are known to be in error.[5] Sir Richard Burton claimed that Jews circumcised females up to the year 1000 A.D., and Elizabeth Gould Davis in 1972 wrote that the practice continued to recent times.[6] There is no substance for these claims, yet they are made with impunity.

For a true understanding of Jewish circumcision, it is necessary to go to the original source, the Old Testament. Based upon a biblical injunction, Jews have practiced the rite of circumcision for about 4,000 years.[7] God ordained this practice to Abraham, specifying that it be performed on the eighth day after birth, with a flint knife.[8]

Although both the Old and New Testaments make numerous references to circumcision, none relates to health. The subject is made even more confusing, inasmuch as the Old Testament mentions circumcision in relation to:

Agriculture: The fruit of a tree should not be eaten for three years. "Ye shall count the fruit thereof as uncircumcised."[9]

Bride purchase: David slew 200 Philistine men and brought their foreskins to Saul to obtain Saul's daughter Michal for his wife.[10]

Vengeance: Dinah was seduced by Shechem, a Hivite, and her enraged brothers sought revenge. Under the pretext of allowing Shechem to marry Dinah, provided all the Hivites agreed to circumcision, the operations were performed. While the men recuperated, Dinah's brothers slew every male Hivite.[11]

Obviously these stories have nothing to do with the original convenant between God and Abraham concerning circumcision, and they certainly have nothing to do with health or hygiene. Since the Bible itself presents such divergent views, it is no wonder that theologians, historians, anthropologists, ethnologists, psychiatrists, etc., can write about every conceivable aspect of the subject without feeling the need to provide proof. Professor Erich Isaac wrote (1967) that if all the circumcision theories were listed, understanding of circumcision would not be enhanced, but the reader could ". . . marvel at the imagination of modern social scientists."[12]

Most Jewish writers abjured the health aspects of circumcision, primarily emphasizing its religious character. For example, Moses Maimonides (1135-1204), the celebrated physician, rabbi, philosopher, and scholar, wrote: "No one, however, should circumcise himself or his son for any other reason but pure faith." Maimonides added that the purpose of circumcision was to make Jews more sexually moderate. He went so far as to claim that if a Jewish woman had intercourse with an uncircumcised man, she would not want to leave him.[13] Health benefits are not mentioned at all by this famous Jewish physician.

The key fact expressed in Maimonides' writings is that circumcision is a pure and simple act of faith. Even before Maimonides, this tenet had become so deeply ingrained in religious Jews that when men did not perform the ritual, women accepted responsibility for the task. When Moses neglected to circumcise his son, his wife Zipporah (a non-Jewish Ethiopian) performed the operation herself.[14] Women also performed circumcisions in periods of repression. In 167 B.C., Antiochus ordered the death penalty for anyone performing a circumcision. Yet all through the Maccabean era (circa 200–150 B.C.), Jewish mothers circumcised their sons.[15]

History is replete with stories of secret circumcisions, e.g., men not circumcised in infancy who circumcised themselves or had others perform the operation.[16] These acts were motivated solely by deep religious convictions.

The intensity of this feeling was noted by Dr. Charles Weiss (1962), who commented: "Indeed, so great is the emotional attachment of our people to this rite that it sometimes borders on fanaticism." Weiss gave two examples of such fanaticism—one from the past and one from the present: (1) During the Maccabean period, Jewish mothers opted for the murder of their sons and themselves rather than have them go uncircumcised; (2) In 1958, a Philadelphia mother threatened to commit suicide upon learning that her son had been circumcised by an intern instead of ritually.[17]

There are four aspects of the Jewish practice that clearly attest circumcision's nonmedical status.

1. If a child dies before it is 8 days old, the corpse must be circumcised before it can be interred in a Jewish cemetery.[18] The ritual takes place at the cemetery, just prior to burial.[19]
2. If a child is born without a foreskin, or if no blood is shed during circumcision—both exceedingly rare occurrences—a drop of blood must be drawn from the glans as a symbolic circumcision. (This is known in Hebrew as *hatafath dam berith*.)[20] The nicking of the glans may be done "with a knife, a needle or even the sharpened fingernails."[21]
3. Such a symbolic circumcision is also performed when a convert to Judaism has been previously circumcised.[22] Reform rabbis have tried to abolish this practice.[23]
4. Up to a century or two ago, the linen cloth used in circumcision, presumably stained with blood, was retained and exhibited at the boy's Bar Mitzvah and wedding as proof of his circumcision.[24]

Clearly the intent of this ritual is religious, not medical. This purely religious aspect is also echoed by the present-day Orthodox rabbinate, who openly deny any health reasons for circumcision: " . . . The Orthodox Jewish community . . . is intent on affirming the strictly religious character of circumcision, and thus on eliminating the medical aura surrounding the practice."[25] This is not an isolated comment. Dr. Joseph Miller, a physician, writing in the house organ of the Union of Chassidic Rabbis of the United States and Canada, stated that he refused to accept the role of mohel (ritual circumciser) for Jewish males "in order to uphold [its] purely religious character."[26] He stated: "Many people today believe that . . . circumcision is primarily a health measure. This is not the fact. Circumcision . . . is the symbol of the Covenant between God and the Jewish nation."[27]

This view was similarly echoed by Dr. Charles Merzbach, a French Orthodox Jewish physician.[28] Immanuel Jakobovitz, Chief Rabbi of England, worried about the medical emphasis placed on circumcision, commented that the entire essence of the ritual is that it is religious and not medical.[29]

Despite the clear declarations of Orthodox Jewish writers that circumcision is purely a religious ritual and not a health measure, many present-day physicians not only accept the literal interpretation of the Bible, but also interpose their own health beliefs. In 1970, Dr. S. I. McMillen wrote: "Medical researchers . . . agree that . . . freedom [from diseases] results from . . . circumcision . . . which God ordered Abraham to institute 4,000 years ago."[30]

Another example of this type of augmentation was the statement made by Dr. Abraham Ravich (1967), who claimed that Moses was a well-trained and highly competent sanitarian who witnessed the outbreaks of venereal disease among his people following their participation in sexual orgies.[31]

The status of Jewish circumcision was summarized by Professor Erich Isaac in 1967. He claimed that the ritual has been practiced without a clear explanation of its origins in the past or a religious interpretation of its present significance. Professor Isaac further noted, "In their absence, the commonly accepted 'explanation' has been that circumcision confers great medical benefits."[32]

Professor Isaac explained that Jews have been reassured and comforted by the attribution of health benefits and by non-Jewish acceptance of the rite. In other words, the Jewish practice influenced non-Jewish acceptance of circumcision, which, in turn, served to reinforce the Jewish ritual. Professor Isaac's article challenges the health benefits attributed to circumcision: "Its presumed medical and physiological advantages are said to be at best unproven and at worst illusory, and the manner of its performance is said to be frequently incompetent or cruel."[33]

In his reference to incompetence or cruelty, Professor Isaac is referring to ritual circumcision, usually performed in the home, not to hospital circumcisions performed by physicians. How accurate is Professor Isaac in claiming that Jewish ritual circumcision is "frequently incompetent or cruel?" To answer that question, it is necessary to examine the historical development of the surgery itself.

Remondino made a broad categorical statement concerning Jewish methodology: "[Jews] never made any alteration or improvement in the manner of performing the operation."[34] This statement is so totally inaccurate that it is obvious he never attempted even a cursory examination of Jewish circumcision literature.

The Jewish ritual underwent several changes over the centuries. Originally the operation consisted of one and only one element, cutting off the tip of the prepuce. This was called *Milah* and was in use for almost 2,000 years. It was changed during the Hellenic period (circa 300 B.C.–1 A.D.). At that time the Greeks engaged in a concerted effort to convert Jews to paganism. One aspect of this conversion was to obliterate evidence of the simple Milah circumcision by blistering the tip of the remainder of the foreskin in order to enlarge it.[35] So many young Jews adopted this practice that the rabbinate of the period decided to alter the surgery in order to make it impossible for a circumcised male to be made to appear uncircumcised. This was accomplished by a procedure known as *Periah*. The entire foreskin was ablated and the inner lining and frenum torn by the specially sharpened fingernails of the ritual surgeon (mohel)[36]—hardly a sanitary procedure!

The next change, although not universally adopted, occurred during the Talmudic period (circa 500–625 A.D.), when an additional element was added. This was *Messisa* (also spelled *Mezziza* or *Metzitzah*, its phonetic pronunciation) and consisted of moistening the lips with wine and then taking the bleeding penis into the mouth to suck the blood.[37] This was done several times, and a special receptacle was provided to receive the blood that was spit out.[38] Again, hardly a sanitary procedure!

These three parts of the ritual—Milah, Periah, and Messisa—continued in general use until about 100 years ago and are performed to this day in some parts of the world.[39] Not unexpectedly, they have been and are a source of many problems. For example, in 1950, Dr. Eugene A. Hand, an ardent supporter of circumcision, reported 41 cases of Jewish infants contracting tuberculosis from mohels.[40]

For the bulk of Jewish communities, the above surgical procedures were radically changed in the last quarter of the 19th century by the advent of advances in aseptic surgery. Although the total foreskin was still removed, the use of fingernails was often replaced by a knife or scissors. Because the Bible is so explicit as to the use of a knife, Orthodox Jews will not use scissors. Fingernails, as a cutting instrument for the inner foreskin lining and frenum, are still in use. In *The Surgery Of Ritual Circumcision* (1961), Leonard V. Snowman specifically described the use of the fingernails for this purpose.[41] Sucking blood directly from the penis was supposedly discontinued, or at least replaced with a glass tube, to avoid direct mouth-penis contact.[42] As will be noted, this practice, in one form or other, is still followed—albeit very rarely.

The difference in the approach taken by mohels in New York City and London is interesting to note. The 1916 pamphlet by the New York City Milah Board, the group that supervises ritual circumcision, stated in bold type: "Sucking the wound with the mouth is absolutely prohibited and any mohel found resorting to this practice will be barred from the certificated list."[43] No mention was made of a glass tube. The 1961 publication of the Initiation Society of London recommended the use of a glass tube rather than the mouth to suck the blood and warned that: "One who does not perform Metzitzah must be debarred from acting as a mohel."[44] Although mouth-penis contact, whether directly or via a glass tube, has virtually been abandoned, some ultra-Orthodox groups still follow the practice in several parts of the world—even in New York City.

Interestingly, current prayer books used in the ceremony still speak of observing "all the precepts" without specifically delineating them, knowing that all are not carried out literally.

At the time these major alterations were made in the rite (1875-1900), Reform Jews in both the United States and Germany attempted to abolish ritual circumcision altogether. However, the effort largely failed, although Reform Judaism succeeded in at least eliminating the requirement of adult circumcision upon conversion.[45]

With the increase of hospital childbirth in the first decades of the 20th century, many Reform Jews employed physicians rather than mohels to perform the surgery and the ritual came to be considered more of a health rather than a religious procedure. Over the years, even Conservative Jews began to follow this practice. However, Orthodox Jews have never allowed physicians to replace mohels. As noted before, it was this trend that the Orthodox rabbinate railed against.

Although still retaining its religious significance, circumcision is practiced by many Jews today largely for health reasons. However, some nonobservant Jews (and some non-Jews) still occasionally call upon mohels to perform the surgery.

The rationale for the selection of mohels rather than physicians is understandable. Physicians, in their training and practice, may have performed hundreds of circumcisions; this surgery occupies a minor proportion of their time. Mohels, on the other hand, for whom this one procedure is often a full-time and lifetime vocation, may have performed thousands of these operations. Mohels, therefore, are often looked upon as more experienced and skilled in circumcision than physicians. Thus it is important to briefly explore the health aspects of the ritual operation.

Although it is only conjecture, the hot climate of the Biblical areas and the concomitant lack of sanitary facilities might well have given rise to foreskin problems, such as infections, tightness, as well as a vast array of other pathological conditions. Such foreskin problems would be alleviated by simple circumcision. It might also be conjectured that the removal of the entire foreskin, as is usually done in medical circumcision, was found to be a better health procedure. Of course, Orthodox Jews would protest such thinking as sacrilege.

It is important to remember the type of surgical instrument—fingernails—used in this procedure. Some may argue that surgical instruments had not been devised 2,000 years ago. However, the fact is that more than 5,000 years ago in Egypt, China, India, Assyria, and later in Greece and Rome, more advanced surgical techniques and instrumentation were in use.[46] Therefore, it is difficult to argue that the use of sharpened fingernails was either advanced scientific or sanitary methodology.

And what of the practice of sucking the bleeding penis? While condemning the procedure, some physicians contend that it was used to stop bleeding.[47] Not only is there little evidence for this theory, but it was also a largely ineffective method. Furthermore, even in antiquity, surgeons had better methods to stop bleeding, such as pressure, instruments, and medication.[48] According to Dr. H. Speert (1953), Maimonides "staunchly supported this procedure [sucking the bleeding penis] as a prophylactic measure against inflammation."[49]

It is not necessary to belabor the obviously unsanitary procedures employed by mohels until 100 years ago. Serious injuries, disease, and death were associated with these practices and, therefore, centuries ago Jewish theologians ruled that if a son died from the operation or if there was severe bleeding, future sons could be exempted from the surgery.[50]

The United States has had many more problems with ritual circumcision than Europe, since the training and practice of European operators were well established in cities and towns for centuries. But in the 19th century, Jewish immigration and dispersion to distant cities and towns left immigrants to the U.S. isolated in their new communities, without the services of skilled mohels. Not having resident mohels available, Jews employed itinerant mohels who traveled about from town to town to perform the ritual. In some towns, groups of Jewish boys ranging in age from several months to 12 years were transported to the nearest mohel for group circumcisions.[51] Jewish newspapers often carried advertisements for mohels to practice in distant communities. A few unscrupulous unemployed Jews, without any circumcision experience whatsoever, responded to such advertisements. The results were horrendous. In 1871, Dr. Charles P. Russel wrote:

> Within about a month, some half dozen deaths have occurred in this city from hemorrhage after circumcision of Hebrew infants. . . . Numerous unskilled and unscrupulous persons have taken to performing this operation among poor Jews. . . .[52]

These horror stories are a century old and, by and large, refer to self-appointed, inexperienced mohels. However, ritual circumcision problems were not limited to unscrupulous rogues but also occurred with experienced mohels.

Although Dr. Russel described the serious situation as early as 1871, it was not until 1914—43 years later—that Jewish religious authorities established the country's first Milah Board in New York City to supervise circumcision in that city. In collaboration with the New York City Department of Health, the Board issued a pamphlet in 1916 describing the sanitary precautions to be taken to avoid infection.[53] No training school was established, and no system of licensing, inspection, or control was instituted.[54] The establishment of the Milah Board was of little consequence, since its authority was not recognized by many rabbis and many, if not most, practicing mohels refused to submit to examinations. Three years after the Milah Board was established (1917), Rabbi Moses Hyamson, Chairman of the New York City Board, wrote:

> Medical men—Jewish and Gentile—have reported cases . . . where male Jewish children have had to be treated for injuries . . . which were the direct result of circumcision, incompetently performed by unskilled or inexperienced mohalim [mohels].[55]

Some physicians thought that the establishment of the Milah Board remedied the situation. In 1953, Dr. H. Speert wrote: "Since 1914 certification by the Milah Board has been required of all mohels in New York City." Yet in the next two paragraphs, Dr. Speert described the circumstances surrounding the death of an infant in 1946 as a result of the work of a "noncertified mohel."[56]

Although the New York City Milah Board was, and still is, weak and ineffective, it was the first such board established in the United States. The second one was not established until 1954—40 years later—in Philadelphia. As late as 1962, no similar boards existed in Los Angeles, Chicago, Boston, Baltimore, or Cleveland. A Reform rabbi from Hollywood, California, commenting on ritual circumcision, stated in 1958: "There is absolute 'hefker' [lawlessness] in our community without any kind of supervision or organization, either religious or on the part of the State."[57]

A Boston physician, Dr. William Glaser, the son of a mohel, performs ritual circumcisions. He wrote: "I have observed in the past 35 years [that] this group [mohels] are not properly qualified in the surgical judgment and associated techniques involved in this procedure [circumcision]."[58]

A New York City pediatrician, Dr. H. Apfel, raised still another question. He noted that he had observed many problems with ritual circumcision, which, though not fatal, caused suffering to the infants and mental anguish to the parents. Physicians were often called upon to control bleeding in the hospital; however, these efforts were rarely brought to the attention of the parents. When the medical staff was critical of the work of mohels, there were, Dr. Apfel noted, " . . . uncomplimentary reactions from certain religious groups. The parents of the little patients invariably throw their sympathy in favor of the religious side."[59]

Thus, so strong is the religious conviction of some Jews that they refuse to intervene on behalf of their own infants who are injured by ritual circumcision. Moreover, the damage inflicted is often repaired by the hospital staff without disclosure to parents. Such disclosure would, of course, make a prima facie case for a medical malpractice suit against the mohel, attending physician, and the hospital. These are events that have occurred not 100 years ago, but within the past quarter-century. In fact, it was the deaths of 2 infants via ritual circumcision in 1957 that prompted Jewish leaders to conduct a worldwide survey of current Milah practices (ritual circumcision). The final report of this exhaustive study was made by Charles Weiss, M.D., Ph.D., of Philadelphia in 1962.[60]

The research revealed a wide spectrum of practices both within the United States and in many other countries—from skilled operators and aseptic conditions to unskilled mohels using crude, outmoded, and unsanitary procedures. The results ranged from good to horrendous, including mutilation, disease, and death. The researchers recommended proper training and supervision of mohels and worldwide acceptance of aseptic conditions. Lacking nationwide or even citywide authority to enforce their recommendations, it is not possible to know whether the study had any effect in improving the poor conditions described.

As recently as 1972, *Newsweek* carried a report entitled "Rating the Circumcisers," which described a Duluth, Minnesota, infant whose glans had been injured by a man claiming to be a mohel, who later admitted to never having performed a circumcision.[61] The child later required plastic surgery to correct the damage. Problems with ritual circumcision are rarely reported unless they require hospitalization or result in litigation or death. One such death as a sequela of ritual circumcision was reported by two physicians in 1978.[62]

The situation in the United States should be contrasted with that in Britain. A Jewish Circumcision Society was established in England in 1745. It licensed mohels, set up a training school at the Bearstead Memorial Hospital, and is still functioning.[63] Although the British situation is far from perfect, e.g., there is no supervision after licensing, it is vastly superior to the situation in the United States.

In spite of the obvious need, no training school for mohels was established in the United States until 1968.[64] At that time it was estimated that there were 100 practicing mohels in the Greater New York City area. Today most mohels practice in private homes or small hospitals. In 1960, it was estimated that 70% of all ritual circumcisions in the Greater New York City area were performed in private homes.[65] Such home circumcisions, usually performed on the eighth day—after the child has been released from the hospital—mean that no records are kept and control of the mohels' activities is almost nil.

A brief examination of the circumcision practices in Israel is warranted, since it is the only modern Jewish state and circumcision is almost universally practiced there. Among nonreligious Jews, the surgery is often performed by physicians. However, among the more religious Jews, mohels are employed.

Mohels are licensed and lists of approved operators are published by the government—excellent as far as it goes, but such regulations apply mainly in large cities. In small towns inhabited by poor immigrants from Yemen, Algeria, Iraq, etc., older mohels are employed who have no knowledge of modern surgical techniques.[66] The penis-mouth procedure is still employed in such communities, and fatal cases of induced tuberculosis, gas gangrene, tetanus, etc., have been reported. In one case, amputation of the penis was necessary in order to save the child's life.[67]

In 1974, *Pediatrics* carried a report by 4 Israeli physicians describing 3 cases in which mohels had applied bandages too tightly, thus preventing urination. In each case, the parents, alerted by the child's distress, had the error corrected by a private physician before serious harm occurred. The Israeli physicians commented that it was surprising that more of such complications did not occur, since a great many circumcisions are performed in Israel by people who are not medically qualified.[68] A year later, an American physician who had practiced in Israel reported on 2 similar cases.[69]

Such deficiencies in ritual operations in Israel led to a newspaper campaign to regulate mohels nationally. It was pointed out that of the hundreds of practicing mohels, only 130 were government-licensed. The Ministry of Health drafted such a law, but the opposition among Orthodox circles was so great that the measure never reached the Knesset (Parliament).[70] Thus, to this day, ritual circumcision is not regulated on a national scale in Israel.

In summary, there are no substantive data in Jewish circumcision history or practice to support the thesis that circumcision is a health measure or that health benefits are in any way derived from it. Historically, the methods employed in performing the surgery were anything but sanitary or scientific. To this day, little or no control is exercised over its practitioners, who can and do cause harm, even death.

Religious Jews vehemently deny *any* health benefits and insist that circumcision is purely a religious rite. Nonreligious Jews who accept circumcision for its health benefits derive support for that theory from the wide acceptance of routine circumcision by non-Jews. Thus, a brief overview of Jewish circumcision sheds no light as to its health origins and no proof of its purported hygienic benefits in its past or current practice.

17
Female Circumcision

Female circumcision is currently practiced in the United States. The very concept of female circumcision is startling; but that it is encouraged in the United States today is even more startling. The World Health Organization reported (1976) that the United States was the only medically advanced country to practice this surgery.[1] Of course, the frequency of female circumcision is not the same as that of male circumcision, nor is it suggested that it be done routinely. However it is being performed in sufficient and possibly growing numbers in the U.S. to warrant attention. *Cosmopolitan*, with a readership of 7½ million, published an article by two physicians in November 1976, suggesting female circumcision as one of the options open to women to enhance their sexual enjoyment.[2]

The term "female circumcision" is confusing, because it is often applied to a wide variety of female genital surgeries. Originally, anthropologists categorized a number of different clitoral operations performed in primitive societies under the umbrella term "female circumcision." It is important, therefore, to define the term accurately. The prime concern of this chapter is female circumcision as presently practiced in the United States; however, it is important to understand clitoral surgery in general, because many different types of operations were and are performed in the United States and in underdeveloped countries. As will be noted, present-day female circumcision in the United States evolved from British clitoridectomy which, in turn, was derived from underdeveloped societies. American clitoridectomy, even today, seeks sanction in primitive African practice.

Definitions

As defined medically and currently practiced in the United States, female circumcision is similar to its male counterpart. It involves cutting off all or part of the clitoral foreskin, also called the prepuce or hood. This surgery is employed by very few Third World societies and is correctly called female circumcision. It is the least drastic clitoral operation.

Far more often in the Third World, when the clitoral foreskin is removed, part or all of the clitoris is also cut off. This is called clitoridectomy or excision.[3] In many Third World societies, clitoridectomy is further extended to include the cutting away of part or all of the small or large labia. The most drastic operation includes all of the above plus sewing up the genital area (infibulation). This is known as Pharaonic circumcision.[4] The extent of the surgery involved varies from country to country and from one ethnic group to another within a given country.[5]

The following list gives the medical term for each surgical procedure:

- Cutting of all or part of the clitoral foreskin—circumcision;
- Cutting off part of the clitoris—clitoridotomy;
- Cutting off all of the clitoris—clitoridectomy;
- Cutting off part of the labia—partial vulvectomy;
- Cutting off the entire labia—complete vulvectomy.

In discussing American female circumcision, the procedure that the term encompasses should be clearly understood. The tissues involved and the methods employed are described in Appendix A. A clear distinction must be made between the very different categories of clitoral surgery under discussion. In one case—true female circumcision, currently practiced in the United States—only the clitoral foreskin is removed. The operation is elective and its objective is enhancement of a woman's sexual pleasure. The other category includes the various surgeries that are currently practiced in underdeveloped countries and are obligatory religious or puberty rituals. Their net effect is the reduction or suppression of sexual pleasure.

Clitoridectomy and removal of the labia are employed in the United States, but only in extreme cases of disease or severe enlargement (hypertrophy). Ablation of the clitoral foreskin is also performed for medical reasons, e.g., removal of benign or malignant growths or to correct genetic defects. The number of such medical operations is very small and this aspect is not within the purview of this chapter. Our concern is with circumcision for sexual enhancement.

Third World Clitoral Surgery

As in the case of male circumcision, no one knows where, when, how, or why the various female surgeries began. They were known in antiquity and, according to some researchers and folklore, may even predate male circumcision.

Speculation as to the origin of and reasons for primitive genital surgery is rather fruitless. Clitoral surgery has been employed for hundreds, if not thousands, of years. It has been estimated that at the present time there are 20 to 25 million women who have undergone clitoridectomy in Africa alone,[6] and in dozens of other places throughout the world.[7] According to Fran P. Hosken, more girls undergo clitoral surgery today than throughout history.[8] Ms. Hosken is waging a one-woman crusade against female genital mutilation. She publishes *The Women's International Network (WIN) News* to disseminate worldwide information on women's health problems, with special emphasis on clitoridectomy.[9]

Proponents of clitoridectomy present the surgery in a positive light. Jomo Kenyatta, the western-trained leader of Kenya, not only encouraged the surgery but wrote of it in such glowing terms that John Gunther said that Kenyatta made "it sound like a picnic at Vassar."[10] Kenyatta, in his thesis at the London School of Economics under Bronislav Malinowski, described the operation (1962):

> [The person performing the surgery] . . . takes out . . . the operating. . . razor, and in quick movements, with the dexterity of a Harley Street surgeon, proceeds . . . with a stroke . . . cuts off the tip of the clitoris.[11]

Other writers on Africa, such as Colin Turnbull, take an idealized view of African culture and see it as superior to that of the West's. In his recent book, *Man In Africa*, Turnbull described both male and female circumcision and characterized them as displays of courage with no word of criticism.[12] However, in 1972 a French physician provided a very different picture of Pharaonic circumcision as currently practiced in Somalia. (It takes a strong stomach even to read the description.)

> After separating [the] outer and inner lips (labia majora and labia minora) with her fingers, the old woman attaches them with large thorns onto the flesh of each thigh. With her kitchen knife the woman then pierces and slices open the hood of the clitoris and then begins to cut it out. While another woman wipes off the blood with a rag, the woman (or operator) digs with her fingernail a hole the length of the clitoris to detach and pull out that organ. The little girl screams in extreme pain, but no one pays the slightest attention.
>
> The woman finishes the job by entirely pulling out the clitoris and then cuts it to the bone with the kitchen knife. Her helpers again wipe off the spurting blood with a rag. The woman then lifts up the skin that is left with her thumb and index finger to remove the remaining flesh. She then digs a deep hole amidst the gushing blood. The neighbor women who take part in the operation then plunge their fingers into the bloody hole to verify that every remnant of the clitoris is removed.[13]

Thousands of women have died or sustained serious injuries or infections as a result of such surgery.[14] Some Protestant missionaries tried to convince tribal leaders to abandon clitoridectomy, but to no avail.[15] Presbyterian missionaries from Scotland were singularly unsuccessful in Kenya. The rejection of the Presbyterian appeal was as much political as medical. The Presbyterians were viewed by Kenyans as the representatives of British imperialism who were denying Kenya freedom and independence; many of the country's leaders, including Jomo Kenyatta, were jailed by the British. Support of the custom of clitoridectomy was therefore considered an anti-British stance and a matter of national pride.

The attitude of Catholics to clitoridectomy is worthy of special note. Jesuits in Ethiopia banned the ritual in the 16th century because they thought it was a Jewish rite. They later allowed the surgery, but only after the people swore they were not Jews.[16] In the 17th century, the matter was brought before the Pope, who sanctioned the surgery as necessary because women who retained their clitorises could not find husbands and therefore could not have children.[17] Ms. Hosken estimated in 1979 that in Kenya today two-thirds of the Catholic girls have undergone clitoridectomy.[18] Some medical missionaries clitoridectomize tribal women in hospitals under aseptic conditions, using anesthesia.[19]

Proponents of clitoridectomy established a "medical" rationale. A non-excised woman is considered unclean; the clitoris is said to interfere with menstruation, childbirth, and impregnation,[20] and is considered the cause of impotence in males.[21] In sum, the clitoris is dirty, dangerous, and disgusting.[22] By far, the most important "medical" reason for clitoridectomy is the claim that the clitorises of Third World women, if not cut off, will grow to monumental proportions. One early traveler in Ethiopia described the clitoris in its natural state as being as "long as a goose's neck."[23] Few carried the exaggeration to that extreme.

What man, in his right mind, would want to marry a dirty, ugly woman who was sterile and who would make him impotent? Jomo Kenyatta wrote that: "No Kikuyu would think of marrying an uncircumcised girl."[24] But Kenyatta and others added another aspect: clitoridectomy was said to subdue sexual urges and make the woman more faithful.[25] The reduction of female sexuality was, and is, an important element in the acceptance of clitoridectomy in underdeveloped countries.

One African tribal leader provided a fascinating rationale:

> A woman has two different and separate areas where she experiences desire and excitement: the clitoris and the vagina.
>
> God has given woman a clitoris so she can enjoy it before marriage and still remain pure . . . One does not cut off the clitoris in small girls because they use it to mastur-

bate. Only when they are ready to procreate is it removed—and once it is they feel deprived. Their desire then is concentrated in one place only and they promptly get married.[26]

The similarity of this differentiation between the clitoris and vagina is startlingly akin to that of Freud's. Freud maintained that the clitoris was the initial source of sexual pleasure, but as the woman matured emotionally and sexually, the vagina replaced the clitoris as the source of orgasm.[27]

The acceptance of clitoridectomy is not limited to tribal leaders. One African man, responding to an attack on this surgery by African physicians, wrote:

> ... an uncircumcised woman is much more interested in sex, and this would undermine the family. ... It would be too hard on a man to regularly satisfy all his wives ... where circumcision is not practiced debauchery and prostitution are the rule.[28]

Nor is this view held only by African males. Two American writers (1977) reported a more extreme position with regard to clitoral hypertrophy and hypersexuality among African women. They stated that social scientists postulate that primitive man actually killed off those women who had a high sex drive: "For the sexually insatiable woman would neither work the fields nor care for the family, but would prowl around in endless quest for men to gratify her."[29] No source is given for this statement, nor is any proof offered.

Until recently, no one bothered to verify or challenge these "facts." However, Ms. Hosken reported that thousands of Ethiopian women, examined in family planning clinics, revealed *no* unusual clitoral hypertrophy. Nor have thousands of African women who refused clitoridectomy in recent years exhibited bizarre sexual behavior.[30] The propagation of the hypertrophy and nymphomania myths is racist. The myth still persists that black men have enormous penises, insatiable desires, and unlimited capacity, and the same myth is also applied to black women. Both, of course, are untrue.

There is no doubt that the circumcision and clitoridectomy procedures described above continue to be practiced. The *New York Times* reported in 1974 that Islam also "tolerates female circumcision"[31] and in 1977 that 90% of Somalian teenagers had undergone Pharaonic circumcision including infibulation.[32]

Many Westerners have been shocked by this mutilation of women and have protested against the practice, among them the London *Spectator* (1949), John Gunther (1953) and Shirley Maclaine (1971).[33] The *New York Times* and the *Paris Match* carried articles in 1977 describing the practice and the protest.[34] Yet, according to Fran P. Hosken, no African leader has spoken out against clitoridectomy.[35]

Recently, women in many parts of the world have protested this ritual. In reporting the proceedings of the First International Tribunal on Crimes Against Women, 1976, the *New York Times*, stated that the most impressive testimony was provided by Third World women who reported on the practice of clitoridectomy in many African and Arab countries.[36] What is new about the clitoridectomy protest is that it is coming from many Third World women themselves, who are struggling against these practices in their own countries and in the international arena. The elimination of centuries-old practices, especially those that are degrading to women, is often a difficult and protracted effort. For example, in Moslem countries some women who took off their veils were murdered, often by their husbands. In many African countries, a woman who is not excised (clitoridectomized) is considered illegitimate and cannot inherit money, cattle, or land.[37]

Some customs have been banned. In the Upper Volta, scarification is prohibited.[38] Ethiopia banned cutting off the uvula, the U-shaped tissue in the back of the throat.[39] In some areas, the elaborate excision rituals have been abandoned, but the surgery has been retained.[40]

Some similarities between African clitoridectomy and Jewish circumcision practices are startling. In Ethiopia, the operation on girls is performed on the eighth day.[41] In some areas of Nigeria the clitoris is nicked, not ablated, to draw blood.[42] In several countries the infant is named after the excision ceremony.[43] Whether these similarities are simply coincidences or a reflection of a common origin is unknown.

The World Health Organization (W.H.O.) held a seminar on clitoridectomy and infibulation in Khartoum, Sudan, in February 1979, under the title "Traditional Practices Affecting the Health of Women."[44] Most of the male delegates wanted the traditional practices maintained and argued that the surgery should be done in hospitals. The women delegates were adamant in calling for total discontinuance of the practices. Although the attendance was sparse (10 countries), resolutions were passed calling for the abolition of all female genital mutilation. This does not mean that such surgeries will cease forthwith, but it is at least the first step by the W.H.O. to eliminate the practices.

If the lack of more vigorous African protest against excision is difficult to comprehend, it should be borne in mind that when clitoridectomy was introduced in the United States and practiced on a large scale, there were no significant protests from women or men. It may seem unfair to compare American and Third World clitoridectomy, because there was little or no pain involved in the American surgery. Although pain is a serious factor in the primitive surgery, it was not of any consequence in the United States, since any surgery to the clitoris and/or adjacent tissues was and is performed under anesthesia. The critical factor is that clitoridectomy, whether performed as an initiation rite or as a medical procedure to stop masturbation, etc., is dehumanizing.

Clitoral Surgery in the United States

It is one thing to censure American medical practice a century ago; the fact is that needless clitoridectomies are still performed in the United States—without protest.

For example, occasionally a girl is born with an overly large clitoris that requires surgical repair since it could be a source of both physical and emotional problems later on. In such cases, the standard procedure is to shorten the clitoris, largely by imbedding it in the surrounding tissue, making certain that there will be minimal interference with its sexual function. In 1964, 3 surgeons from the Columbia Presbyterian Medical Center in New York reported that they had successfully treated 15 such cases by this method.[45] However, 2 years later the American medical journal *Surgery* reported on a very different type of treatment for the same problem. Not only was the entire clitoris cut off but the total root and nerve system was extirpated. The authors included a photo of a completely dissected clitoris to illustrate the meticulousness of the surgery.[46] This article did not refer to one isolated case performed in a backwoods hospital, but to 47 cases reported on by the Boston Children's Hospital and the *Harvard Medical School*.

What is important about the Harvard report is that the authors did make reference to the previously mentioned surgical alternative—but only referred to one case 10 years earlier, stating that they were awaiting its outcome. They totally ignored the 15 cases reported in 1964. In fact, the moderate surgical approach was scoffed at:

> We have a strong feeling that these half-way measures are much less satisfactory than complete clitorectomy.[47]

> . . . a clitoris is not necessary for normal sexual function.[48]

The alleged proof for this statement came from studies of clitoridectomized African women. The authors noted: " . . . normal sexual function is observed in these females."[49] In other words, African clitoridectomy provided the sanction for the American operation.

It is true that a woman without a clitoris can have coitus and even orgasm. But to call that "normal sexual function" is quite another matter. "Normal" sexual functioning as a result of clitoridectomy was discussed by Egyptian psychiatrist Dr. Laila Takla, who has been criticized and ostracized because of her campaign against routine clitoridectomy in her country. In describing her own sexual problems as a result of clitoridectomy at age 7, she stated (1978): "I never had an orgasm with my first two husbands. . . . [my present husband] is the only liberated man I know . . . it takes practice, after a clitoridectomy, to have one [an orgasm], but now I can."[50] Normality, indeed!

Origins of Clitoridectomy to Treat Masturbation

Clitoridectomy as a medical modality in the treatment of hypertrophy has been used in Europe for almost 2,000 years.[51] The practice admittedly came from Egypt. However, hypertrophy was and is a rare anomaly and the operation, therefore, was performed infrequently.

A hypertrophied clitoris was considered not only unsightly, but also a source of hypersexuality. But hypersexuality in women, while possibly unfeminine, was not considered a disease until the 19th century. Before then, clitoridectomy was reserved for hypertrophy, not hypersexuality. No one, prior to the 19th century, suggested clitoral amputation to treat masturbation. By the 1860s, 3 discrete trends converged leading to the use of clitoridectomy to treat hypersexuality.

1. With the introduction of anesthesia, surgery could be used more easily and was applied in the treatment of many ills.
2. Sexuality came to be considered a major factor in disease etiology. Special emphasis was given to masturbation as a cause of physical and emotional diseases that could result in insanity and even death.
3. Through all of recorded history, people visited, traded, and fought with each other. This was certainly true in the Mediterranean area, which included Egypt, Turkey, and North Africa, whose customs were known in Europe. The 16th, 17th, and 18th centuries were eras of great travel, exploration, and conquest by Europeans. Explorers, travelers, missionaries, soldiers, and others visited hitherto unknown lands, returning with accounts of exotic practices that were widely publicized. Anthropology, based upon these travels, began to emerge as a fledgling science.

Genital surgery was of special interest, particularly clitoridectomy. Arab, Egyptian, and other African women, it was reported, had enormous clitorises. If not lopped off, the organ would grow to grotesque proportions. More important, or perhaps related to size, was the rampant sexual drive attributed to such nonexcised women. Clitoridectomy allegedly suppressed this hypersexuality.

What a coincidence! On the one hand was the fear of female sexuality and on the other hand was the means to suppress it. There was ample "logic" to medical clitoridectomy. If masturbation had such a devastating effect on women, then the major masturbatory organ—the clitoris—should be removed.

Ms. F. P. Hosken denied (1979) the African origin of clitoridectomy. She stated: "Clitoridectomy was introduced quite independently of existing African practices, which were probably entirely unknown to the Western surgeons involved, some of whom prided themselves on having 'invented' this procedure. . . . "[52]

While it is true that some physicians claimed the "invention," that falsehood was the least important of which they were guilty. There are many European references to clitoral surgery in Arabia, Egypt, and Africa in the 19th century and earlier, of which the medical establishment must have been aware. Sir Richard Burton (1821-1890), perhaps the most prolific writer on sexual customs in underdeveloped countries, began to lecture and write in 1842 and published 3 volumes about his travels in 1855-1856, prior to the introduction of clitoridectomy in England as a treatment for masturbation.[53]

The relationship between medical and primitive clitoridectomy was admitted by Remondino (1891): " . . . It is safe to assert that a strict adherence . . . to some of the African customs for females would surely relieve all these cases that might come under the caption of results of reflex neuroses."[54] Actually, detailed descriptions of the African rites were published in the American medical press as late as 1920.[55]

The earliest mention of clitoridectomy in the 19th century was in Berlin in 1822.[56] There are indications that other European surgeons employed clitoridectomy to treat masturbation.[57] Dr. Gustav Braun employed the surgery in Vienna for a brief period in the 1860s. By the 1890s, some French physicians were not only removing the clitoris but amputating the labia minora, as well. But the reaction against this surgery was so strong in France that it was prohibited by law.[58]

The only country in Europe where clitoridectomy took hold on a large scale, but only for a limited period, was England. The one name primarily associated with the English experience was Dr. Isaac Baker Brown (some writers erroneously use the name Brown Baker).

Clitoridectomy in England

Isaac Baker Brown (1812-1873) was considered one of the ablest and most innovative gynecological surgeons in England. He was graduated with honors from the Royal College of Surgeons in 1834 and, upon examination, was admitted as a Fellow of the Royal College of Surgeons in 1848. He was also a Fellow of the Obstetrical Society of London and, at the zenith of his reputation, in 1865, was elected President of the Medical Society of London.[59] In 1854 he published *Surgical Diseases of Women*, which was well received and went through 3 editions. In 1858, he founded a private hospital, the London Surgical Home, with 20 beds; in 1861 the capacity was increased to 34 beds. All types of gynecological surgery were performed and the hospital had 3,417 visits from physicians from all over the world to observe his techniques (several physicians came more than once).

It is not clear precisely when Dr. Brown "invented" clitoridectomy and when he began to practice the surgery. Nor is there any certainty of the numbers of women so treated. In the 9 years of the London Surgical Home's existence, with a bed capacity of from 20 to 34, it is possible that several hundred, or perhaps several thousand, such surgeries were performed. One gynecologist said Dr. Brown "operated in an enormous number of cases. . . . "[60]

What is clear is that Dr. Brown was seeking a surgical solution to the vexing mental disorders of women. According to the doctor, the main culprit was masturbation, which caused 8 problems, starting with hysteria and spinal irritation, culminating in mania and death. The treatment was clitoridectomy.[61]

In March 1866, he published a slim volume entitled *The Curability of Certain Forms of Insanity, Epilepsy, Catalepsy and Hysteria in Females*. From that moment on, the British medical establishment lowered the boom on Brown. The claimed cures were denied; clitoridectomy was called quackery. A demand was made that 20 cases be put to review by other doctors, and that all such surgery cease, pending review. This was serious enough; but Dr. Brown's peers went further:

1. He was accused of giving an interview to the *London Standard*, a popular newspaper.
2. Such popularization violated professional ethics, and excited the attention of women to the "dirty subject" of masturbation.
3. Brown deigned to print the title page of his book in gold leaf.
4. He was charged with operating an unlicensed insane asylum.

After a heated and often intemperate debate, on April 3, 1867, Dr. Brown was expelled as a Fellow of the Obstetrical Society. Three weeks later, April 21, 1867, Dr. Brown resigned as President of the London Medical Society and on August 3, 1867, he resigned from the London Surgical Home.[62] His career in shambles, he became ill shortly thereafter and died in 1873. Thus, one year after the publication of his book on clitoridectomy, Dr. Isaac Baker Brown was disgraced and clitoridectomy fell into disrepute in England.

Clitoridectomy in the United States

Although communication between the United States and England was slow in the 1860s, the American medical establishment was aware of advances in British medicine and surgery. The very year that Dr. Brown came under attack in England—1866—an American medical journal noted:

> One of the aspiring surgeons of the day in England, Dr. Isaac Brown Baker, [sic] practices excision of this organ [clitoris] for the relief of epilepsy, and other nervous affection of women.

[Since these views were publicized, there had] occurred a warm and elaborate discussion of the whole subject in the English journals.[63]

The editor of the journal commented that British medical opinion overwhelmingly opposed the surgery and he added his own words of severe criticism.[64] It would be understandable, despite the caveats, that some American physicians might have been attracted to clitoridectomy in 1866 and 1867, prior to Dr. Brown's downfall. But that was not to be. American physicians not only adopted clitoridectomy for many years, they embellished it. By the early 1870s, two noted American surgeons, J. Marion Sims and Horatio Storer, combined clitoridectomy with oophorectomy (removal of the ovaries).[65] There are no records of the number of such clitoris-ovary operations performed in the 1870s; the figure is likely in the thousands. Although the combined clitoris-ovary removal surgery was largely discontinued by 1880, clitoridectomy continued on a large scale until the 1890s. Its popularity finally ceased about 1910, because it failed to cure the "diseases" of hypersexuality and masturbation.[66] Wayland Young reported (1964) that the 1940 *Roman Catholic Manual for Confessors* recommended cauterization or amputation of the clitoris as a cure for "the vice of lesbianism."[67]

Some 20 years after clitoridectomy was banned in England, a British gynecologist apologized (1888) for its inventor, Dr. Brown, saying that he was "injudicious . . . due to the fact that he was suffering from extensive cerebral softening."[68] In contrast, an 1894 American medical journal paid tribute to Dr. Brown for introducing clitoridectomy and described the operation as performed on a 7-year-old girl because " . . . she masturbated and was nervous and reluctant to answer questions."[69]

The "medical" test for hypersexuality, proof of the need for clitoridectomy, was simple—and obscene. The patient's breasts and/or clitoris were stroked. If orgasm was induced, this was proof positive of hypersexuality, and the need for surgery.[70]

It is important to contrast the use of clitoridectomy in England and the Continent with its use in the United States. In all other countries the use was short-lived; in the United States the surgery was in vogue for almost 50 years. No other country compounded the horror by removing the ovaries. The compelling question is: Why—Why only in the United States?

The complete history of clitoridectomy practice in the United States has yet to be written. It should be noted that by the 1860s gynecology had not evolved as a full medical specialty. (That recognition was not achieved until 1889, when Dr. Howard Kelly established the first Department of Gynecology at the Johns Hopkins Medical School.) Almost every type of female disorder was attributed to sexuality, and the knowledge of female sexuality was crude. Isaac Harvey, in *Eternal Eve*, presented the following quotes from mid-19th century medical texts:

[Uterine cancer occurred more frequently in women] with an erotic temperament . . . [who were] tormented by venereal desires . . . [who engaged in] excess(ive) masturbation . . . [and who] pass their lives in crowded parties.

Immoderate coitus and excessive sexual excitation are not without importance in the aetiology of cancer.

[Leucorrhoea, a whitish vaginal discharge, was caused by] erotic reading . . . and solitary pleasures.

[Ovaritis was thought to be due to the conflict] between the impulse of passion and the dictates of duty [and] intemperate . . . indulgence, [or] involuntary abstinence in a single woman of strong passion.

[Inflammation of the uterus was believed to be caused by] masturbation, excessive coitus . . . abstinence, ice-cream to excess . . . and tight corsets worn while reading French novels.[71]

These notions were accepted by European as well as American physicians; they accounted, at least in part, for the ready acceptance of drastic clitoral surgery; no other cures were suggested or available. Degrading attitudes to women, in general, and immigrants, blacks, and the "lower classes," in particular, plus the desire for surgical experimentation may well have been contributing factors to the medical history of the period.

Female Circumcision to Cure Masturbation

Clitoridectomy was an abysmal and abominable failure. As American physicians slowly realized this truth, it was necessary to find a solution to the ever-present problem of masturbation. Again the "cure" was found in surgery—circumcision—leaving the clitoris intact, but removing the clitoral foreskin. If male circumcision could be used to prevent or cure masturbation, the equivalent female operation should have a similar effect, or so it was thought. Female circumcision came into use in the late 1880s and was widely employed up to 1937.[72]

Actually, clitoridectomy coexisted with circumcision for several decades. For example, in 1894, Dr. A. J. Block employed very different means to treat female masturbation. A 14-year-old girl was circumcised, but a 2½-year-old girl had her clitoris cut off because Dr. Block found that not only had the 2½-year-old masturbated, but the baby's mother and grandmother did also. Ergo, more drastic therapy was called for.[73]

Female circumcision was advocated on the grounds that denying it to females meant denying their equality with males. Some physicians described the scars of female circumcision as "pretty as dimples."[74] Articles in the American medical press, including the *Journal of the American Medical Association*, expressed the view that "many women need circumcision," without providing empirical evidence.[75]

Actually, American medicine went through a circumcision craze from 1890 to the early 1920s. The members of the Orificial Surgical Society (see Chapter 4) were the self-appointed zealots. Their literature suggests an even greater interest in female circumcision than in male circumcision. Certainly they expanded the list of "diseases" to be cured by the operation, e.g., to kleptomania and hiccoughs. Although the Orificialists officially went out of business in 1923, many practitioners continued to function well into the 1930s. Dr. Alan F. Guttmacher noted (1956) that female circumcision was occasionally performed to stop masturbation in the 1930s and even in the 1940s. However, he added: "The pathological behavior for which it was deemed curative . . . [is] now more wisely handled through psychotherapy."[76]

The rationale for male circumcision was that besides eliminating masturbation, it improved hygiene and prevented venereal diseases and cancer. These "health" factors were applied only to males and were completely ignored for females, despite the fact that the rationale is really identical for both sexes.

Male circumcision is suggested for ease of hygiene. Yet, as discussed in prior chapters, the external female genitalia are, if anything, more difficult to keep clean, and are subject to even greater problems than the male's. Smegma, identical to the male's, is secreted under the clitoral foreskin. If proper hygiene is not maintained, the smegma can accumulate, causing irritation, infection, scar tissue, and adhesions.[77] This can result in painful coitus (dyspareunia).[78]

Male circumcision is also recommended to prevent venereal diseases. As in the case of the male organ, primary syphilis can affect the clitoris and adjacent tissues. Presumably, venereal disease germs can hide under the clitoral foreskin as well as they can under the penile foreskin. Similarly, male circumcision is urged to prevent cancer of the penis, yet cancer of the clitoris and labia occur more frequently than does penile cancer.

Clitoral neglect by patient and/or physician can also cause problems in older women, as several authors have noted:

> [Because vaginal and clitoral lubricating secretions diminish with age] . . . The clitoral area of older women is often more sensitive to trauma or irritation. . . . [79]
>
> The clitoris should be carefully inspected since it is a favorite site of [external genital] malignancy in the elderly.[80]

(No one has studied the effect in the postmenopausal period of clitoral circumcision.)

Thus, if the arguments for male circumcision are valid, there is even greater reason to suggest routine infant female circumcision to prevent these physical ailments. However, such reasons have not been propounded.

There would appear to be a double standard—great "benefits" for the male and ignored "benefits" for the female. An example of this double standard is reflected by David Reuben (1974), who is ardently in favor of male circumcision, but has this advice for women: "Considering that cancer of the clitoris isn't much of a problem, and that V.D. of the clitoris is not exactly overwhelming, female circumcision doesn't seem to be an important operation these days...."[81] Dr. Reuben failed to mention that these disease entities had nothing to do with the reason female circumcision was being recommended in 1974, that is, solely to enhance a woman's sexual pleasure. This is the current key issue, which Dr. Reuben, a psychiatrist, did not even consider.

It is worth noting that some women who reject female circumcision accept the claimed benefits of male circumcision. For example, Ms. F. P. Hosken, who is violently opposed to Third World clitoral surgery, accepts male circumcision for fallacious reasons, including general health benefits and orgasmic delay, and because it is not painful since the foreskin has few nerve endings.[82]

Before discussing the current use and objectives of female circumcision, it is important to discuss other operations performed on the female genitalia to suppress or enhance female sexuality.

Other Female Genital Surgery

To prevent masturbation, the labia were infibulated (sewn together). Here, there was sexual equality; the male foreskin was dealt with similarly. The practice was recommended up to 1905.[83] This operation is of particular interest because it has no medical precedent. Infibulation was clearly derived from Africa, although it was never used there to prevent masturbation.

Thus far, the objective of all clitoral surgery was to suppress sexuality. However, after the turn of the century, largely under the influence of Freud, growing attention was paid to women's sexual needs and emotions. Greater importance was given to the clitoris in a positive sense as a source of intense sexual pleasure, although, according to Freud, the clitoris is always subservient to the vagina.

Concerned over the lack of female sexual fulfillment, Dr. Marie Bonaparte, one of Freud's disciples, hypothesized that one of the causes was that the clitoris might be poorly positioned. She believed that if the distance between the clitoris and the meatus (urinary opening) was too great, it would prevent proper stimulation in coitus and thereby preclude orgasm. In fact, Dr. Bonaparte maintained that a physical measurement of such distance would be an indication of a woman's sexual responsiveness; i.e., if the distance was short, the woman would likely be orgasmic, if the distance was long, the woman would likely be nonorgasmic. Dr. Bonaparte first published her observations in 1924.[84] Since Dr. Bonaparte believed that orgasmic problems had a physical basis, she reasoned that they could therefore be corrected surgically. Dr. Bonaparte suggested severing the tissues on each side of the clitoris in order to lower the organ and bring it closer to the meatus, thereby increasing sexual pleasure.

In 1932, Dr. Joseph Halban of Vienna devised such an operation and performed it on five women. The results were less than optimal: in 1 case the results were clearly negative; 2 cases were lost to follow-up, while the remaining 2 cases showed "generally favorable though not decisive results." Based upon this limited sample and far from outstanding results, Dr. Bonaparte continued to support this surgery but cautioned that the " . . . operation should only be tried in . . . selected cases. . . . "[85]

Such surgery could be relegated to insignificant medical history, except for the fact that it is still being recommended and publicized in the lay press. In her book *The Search for the Perfect Orgasm* (1973), Jodi Lawrence noted: "Other magic that a plastic surgeon can perform to add to sexual pleasure . . . [includes] reconstructure of muscles to lower the clitoris. . . . "[86]

In recognition of the popularization of such surgery, articles in the medical press, as recently as 1974, have disclaimed the importance of the relative position of the clitoris.[87] But the surgery marches on! In his book *Sexual Behavior in the 1970's* (1975), Morton Hunt stated: "Certain sex researchers in the 1970's even recommend surgical operations to free or move the clitoris."[88] And the following statement was found in the November 1976 issue of *Cosmopolitan:*

> [The clitoris] factor in female sex response is not so much size as placement. There is great variance in the distance between the clitoris and the top of the vaginal opening; the farther away, the less likely it is to be rubbed by the penis during intercourse.[89]

Although this surgical procedure has been recommended on and off for over 50 years, there is not a shred of evidence to support the claimed benefits. For that matter, there are no records of the number of such operations performed; it is probably a very rare procedure. What is important is that the mythology still persists, and that women are given the impression that quick and simple surgical solutions, for what may be deep-seated emotional problems, are readily available.

The surgery to lower the position of the clitoris is often combined with female circumcision. Drs. Isenberg and Elting claimed: " . . . size has nothing to do with sensitivity—the position and accessibility of the clitoris are prime factors in ease of orgasm."[90] So now it is not only position but accessibility that counts! The theory is that the foreskin hides the clitoris and holds it down, and so circumcision will release the clitoris, which will therefore be more accessible to touch, making the sexual response both more rapid and more rewarding. There is no scientific evidence to support such claims.

The Clitoris and Orgasm

It is well known that a large proportion of women suffer from some form of orgasmic dysfunction—they either have a total inability to achieve orgasm or they do so only rarely. Female circumcision and other such surgeries are being presented as quick surgical solutions to what often are deep-seated emotional problems. They are offered to the public as pathways to an orgasmic Nirvana, but they are not based on fact or even elementary research.

In discussing male circumcision, it was pointed out that there is still much unknown about the penis and the sexual function of the foreskin, and that the physical and sexual effects (if any) of circumcision are uncertain. If this is true for male circumcision, it is much more so for female circumcision. The clitoris and its foreskin are identical to the penis and its foreskin in cell structure, nerve distribution, and blood supply. Clitoral sensitivity is even greater, because approximately the same number of nerves are concentrated in a smaller area. Therefore, how will cutting off the erogenous clitoral foreskin, thereby exposing the clitoris to a toughening process (as was described for male circumcision), affect a woman's orgasm? According to the theory applied to males, orgasm should be retarded. However, the new claimed benefit of female circumcision is that orgasm is hastened and more intense. Both theories cannot be correct since they are contradictory. Both are false.

There is little understanding of the vascular and neurological function of the clitoris. For a variety of reasons, the organ is seldom examined.[91] The primary impediment to such examination is that it might be construed as a sexual advance by the physician, who is usually a male. Examination of the penis is obviously easier and the physician is also usually a male. And yet, as noted, the clitoris and its foreskin are subject to the same pathologic conditions as their male counterparts.

The encouragement of female circumcision is based upon the wrong approach to the right problem. Sexual dysfunction has been discussed in medical literature for centuries—but the emphasis was almost always on male dysfunction. There were two reasons for this.

1. A malfunctioning or nonfunctioning penis limited or prevented its role in reproduction. A male orgasm was essential for conception. Female sexual dysfunction or nonfunctioning had little to do with reproduction. A nonorgasmic woman could conceive. Female infer-

tility was a major concern, but not female sexual responsiveness.
2. The male's right to sexual enjoyment was taken for granted; it was a male prerogative. A woman's enjoyment of sex was not only discouraged but frowned upon; female masturbation and hypersexuality were considered "diseases," to be treated by surgery.

One of the objectives of the Women's Liberation movement is to achieve sexual as well as economic, social, and political equality with men. There has been an increasing awareness of both the need and the desire for sexual fulfillment. Women's "consciousness-raising" groups have gained wide acceptance and sexual problems are openly discussed. In addition, various psychotherapeutic modalities are being utilized in search of solutions to women's lack of sexual responsiveness.

It has only been during the past half-century that attention has been given to female sexuality and it was not until the mid-1960s that serious attention began to be paid to female sexual physiology. Drs. Gene G. Abel, et al. (1979) noted this fact. Their search of the literature relating to studies of clitoral and vaginal response to orgasm revealed 9 articles, none of which was published prior to 1970. Although diagnostic procedures have been developed for males, they noted that " . . . similar . . . procedures are almost nonexistent for females."[92]

Lack of even elementary knowledge of female sexual physiology was revealed in a question-and-answer section of a medical journal in 1977. A physician asked the following question: "At the time of orgasm, does the clitoris undergo spasmodic contractions comparable to that of the penis?" Dr. Thomas P. Lowry replied: "Probably not," explaining that since the clitoris normally retracts into surrounding tissues during orgasm, observation of this process is difficult.[93] Thus in 1977 there was no certainty about clitoral response to orgasm.

Clitoral stimulation is an important factor in coitus, but it is a highly individualized response. Dr. Barbara Schneidman wrote (1977): "The amount of pressure in direct clitoral stimulation that women prefer varies with each woman."[94]

Dr. Mary Jane Grey noted (1978): "Some women enjoy direct stimulation of the glans, but others may find this organ so sensitive that direct stimulation is painful."[95] This was reiterated by Dr. Lonnie G. Barbach (1978), who pointed out that genital stimulation is highly individualized for both men and women, and stated that there is no single type of clitoral stimulation preferred by all women.[96] Dr. Fred Seligman noted (1978): "Having the clitoris stroked manually is very individual to each woman. In general, the head [glans] of the clitoris is extremely sensitive and many women prefer indirect stimulation of the clitoral area."[97]

Dr. Marcia J. Coleman addressed (1979) the question of the role of penile thrusting to clitoral stimulation:

> The enjoyment of penile movement results from traction placed indirectly on the labia and clitoris. Thrusting movements may cause too direct clitoral stimulation for some women, although this depends upon the couple. A circular motion of the penis in the vagina places a more indirect traction on the clitoris and may be more pleasurable to some women who cannot tolerate direct clitoral touching.[98]

Dr. Caroline Preston noted: "We know that for some older women [age 55 and older] orgasmic contractions are experienced as painful."[99]

The issue of clitoral functioning is further complicated by the presentation of inaccurate information. For example, Dr. David Reuben claimed in 1969 that the clitoris enlarged after menopause. This error was corrected in later editions of his book.[100]

Obviously, there is little knowledge of the clitoris, nor even universal agreement on its role in coitus; it is very highly individualized. Nevertheless, many physicians generalize that in intromission pressure is brought to bear on the lower vaginal entrance, which causes a downward motion of the clitoral foreskin that stimulates the clitoris. This view is opposed by Shere Hite and other sex researchers. They claim that there is ample evidence that a large proportion of American women do not experience orgasm via coitus.[101]

Dr. Merle S. Kroop (1977) agreed, and noted: "A woman who complains of coital anorgasmia [absence of orgasm] is unable to achieve orgasm by the indirect stimulation of penile thrusting and requires direct clitoral stimulation." She claimed that approximately 50% of American women fall into this category and that sex therapists are "becoming increasingly reluctant" to consider this type of anorgasmia as a dysfunction.[102]

For that matter, even the descriptions of dysfunction are undergoing change. The term "frigidity" has been dropped by the American Psychiatric Association *Diagnostic Manual* because: "It is an outmoded, imprecise term that no longer has a place in medical terminology."[103] However, as will be seen later, the term is still bandied about.

There is no research to validate the use of female circumcision. The claims for this surgery simply reflect the mythology associated with the male procedure. For centuries men have been concerned about penile size. To this day, the fear of having a smaller than normal penis is still a source of anxiety.[104] This fear is reflected in women's concern over clitoral size; however, here the concern takes two forms: fear that the clitoris is too large or that it is too small. The medical profession has been concerned with both situations and has suggested a variety of treatment modalities. If grotesquely large, full or partial excision may be recommended,[105] or the less drastic measure of imbedding the clitoris in the surrounding tissue.[106] If too small, hormones may be recommended. One writer suggested the use of hormones for enlarging the clitoris, especially if the woman is large-breasted.[107] Most hormones are generally injected or ingested, but, according to one physician, clitoral enlargement may be achieved by topical application of the male hormone testosterone. However, the physician warned that this may make the clitoral glans painfully sensitive.[108]

Except in rare cases, the size of the penis or clitoris falls within a rather broad normal continuum and within this size continuum, the organ usually functions adequately. More frequently the difficulty is emotional, not physical, and there are always risks in surgery and in the use of hormones. Emphasis on clitoral anatomy is treacherous. Recent findings have confirmed enormous individual anatomic differences. Everyone accepts individual differences in fingerprints, body and organ size, etc.; however, Dr. R. J. Williams reported: " . . . some anatomical features have been depicted as normal in medical textbooks for generations yet they probably apply to only 15 percent of the population."[109] If this applies to the heart, stomach, liver, etc., it certainly also applies to the clitoris.

Many women find direct clitoral stimulation to be painful.[110] This is particularly true when stimulation is continued beyond the point of orgasm. In fact, at that point the clitoris recedes deep into the surrounding tissues. What happens when the protection of the clitoral foreskin is removed is not known, nor has it ever been mentioned in the medical literature. It is within the context of myths, minimal information, and much misinformation that the present-day practice of female circumcision is discussed. Despite the obvious confusion, there are some physicians ever ready with the scalpel to solve problems of female sexuality.

Present-Day Female Circumcision in the United States

The difficulty in discussing female sexual dysfunction and the possible role that circumcision may play in its alleviation is due to the fact that the subject has never been researched. Some women have been attracted to this quick surgical solution for solving sexual problems and for attaining greater sexual fulfillment and gratification. However, there are several unanswered questions, such as the degree to which circumcision may have become a fad; whether some women who are orgasmic undergo the operation to increase the intensity of their response; and whether after so much touting of the virtues of male circumcision, some women might feel deprived of such "benefits" and decide to be circumcised. Whatever the reasons for the acceptance of female circumcision, there are no accurate data available as to the number of such surgeries performed each year.

Government statistics for the years 1968, 1973, and 1977 indicate that approximately 5,000 operations were performed annually on the external female genitalia; of these possibly 2,000 to 3,000 were circumcisions.[111] However, this number represents women who have had the operation done in hospitals. According to one study, the ratio of this operation performed in doctors' offices to hospitals is about 50:1.[112] The 50:1 figure is not projectible; if it turns out to be reasonably accurate, then more female circumcisions are performed than are noninfant male circumcisions.

Regardless of the actual number of adult female circumcisions performed, the figure is small in comparison to those done on their newborn male counterparts—so far. Nevertheless, female circumcision is being written about in positive, glowing terms. A physician-nurse, husband-wife team reported that a California physician has been doing the procedure for "excessive foreskins," for 20 years and claimed that an "incredible number of marriages" have been saved.[113] One female author claimed that the surgery would make the clitoris more prominent, allowing for greater sexual sensation.[114] A male physician reported an equivocal result from using female circumcision as a cure for "frigidity." Although the woman remained incapable of orgasm, she turned into a "hussy," making frequent sexual demands, to the delight of her husband.[115] The important fact is that the concept is being disseminated in the lay press and is being encouraged by some physicians.

Female circumcision received one of its biggest boosts in an article entitled "Circumcision for Women—The Kindest Cut Of All," which appeared in a 1973 issue of *Playgirl* magazine. The author related the story of her own circumcision and its glowing results.[116] The magazine at that time had a circulation of 1,420,000, with a readership estimated at 6,000,000.[117] One-and-a-half years later, *Playgirl* published a second article by the same author under the heading, "$100 Surgery For A Million Dollar Sex Life," in which circumcision was again extolled.[118] Several months later, a physician wrote to the magazine praising their coverage of the subject, and stated that he soon would complete his fiftieth such operation. The physician commented that "probably ten to fifteen percent of all women could benefit sexually from it."[119]

In November 1976, *Cosmopolitan* magazine published an article describing operations that are now being performed more frequently to improve sexual response. Female circumcision headed the list—with the claim that it could benefit 10% of all women with a noncooperative clitoris.[120]

It is, of course, impossible to gauge the effect of these articles on readers. However, it would appear that physicians and therapists are receiving inquiries about such surgery from their patients. Physicians' replies to inquiries appeared in *Medical Aspects of Human Sexuality* in 1974 and 1976. In 1974, two sex therapists (a husband-wife team), wrote that it was their professional opinion that clitoral dysfunction is 90% psychological and less than 10% organic. (The anatomical dysfunctions are largely adhesions caused by poor hygiene and easily remedied by washing, lubrication, etc.) Furthermore, they noted, there is little scientific information upon which a sex therapist could base his assurance to a woman with a sexual dysfunction that she could be cured by circumcision or hormones.[121] Then in 1976, Dr. Johanna F. Perlmutter, an obstetrician and gynecologist, argued strongly against female circumcision and concluded with the statement that: "Surgical procedures to enhance orgasmic response in the female are not effective and will invariably precipitate genuine problems that are iatrogenic [caused by medical treatment] in their etiology."[122]

Others denied the effectiveness of the operation. Dr. John W. Huffman claimed (1976) that he had seen no change in the sexual reactions of women who were circumcised.[123] Dr. Lawrence S. Jackman made this point (1978):

> Clitoral adhesions have been alleged by some sex therapists to play a significant role in the etiology of unsatisfactory sexual response in women. Recommendations for lysis [loosening] of these adhesions, or scar tissue, between the clitoris and underlying hood and even clitoral circumcision have been made. Significant improvement in sexual response after these procedures has been claimed but, to my knowledge, never documented by the usual criteria of controlled scientific clinical research.[124]

Dr. Takey Crist recorded her experience with female circumcision (1977) and cautioned against its use on nonorgasmic women. She noted:

> [Female circumcision] may be indicated to enhance sexual stimulation in certain selected cases. In our practice [Crist Clinic for Women, Jacksonville, N.C.] 15 patients were selected for this procedure.
>
> Patients who have undergone this procedure have generally commented that they have enhanced sexual response. The procedure should never be considered routine, but clitoral circumcision may have its place in certain select women. We do not consider it appropriate for nonorgasmic women.[125]

Dr. Martin Shepard, in his book *Ecstasy* (1977), also argued against female circumcision for nonorgasmic women. He commented: "Failure of women to achieve orgasm is almost never due to physical dysfunction; its cause is psychological."[126]

In spite of the differences of opinion, lavish claims abound and the surgery continues to be performed. Despite the absence of substantiating data, Dr. Karen E. Paige wrote (1978) that "the operation is not uncommon."[127] Indicative of the regard in which female circumcision is held is the decision made by the National Blue Shield Association on May 18, 1977, which stated that henceforth they would no longer pay for a number of procedures considered "obsolete or ineffective," such as surgery for asthma and high-blood pressure, and female circumcision. The Blue Shield research department was unable to estimate the total number of female circumcisions they had paid for annually.[128]

With any surgery there may be problems. Dr. Paige reported on one California woman who sued her doctor in 1977 for circumcising her to cure her "sexual insensitivity." Several physicians testified at the trial. One said he could "see no reason" for the surgery; another said "it is a matter of judgment."[129]

Drs. Isenberg and Elting, who wrote the 1976 article for *Cosmopolitan* magazine, favored the surgery for some women but added a cautious note:

> Some women want their clitoris to stand erect like the male penis. The clitoris is more sensitive than the penis however, its surrounding tissue protects it. To expose it to unnecessary trauma would be to dull the very sensitivity you hope to increase.[130]

In addition to this warning, they also cautioned that differences of opinion about this surgery exist among physicians.

> There is considerable debate by surgeons over the necessity for this surgery. It is probably true that noncooperation of the clitoris is 90 percent psychological and 10 percent physical, but that doesn't make it any less real, nor the cure rate more abstract.[131]

Based upon this reasoning, they concluded:

> [If clitoral noncooperation] is what you suspect to be at the heart of your sexual problems, you might just be one of the 10 percent to find relief in female circumcision.[132]

Female Circumcision Research

Putting aside the pros and cons, it is important to examine the so-called "research" conducted in this field to try to prove the validity of female circumcision. According to Dr. R. Cook of the World Health Organization, there have been only two studies reported in the American medical literature.[133] The first study, by Dr. W. G. Rathmann, was published in 1959 and the second, by Dr. Leo Wollman, in 1973.[134]

Dr. Rathmann, in addition to publishing his research, invented a new surgical clamp for the operation. His discussion of female circumcision is most "enlightening." Using the anthropologist Felix Bryk as a reference,[135] Dr. Rathmann noted the origin of female circumcision in antiquity and stated in the opening paragraph of his article: "The value of this procedure in improving function has been accepted by various cultures for the past 3,500 years."[136] However, Felix Bryk was discussing clitoridectomy and other genital surgery. The improvement of a woman's sexual pleasure was not mentioned in his work.

According to Dr. Rathmann, indications for the necessity of circumcision are: The inability to have an orgasm and/or an anatomic or mechanical factor in need of correction. These indications were claimed to be important if psychosomatic problems are elicited or "if the problem of divorce is present." Dr. Rathmann described one patient who had 5 divorces and stated that her surgery saved the sixth marriage.[137] If the problems are "based on abnormal anatomy," female circumcision "patients are often permanently cured," Dr. Rathmann stated. He noted: "The two common problems that make the highly sensitive area of the clitoris unable to be stimulated are phimosis [adhesions] and redundancy [overly long foreskin]."[138]

Although Dr. Rathmann specified the degree of adhesions, he did not suggest alternative treatment modalities. He defined redundancy as the clitoral foreskin's extending from ¼ " to 1 " beyond the clitoral glans. Redundancy, he claimed, "can prevent contact and be harmful."[139] However, he noted: "Routine circumcision because of a functional problem alone, without the proper anatomic indications, will probably be of no benefit and might be harmful."[140]

In addition to the basic indications for surgery—phimosis and redundancy—Dr. Rathmann listed situations that would indicate the need for circumcision even though less phimosis or redundancy were present:

1. If the patient is quite adipose . . . this operation may help cure her adiposity by relieving psychosomatic factors.
2. If the husband is unusually awkward [the surgery] should at times make the clitoris easier to find.
3. If the clitoris is quite small . . . a circumcision might help by making it more accessible.[141]

The contraindications for surgery that Dr. Rathmann gave were "frigidity from psychologic causes" and "excessive psychoneurosis."[142] With this as background, Dr. Rathmann then presented his data. His data were based upon a questionnaire mailed to women that he had circumcised during the past 15 years. A total of 112 questionnaires were completed and returned by the patients. The query asked was simple. In addition to the date of surgery, the women were asked: Could you have an orgasm prior to surgery? Yes/No. If yes, has the orgasm improved? If no, are you able to orgasm now?[143]

There was no information about the total number of circumcisions that Dr. Rathmann performed, including the period earlier than the prior 15 years, nor was the number of operations performed during the 15-year period given. Thus, there was no information as to the total number of questionnaires that were sent out. Simply being told that 112 questionnaires were completed and returned does not provide the necessary denominator for the research, and the projectibility of the data is nil. If 112 questionnaires were mailed and 112 answered, that would be a 100% response; if 224 were mailed and 112 answered, that would be a 50% response; if 1,120 were mailed and 112 answered, that would be only a 10% response, etc. Denying such information invalidated the results, since it does not provide even the vaguest idea of the projectibility of the material, or of sampling bias.

The only data that Rathmann presented were as follows: Of those who had never experienced an orgasm prior to circumcision, there were 73 responses. Of these, surgery was successful in 64 cases (87.6% in the "orgasm now" category); and not successful in 9 cases (12.4% in the "Do not orgasm now" category). Of those who had experienced orgasm with difficulty prior to circumcision, there were 39 responses. Of these, the surgery produced improvement in 34 cases (87.5%); and no improvement in 5 cases (12.5%).

Based upon this study, Dr. Rathmann concluded that satisfactory improvement should be expected in 85% to 90% of the cases, if the patients are carefully selected.[144]

Dr. Rathmann's study ignored many important elements:

1. What is the effect of circumcision over time?
2. Is there a difference in response in relation to the ages of the patients at the time of surgery?
3. Does "orgasm" refer to clitoral orgasm, vaginal orgasm, or both?
4. Is orgasm as a result of coitus or masturbation?
5. Does orgasm occur 10% or 90% of the time coitus is attempted?
6. How often does coital opportunity occur—4 times weekly with an orgasm 50% of the time, or once a month with orgasm 100% of the time?
7. Is the orgasm mild or intense, single or multiple?

The absence of proper data collection and analysis makes it impossible to draw any conclusions from this research.

In the other American study of female circumcision, Dr. Wollman reported on 100 patients referred to him by psychotherapists for evaluation to determine if they were good candidates for circumcision.[145] Of the 100 women: 68 were circumcised, 28 were deemed not to be in need of circumcision and therefore were not circumcised, and 4 refused to be treated by circumcision.

Dr. Wollman could have reported his findings with respect to the 68 women who underwent the surgery, and he could have compared these results with the 32 women who were not circumcised. This was not done. His data presentation is difficult to follow. *All* of the tabular material is listed under the heading: "Statistical Analysis of One Hundred Cases." This is valid, to show the demography of the 100 referrals. However, the figures provided in the tables do not indicate whether the numbers refer to individuals among the 100 cases or to percentages of the 68 women who were circumcised. No table is headed with the % symbol or the words "percent" or "percentage." Thus, despite the heading "100 Cases," it must be assumed that Dr. Wollman meant percentages of the 68 circumcised patients. Otherwise the data make no sense.

Demographic characteristics were given by age, occupation, marital status, and religion. The average age was 28, ranging from a low of 16 to a high of 54. Other than demographics, the tabular material showed sexual activity, subjective assessment, period of follow-up, and where the surgery was performed.

The doctor stated that the 100 referrals were "consecutive." The inference usually made in such situations is that the referrals took place within a finite time span, e.g., 1 or 2 years or less. This is a valid research technique, because it means that the element of time is not an independent variable that has to be taken into account. However, the report showed that the longest follow-up was 20 years. This means that the 100 "consecutive" referrals covered a 20-year period, which seriously biased the research. Coital frequency, especially over a 20-year span, will often change, due to a host of related factors such as health, age, fatigue, partner availability, etc. Moreover, measuring the effect of circumcision within one year of surgery may be very different from measuring the effect over 20 years. Dr. Wollman stated that 64 patients were followed for more than 5 years, but the doctor did not make clear whether the 64 were from the total of 100 referrals or from the 68 operated upon; if it was from the latter group, it means that only 4 operations were performed by him during the last 5-year period (68 minus 64).

The section of Dr. Wollman's report that is the most difficult to understand, however, is the data on sexual activity and the subjective assessment of results. Under the heading "Sexual Activity," Dr. Wollman reported that "before treatment" sexual activity was engaged in an average of 3 times weekly, and "after treatment" the frequency averaged 5 times a week. Under the heading "Orgasm Attained," the report showed that 49 achieved orgasm prior to treatment and 92 after treatment. In the absence of data clarification (Do the numbers refer to cases or percentages of cases?) it is impossible to understand the figures. If 92 *patients* attained orgasm "after treatment" but only 68 were circumcised, what "treatment" accounted for the results in the 24 cases who were not circumcised (92 minus 68)? It seems obvious that Dr. Wollman meant these figures to be percentages. If 49% were able to attain orgasm before circumcision and had an average coital frequency of 3 times weekly, why were they circumcised? An average coital frequency change of from 3 to 5 times weekly hardly seems to be an important measure of success. Moreover, coital frequency is not a reliable measure of sexual fulfillment. Nor, for that matter, is orgasm attained as it is presented here, since it is not specified whether orgasm was attained in every coital experience, 50% of the time, or whether it represented multiple orgasms. As to patients' subjective assessments, the report showed that 92 improved, 7 reported no change, and one was worse. "Improved" was measured by increased intensity, more rapid response, or a greater number of orgasms.

Dr. Wollman provided only one reference for substantiation—his own article in the same journal, of which he is the editor. He expressed the opinion that clitoral sensitivity was greater when there was no tissue covering the glans and that the "ideal result" of the surgery was the improvement both in the quality and speed of orgasm. In conclusion he stated that female circumcision has a definite place in the treatment of frigidity, particularly in women with "cryptic" (hidden) clitorises. This conclusion is at odds with other pro-circumcision advocates, who caution against using this surgery for "frigidity." Dr. Wollman cautioned that in rare instances a hematoma (accumulation of blood) as large as a "goose egg" may occur, but claimed that the condition is easily remedied.

The Wollman study is important in a discussion of female circumcision, because it is only the second published American research paper, and it was supposedly based upon a reasonable number of patients who were followed up over time. However, as noted, the weaknesses of the research negate any real value it might have.

One physician accurately summed up the controversy over the usefulness of female circumcision to improve sexual satisfaction: "Detailed, reproducible, or controlled studies have not been reported and this hypothesis is untested."[146] Until ample evidence is available to prove the efficacy of female circumcision, there is nothing to recommend it. Like its male counterpart, it belongs in the category of unnecessary surgery, except in rare circumstances.

Beyond Female Circumcision—The "Surgery of Love"

As we have seen, the medical profession employs female circumcision with no empirical evidence of its benefit. An extreme example of how far female genital surgery can be carried is provided by the work of James C. Burt, M.D., of Dayton, Ohio.

Dr. Burt believes in female circumcision. He also accepts the thesis that a woman's sexual response is determined by the distance between the clitoris and the vagina. His solution is *not* to move the clitoris closer to the vagina, but to move the vagina closer to the clitoris, and perform circumcision.

In 1975, Dr. Burt published *Surgery of Love,* describing the history, rationale, and "success" of this operation.[147] Barbara Demick, a news reporter, interviewed him and published comments from the medical and health profession in 1978.[148] Dr. Burt's sexual philosophy is simple and sexist. Ms. Demick quoted Dr. Burt: "In males with impotence, the impotence is female's impotence, that is, female caused. . . . " According to Ms. Demick, Dr. Burt believes that if a woman cannot climax, it is her own fault. She therefore has to resort to—to use Dr. Burt's own terminology—"female homosexual clitoral manipulation," or oral sex.

Some of the chapter headings in his book reveal his philosophy: "Every Man Can Be A Stud"; "Your Own Private Sexpot In Your Own Private World"; "Any Man At Any Age Can Love His Woman To Exhaustion."

Dr. Burt became involved in vaginal surgery through his experiences of sewing the vagina tightly after episiotomy. This, he described, was fine for the man, but painful for the woman, because it changed the angle of entry, causing the penis to press against the large pubococcygeal muscle, located at the floor of the pelvis. He concluded that: "The obvious solution was to cut the damn muscle."[149] And so he did. This vaginal reconstruction is major surgery (at $1,500 + hospitalization). There are no clinical data upon which to base this operation. It has been scathingly attacked from all quarters, but Dr. Burt appears on radio and television; the inquiries pour in and the surgery is regularly performed.

Dr. Burt claims to have performed the vaginal tightening operation on 4,000 women, some admittedly without their knowledge. Since 1975, he claims to have performed 200 total vaginal reconstructions, including circumcision, producing what he calls the "Mark II vagina."

It is a sad commentary on American medicine that Dr. Burt can function in this manner with no control over his activities. It is also a sad commentary on American society that women can be led to believe: (1) that they are the sole source of sexual problems; (2) that the problem is not emotional, but purely physical; (3) that the physical problem lies in their inadequate anatomy; and (4) that such drastic surgical solutions are the answer.

18
An Appeal to Reason

Circumcision is a unique phenomenon. Its origins in antiquity are obscure, its original objectives unknown, its spread to all continents a source of speculation; yet this operation, this first ritual surgery devised by humans, is still in use. As a ritual, circumcision has been practiced for thousands of years. It is so deeply ingrained among many groups that there is little likelihood of the practice soon being abandoned.

But circumcision is more than merely ritual surgery. As a therapeutic measure, to correct a true defect, it is accepted worldwide. In the U.S., circumcision is allegedly employed therapeutically—to correct a pseudodefect. A third aspect, prophylaxis, has taken on even greater significance in the United States, where many more operations are performed for prophylactic reasons than for religious or therapeutic ones.

Thus the American practice is trifaceted; a religious rite, a therapeutic measure, and a prophylactic operation. No other surgical procedure can make such a claim. In fact, according to Dr. David Grimes, "Newborn circumcision eludes classification."[1] (Surgery is classified into four areas: repair of wounds, extirpation of diseased organs or tissue, reconstructive surgery, and physiologic surgery. Prophylactic circumcision fits none of these classifications.)

A century ago, ignorant of disease etiology, physicians introduced male circumcision to cure almost every disease imaginable. Despite later knowledge that most diseases did not have the remotest connection with this surgery, the practice was continued with ever-increasing frequency. Now when *all* claims for ills supposedly prevented by circumcision have been shown to be illusory, the surgery still continues unabated. The prophylaxis theories are myths; they are no longer acceptable hypotheses. In fact, the entire concept of "health" circumcision in the United States is beyond the bounds of medicine. Dr. Lendon Smith claimed (1969) that: "Circumcision now seems to be a national cultural trait in the United States."[2] This "national cultural trait" endows circumcision with mystical prophylactic powers and an entire health philosophy has been accreted around it. But the very concept of a "national cultural trait" is in error, because it obscures the real reason for the acceptance of circumcision in the United States. The issue is further clouded by some of the psychiatric approaches to circumcision.

Bruno Bettelheim, in his book *Symbolic Wounds* (1962), stated:

> At the end of this study, I am still unable to explain circumcision fully and unequivocally. There is much evidence that women impose* or desire it; but there is also much reason to believe it is desired by men—either because it gives them symbolically the capabilities of women, or because it emphasizes their masculinity by making the glans permanently more visible. . . . [3]

Dr. Bettelheim continued:

> In any case all the explanations that appear most plausible to me seem to originate in the great biological antithesis that creates envy and attraction between the two sexes.[4]

He went on to discuss circumcision in relation to penis envy and castration anxiety, and paraphrased Freud:

> . . . he [Freud] looked to racial memory traces for its cause and concluded that we are born with a fear of losing our sex organs. I believe, instead, that our desire for the characteristics of the other sex is a necessary consequence of the sex differences.[5]

Attributing circumcision to penis envy and/or castration anxiety "explains" why women "impose" it, but does not take into account the simple fact that circumcision is not practiced by 75% of the human race. Is it possible that 75% of the world's population is unaware of sex differences and therefore do not suffer either penis envy or castration anxiety? There are no empirical data to support the Bettelheim thesis on this question.

The acceptance of the American circumcision practice for health reasons is based upon ignorance of the facts and fear; fear of taking issue with a well-entrenched custom. Pessimism about changing the situation was noted by two physicians in 1963: "One would hope the situation might change in the next century—but do not bet on it!"[6]

A New York City newsweekly, *The Village Voice,* published an article on circumcision in 1975 by Sylvia Topp, who conducted a series of interviews. She found in telephone interviews with a random sample of 10% of

*Note the sexism. Both men and women desire it; only women *impose* it.

Manhattan obstetricians that more than half of them believed that circumcision is unnecessary. Nevertheless, they performed the operation on over 90% of the males they delivered in the belief that parents strongly desired the surgery—so much so that, in their opinion, it would have been useless to try to convince the parents to reject the surgery. They therefore made no effort to do so.[7] On the other hand, interviews with a nonrandom sample of mothers that Ms. Topp conducted revealed almost a diametrically opposite point of view: 2 out of every 3 mothers stated that if the doctor had suggested not circumcising the child, they would have accepted his opinion. The others were not certain what they would have done.[8]

There is, furthermore, a strange issue of medical "turf" in the employment of obstetricians to do circumcisions. The American Board of Obstetrics and Gynecology warned that: "Physicians who assume responsibility for the health of male patients for operative or other care will not be regarded as specialists in obstetrics-gynecology."[9] And yet thousands of routine circumcisions are performed annually by Board Certified obstetricians-gynecologists. These specialists seldom see the circumcision patient for follow-up. Dr. Grimes suggested that it would be better to have the circumcision performed by the child's physician, rather than the mother's, because better postoperative care could be provided, which would result in fewer complications.[10]

Dr. Edward B. Feehan (1977) suggested a profit motive in that there are communities in which the obstetrician provides all care for the newborn. The decision to do so is probably motivated by "custom and economics."[11]

The question of monetary gain has been mentioned only briefly. While this may be a factor for some, most physicians perform the surgery either in the mistaken belief that it may do some good or because of the lingering fear that not doing it may cause harm. The charge of venality is easy to make but difficult to document. Moreover, opposition to routine circumcision should not be sidetracked by such an extraneous issue, but should instead be argued on the merits of the procedure. However, as Dr. D. Grimes (1978) commented, no one has determined the "cost-effectiveness ratio."[12] Grimes estimated that the cost of all newborn circumcisions in the United States ranged between $50,000,000 and $200,000,000 annually, plus the millions of personnel hours required, and suggested this money could be more wisely spent for immunization and health education.[13]

This state of affairs is not unique to circumcision. According to a 1978 Congressional Committee, the results of accepting the concept that "The doctor knows best" were 2 million unneeded operations, a loss of more than 10,000 lives, and a cost of $4 billion in 1977 alone. Perhaps the most alarming aspect of this surgical scandal is that it is not a new development but is, instead, a frequently told story about which little corrective action has been taken. The *New York Times* reported (1978) that Rep. John Moss noted that there has *not* been a significant decline in unnecessary surgery, although this matter had been called to public attention 3 years ago.[14]

If the medical establishment moves this slowly in respect to major surgery, it should come as no surprise that the situation vis-à-vis circumcision—minor surgery—may not change even in the next century. The medical profession often stresses how much it knows, but seldom admits how little is known. Dr. Ernest W. Saward, Associate Dean of the Rochester School of Medicine, recently wrote (1977):

> The impression is often obtained from medical scientists and from the press that the scientific knowledge upon which medical practice is based is vast. If we look carefully, however, it appears more as an archipelago of knowledge in a sea of ignorance. And the efficaciousness in medical practice of much that we think we know has never in fact been substantiated.[15]

Dr. H. H. Hiatt (1975), listing numerous procedures that were in vogue in the recent past but are no longer used, noted that because they remained on the "medical commons" too long, valuable health resources were squandered.[16] Dr. Grimes, commenting on Dr. Hiatt's study, stated that when certain medical practices were discontinued, it was not because they were necessarily replaced by improved methods, but because it was found that they were of no benefit to the patient.[17] Dr. Hiatt decried the fact that when a medical procedure has been widely adopted, it is not given up even after there is proof that the procedure has no value.[18] He further commented that physicians should use techniques only when they are quite certain that they will do good. Physicians should not be in the position of demonstrating that a procedure is merely not dangerous.[19]

The editor of the *Australian Journal of Medicine* declared (1971) that some medical procedures take a long time to die, and that of all procedures which should have passed from the scene, neonatal circumcision is "among the most stubborn."[20]

According to a health consumer publication (1977), tonsillectomy and adenoidectomy (T and A) are also cases in point.

> Despite the prevalence of T and A, very few studies have been done to determine its value.
>
> Sixty percent of all T and A are done by surgeons who are not Board certified.
>
> ... 685,000 T and As were performed in 1975 at a cost of up to 350 deaths and at least an equal number of serious, nonfatal complications. . . . [21]

The medical profession admits that too many T and A's have been and are performed unnecessarily. Yet the operation continues, although at a diminishing rate. Therefore, it is probably asking too much to expect that the profession would also admit that millions of circumcisions have been and are needlessly performed. Circumcision is not innocuous; trauma, morbidity, and mortality do occur. Moreover, the tissue removed is little understood. The prepuce, like the earlobe, has long been considered a useless appendage. However, the earlobe is at least useful for ornamentation. There is evidence in acupuncture that the earlobe is useful for anesthesia and/or therapy. If the earlobe is a useful part of the body, what about the prepuce?

A few years ago (1974) two sex therapists made a cogent observation: "At any given moment in history, the things people do, even their thoughts and opinions, are largely governed by what their societies find acceptable."[22]

Unfortunately, tradition dies hard in medicine. It took decades for Semmelweis' theories of simple childbirth sanitation to be adopted, and decades before Freud's Viennese colleagues would even seriously consider his theories. Natural childbirth is still often frowned upon. Psychiatrist Mary Jane Sherfey, in addressing the question of the medical profession's slowness to accept change, quoted the famous German physicist Max Planck: "A new scientific truth does not triumph by convincing its opponents and making them see the light, but rather because its opponents eventually die off, and a new generation grows up that is familiar with it."[23]

Bertrand Russell put it another way: "I venture to propose . . . a doctrine which may, I fear, appear wildly paradoxical and subversive. The doctrine in question is this: That it is undesirable to believe a proposition when there is no ground whatsoever for supposing it true."[24]

But circumcision has gone far beyond the bounds of reason or medicine and has involved the least likely government agency.

Probably the most outrageous circumcision "study" of the century was reported in the *New York Times* in 1977.[25] The Central Intelligence Agency (C.I.A.) reported that in 1961 it had arranged to have 15 boys, aged 5 to 7, circumcised. The boys were from low-income families; their ethnic backgrounds were not identified. The *New York Times* article stated that the objective of the research was to determine whether castration anxieties were caused by circumcision. The C.I.A. documents were "heavily censored"; however one report noted that the research sought to determine whether such "emotional disorders" as homosexuality were related to castration complexes. Queries to the C.I.A. revealed that the research findings had been destroyed. No information was available as to whether parental consent had been requested or given. Clearly this "study" represents surgical and psychiatric experimentation with human subjects in violation of accepted medical practices and government regulations.

The *New York Times* reported the story without immediate or delayed comment. So did the *Washington Post*. A few days later, Richard Cohen, a *Washington Post* columnist, wrote a blistering attack not only on the C.I.A. but on the silence that had ensued:

I waited for some Senator or Congressman to yell bloody murder. Nothing. I waited for an editorial, somebody maybe asking what business it was of the C.I.A.'s to find out anything about circumcision. Nothing.[26]

The press carried no criticism or protest from any section of the medical establishment, or any government official, of this prostitution of a surgical technique or of the surgeons who performed the operations. It is not that the C.I.A. is immune to criticism. In recent years hundreds of this agency's cloak-and-dagger acts have been attacked—from the media to the pulpit to Congress. Why then no comment when the issue is circumcision? Is the subject sacrosanct?

The status of American circumcision practice was summarized by Dr. Karen E. Paige in 1978:

> When a custom persists after its original functions have died, it may be accorded the status of ritual.
>
> When the same operation is variously reputed to accomplish antithetical goals—in the case of circumcision, to repress sexuality and to liberate it, to make the penis or clitoris less sensitive and more sensitive—we can be sure we are dealing with ritual, not rational thinking. It is astonishing that such a little bit of skin carries such a great load of power.[27]

Thus, both male and female circumcision are described as ritual, not rational. At least the male operation maintains an aura of medical benefit, and sexual enhancement (reduction of premature ejaculation) is claimed as an incidental advantage. In female circumcision, however, no health benefits are suggested; the rationale is strictly limited to improved sexual response.

In other words, if a woman is sexually unresponsive or responds poorly, the onus lies with her or, more to the point, with her genital anatomy—allegedly easily corrected by surgery. This sexual vicitimization of women—placing the blame solely upon their sexual anatomy and urging surgical remedy—is not abating, it is increasing.

With respect to male circumcision, there is some evidence that pediatricians are becoming more outspoken in their opposition. Dr. Sydney S. Gellis writing in the *American Journal Diseases of Children* (1978) made an impassioned plea for physicians to be more outspoken in discouraging newborn circumcision. He concluded the article with these words: ''Down, I say, with . . . circumcision. . . . ''[28] (The full quote is ''Down, I say, with both circumcision and Fournier's syndrome.'' Fournier's syndrome is gangrene of the genitalia occasionally associated with circumcision. Dr. Gellis maintained that the term gangrene is sufficiently clear. To call it by a specific name obscures the situation.)

Certainly, the medical profession has the responsibility to conduct and to encourage research into all aspects of circumcision or any other surgery. For that matter, enlightened health consumers must also take responsibility to ask questions and to question answers. This volume is only an initial effort to review available information; much more work needs to be done. Hopefully, this book will encourage others to explore the subject and demystify it. Not to do so leaves the field wide open to abuse.

The medical profession bears responsibility for the introduction of prophylactic circumcision without scientific basis in the past and for its continued use and rationalization without scientific basis in the present. The profession seems to accept circumcision as a "national cultural trait" as much as do lay people. With evidence at hand to disprove the prophylactic benefits of the surgery, the medical profession has the responsibility to discourage this practice. The pretense of neutrality is a negative stance.

Today circumcision is a solution in search of a problem. The operation, as prophylaxis, has no place in a rational society. The final conclusion to be drawn is that routine infant health circumcision is archaic, useless, potentially dangerous, and therefore should cease.

Appendix A
What Is Circumcision?

Penile Structures

External penile structures can be more easily understood by first describing a circumcised penis. Its outward appearance is that of a cylinder, rounded at the end. Four parts are visible, namely: the shaft, which makes up the major length of the organ; the glans or rounded head at the end; the sulcus, or groove, which separates the glans from the shaft; and the meatus, or opening at the tip of the glans, which permits passage of fluids (see Figure 1).

An uncircumcised penis has each of the four parts mentioned above plus a foreskin. The foreskin, or prepuce, can be visualized as cone-shaped with the base of the cone encircling the penile shaft, close to the groove. The foreskin is also attached to the underside of the glans at a ridge called the frenum, which is observable on either a circumcised or uncircumcised penis. Usually, the foreskin covers the glans completely, although in some cases it may only cover it partly or it may extend beyond it, as there are variations from person to person. Though the foreskin is cone-shaped, the tip is not pointed but is instead blunt and has an opening. Because the foreskin fits snugly over the glans, which is often wider than the shaft, the foreskin appears to bulge at the widest part of the glans (see Figure 2). Thus the foreskin can be visualized as a soft, pliable, cone-shaped tissue, which is open at the end to permit the passage of fluids from the meatus. The opening is expandable in order to allow for the protrusion of the glans in erection, for washing the glans, and for urination in noninfants.

Actually, the foreskin is composed of two distinct layers of tissue, almost like a lined sleeve. The inner layer starts from the foreskin opening at the tip, where it is joined to the outer foreskin layer, and continues under the outer layer to cover the glans (see Figure 3). The inner layer is attached to the shaft near the groove, or sulcus, as well as to the underside of the glans at the frenum.

Unlike the inner layer, the outer layer of the foreskin is simply an extension of the external skin of the penile shaft, which continues over the glans until it joins the inner layer at the opening at the tip of the foreskin. The outer layer does not come into direct contact with the glans.

The two foreskin layers are different in structure and function. The texture of the outer layer is identical to the rest of the penile shaft skin and, as with all penile skin, it is erotogenic. The texture of the inner lining is more like that of a mucous membrane and it is kept moist by the secretion of smegma, which its cells produce. The inner layer also contains specialized nerve cells which make it one of the most erotogenic of all male body tissues. (The inner lining of the clitoral foreskin is similarly endowed.)

When an uncircumcised penis is flaccid (not erect), the entire organ is covered with a continuum of skin from the base (at the abdomen) to the meatus. In a circumcised penis, the external skin ends near the groove, which is usually exposed, as are the glans and the meatus.

There is much confusion concerning erection and circumcision for two reasons: (1) all penises, when erect, are superficially identical in appearance, but upon closer examination, many differences can be noted; (2) there are many myths about the foreskin and erection.

The erect penis with a foreskin is *not* longer, thicker, or firmer than its circumcised counterpart. However, there is a difference in the distribution of erotogenic tissue, but there is neither firm knowledge nor tentative experimental evidence to demonstrate differences in sexual pleasure and function solely in terms of the presence or absence of the foreskin.

When circumcision is performed, care must be exercised not to remove too much foreskin; that is, ample skin should be left on the shaft. Therefore, in the flaccid state, a circumcised penis appears to have an overabundance of shaft skin (see Figure 1). When the penis becomes erect, it is the inner shaft structure that elongates, and the seemingly excess external shaft skin allows for this lengthening. The erect circumcised penis is shown in Figure 4.

In the uncircumcised penis, as well as in the circumcised penis, the inner shaft elongates in erection. This causes the external shaft skin to stretch to accommodate the increase in penile size. As erection continues, the glans begins to protrude through the opening at the tip of the foreskin, which, since it is soft and pliable, can easily stretch to accommodate the protruding glans. The outer foreskin layer does not shift position; it is the glans that moves outward to extend beyond the foreskin. The outer foreskin, then, no longer covers the glans but remains a continuation of the elongated penile shaft skin (see Figures 5A and 5B). However, since the outer foreskin layer is attached to the

Figure 1. Diagrammatic Representation of the Circumcised Penis in the Relaxed State.

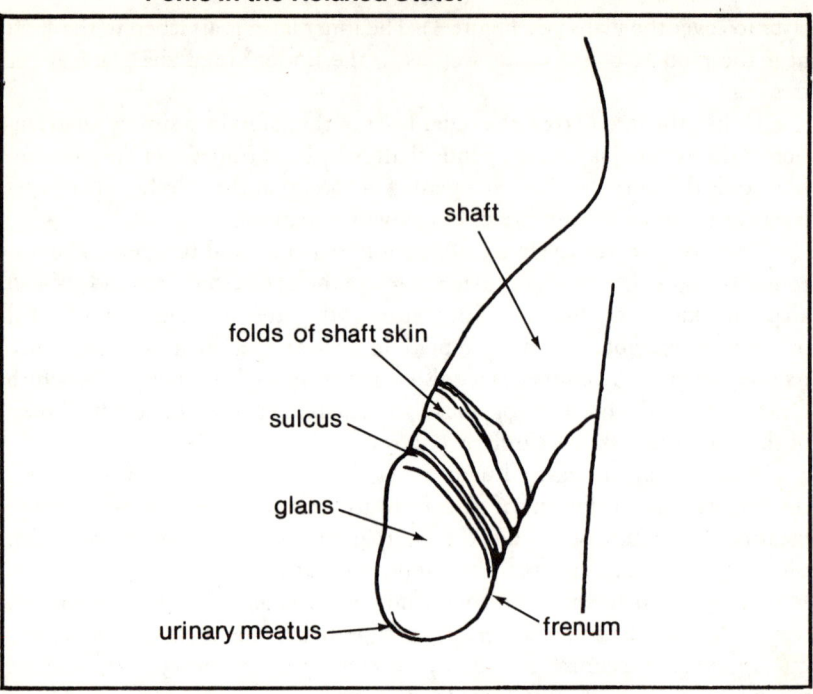

Figure 2. Diagrammatic Representation of the Uncircumcised Penis in the Relaxed State.

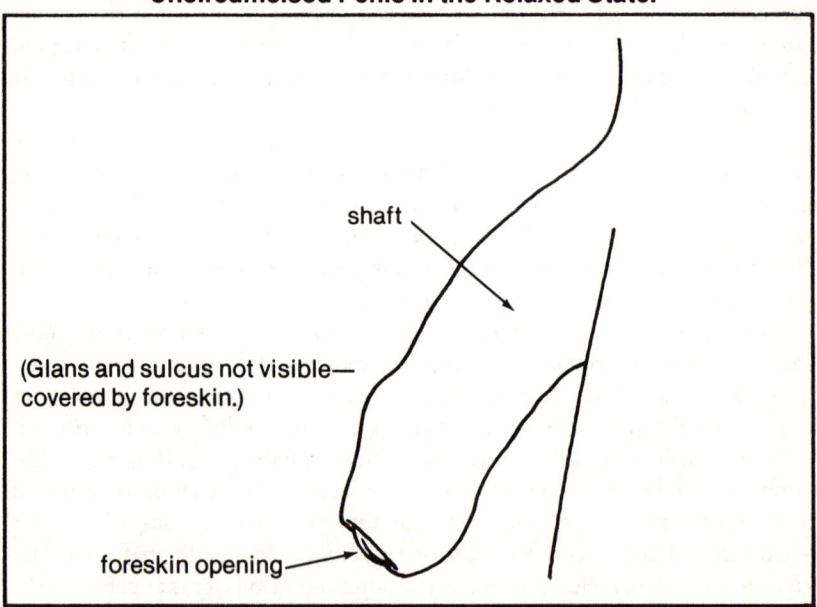

Figure 3. Diagrammatic Representation of the Inner and Outer Foreskin Layers.

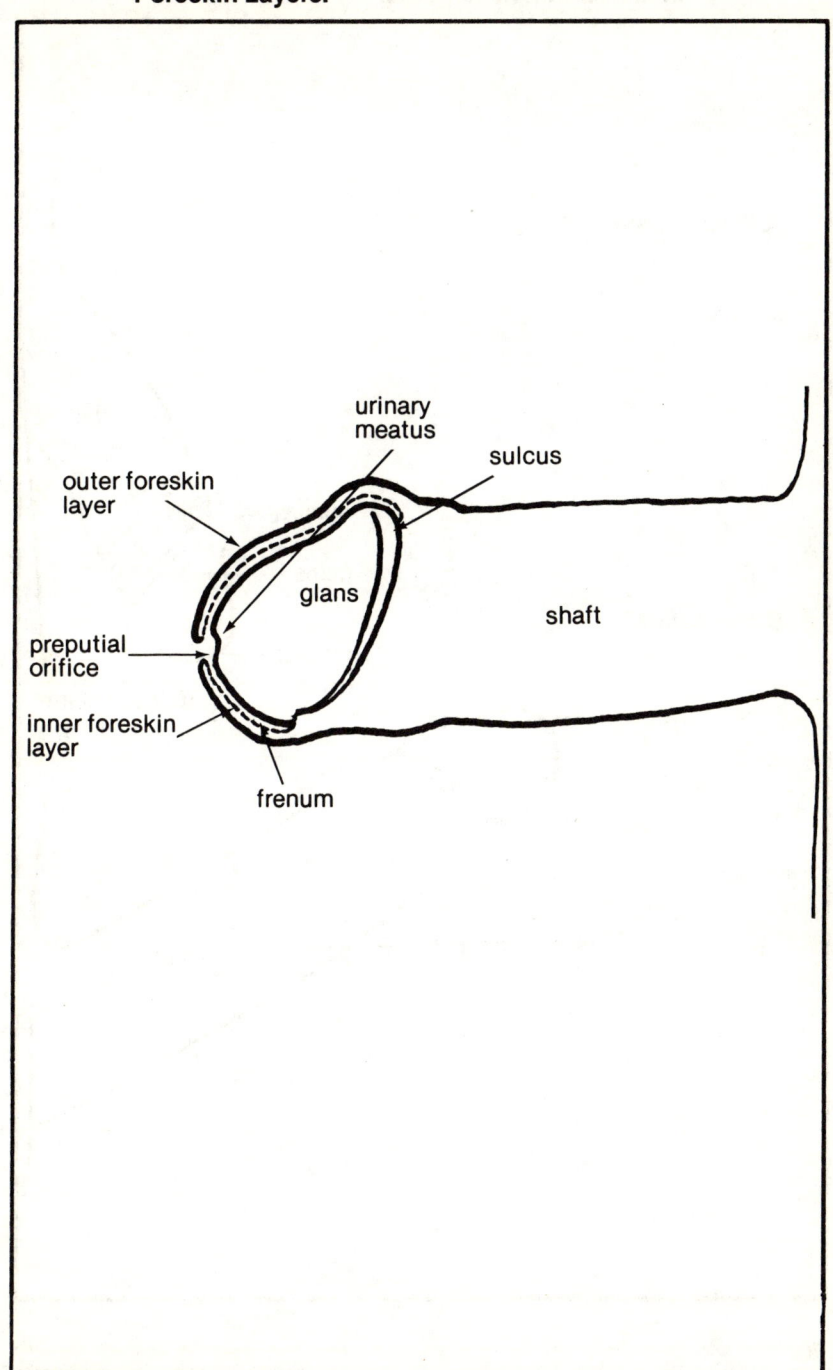

Figure 4. Diagrammatic Representation of Erectile Process in the Circumcised Penis.

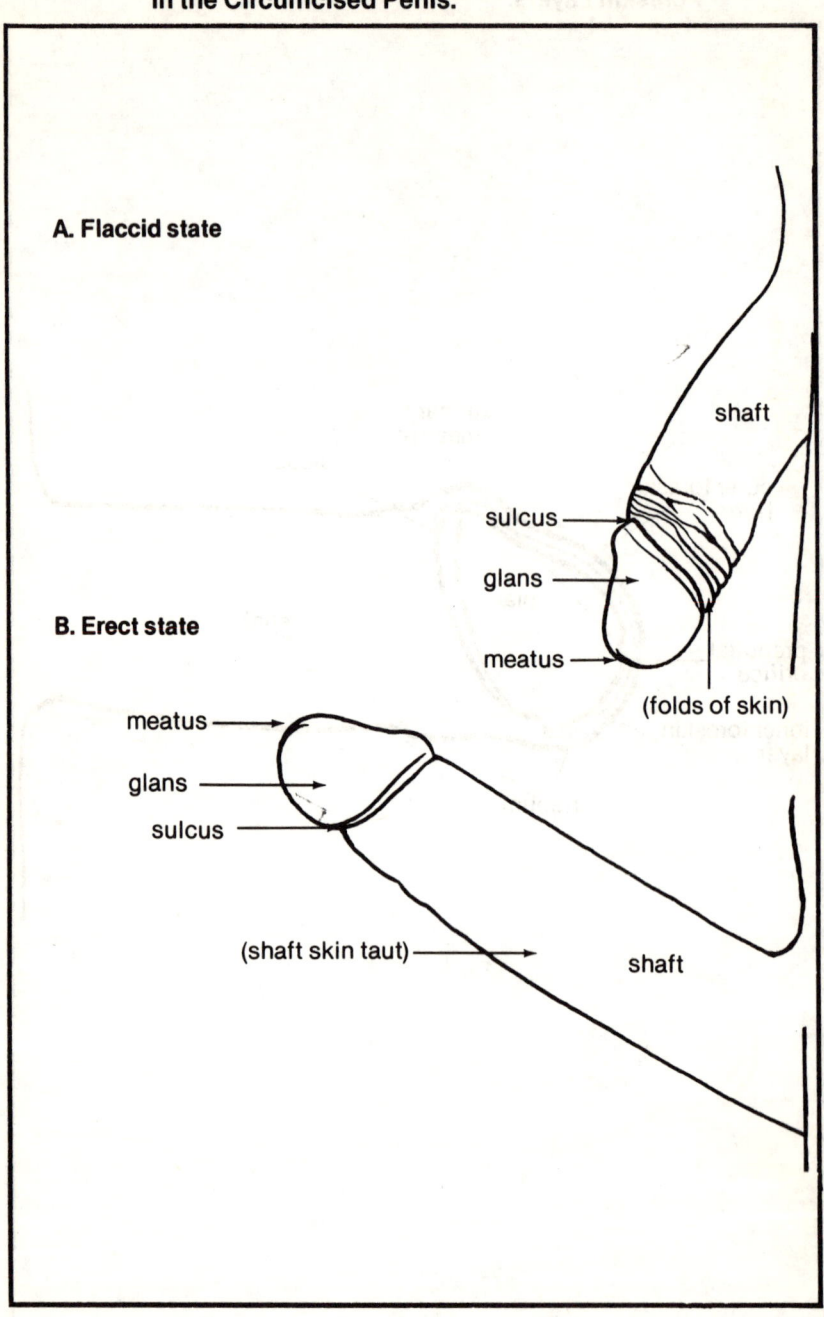

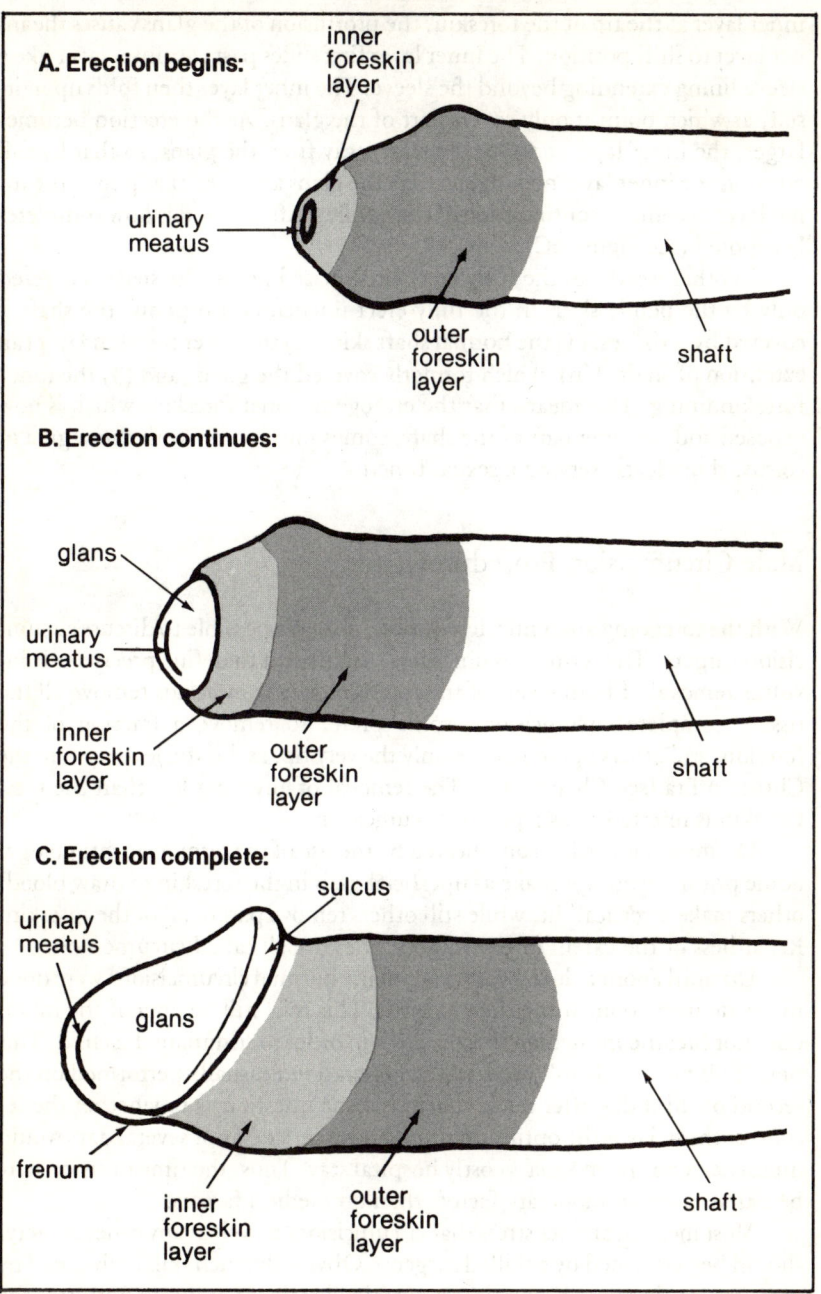

Figure 5. Diagrammatic Representation of the Erection Process in the Uncircumcised Penis.

inner layer at the tip of the foreskin, the protrusion of the glans causes the inner layer to shift position. The inner layer first slides past the outer layer like a sleeve lining extending beyond the sleeve. The inner layer then folds upon itself, at which point it only covers part of the glans. As the erection becomes larger, the inner layer continues to shift away from the glans, so that by full erection the inner layer no longer covers the glans at all. At that point, the inner layer becomes a continuation of the penile shaft skin and is now completely exposed (see Figure 5C).

In other words, in the fully erect circumcised penis, the shaft is covered only by the penile skin. In the fully erect uncircumcised penis, the shaft is covered by 3 tissues: (1) the normal shaft skin; (2) the outer foreskin layer (an extension of shaft skin), which formerly covered the glans; and (3) the inner foreskin lining. This means that the erotogenic inner foreskin, which is now exposed and covering part of the shaft, comes into contact with the vagina in coitus, thus clearly serving a sexual function.

Male Circumcision Procedures

With the foregoing anatomic description, it is now possible to discuss circumcision surgery. The term "circumcision" is difficult to define precisely. It involves removal of both layers of the foreskin. Most physicians remove all the tissue (complete circumcision); some prefer to remove a fraction of the foreskin, still others opt to remove only the very tip, as did the Jews prior to the Christian Era (see Chapter 16). The removal of anything less than the total foreskin is referred to as a partial circumcision.

Definition is further complicated by the use of the term in anthropology. Some primitive groups make a superficial gash in the foreskin to draw blood; others make a vertical slit, while still others remove part or all of the foreskin. Regardless of the extent of the surgery, they are all called circumcision.

Up until about a dozen years ago, many hospital circumcisions were done in the delivery room at the time of birth. This may still be done if the infant does not breathe immediately after birth in order to stimulate the child. This practice is now rarely followed and the operation is usually performed on the second or third day after birth. There is some question as to whether the second or third day is the optimum time; however, a delay of several days would unduly extend the mother's costly hospital stay. Thus, the time decision may be based more on monetary factors than on medical factors.

Most medical articles stress that circumcision, as well as any other surgery, should be performed by a skilled surgeon. Obviously, such skill is obtained by practice. Yet in many hospitals, an untrained resident or intern performs the surgery, often with no attending physician present. Although this is technically illegal, it is a common practice in many types of surgical procedures. Certainly, a medical novice performing his first circumcision cannot be expected to be as competent as one performing his hundredth.

There are a number of methods employed to remove the foreskin. They fall into two major categories: direct surgery and a squeezing technique; each has several variations. Presurgery preparations are as follows:

1. The infant must be restrained to avoid injury. This is usually accomplished by a specially designed Y-shaped board with Velcro straps to secure the infant firmly to the board. The body and hands are held by the base of the Y and the legs by the arms of the Y.
2. The genital area is cleaned and a sterile environment established—instruments, gloves, masks, etc. The importance of this is obvious, yet the frequency of infections suggests that maximum care may not always be exercised.
3. In newborn circumcision, anesthesia is usually not employed; to do so can involve additional risk. In many operations, the anesthesia is as dangerous as the surgery. Some physicians attempt to lessen the pain of circumcision by providing the infant with a piece of gauze to suck on which has been soaked in wine or whiskey diluted with sugar water. However, most physicians make no effort to reduce pain. For older children or adults, local or general anesthesia is used.
4. In any circumcision procedure, the foreskin must first be separated from the glans, forcibly if necessary.

Direct Surgery

In direct surgery, the foreskin is held by clamps and pulled away from the glans. One blade of a scissor (or a scalpel) is inserted between the foreskin and glans and the foreskin is first cut along its full length from the tip to the sulcus (groove). The incision is spread apart to expose the glans. Then, using a scalpel or scissors, the foreskin is completely cut off close to the groove (see Figure 6). Bleeding, if not profuse, is usually controlled by pressure; stitches are rarely required except in older children or adults. Proponents of this free-hand surgery claim that they have full control of the operation since the field of vision is not obstructed, thereby minimizing the problem of removing too much or too little of the foreskin. The procedure usually takes less than 5 minutes. Almost all adolescent and adult circumcision is performed by direct surgery.

Squeeze Technique Using the Gomco Clamp

In the squeeze technique, the foreskin is literally squeezed off. The advantage claimed for this method is that bleeding is minimized, thus reducing the possibility of infection.

Figure 6. Diagrammatic Representation of Circumcision by Direct Surgery.

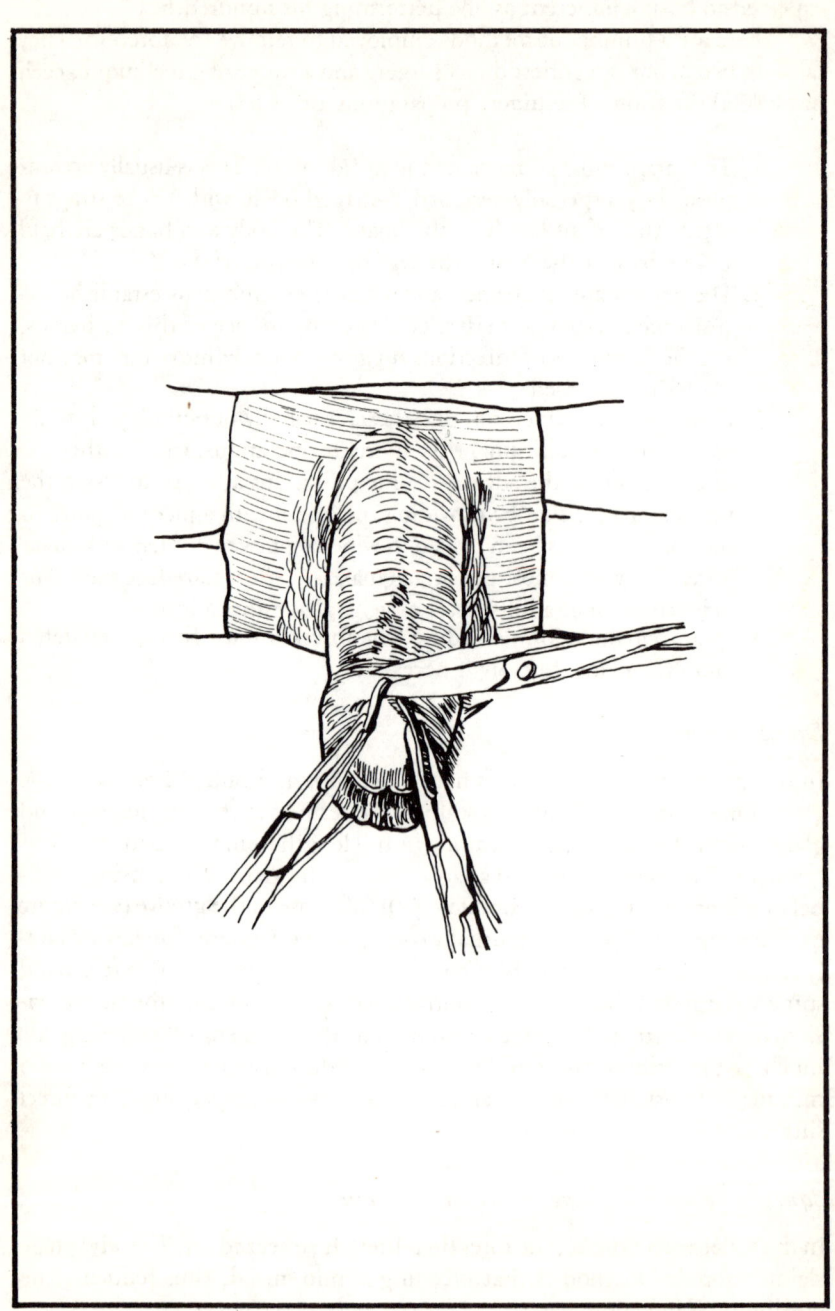

The Gomco clamp consists of three parts (see Figure 7):

1. A flat metal plate (1" × 4") with a hole near one end.
2. A circular metal cap, shaped like a hand bell (approx. 3/8" high and 3/8" diameter) and open at one end to cover the glans. The closed end is attached to a handle, which has a flange perpendicular to it at the opposite end to connect the handle to the screw device.
3. A screw type device, which is attached to the plate to squeeze the cap against the hole in the plate.

In the Gomco method, the foreskin is first cut lengthwise to expose the glans (see Figure 7A). Then the cap is placed over the glans (Figure 7B) and the foreskin is pulled over the cap, stretched, and firmly tied to the cap handle (Figure 7C). The hole in the base plate is placed over the cap handle, and the flange on the handle is fitted into a groove in the screw device (Figure 7D). The foreskin is now firmly held between the metal cap and the rim of the hole in the metal plate. By turning the screw device, the handle and cap are raised, squeezing the foreskin tightly against the plate opening (Figure 7D). While the clamp is squeezing the base of the foreskin, the bulk of the foreskin is cut off (Figure 7E). The clamp remains in place for at least 5 minutes, and when it is released, the base of the foreskin usually can be easily separated from the penile shaft. The entire procedure takes about 10 minutes from the original vertical slit to releasing the clamp.

Squeeze Technique Using the Plastic Bell

This variation of the squeeze technique employs a device called the Plastibell, which consists of a round cap with an attached handle (see Figure 8). Unlike the Gomco cap, the Plastibell has a urine opening and a deep groove. As the name implies, the device is made of sturdy plastic. The principle of this method is almost identical to that of the Gomco clamp, except that the squeezing is done by means of a string.

First the foreskin is slit vertically, exposing the glans (Figures 8A and 8B). Then the cap is inserted under the foreskin and over the glans (Figures 8C and 8D). The foreskin is pulled up over the cap and on to the handle. A string is tied tightly around the foreskin (like a tourniquet), pressing the foreskin base into the cap groove. After about two minutes of squeezing, the foreskin extending beyond the cap is cut off (Figure 8E) and the handle is separated from the cap (Figure 8F). This leaves the cap intact with the base of the foreskin still fastened tightly to it. This position is maintained for 5–10 days, after which time the foreskin usually falls off by itself. (There is an opening in the cap to allow for the passage of urine.) This procedure takes between 5 and 10 minutes from the vertical slit to the removal of the excess foreskin.

Figure 7. Diagrammatic Representation of Circumcision with the Gomco Clamp.

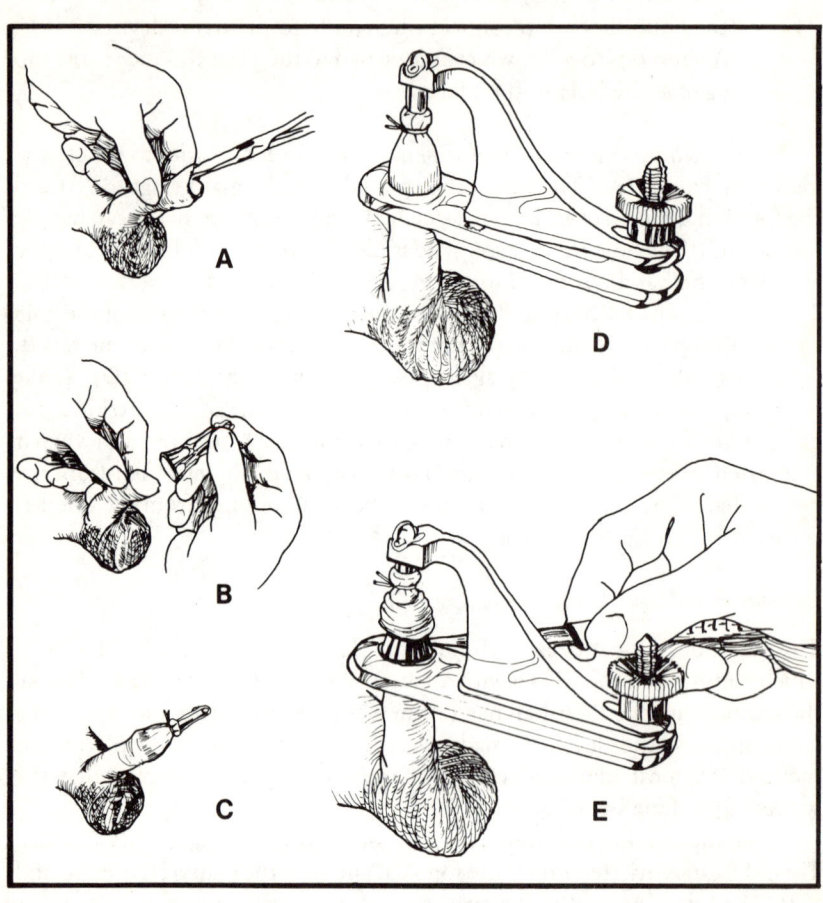

Figure 8. Diagrammatic Representation of Circumcision with the Plastic Bell.

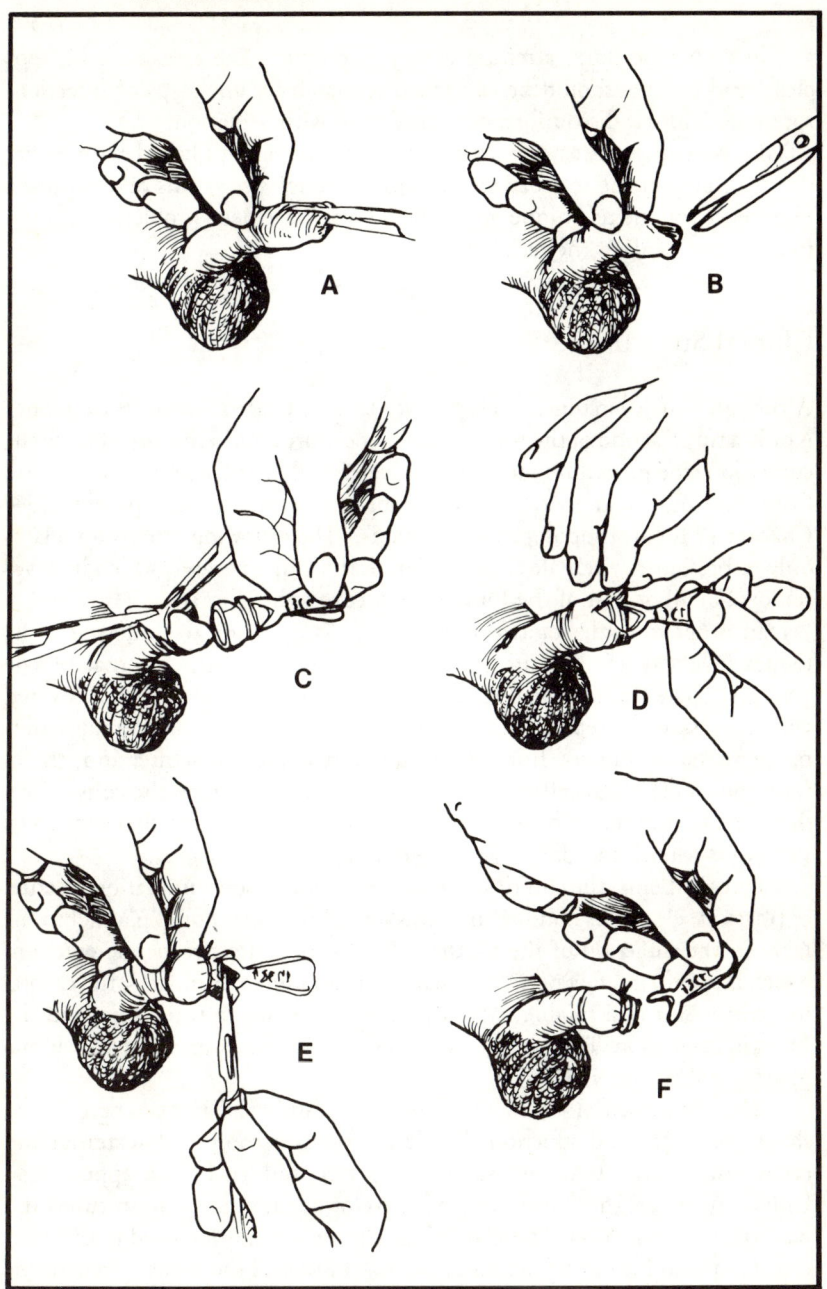

In each procedure, aftercare is very important. The area must be kept clean and parents should be cautioned to watch for any signs of infection, soreness, unusual discomfort, or interference with urination.

In general, satisfactory circumcision can be accomplished with either direct surgery or the squeeze techniques, although physicians may express a preference for one technique or another. There have been problems reported in reference to all of the techniques.

Clitoral Structure

Although female circumcision is practiced in the United States, its frequency is only a tiny fraction of the total of male procedures. As in the case of male circumcision, the procedure must be clearly defined in order to avoid confusion from the loose and inaccurate usage of the term in anthropology. (See Chapter 17 for anthropological definitions.) The following discussion relates only to present-day female circumcision in the United States, which involves removal of all or part of the foreskin that covers the clitoris.

In order to understand this surgery, it is necessary to understand the tissues involved. (See Figure 9 for a representation of the external female genitalia.) The clitoris is analogous to the penis and, like the penis, is covered with a foreskin or prepuce, often called a hood. Both male and female external genitalia are derived from identical embryological structures and, therefore, consist of similar cell and nerve tissues. Thus, the clitoris also consists of a shaft, glans, and foreskin. As does the male's, the clitoral foreskin consists of two layers—inner and outer. The inner layer produces smegma.

Like the penis, the clitoris is a sexual organ and upon stimulation, mental or physical, elongates and becomes thicker. Clitoral erection is parallel to the labia in the direction of the urethra. This is in contrast to penile erection, which is approximately perpendicular to the abdomen. Similarly, the clitoral foreskin is soft and pliable, which permits the glans to extend beyond the foreskin in erection. The foreskin can easily be pulled back to expose the clitoral glans and shaft for washing.

The clitoris differs from the penis in a number of respects, e.g., size, shape, position, and function. While the penis is completely external and easily visible, the clitoris is usually completely hidden by the upper labia. Unlike the penis, the clitoris does not envelop the urethra (urinary tube) and has no urinary function. The shaft of the clitoris is firmly attached to the adjacent tissues and is but a fraction of the size of that of the penis. (As with the penis or any other body structure, there is a wide variation in normal clitoral length, width, foreskin, and erectile state.) Furthermore, the clitoral foreskin does not encircle the organ; instead, it is relatively flat and shaped like an isosceles triangle, with its apex at the base of the clitoris.

Figure 9. Diagrammatic Representation of the Female External Genitalia.

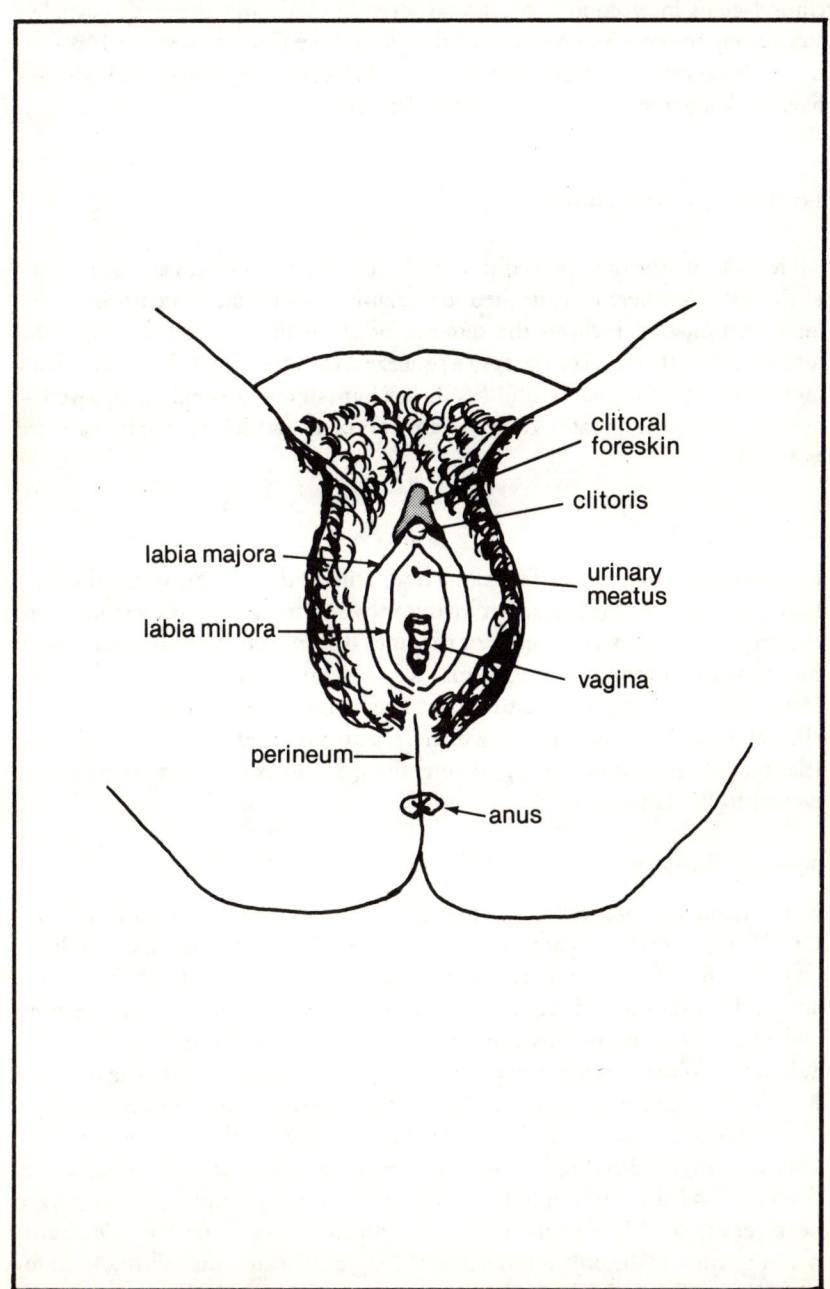

The arms of the triangle are attached to the labia. The base is unattached and may be pulled back to expose the clitoris or to permit the protrusion of the clitoral glans in erection. The clitoral foreskin may cover the shaft partially, completely, or even extend beyond the glans. (See Figures 10A and 10B.)

Clitoral myths abound, but clitoral and foreskin size, shape, and position have no known relationship to sexual pleasure.

Female Circumcision

All female circumcision procedures involve cutting the foreskin along the arms of the triangle where it is attached to the labia. As with male circumcision, female circumcision involves the removal of all or part of both layers of the foreskin, via either direct surgery or a squeeze technique. Since this surgery is almost always performed in adulthood, local anesthesia is usually employed—general anesthesia is rare. A sterile environment and judicious aftercare are essential.

Direct Surgery

Lines are drawn on the foreskin along both arms of the triangle where the foreskin is attached to the labia. An incision (by scalpel or scissors) is made from the base to the apex along each of the lines drawn, thus removing the entire foreskin. An alternative method may also be employed. An incision is made from midpoint in the base to the apex. The incision is separated, exposing the clitoral shaft. The two flaps, which remain attached to the arms of the triangle, are then removed by cutting along the lines where the flaps are attached to the labia.

Squeeze Technique

As the name squeeze technique implies, the foreskin is squeezed off. In 1959, Dr. W. G. Rathmann patented a clamp-type device, which looks like large lockable pliers.[1] At one end are the two handles to control and lock the device, and at the opposite end are two hollow metal triangles. The device is opened and one hollow triangle is inserted between the clitoris and the foreskin. When this lower triangle is in place, the upper triangle is pressed against the lower one by means of the pliers device and locked into position. After about 5 minutes of squeezing, the foreskin is cut off alongside the inner edges of the hollow triangle. Bleeding is controlled by stitches and healing usually takes from 1 to 2 weeks. Although the operation is relatively simple, problems have been reported with both direct surgery and the squeeze method. Dr. Rathmann's article is the only reference to the squeeze technique. Virtually all female circumcisions in the United States are performed via direct surgery.

Figure 10. Diagrammatic Representation of the Clitoris and Its Foreskin.

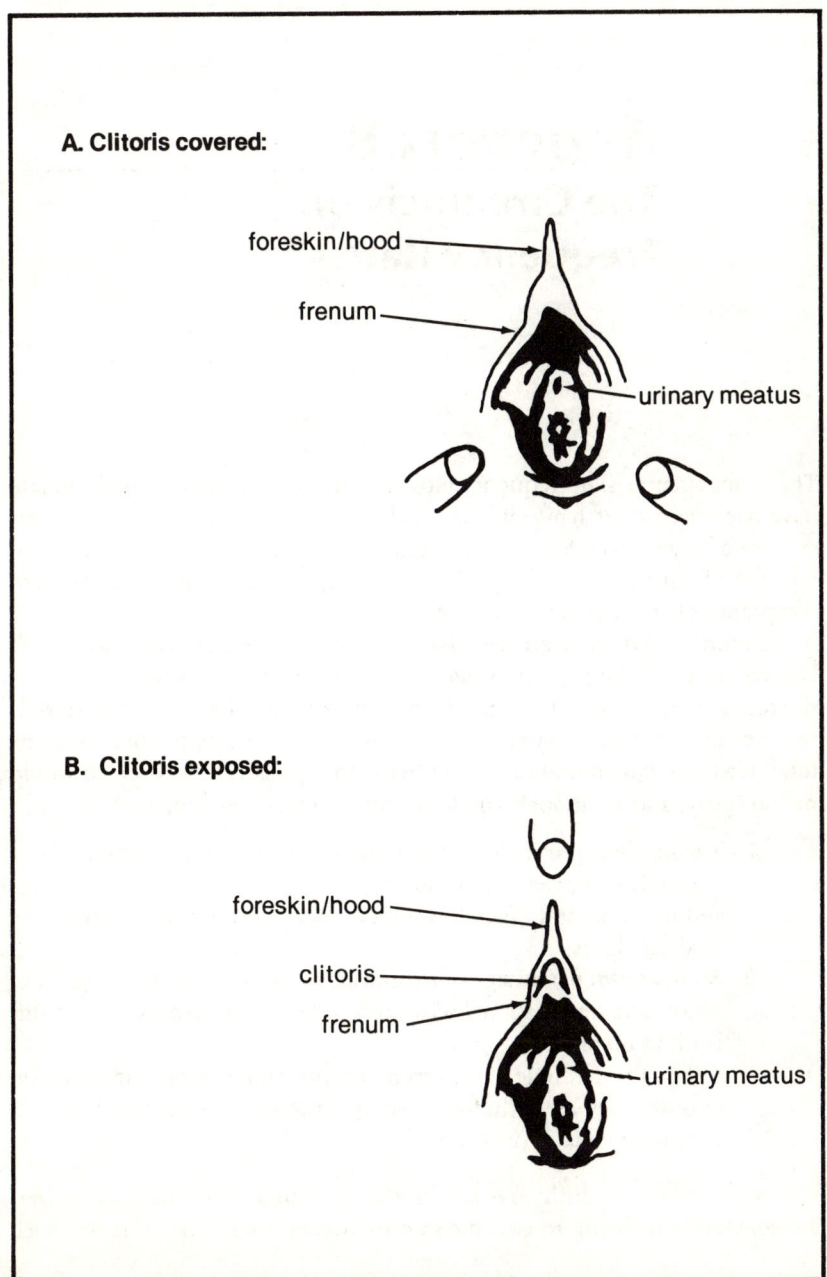

Appendix B
The Circumcision Frequency Rate

The terms circumcision frequency rate, frequency rate, and circumcision rate have been used interchangeably throughout the text. They refer to the percentage of newborn males circumcised in a given time period. An understanding of the frequency rate is helpful in providing an indication of the degree of acceptance of the practice over time.

Unfortunately, accurate records of the circumcision frequency rate for the United States are simply not available. Circumcision surgery was and is considered too unimportant to maintain national statistics. Accurate records could be obtained by (1) a national census or (2) a sample representative of the total newborn male population. Neither plan is practicable. A census would be too costly, and a national sample is close to impossible because:

1. It would have to include a representative sample of many types of hospitals (proprietary, voluntary, municipal, and federal) by size and location, and many hospitals do not record circumcision on the medical charts.[1]
2. An unknown percentage of circumcisions are performed in physicians' offices and on a national scale such individual records would be difficult to obtain.
3. Although the federal government maintains some circumcision records, they are only for those operations performed in hospitals after the neonatal period.[2]

And yet, although there is an absence of accurate national data, writers are constantly referring to circumcision frequency on a national scale. Such

The Circumcision Frequency Rate

rates are based upon educated guesses and nothing more. Some accurate data do exist, but they usually represent an individual hospital at a specific point in time. It is impossible to extrapolate from a given hospital to the entire nation. Some studies provide accurate data for limited samples, which are also not nationally projectible.

Sometimes small samples can be useful in discerning trends and for comparison to statistics obtained from larger studies. For instance, a study in a Canadian hospital showed that in 1952 the circumcision rate was 50% and that in 1962 it was 48%.[3] This compares closely to the reported frequency in 1947 in the Canadian army of 52%.[4]

A national census for 1972 was conducted by the British Department of Health and Social Security, utilizing the records of 400,000 males less than one year old.[5] This number represented almost all boys born that year and the data are, therefore, reliable. The circumcision frequency rate was 0.41%. In the United States, two studies involving rather large numbers of case records (10,000 each) were conducted and the results were as follows: For the year 1950, Columbia Presbyterian Hospital in New York City had a circumcision frequency rate of 75%.[6] For the year circa 1964, Highland Park Hospital in Rochester, N.Y., had a frequency rate of 90% +.[7] Replies to inquiries from 18 American teaching hospitals indicated a circumcision rate of 85% for the 14,000 boys born in those hospitals in 1974.[8] This cannot be taken as a reliable *national* statistic because these 14,000 male births represented less than 1% of American male children born that year. Moreover, the degree to which teaching hospitals reflect all hospitals in regard to circumcision is unknown. A smaller sample, limited to one hospital in California, was provided by Dr. D. Hovsepian for 1949 and 1950.[9] It showed that of 1,878 live male births, 93% were circumcised at birth and an additional 5% within a few days, making a total rate of 98%.

In addition to such limited data, national circumcision frequency figures for the past 10 years are mentioned in medical and lay publications. Selected figures are shown in Table B-1.

Based upon the limited sample statistics in Table B-1 and the *guesstimates* of others, some general conclusions can be drawn:

1. Circumcision was not universally adopted in the United States in any given year or decade. Its acceptance was minimal at first (about 1870), but increased steadily over the next 100 years.
2. It would appear that circumcision was first adopted in large city hospitals and then later was adopted by the rural hospitals.
3. There is no indication of a sharp drop or even a modest decline in the circumcision rate in the United States during any period within the past century.

It is of little significance whether the figures given have an error term of plus or minus 5% or even 10%—the important thing is the trend. Using all data and estimates available, Table B-2, estimated circumcision rates during the past 100 years, was compiled. If anything, Table B-2 errs on the side of caution, using lower percentages.

Table B-1 Selected Male Circumcision Figures

Year	Frequency	Source
Before 1870	8%	Patel[10]
1910	56%	Patel[10]
1930s	75% of middle class	Paige[11]
1941	75% in urban hospitals	Guttmacher[12]
1949-1950	98% in one hospital	Hovsepian[13]
1950	75% in one hospital	Garvin and Persky[14]
1950s	50% plus—of all children	Paige[11]
1954	85% in private hospitals	*Time* magazine[15]
1954	20%-30% of all boys	Holt[16]
1965	90%+ in one hospital	Kariher[17]
1966	60%-97%	Patel[10]
1966	routinely recommended for 95% of newborns delivered in hospitals	Masters and Johnson[18]
1968	60%-90%	*Good Housekeeping*[19]
1970	80%	*Time* magazine[20]
1971	80%	Williams[21]
1963-72	94% in one hospital	Gee and Ansell[22]
1972	90%	*Newsweek* magazine[23]
1973	85%	Morris[24]
1973	60%-97%	Klauber[25]
1973	80%	Grimes[26]
1974	98% U.S. Army Airforce hospitals	Schwark[27]
1974	80% Hospital record study	Wirth[28]
1976	87% California medical program	Paige[11]

Table B–2 Estimated Male Circumcision Rates in the United States

Year	Frequency (%)
1870	5%
1880	10%
1890	15%
1900	25%
1910	35%
1920	50%
1930	55%
1940	60%
1950	70%
1960	75%
1970	80%
1979	85%

Appendix C
The American College of Obstetricians and Gynecologists (ACOG) Position on Circumcision

In December 1978 the Executive Board of ACOG issued a statement of policy headed "STATEMENT ON NEONATAL CIRCUMCISION." The opening sentence reads:

> The American College of Obstetricians and Gynecologists supports the position of the AAP [American Academy of Pediatrics] ad hoc Task Force on Circumcision (1975) that "there is no absolute medical indication for routine circumcision of the newborn."

Unlike the AAP which made its 1975 position public by publishing it in *Pediatrics,* its official journal, thereby achieving wide dissemination, ACOG sent the STATEMENT ON NEONATAL CIRCUMCISION only to its own members via the ACOG *Newsletter.* The Statement was not published in the ACOG *Journal* and is not listed in the *Index Medicus.* The medical community is therefore not generally aware of the change in the ACOG position on circumcision. The matter was called to my attention by sheer coincidence 1½ years after the fact. To my knowledge, this is the first time that the ACOG position is made public.

Notes to Chapters

2 The Circumcision Mystique*

1. Gerald Oster, "The Modern Look of Ice Age Art," *Natural History*, vol. 87, no. 8, Oct. 1978, p. 108.
2. Ashley Montague, "Circumcision," *Encyclopedia Britannica* (Chicago: William Benton, 1973), vol. 5, p. 800.
3. Leonard V. Snowman, "Circumcision," *Encyclopedia Judaica* (Jerusalem, Israel: Macmillan Co., 1971), vol. 5, p. 568.
4. Richard A. Gould, *Yiwara* (New York: Scribner's, 1969), pp. 110, 112-3, 117, 119, 209.
5. Subincision is obviously a painful ordeal. It was so described by Gould (above) and others. See *The Making of Man*, edited by V. G. Calverton (New York: Modern Libr., 1931), p. 292. However Felix Bryk, *Circumcision in Man and Woman*, originally published 1930, reprinted (New York, AMS Press, 1974), quotes a German anthropologist, Eylmann (1908), who wrote, ". . . primitive people, like the Australians . . . are much less sensitive to bodily pain than we. . . ." (p. 98). Bryk also quotes Otto Stoll (1908): "The indifference to foreign bodily pain prevailing among primitive peoples . . . " (p. 142). These statements are myth, not fact.
6. Richard F. Burton, *Personal Narrative of a Pilgrimage to Al-Medinah and Mecca*, originally published, 1893. Reprinted 1962 (New York: Dover), vol. 2, p. 110.
7. Gould, *Yiwara*, p. 112.
8. "The Redundant Maya," *Scientific American*, vol. 238, no. 5, May 1978, p. 96.
9. For a fuller discussion of the Jewish circumcision rituals, see Chapter 16.
10. Genesis, 17: 10-14.
11. Acts, 15: 1-31.
12. Acts, 16: 3.
13. Robert P. Bolande "Ritualistic Surgery: Circumcision and Tonsillectomy," *New England Journal of Medicine*, vol. 280, no. 11, March 13, 1969, pp. 591-592.
14. *Encyclopedia Britannica*, vol. 5, p. 799.
15. Sigmund Freud, *Moses and Monotheism* (New York: Vantage Books, 1959), p. 34.

*There are no notes to Chapter 1: Questions to Answer; Answers to Question.

16. Snowman, "Circumcision," *Encyclopedia Judaica*, vol. 5, p. 572.
17. Ibid., pp. 575 and 577.
18. Eugene A. Hand, "History of Circumcision," *Journal Michigan State Medical Society*, vol. 49, no. 5, May 1950, p. 573, 574.
19. Robert Briffault, *The Mothers*, abridged (New York: Macmillan, 1959), p. 398.
20. Vern L. Bullough, *Sexual Variance in Society and History* (New York: Wiley, 1976), p. 60.
21. *Women's International Network News*, vol. 3, no. 1, Winter 1977, p. 26. (Also see Chapter 17 on Female Circumcision.)
22. *Encyclopedia Judaica*, vol. 5, p. 576.
23. Felix Bryk, *Circumcision in Man and Woman* (New York: AMS Press, 1974), pp. 23-28. This was originally published in 1930. See also Peter Charles Remondino, *History of Circumcision From The Earliest Times To The Present*, 1st ed. (New York: AMS Press, 1974), pp. 70-75. Originally published in 1891.
24. August Forel, *The Sexual Question* (Brooklyn: Physicians and Surgeons Book Co., 1931), p. 348. Originally published in German in 1906. Dr. Forel spelled the name Blaubekin and claimed the nun became psychotic.
25. L. H. Gray, "Circumcision," *Encyclopedia of Religion and Ethics* (New York: Scribner's, 1959), vol. 10, pp. 659-680.
26. J. C. Frazer, "The Origin Of Circumcision," *Albany Review* (London, England), vol. 4, 1904, p. 209.
27. Gould, *Yiwara*, p. 116.
28. Gray, *Encyclopedia of Religion and Ethics*, p. 663.
29. Act V, Scene 2.
30. Sutor was a French army surgeon who traveled extensively to colonial outposts and wrote under the pen name of Jacobus X. His book, *Wanderings in Untrodden Fields of Anthropology*—the French title was, *L'Amour Aux Colonies* (Paris, France: I. Liseau, 1893)—was expanded for its 1898 English-language edition and was republished in Paris in 1935 in five volumes under the title, *L'Ethnologie du Sens Genitale*. (See footnote 31 below for source of information about Sutor.)
31. Allen Edwards and R. E. L. Masters, *The Cradle of Erotica* (New York: Julian Press, 1963), pp. 15 and 16.
32. Ibid., p. 15.
33. Ibid., p. 65
34. Ibid., p. 16.
35. Ibid., p. 45.
36. Ibid., p. 55.
37. Ibid., p. 235.
38. In writing this book the author queried many people about their knowledge and attitude to circumcision. Surprisingly, several men responded with the "fact" that circumcision permits the penis to achieve maximum size, since the foreskin retards growth. Also see Remondino, *History of Circumcision*, p. 187; and R. J. Valentine (a pseudonym), "Adult Circumcision: A Personal Report," *Medical Aspects of Human Sexuality*, vol. 8, no. 1, Jan. 1974, p. 33.
39. Edwards and Masters, *Cradle of Erotica*, p. 89.
40. Abraham Ravich, *Preventing V.D. and Cancer by Circumcision*, (New York: Philosophical Library, 1973), pp. 155 and 156.

41. Wayland Young, *Eros Denied*, (New York: Grove Press, 1964), p. 322.
42. Ibid., p. 322, quoting from Gunnar Myrdal, *An American Dilemma* (New York, 1944).
43. Ibid., p. 323.
44. Ibid., p. 324.
45. Bryk, *Circumcision in Man and Woman*, p. 102.
46. Ibid., p. 105.
47. Remondino, *History of Circumcision*, p. 162.
48. "Circumcision & V.D.," *Newsweek*, vol. 30, no. 3, July 21, 1947, p. 49.
49. William H. Masters and Virginia E. Johnson, *Human Sexual Response* (Boston: Little, Brown, 1966), p. 190.
50. Remondino, *History of Circumcision*, p. 270.
51. The word "infibulation" is derived from *fibula*, or clasp, used in ancient Rome. Passed through the foreskin or labia, it prevented sexual intercourse among slaves.

3 The Medical Mystique

1. George W. Kaplan, "Circumcision—An Overview," *Current Problems In Pediatrics*, vol. 7, no. 5, March 1977, p. 3.
2. Boyce Rensberger, "Fraud in Research is a Rising Problem In Science," *New York Times*, Jan. 23, 1977, p. 1.
3. Charles C. Sherman, "Circumcision," *The New Schaff Herzog Encyclopedia of Religious Knowledge*, (Grand Rapids: Baker Book House, 1967), vol. 3, p. 119.
4. More may exist, but they do not appear in any publication index for trade or scientific books or in medical or general library card files. Anthropological and religious books are not included. Two additional books should be noted. In 1967 the Brandon House (North Hollywood, Calif.) published *Sex and Circumcision*, by Felix Bryk. Ostensibly a new book, the publication was actually a reprint of *Circumcision in Man and Woman*, by the same author, written in 1930 in German and published in the United States in 1934 (New York, American Ethnological Press) (later reprinted by AMS Press, 1974). This is an ethnological study. The other book, *Routine Circumcision: The Tragic Myth* by Nicholas Carter (London, England: Londimium Press, 1979), is a brief volume (144 pages), containing many accurate reports from the circumcision literature and reflecting some painstaking research. As such, it would ordinarily be welcomed as a contribution to the circumcision debate. Unfortunately, the work is seriously flawed. Mr. Carter is vehemently opposed to routine newborn circumcision. However, his presentation is so filled with rhetoric and outrage that it obscures much of his positive reporting. This tone is reflected early in the volume, where reasons for American circumcision practices are given, among them, "the neurotic, sexually frustrated woman who derives satisfaction from the mutilation of the male organ" p. 27. Circumcision is described as "mutilation" throughout the book, or by such terms as "psychologically compelling mutilation," the "desire to mutilate," and "self-mutilation." His handling of data is questionable. As an example, with regard to cervical cancer, Mr. Carter confuses incidence with death rate

and claims that both have dropped (p. 45). The facts are that the death rate has dropped but the incidence has risen. Finally, when Mr. Carter ventures into psychology and psychiatry, he makes many unsubstantiated generalizations and suggests that a long list of conditions may be related to circumcision: homosexuality, autism, hyperkinesis, learning disabilities, dyslexia, allergies, skin conditions, stammering, stuttering, and sudden infant death. (pp. 90, 112, 113, 115)

 5. Herbert Now, *The Barbarity of Circumcision As A Remedy For Congenital Abnormalities* (London: J. and A. Churchill Co., 1890).

 6. M. Clifford, *Circumcision: Its Advantages And How To Perform It* (London: Churchill Co., 1893).

 7. Peter Charles Remondino, *History of Circumcision From The Earliest Times to the Present* (Philadelphia: F. A. Davis Co., 1891; republished, 1st ed. (New York: AMS Press, 1974), p. 10.

 8. Ibid., p. 114.

 9. Ibid., p. 52.

 10. Ibid., p. 49.

 11. See the *New York Public Library and Branches, Catalogue 1978, Vol. A-Cit.* This catalogue lists the 1974 publication date without indicating that it was first published in 1891. The 1979 subject catalogue lists *no* book on circumcision.

 12. Robert J. Valentine (a pseudonym). "Adult Circumcision: A Personal Report," *Medical Aspects of Human Sexuality,* vol. 8, no. 1, Jan. 1974, p. 42. Dr. Lester Persky, a urologist, (though an ardent supporter of circumcision) was so angered by Dr. Valentine's outrageous claims that he wrote a reply in the same issue of the journal, page 50, to remind Dr. Valentine that " . . . the greatest sex organ lies between the ears."

 13. Joseph Lewis, *In the Name of Humanity,* 2nd ed. (New York: Eugenics Publishing, 1956), pp. 84, 91.

 14. Ibid., pp. 106, 110, 138, 142.

 15. John M. Foley, *The Practice of Circumcision: A Reevaluation,* 1st ed. (New York: Materia Medica Press, 1966), pp. 4, 5.

 16. Abraham Ravich, *Preventing V.D. and Cancer By Circumcision,* 1st ed. (New York: Philosophical Library, 1973).

 17. Ibid., pp. 80, 81, 87, 88, 94, 99, 155–156.

 18. Ibid., p. 159.

 19. Ibid., p. 158.

 20. Ibid., p. 149.

 21. Ibid., p. 47.

 22. Ibid., p. 99.

 23. Ibid., pp. 45–46.

 24. "Circumcision and V. D.," *Newsweek,* vol. 30, no. 3, July 21, 1947, p. 49.

 25. Robert P. Bolande, "Ritualistic Surgery: Circumcision and Tonsillectomy," *New England Journal of Medicine,* vol. 280, no. 11, Mar. 13, 196, pp. 591, 592. "Morgan" is a reference to William K. C. Morgan's "The Rape of the Phallus," which appeared in *Journal of the American Medical Association,* vol. 193, no. 3, July 19, 1965, p. 124.

 26. Ibid., p. 593.

27. R. S. Ganelin, Letter to Editor, *New England Journal of Medicine*, vol. 280, no. 19, May 8, 1969, pp. 1076-1077.

28. Nelson, Vaughn, and McCay, *Pediatrics*, 10th ed. (Philadelphia: Saunders, 1975), p. 1370.

29. Meredith F. Campbell, *Urology*, 2nd ed. (Philadelphia: Saunders, 1963), vol. 3, p. 1974.

30. O. Swenson, *Pediatric Surgery* (New York: Appleton-Century-Crofts, 1958), p. 547.

31. Willard E. Goodwin, Letter to Editor, *Journal of the American Medical Association*, vol. 214, no. 2, Oct. 12, 1970, p. 375.

32. J. A. Little, Reply to Query, *Journal of the American Medical Association*, vol. 194, no. 3, Oct. 1965, p. 319.

33. Robert A. Shaw and W. O. Robertson, "Routine Circumcision," *American Journal Diseases of Children*, vol. 106, no. 2, Aug. 1963, pp. 216-217.

34. A. G. M. Campbell, et al., "Circumcision," *Patient Care*, vol. 5, no. 13, July 15, 1971, p. 56.

35. Morgan, p. 123.

36. Boyce Rensberger, "Unfit Doctors Create Worry in Profession," *New York Times*, Jan. 26, 1976, p. 1; Jane E. Brody, "Incompetent Surgery Is Found Not Isolated," *New York Times*, Jan. 27, 1976, p. 1; Boyce Rensberger, "Few Doctors Ever Report Colleagues' Incompetence," *New York Times*, Jan. 29, 1976, p. 1; Richard D. Lyons, "A.M.A. Meets Here, Facing New Pressure," *New York Times*, June 24, 1973, p. 1. Senator Edward Kennedy reported that Massachusetts has as many neurosurgeons as Great Britain, and they each perform the same number of operations each year, but England has eight times as many people.

37. Ronald S. Illingworth, *The Normal Child*, 4th ed. (Boston: Little, Brown, 1968), p. 98.

38. Editorial, *Journal of the American Medical Association*, vol. 185, no. 10, Sept. 7, 1963, p. 780. Copyright 1963, American Medical Association.

39. Morgan, p. 123.

40. W. K. C. Morgan, Reply to Dr. J. Greenblatt, *American Journal Diseases of Children*, vol. 111, no. 4, April 1966, p. 448.

41. E. Noel Preston, "Whither the Foreskin?", *Journal of the Medical Association*, vol. 213, no. 11, Sept. 14, 1970, pp. 1853-1858.

42. Jack R. Harnes, "The Foreskin Saga," *Journal of the American Medical Association*, vol. 217, no. 9, Aug. 30, 1971, p. 1241.

43. Kaplan, "Circumcision—An Overview," p. 31.

44. "Report of the Ad Hoc Task Force on Circumcision," *Pediatrics*, vol. 56, no. 4, Oct., 1975, p. 610. Copyright American Academy of Pediatrics 1975.

45. Lester Persky, Reply to Query, *Medical Aspects of Human Sexuality*, vol. 11, no. 2, Feb., 1977, p. 92.

46. Benjamin Spock, Letter to Editor, *Moneysworth*, vol. 5, no. 5, Mar. 29, 1976, p. 12. Reprinted by permission of the publisher.

47. R. Dagher, M. L. Selzer, and J. Lapides, "Carcinoma of the Penis and the Anti-Circumcision Crusade," *Journal of Urology*, vol. 110, no. 1, July 1973, pp. 79, 80.

48. See note 38.

49. Karen E. Paige, "The Ritual of Circumcision," *Human Nature,* vol. 1, no. 5, May 1978, p. 44, pp. 46-47.

4 Why Only in the United States?

1. Desmond Morris, *Intimate Behavior* (New York: Bantam Books, 1973), p. 243.
2. Ronald S. Illingworth, *The Normal Child,* 4th ed. (Boston: Little, Brown, 1968), p. 98.
3. Hawa Patel, "The Problem of Routine Circumcision," *Canadian Medical Journal,* vol. 95, no. 11, Sept. 10, 1966, p. 579.
4. Roscoe L. Wall, Jr., "Routine Circumcision? Recent Trends and Concepts," *North Carolina Medical Journal,* vol. 29, no. 3, March 1968, p. 103.
5. Patel, "Routine Circumcision," p. 579.
6. Charles Weiss, "Circumcision In Infancy," *Clinical Pediatrics,* vol. 3, no. 9, Sept. 1964, p. 560.
7. Patel, "Routine Circumcision," p. 579.
8. M. P. M. Richards, J. F. Bernal, and Yvonne Brackbill, "Early Behavioral Differences: Gender or Circumcision?," *Journal of Developmental Psychobiology,* vol. 9, no. 1, Jan. 1976, p. 91.
9. Weiss, "Circumcision in Infancy," p. 560.
10. Richards et al., "Early Behavioral Differences," p. 93*f.*
11. W. K. C. Morgan, "Penile Plunder," *The Medical Journal of Australia,* vol. 1, May 27, 1967, pp. 1102-1103.
12. Editorial Comments, *The Medical Journal of Australia,* 58th Year, vol. 2, no. 4, July 24, 1971, p. 175.
13. Ibid.
14. See note 5.
15. John L. Wirth, "Statistics on Circumcision in Canada and Australia," *American Journal of Obstetrics and Gynecology,* vol. 130, no. 2, Jan. 15, 1978, pp. 236-239. The Australian figures cover those births compensated by the Health Service. The Canadian figures are a nonweighted average of all provinces.
16. R. Burger and T. H. Guthrie, "Why Circumcision?" *Pediatrics,* vol. 54, no. 3, Sept. 1974, pp. 362-364.
17. Medical libraries the world over carry publications from almost every other country. The *Index Medicus,* which is used world-wide, lists articles published in almost every country. Thus every major medical library in the world carries American publications and vice versa. In fact, foreign physicians are more likely to be familiar with American medical literature than American physicians are with foreign medical literature. There are probably more medical journals published in the United States than the rest of the world put together.
18. Editorial Comment, "Science For the Citizen," *Scientific American,* vol. 229, no. 3, Sept. 1973, p. 64. Regarding infant mortality, 14 countries had a lower rate than the United States, including Sweden, Japan, France, Canada, Great Britain, and East Germany.

19. Richard J. Gelles, "Violence Toward Children in the United States," *American Journal of Orthopsychiatry*, vol. 48, no. 4, Oct. 1978, pp. 580–592.

20. Barbara Campbell, "Children's Abuse Target of Drive," *New York Times*, Aug. 15, 1976, p. 60. In 1973, 50,000 American children died and 300,000 were permanently injured by child abuse.

21. "Hunger's Lifelong Effects," *New York Times*, (sec. IV: p. 5) May 5, 1974. Moreover, 75% to 85% of the reported mentally defective and retarded children born in the United States each year are born in poverty, and many of these problems are directly attributable to malnutrition.

22. John J. Witte, *Health Education Report*, vol. 1, no. 7, Nov.–Dec. 1974. This report is issued by the Center for Disease Control, Department of Health, Education and Welfare.

23. Catherine V. Richards, *Children Today*, vol. 5, no. 4 July/Aug. 1976, p. 31. Book review of John G. Cull and Ricard E. Hurdy (Eds.), *Problems of Runaway Youth*, (Springfield, Ill.: Charles C Thomas, 1976).

24. Dr. Valdemar Kirkland, Assistant Director of the National Health Service, Oslo, Norway. Personal interview, August 1973.

25. Dr. Dag Riis, Director of an Oslo well-baby clinic, Oslo, Norway. Telephone interview, August 1973.

26. A. J. Wabrek and C. J. Wabrek, "Dyspareunia," *Journal of Sex and Marital Therapy*, vol. 1, no. 3, Spring 1975, p. 235.

27. A. S. Härö, Director, Department of Planning and Evaluation, The National Board of Health, Helsinki, Finland. Private correspondence, Oct. 24, 1973.

28. Vern L. Bullough, *Sexual Variance in Society and History* (New York: Wiley, 1976), p. 542.

29. Benjamin Rush, *Medical Inquiries and Observations Upon the Diseases of the Mind* (Philadelphia: Kimber and Richards, 1812), p. 347.

30. Ibid.

31. Sylvester Graham, *A Lecture to Young Men on Chastity, Intended also for the Serious Consideration of Parents and Guardians*, 10th Edit. (Boston: C.H. Pierce, 1848).

32. Bullough, "Sexual Variance," p. 543.

33. Ibid., p. 546.

34. John Duffy, "Masturbation and Clitoridectomy," *Journal of the American Medical Association*, vol. 186, no. 3, Oct. 19, 1963, p. 248.

35. Bullough, pp. 542–549.

36. Ibid., p. 545.

37. Ibid.

38. Ibid.

39. Lee Coleman, "Problem Kids and Preventative Medicine," *American Journal of Orthopsychiatry*, vol. 48, no. 1, Jan. 1978, p. 68.

40. Bullough, "Sexual Variance," p. 546.

41. Ibid., p. 540.

42. Ibid., p. 542.

43. Ibid., p. 548.

44. Ibid., p. 549.

45. Ibid. For a complete list of anti-masturbation patents see Bullough, pages 561 and 562.
46. Ibid., p. 546.
47. John Duffy, p. 247.
48. Ibid, p. 248.
49. Ibid.
50. Ibid., p. 246.
51. Bullough, "Sexual Variance," p. 552.
52. Stephen Kern, *Anatomy and Destiny* (Indianapolis: Bobbs-Merrill, 1975), p. 42.
53. Bullough, "Sexual Variance," pp. 552-553.
54. George T. Klauber, "Circumcision and Phallic Fallacies, or the Case Against Routine Circumcision," *Connecticut Medicine,* vol. 37, no. 9, Sept. 1973, p. 445.
55. Nora Ephron, *Crazy Salad—Some Things About Women* (New York: Bantam Books, 1976), pp. 84-85. Mum was the first trademark brand a few years after 1870. Odo-ro-no was introduced in 1914.
56. René Spitz, "Authority and Masturbation," *Psychoanalytic Quarterly,* vol. 21, no. 4, 1952, pp. 502-503. The Sachs book was *Treatise on Nervous Diseases of Children,* (New York: William Wood, Co., 1905). The "leading textbook on pediatrics" referred to was by L. E. Holt, *Diseases of Infancy and Childhood,* (New York, Appleton Century, 1897), which was published in updated editions until 1936.
57. Aubre de L. Maynard, *Surgeons to the Poor* (New York: Appleton-Century-Crofts, 1978), p. 3.
58. E. H. Pratt, *Orificial Surgery and Its Application to Chronic Diseases* (Chicago: Halsey Bros., 1890).
59. E. H. Pratt, *Orificial Surgery,* (Kansas City, Kan.: Western Baptist Publications Co., 1925).
60. Spitz, "Authority and Masturbation," p. 503.
61. Ibid., p. 504.
62. Ibid., p. 503.
63. C. S. Eaton, "Circumcision for Headaches," *Journal of Orificial Surgery,* vol. 8, no. 8, Feb. 1900, pp. 369-370.
64. M. K. Kreider, "A Few Cases of Circumcision," *Journal of Orificial Surgery,* vol. 6, no. 1, July 1897, p. 8.
65. C. B. Walls, "Circumcision—Is It A Fad?," *Journal of Orificial Surgery,* vol. 5, no. 4, Oct. 1896, pp. 507-508, 511.
66. T. E. Costain, "Circumcision," *Journal of Orificial Surgery,* vol. 9, no. 1, July 1900, pp. 160-161.
67. Bullough, "Sexual Variance," p. 547.
68. S. L. Kistler, "Rapid Bloodless Circumcision of Male and Female and Its Technic," *Journal of the American Medical Association,* vol. 54, no. 22, May 28, 1910, pp. 1782-1783.
69. Lester Persky, Reply to a Query, *Medical Aspects of Human Sexuality,* vol. 11, no. 2, Feb. 1977, p. 92.

5 The Circumcision Decision: Is It Informed Consent?

1. J. E. Wright, "Non-Therapeutic Circumcision," *The Medical Journal of Australia,* vol. 1, no. 22, May 27, 1967, p. 1086.
2. A. G. M. Campbell, et al., "Circumcision," *Patient Care,* vol. 5, no. 13, July 15, 1971, p. 71.
3. Edward B. Feehan, Letter to the Editor, *Pediatrics,* vol. 60, no. 4, Oct. 1977, p. 566.
4. Robert A. Shaw and W. O. Robertson, "Routine Circumcision," *American Journal Diseases of Children,* vol. 106, no. 2, Aug. 1963, pp. 216–217.
5. Hawa Patel, "The Problem of Routine Circumcision," *Canadian Medical Journal,* vol. 95, no. 11, Sept. 10, 1966, p. 581.
6. Deron Hovsepian, "The Pros & Cons of Routine Circumcision," *California Medicine,* vol. 75, no. 5, Nov. 1951, p. 360.
7. George W. Kaplan, "Circumcision—An Overview," *Current Problems in Pediatrics,* vol. 7, no. 5, March 1977, pp. 14-15.
8. June V. Schwartz and Emma R. Botts, *The Very New Baby: The First Days of Life* (New York: Public Affairs Pamphlets), No. 553, 1977.
9. A. G. M. Campbell, et al., "Circumcision," p. 57.
10. M. Terris, F. Wilson, and J. H. Nelson, "Relation of Circumcision to Cancer of the Cervix," *American Journal of Obstetrics and Gynecology* vol. 117, no. 8, Dec. 15, 1973, pp. 1056–1057.
11. Abraham M. Lilienfeld and Saxon Graham, "Validity of Determining Circumcision Status by Questionnaire as Related to Epidemiological Studies of Cancer of the Cervix," *Journal of the National Cancer Institute,* vol. 21, no. 4, Oct. 1958, pp. 713–720.
12. Barbara Seaman, "Circumcision, The Pros & Cons," *Woman's Day,* Aug. 1976, p. 40.
13. Alan F. Guttmacher, "Should the Baby Be Circumcised?," *Parents' Magazine,* vol. 16, no. 9, Sept. 1941, p. 26.
14. "Circumcision and Venereal Disease," *Newsweek,* vol. 30, no. 3, July 21, 1947, p. 49.
15. "Information for Mothers," Reply to Query, *Hygeia Magazine,* vol. 25, Nov. 1947, p. 819.
16. "Circumcision & Cancer," *Time* magazine, vol. 63, no. 14, Apr. 5, 1954, p. 96.
17. L. E. Holt, Jr. "Circumcision," *Good Housekeeping,* vol. 139, Aug. 1954, p. 128.
18. Ibid., p. 129.
19. Ibid.
20. E. J. Wilkes, "Should Your Son Be Circumcised?," *Parents' Magazine,* vol. 34, no. 2, Feb. 1959, p. 50.
21. "Circumcision Urged To Prevent Cancer," *Science Newsletter,* vol. 86, no. 18, Oct. 31, 1964, p. 281.
22. "The Medical Controversy Over Circumcision," Editorial, *Good Housekeeping,* vol. 167, Sept. 1968, p. 179.

23. E. Noel Preston, "Whither the Foreskin?" *Journal of the American Medical Association*, vol. 213, no. 11, Sept. 14, 1970, pp. 1853-1858.
24. Jane E. Brody, "A Restudy Urged on Circumcision," *New York Times*, Sept. 20, 1970, p. 19.
25. "Report of the Ad Hoc Task Force on Circumcision," *Pediatrics*, vol. 56, no. 4, Oct. 1975, p. 611. Copyright American Academy of Pediatrics 1975.
26. Barbara Yunker, "New Policy on Circumcision," *Good Housekeeping*, Vol. 182, No. 2, Feb., 1976, p. 40.
27. Barbara Seaman, "Circumcision," pp. 40, 152.
28. Alice Lake, "Circumcision: Is It Necessary?," *McCall's*, vol. 103, no. 9, June 1976, p. 36.
29. Andrew Kapuciunas, "Pediatricians Score Circumcision As Needless and Risky," *Moneysworth*, Jan. 19, 1976, p. 1.
30. Letters to the Editor, *Moneysworth*, Mar. 29, 1976, p. 12.
31. Jane E. Brody, "Pros and Cons of Circumcision," *New York Times*, Jan. 24, 1979, p. C13.
32. Benjamin Spock, *Baby and Child Care*, (New York: Pocket Books, 1946), p. 18.
33. Ibid., p. 17.
34. Benjamin Spock, *Baby and Child Care*, (New York, N.Y.: Hawthorne Books, 4th Edit., 1976), p. 191.
35. Benjamin Spock, Letter to Editor, *Moneysworth*, March 29, 1976, p. 12.
36. Virginia E. Pomerantz and Dodi Shultz, *The Mother's Medical Encyclopedia* (New York: Signet Reference Books, 1972), p. 99; David T. Hellyer, *Your Child and You* (New York: Delacorte Press, 1966), pp. 32-33.
37. Gideon G. Panter and Shirley Mitter Linde, *Now That You've Had Your Baby* (New York: David McKay, 1976), pp. 18-19.
38. R. H. Pontell, J. F. Fries, and D. M. Vickey, *Taking Care Of Your Child*, (Reading, Mass.: Addison Wesley, 1977), p. 29.
39. John LaPlace, *Health* (New York: Appleton-Century-Crofts, 1972), p. 208.
40. The use of redundancy as an excuse for circumcision dates back before the turn of the century. The founder of the Orificial Surgical Society, E. H. Pratt, wrote in "The Orificial Philosophy," *Journal of Orificial Surgery*, vol. 2, no. 12, June 1894, p. 528: "The foreskin which completely covers the glans in the relaxed state is too long. . . . A redundant foreskin is most common." Virtually all foreskins completely cover the glans in the relaxed state; it certainly is "most common." That does not make them "too long."
41. The Boston Women's Health Book Collective, *Our Bodies Ourselves*, 1st ed. (New York: Simon & Schuster, 1973), p. 265.
42. The Boston Women's Health Book Collective, *Our Bodies Ourselves*, 2nd ed. (New York: Simon & Schuster, 1976), p. 145.

6 The Ill-Fated Foreskin: Is It All Bad?

1. W. H. Masters and V. E. Johnson, *Human Sexual Response*, 1st ed. (Boston: Little, Brown, 1966).

2. "W.H.O. Urges Sex Education for Medics," *Washington Post,* Feb. 16, 1975, Sec. L, p. 15.

3. Mary Jane Sherfey, in "Some Biology of Sexuality," *Journal of Sex and Marital Therapy,* vol. 1, no. 2, Winter 1974, p. 103, commented: "Since Masters and Johnson, there has been no research, that I know of on these mysterious muscles of the orgasm." W. Charles Lobitz, in Reply to a Query, *Medical Aspects of Human Sexuality,* vol. 10, no. 11, Nov. 1976, p. 115, stated: "Despite the research of Masters and Johnson and others, relatively little is known about the neurophysiology of sexual response." Michael L. LaRocque, in Reply to a Query, *Medical Aspects of Human Sexuality,* vol. 10, no. 3, March 1976, p. 125, noted: "The precise mechanism releasing the erectile state has not been elucidated." Bernard H. Smith, in Reply to a Query, *Medical Aspects of Human Sexuality,* vol. 10, no. 7, July 1976, p. 86, said: "The hemodynamics of penile erection and detumescence are delicate and ill understood."

4. D. Gairdner, "The Fate of the Foreskin," *British Medical Journal,* vol. 2, Dec. 24, 1949, p. 1433.

5. Deron Hovsepian, "The Pros and Cons of Routine Circumcision," *California Medicine,* vol. 75, no. 5, Nov. 1951, p. 359.

6. J. E. Wright, "Non-Therapeutic Circumcision," *Medical Journal of Australia,* vol. 1, no. 22, May 27, 1967, p. 1086.

7. R. S. Illingworth, *The Normal Child,* (Boston: Little, Brown, 1972), pp. 110–111.

8. Peter Charles Remondino, *History of Circumcision from the Earliest Times to the Present,* 1st ed. (New York: AMS Press, 1974), pp. 218, 246. Originally published in 1891 by F. A. Davis, Philadelphia.

9. Robert J. Valentine (a pseudonym), "Adult Circumcision: A Personal Report," *Medical Aspects of Human Sexuality,* vol. 8, no. 1, Jan. 1974, pp. 42, 48.

10. George W. Kaplan, "Circumcision—An Overview," *Current Problems in Pediatrics,* vol. 7, no. 5, March 1977, pp. 23–24.

11. Gairdner, "The Fate of Foreskin," pp. 1434, 1435.

12. Meredith F. Campbell, *Urology,* 2nd ed. (Philadelphia: Saunders, 1963) vol. 3, p. 1974.

13. Howard C. Mofenson and J. Greensher, "Penile Trauma in Boys," *Medical Aspects of Human Sexuality,* vol. 9, no. 8, Aug. 1975, p.71.

14. Wright, "Non-Therapeutic Circumcision," p. 1083.

15. Editorial, *Journal of the American Medical Association,* vol. 224, no. 10, June 4, 1973, p. 1414.

16. Howard C. Mofenson, Letter to the Editor, *Journal of the American Medical Association,* vol. 225, no. 11, Sept. 10, 1973, p. 1388.

17. A. J. Thomas, Reply to a Query, *Medical Aspects of Human Sexuality,* vol. 10, no. 8, Aug. 1976, p. 74.

18. Mofenson and Greensher, "Penile Trauma," p. 71.

19. Kermit Krantz, Reply to Query, *Medical Aspects of Human Sexuality,* vol. 12, no. 2, Feb. 1978, p. 139.

20. W. H. Masters and V. E. Johnson, "Orgasm, Anatomy of the Female," *The Encyclopedia of Sexual Behavior,* 1st ed. (New York: Jason Aronson, 1973), p. 789.

21. William O. Robertson, Jr., Comments, *Medical Aspects of Human Sexuality,* vol. 8, no. 1, Jan. 1974, p. 48.

22. C. J. Falliers, Letter to Editor, *Journal of the American Medical Association*, vol. 214, no. 12, Dec. 21, 1970, p. 2194.
23. Gordon M. Shepherd, "Microcircuits in the Nervous System," *Scientific American*, vol. 238, no. 2, Feb. 1978, p. 93.
24. Richard D. Keynes, "Ion Channels in the Nerve Cell Membrane," *Scientific American*, vol. 240, no. 3, March 1979, pp. 126-135.
25. Moses Maimonides (1135-1204), *The Guide for the Perplexed*, (New York: Dover Publications, 1956), p. 378.
26. H. Speert, "Circumcision of the Newborn," *Obstetrics/Gynecology*, vol. 2, no. 2, Aug. 1953, p. 166.
27. Lester Persky, Comment, *Medical Aspects of Human Sexuality*, vol. 8, no. 1, Jan. 1974, p. 55.
28. Valentine, "Adult Circumcision," p. 33.
29. Masters and Johnson, *Human Sexual Response*, p. 190.
30. Ibid., p. 191.
31. Shepherd, "Microcircuits," p. 97. Pheremones were one of the scents studied in the neurology of the olfactory nerves.
32. "A Sexually Attractive Secretion," *New York Times*, Dec. 29, 1974, p. E-9.
33. Dr. Alex Comfort, Quoted in Reply to a Query, *Playgirl*, Nov. 1975, p. 14.
34. O. S. Colp, "Anomalies of Male Genitalia," *Medical Aspects of Human Sexuality*, vol. 8, no. 9, Sept. 1974, p. 131; *Proceedings of the Society of Experimental Biology and Medicine*, vol. 75, no. 2, 1950, p. 370. Quoted by Saul Benison, Letter, *Journal of the American Medical Association*, vol. 194, no. 3, Oct. 18, 1965, p. 197.
35. Speert, "Circumcision of Newborn," p. 167.

7 Therapeutic Circumcision: The Tight Foreskin

1. D. Gairdner, "The Fate of the Foreskin," *British Medical Journal*, vol. 2, Dec. 24, 1949, pp. 1433-1437.
2. Jacob Øster, "Further Fate of the Foreskin," *Archives of Diseases of Childhood*, vol. 43, no. 228, April 1968, pp. 200-203.
3. Ibid., p. 201.
4. Ibid., p. 202.
5. "Report of the Ad Hoc Task Force on Circumcision," *Pediatrics*, vol. 56, no. 4, Oct., 1975, p. 610. Copyright American Academy of Pediatrics 1975.
6. M. P. M. Richards, J. F. Bernal, and Yvonne Brackbill, "Early Behavioral Differences: Gender or Circumcision?," *Developmental Psychobiology*, vol. 9, no. 1, Jan. 1976, p. 93.
7. *Stedman's Medical Dictionary*, 23rd ed. (Baltimore: Williams & Wilkins), p. 1073.
8. *Dorland's Illustrated Medical Dictionary*, 25th ed. (Philadelphia: Saunders, 1974), p. 1182.
9. H. A. Katchandourian and Donald T. Lunde, *Fundamentals of Human Sexuality* 2nd ed. (New York: Holt, Rinehart & Winston, 1972), p. 25.
10. Milton I. Levine and Jean H. Seligmann, *The Parents Encyclopedia of Infancy, Childhood and Adolescence*, 1st ed. (New York: Crowell, 1973), p. 93.

11. Alan F. Guttmacher, *Pregnancy and Birth* (New York: Signet Books, 1962), pp. 239–241.

12. M. H. Flock, et al., *Maternity Nursing Today* (New York: McGraw Hill, 1973), p. 672.

13. Charles Schlosberg, "Thirty Years of Ritual Circumcisions," *Clinical Pediatrics*, vol. 10, no. 4, April 1971, p. 206.

14. George W. Kaplan, "Circumcision—An Overview," *Current Problems in Pediatrics*, vol. 7, no. 5, March 1977, p. 8.

15. Jane E. Brody, "Pros and Cons of Circumcision," *New York Times*, Jan. 24, 1979, p. C13.

8 Penile Hygiene

1. Edwin M. Loeb, "The Blood Sacrifice Complex," *Memoirs of the American Anthropological Association*, No. 30, 1923 (Millwood, N.Y.: Kraus Reprint Co., 1964), p. 14.

2. Ibid., map, unnumbered.

3. O. G. Dodge and J. N. Kaviti, "Male Circumcision Among the Peoples of East Africa and the Incidence of Genital Cancer," *East Africa Medical Journal*, vol. 42, no. 3, March 1965, p. 99.

4. E. Noel Preston, "Whither the Foreskin?," *Journal of the American Medical Association*, vol. 213, no. 11, Sept. 14, 1970, pp. 1853–1858.

5. Jane E. Brody, "A Restudy Urged on Circumcision," *New York Times*, Sept. 20, 1970, p. 19.

6. "Circumcision and V.D.," *Newsweek*, vol. 30, no. 3, July 21, 1947, p. 49.

7. Hawa Patel, "The Problem of Routine Circumcision," *Journal of the Canadian Medical Association*, vol. 95, no. 11, Sept. 10, 1966, p. 579.

8. H. Speert, "Circumcision of the Newborn," *Obstetrics and Gynecology*, vol. 2, no. 2, Aug. 1953, p. 170.

9. M. Calnan, J. W. B. Douglas, and H. Goldstein, "Tonsillectomy and Circumcision: Comparisons of Two Cohorts," *International Journal of Epidemiology*, vol. 7, no. 1, March 1978, p. 82.

10. Karen De Witt, "U. S. Bridges the Dental Health Gap," *New York Times*, July 30, 1978, p. E11.

11. *Health Facts*, (New York: The Center for Medical Consumers and Health Care), vol. 2, no. 10, July/August, 1978, p.1, noted: "By age 65, 50% of all Americans will be toothless." *Survey of Needs for Dental Care* (Chicago: American Dental Association, 1965), pp. 10, 13, 15, 17, revealed: 80.6% of 6,048 white women and 80.1% of 5,379 white men in the study were in need of dental care. Among blacks the need was greater. Nearly 9% required treatment for periodontal (gum) disease. Among those aged 10–14, about one-fourth were considered to be in need of correction for malocclusion. De Witt (see note 10 above) noted that 50% of Americans do not get annual dental check-ups, although such care is available to 94% of the population. Thomas McGuire, in *The Tooth Trip* (New York: Random House), 1972, p. 226, noted that an army survey revealed that the dental requirements of every 100 inductees included: 600 fillings, 112 extractions, 40 bridges, 21 crowns, 18 partial dentures, and

1 full denture. See also P. I. Murphy and R. C. Murphy, "The Perils and Pitfalls of Dentistry," *The New York Times*, Apr. 29, 1979, magazine section, pp. 110-126.

12. Robert Claiborne, "The Great Health Care Rip-off," *Saturday Review*, Jan. 7, 1978, p. 10.

13. "It Costs Too Much" (editorial), *Health Security News*, vol. 7, no. 1, June 1, 1978, p. 2.

14. Harold M. Schmeck, Jr., "Lack of Immunization Policy Endangers Health, Panels Say," *New York Times*, Apr. 4, 1977, p. 32, noted: " . . . From 1964 to 1975 the percentage of young children immunized against polio dropped from roughly 79 percent to 65 percent." *A National Health Service, Questions and Answers* (New York: Committee For a National Health Service), July 1977, p.3, stated that although Medicare has done much to provide a portion of the cost of treating existing illness among the elderly "Preventive services were deliberately exluded in Medicare. No immunizations were allowed even though the elderly are most likely to die from influenza. And no periodic examinations were included." Daniel S. Martin, "Cancer; a Clamour for Cures," *New York Times*, June 17, 1978, p. A17, commented: "Admittedly, we may be living in a sea of carcinogens." "A Survey Scrubs Myths About Lice," *Moneysworth*, Feb. 1978, p. 3. printed a statement made by Norcliff Thayer, Inc., a manufacturer of a lice remedy: "The incidence of head lice infestation has reportedly increased from 250,000 cases in 1963 to 5,000,000 in 1977." *Consumer Health Perspectives* (New York: Consumer Commission on the Accreditation of Health Services), vol. 5, no. 1, April 1978, p. 2, stated that the Robert Wood Johnson study (1977): "Indicates that 24 million people, or 12% of the population, have neither a physician nor a source of regular care, such as a clinic. . . . In rural areas 145 counties are without a physician. . . .

15. Wayne King, "Poverty and Disease in Carolina Low Country Belie the New South Boom," *New York Times*, Apr. 1, 1977, p. 1.

16. Jane E. Brody, "Personal Health," *New York Times*, Nov. 9, 1977, p. C17.

17. Alexander Leaf, "Getting Old," *Scientific American*, vol. 229, no. 3, Sept. 1973, p. 46. Among the Vilcamba in Equador, a large number of people were over 100 years old. "When we asked various villagers how long it had been since they last bathed, the responses showed that many had not done so for two years. (The record was ten years.)"

18. Isaac Harvey, *Eternal Eve* (Garden City, N.Y.: Doubleday, 1951), p. 437.

19. "Governor West Dedicates Bathroom in Carolina Drive for Plumbing," *New York Times*, June 4, 1972. In the 1970 census, 149,300 houses in South Carolina were without "adequate plumbing." James T. Wooten, "Plains, Ga., Presents 2 Contrasting Faces Typical of the South," *New York Times*, Dec. 20, 1976, p. B1. "More than two-thirds of the houses on the south side of the tracks have no indoor plumbing."

20. W. J. Gadpaille, Reply to Query, *Medical Aspects of Human Sexuality*, vol. 10, no. 9, Sept. 1976, p. 84.

21. The Boston Women's Health Book Collective, *Our Bodies Ourselves* (New York: Simon & Schuster, 1973); M. S. Kennedy, "The Sexual Revolution Just Keeps On Coming," *Mother Jones*, vol. 1, no. 9, Dec. 1976, p. 25.

22. Junius Ellis, " 'Sexually Complete' Boy Dolls The Big Thing For Christmas," *Moneysworth*, vol. 7, no. 2, Dec. 20, 1976, p. 12.

23. Doris E. Fiedler, "Female Sexual Hygiene," *Medical Aspects of Human Sexuality*, vol. 9, no. 10, Oct. 1975, p. 83.

24. Peter Charles Remondino, *History of Circumcision From The Earliest Times To The Present*, 1st ed. (New York: AMS Press, 1974), p. 263. Previously published by F.A. Davis, Philadelphia, in 1891.

25. Benjamin Spock, *Baby and Child Care* (New York: Pocket Books, 1946), p. 18.

26. Gloria Whorton, "Should Your Child Be Circumcised?," *Life and Health*, vol. 74, April 1959, p. 33.

27. Patel, "Routine Circumcision," p. 578.

28. John M. Foley, *The Practice of Circumcision: A Reevaluation*, 1st ed. (New York: Materia Medica Press, 1966), p. 5.

29. H. C. Mofenson and J. Greensher, "Penile Trauma in Boys," *Medical Aspects of Human Sexuality*, vol. 9, no. 8, Aug, 1975, p. 71.

30. Patel, "Routine Circumcision," p. 578.

31. R. J. Valentine (A pseudonym), "Adult Circumcision: A Personal Report," *Medical Aspects of Human Sexuality*, vol. 8, no. 1, Jan. 1974, p. 40.

32. "Japanese Officer Model of Health After 30 Years In the Jungle," *New York Times*, Apr. 24, 1974, p.1.

33. C. H. Garvin and L. Persky, "Circumcision: Is It Justified In Infancy?," *Journal National Medical Association*, vol. 58, no. 4, July 1966, p. 234.

34. John Vinocur, "Survey Indicates the German Self-Image Is More Wish Than Reality," *New York Times*, Dec. 13, 1978, p. A14.

35. "Popular Pamphlet Helps Nigerians Going to Britain," *New York Times*, Apr. 16, 1979, p. A10.

36. R. Dagher, M. L. Selzer, and J. Lapides, "Carcinoma of the Penis and the Anti-Circumcision Crusade," *Journal of Urology*, July, 1973 vol. 110, p. 80.

37. B. M. Osborne et al., *Foundations of Health Science*, (Boston: Allyn and Bacon, 1968), pp. 294-295.

38. "Report of the Ad Hoc Task Force on Circumcision," *Pediatrics*, vol. 56, no. 4, Oct. 1975, p. 611. Copyright American Academy of Pediatrics 1975.

39. Ibid., p. 610.

40. Preston, "Whither the Foreskin?," p. 1857.

41. D. Gairdner, "The Fate of the Foreskin," *British Medical Journal*, vol. 2, Dec. 24, 1949, p. 1434.

42. J. Øster, "Further Fate of the Foreskin," *Archives Diseases of Childhood*, vol. 43, no. 228, April 1968, p. 202.

43. Jack G. Shiller, *Childhood Illness—A Common Sense Approach* 4th ed. (New York: Stein and Day, 1973), p. 169.

44. L. King, R. Morris, H. Pearson, "Circumcision: Rite, rational or both?," *Patient Care*, vol. 12, no. 5, March 15, 1978, p. 96.

9 Circumcision and Venereal Disease

1. "Circumcision and V. D.," *Newsweek*, vol. 30, no. 3, July 21, 1947, p. 49.

2. Rabbi Samuel Glasner, "Judaism and Sex," *Encyclopedia of Sexual Behaviour*, (New York: Jason Aronson, 1973), pp. 580–581.

3. Alan F. Guttmacher, "Should The Baby Be Circumcised?," *Parents' Magazine*, vol. 16, no. 9, Sept. 1941, p. 76.
4. "Information for Mothers," *Hygeia* magazine, vol. 25, Nov. 1947, p. 819.
5. See note 1.
6. Alexander W. Young, Jr., "Vulvar Conditions Caused by Sexually Transmitted Diseases," *Medical Aspects of Human Sexuality*, vol. 12, no. 10, Oct. 1978, p. 23.
7. Gennell Subak-Sharpe, "The Venereal Disease of the New Morality," *Today's Health*, vol. 53, no. 3, March 1975, p. 42; M. W. Rytel, Reply to Query, *Medical Aspects of Human Sexuality*, vol. 11, no. 1, Jan. 1977, p. 14.
8. M. S. Amstey, "Herpes V. D.—A Serious Problem In Pregnancy," *Medical Aspects of Human Sexuality*, vol. 8, no. 8, Aug. 1974, p. 128.
9. Subak-Sharpe, "Venereal Disease of New Morality," p. 42.
10. Earl Ubell, "Venereal Disease, The Search of a Way to Control the Plague," *New York Times*, April 16, 1972, p. E14.
11. R. L. Green, "Anaphylactic and Pseudoanaphylactic Reactions to Penicillin in the Treatment of Venereal Disease," *Medical Aspects of Human Sexuality*, vol. 11, no. 2, Feb. 1977, p. 83.
12. H. Pariser, "Need for Routine Testing for Gonorrhea," *Medical Aspects of Human Sexuality*, vol. 10, no. 9, Sept. 1976, p. 144; "Venereal Disease Cases Reported Down in 1977," *New York Times*, Jan. 29, 1978, p. A24.
13. Harold M. Schmeck, Jr., "Scientist Who Predicted Penicillin-Resisting Gonorrhea Is Tracking Its Cause," *New York Times*, June 29, 1977, p. A16.
14. P. J. Wiesner, Reply to Query, *Medical Aspects of Human Sexuality*, vol. 12, no. 1, Jan. 1978, p. 135.
15. Jon C. Lochner, "Secondary and Latent Syphilis," *Medical Aspects of Human Sexuality*, vol. 13, no. 1, Jan. 1979, p. 117.
16. "Syphilis Cases Decline," *New York Times*, Dec. 4, 1977, p. 69.
17. C. H. Garvin and L. Persky, "Circumcision: Is It Justified In Infancy?," *Journal of the National Medical Association*, vol. 58, no. 4, July, 1966, p. 237.
18. Jane E. Brody, "A Restudy Urged On Circumcision," *New York Times*, Sept. 20, 1970, p. 19.
19. Marvin S. Eiger, "The Case for Circumcision," *Today's Health*, vol. 50, no. 4, April 1972, p. 15.
20. Abraham Ravich, *Preventing V.D. and Cancer by Circumcision*, 1st ed. (New York: Philosophical Library, 1973).
21. David Reuben, *How To Get More Out Of Sex* (New York: Bantam Books, 1974), p. 6.
22. John J. Secondi, *For People Who Make Love—A Doctor's Guide To Sexual Health* (New York: Taplinger, 1975), p. 152.
23. R. G. Wendel, et al., "Prostatic Conditions Caused by Gonorrhea," *Medical Aspects of Human Sexuality*, vol. 11, no. 1, Jan., 1977, p. 59.
24. "A Basic 'Fact' About Syphilis May Be Wrong," *New York Times*, Aug. 15, 1974, p. 8.
25. Meredith F. Campbell, *Urology*, 2nd ed. (Philadelphia: Saunders, 1963), Vol. 3, p. 2773.

26. A. W. Hoke, "Chancroid," *Medical Aspects of Human Sexuality*, vol. 11, no. 2, Feb. 1977, p. 81.

27. Lester Persky, Reply to Query, *Medical Aspects of Human Sexuality*, vol. 13, no. 2, Feb. 1979, p. 43.

28. Elizabeth Barrett-Connor, "Personal Prophylaxis for Venereal Disease," *Medical Aspects of Human Sexuality*, vol. 12, no. 5, May 1978, p. 154.

29. P. K. Taylor and P. Rodin, "Herpes Genitalis and Circumcision," *British Journal of Venereal Disease*, vol. 51, no. 4, Aug. 1975, p. 276.

30. George W. Kaplan, "Circumcision—An Overview," *Current Problems in Pediatrics*, vol. 7, no. 5, March 1977, p. 10.

31. Karen E. Paige, "The Ritual of Circumcision," *Human Nature*, vol. 1, no. 5, May 1978, pp. 40–48.

32. Joseph R. Valinoti, Letter to Editor, *Human Nature*, vol. 1, no. 8, Aug. 1978, pp. 6 and 8.

33. Robert L. Johnson, Reply to a Query, *Medical Aspects of Human Sexuality*, vol. 12, no. 8, Aug. 1978, p. 116.

34. R. H. Kampmeier, "Sexual Aspects of Cytomegalic Inclusion Disease," *Medical Aspects of Human Sexuality*, vol. 12, no. 7, July 1978, p. 98.

35. N. J. Fiumara, "Unusual Anatomic Locations of Sexuality Transmitted Infections," *Medical Aspects of Human Sexuality*, vol. 13, no. 2, Feb. 1979, pp. 127-128.

36. Hoke, "Chancroid," p. 81.

10 Circumcision and Cancer

1. American Cancer Society, *1978 Cancer Facts and Figures* (New York, 1977), p. 10.

2. United States Department of Commerce, Bureau of the Census, *Statistical Abstract of the United States 1975*, 96th ed., (Washington, D.C.: 1975), p. 64.

3. John K. Mustard, "Cancer: Our Overloaded Time Bomb," Letter to Editor, *New York Times*, Dec. 9, 1975, p. 40. The writer claims that the normal growth has been 1% annually, but that in 1975 the increase was 5%, a possible forerunner of an explosive increase.

4. American Cancer Society, "1978 Cancer Facts" p. 3.

5. Editors, "Occupational Medicine," *M.D. Medical Newsmagazine*, vol. 19, no. 8, Aug. 1975, p. 70.

6. Lawrence K. Altman, "Surveillance Widens for Cancer Research," *New York Times*, May 11, 1977, p. A13.

7. Harold M. Schmeck, Jr., "Environmental Factors in Cancer Are Hinted in Atlas on Nonwhites," *New York Times*, Jan. 6, 1977, p. 18.

8. Dr. Philip Strax, quoted in Letter to Editor, *New York Times*, Magazine Section, Nov. 21, 1976, p. 73.

9. Schmeck, "Environmental Factors in Cancer."

10. Lorraine J. Carbary, "Circumcision: Ancient Rite, Modern Operation," *Nursing Care*, vol. 8, no. 10, Oct. 1975, pp. 26-27.

11. American Cancer Society, *1978 Cancer Facts*, p. 17.

12. S. I. McMillen, *None of These Diseases* (Old Tappan, N.J.: Spire Books, 1970), p. 17.

13. Dr. Abraham Ravich, *Preventing V.D. and Cancer by Circumcision* (New York: Philosophical Library, 1973), p. 38.

14. Marvin S. Eiger, "The Case for Circumcision," *Today's Health*, vol. 50, no. 4, April 1972, p. 15.

15. Jane E. Brody, "Cancer as a Venereal Disease," *New York Times*, Sept. 29, 1968, Sec. IV, p. 8.

16. Jane E. Brody, "Cervical Cancer May Be Venereal," *New York Times*, April 4, 1971, p. 30.

17. Ravich, *Preventing V.D. and Cancer*, pp. 111, 114.

18. The reason for this lack of proof is understandable; it would take about 50 years of large-scale circumcision practice among non-Jewish males to reflect a noticeable drop in the cervical cancer rate. In the 1940s, the risk of cervical cancer was greatest between the ages of 40–50, which meant that a woman would have to have been born between 1890 and 1900. Her husband, most likely, would have been born in 1890 or earlier, at which time the circumcision rate among non-Jewish men did not exceed 15%. (See Appendix B.)

19. E. L. Wynder, et al., "A Study of Environmental Factors In Carcinoma of the Cervix," *American Journal of Obstetrics and Gynecology*, vol. 68, no. 4, Oct. 1954, pp. 1016–1046.

20. "Circumcision and Cancer," *Time* magazine, vol. 63, no. 14, April 5, 1954, p. 96.

21. David Reuben, *How To Get More Out Of Sex* (New York: Bantam Books, 1975), p. 5.

22. Ibid, p. 6.

23. Wynder, et al., "Environmental Factors in Carcinoma," p. 1046.

24. Ibid., p. 1032.

25. Ibid., p. 1022.

26. M. Terris, et al., "Relation of Circumcision to Cancer of the Cervix," *American Journal of Obstetrics and Gynecology*, vol. 117, no. 8, Dec. 15, 1973, pp. 1056–1057.

27. Abraham M. Lilienfeld, and Saxon Graham, "Validity of Determining Circumcision Status by Questionnaire as Related to Epidemiological Studies of Cancer of the Cervix," *Journal of the National Cancer Institute*, vol. 21, no. 4, Oct. 1958, pp. 713–720.

28. Terris, et al., "Circumcision and Cancer of the Cervix," p. 1062.

29. J. Atkin-Swan and D. Baird, "Circumcision and Cancer of the Cervix," *British Journal of Cancer*, vol. 19, no. 2, June 1965, p. 226.

30. "Prevention of Cancer," *World Health Organization Technical Report Series 276*, 1964, p. 18.

31. Aitken-Swan and Baird, "Circumcision and Cancer" p. 217.

32. E. Noel Preston, "Whither the Foreskin?," *Journal of the American Medical Association*, vol. 213, no. 11, Sept. 14, 1970, p. 1856.

33. Alfred Plaut and Alice C. Kohn-Speyer, "The Carcinogenic Action of Smegma," *Science*, vol. 105, no. 2728, Apr. 11, 1947, p. 392.

34. Ravich, *Preventing V.D. and Cancer*, p. 17.
35. Jane E. Brody, "Cancer of Cervix Linked to Virus," *New York Times*, Sept. 21, 1968, p. 1. See also notes 15 and 16; also "Findings Said to Bolster Evidence Tying Virus to Cervical Cancer," *New York Times*, Nov. 16, 1971, p. 38.
36. Keen A. Rafferty, Jr., "Herpes Viruses and Cancer," *Scientific American*, vol. 229, no. 10, Oct. 1973, pp. 26-33; John J. Holland, "Slow, Inapparent and Recurrent Viruses," *Scientific American*, vol. 230, no. 2, Feb. 1974, pp. 33-40.
37. William A. Knaus, "Viruses of Love," *New York Times*, Magazine Section, Oct. 17, 1976, pp. 60-68.
38. Jane E. Brody, "Cervical Cancer Linked to Males," *New York Times*, April 5, 1973, p. 27; Rafferty, "Herpes and Cancer," p. 33.
39. McMillen, *None of These Diseases*, p. 19.
40. William J. Hennessy, "Granuloma Inguinale," *Medical Aspects of Human Sexuality*, vol. 11, no. 1, Jan. 1977, p. 119.
41. American Cancer Society, *1978 Cancer Facts*, p. 10, footnote.
42. Ibid., p. 17.
43. Ibid.
44. Brody, "Cancer as a Venereal Disease," Sec. IV, p. 8.
45. James A. Sebastian, Reply to Query, *Medical Aspects of Human Sexuality*, vol. 13, no. 4, April 1979, p. 117. Evidence that the onset of sexual activity in early adolescence may be related to cervical cancer comes from a study of 750 Taiwanese prostitutes. Contrary to expectation, their cervical cancer rate was relatively low. In Taiwan almost all girls remain at home under close family supervision until age 18. It was rare to find a prostitute who was sexually active prior to that age. Also see J. L. Rauh and R. L. Burket, "Adolescent Sexual Activity and Resulting Gynecological Problems," *Medical Aspects of Human Sexuality*, vol. 13, no. 4, April 1979, p. 56, and Kirsten Blanch, "Cervical Cancer: A Shocking New Theory," *Pageant*, vol. 30, no. 10, April 1975, p. 50.
46. American Cancer Society, *1978 Cancer Facts*, p. 10.
47. Eiger, "Case for Circumcision," p. 15.
48. The list, starting with rank order 33, includes Yugoslavia, Greece, Bulgaria, Mexico, Iceland, Mauritius, Japan, Hong Kong, Philippines, El Salvador, Honduras and Thailand.
49. A. Apt, "Circumcision and Protastic Cancer," *Acta Med. Scand.*, vol. 178, 1965, pp. 493-504.
50. Preston, "Whither the Foreskin?," p. 1857.
51. George W. Kaplan and Vincent J. O'Conor, Letter to Editor, *Journal American Medical Association*, vol. 196, no. 9, May 30, 1966, p. 123-124.
52. L. M. Franks, "Etiology, Epidemiology and Pathology of Prostatic Cancer," *Proceedings of the National Conference on Urologic Cancer* (New York: American Cancer Society, 1973), p. 1092-1095.
53. "Trends in Cancer Incidence in Norway 1955-1967," *The Cancer Registry of Norway* (Oslo, Norway: Universitetsforlager, 1972), p. 34. The total age-adjusted rate per 100,000 of prostatic cancer was 41.2 in 1955 and 49.1 in 1967.
54. American Cancer Society, *1978 Cancer Facts*, p. 7. Prostatic cancer occurring between 1956-1975 would have largely affected men age 60 and older, i.e., men born between 1890-1915 or earlier. Although the circumcision rate was relatively low in

1890, it increased by 1915 to a point where it should show up statistically during the period in question (1950-1975). Even if no decrease was noted, the rate should have stabilized. Instead it rose appreciably, demonstrating no link to circumcision.

55. Mark A. Silvert, Reply to Query, *Medical Aspects of Human Sexuality*, vol. 12, no. 8, Aug. 1978, p. 74.

56. Abraham Ravich, "The Relationship of Circumcision to Cancer of the Prostate," *Journal of Urology*, vol. 48, 1942, p. 298.

57. Fred Rosner, "Circumcision: Attempt at Clearer Understanding," *New York State Journal of Medicine*, vol. 66, no. 22, Nov. 15, 1966, p. 2920.

58. Kaplan and O'Conor, Letter to Editor, p. 124.

59. Ravich, *Preventing V.D. and Cancer*, pp. 29, 32, 42, 43.

60. Ibid., p. 29.

61. G. E. Demetrakopoulos, "A Different View of the Facts," *Pediatrics*, vol. 56, no. 2, Aug. 1975, pp. 339-340.

62. Robert Burger and Thomas H. Guthrie, "Why Circumcision?," *Pediatrics*, vol. 54, no. 3, Sept. 1974, pp. 362-364.

63. A. G. S. Philip, "Urologist's Views Challenged," *Pediatrics*, vol. 56, no. 2, Aug. 1975, p. 338; G. G. Carpenter and A. R. Hervada, "More Criticism of Circumcision," *Pediatrics*, vol. 56, no. 2, Aug. 1975, pp. 338-39; M. L. Sorrells, "Still More Criticism," *Pediatrics*, vol. 56, no. 2, Aug. 1975, p. 339.

64. Robert Burger, "Dr. Burger Replies," *Pediatrics*, vol. 56, no. 2, Aug. 1975, pp. 340-341.

65. Ibid.

66.

Estimated Pool of Uncircumcised Men Age 50 and Over (1975)

Age	Total Population	% Uncircumcised	Number Uncircumcised
50-54	4,593,600	45	2,067,120
55-64	9,345,000	60	5,607,000
65 and over	9,172,000	70	6,420,400
		Total	14,094,520

Source: *Statistical Abstract of the United States 1976*, p. 27, for population by age. For frequency rates, see Appendix B.

67. A. L. Wolbarst, "Circumcision and Penile Carcinoma," *Lancet*, vol. 1, Jan. 16, 1932, pp. 150-153.

68. D. Hovsepian, "The Pros and Cons of Routine Circumcision," *California Medicine*, vol. 75, no. 5, Nov. 1951, p. 360.

69. Elliot Leiter and Albert M. Lefkovits, "Circumcision and Penile Carcinoma," *New York State Journal of Medicine*, vol. 75, no. 9, Aug., 1975, p. 1520.

70. O. Swenson, *Pediatric Surgery* (New York: Appleton-Century-Crofts, 1958), p. 547.

71. Burger and Guthrie, "Why Circumcision," p. 362.

72. H. Speert, "Circumcision of the Newborn," *Obstetrics/Gynecology*, vol. 2, no. 2, Aug. 1953, p. 167.

73. Samuel Licklider, "Jewish Penile Carcinoma," *Journal of Urology*, vol. 86, no. 1, July 1961, p. 98.

74. Victor F. Marshall, "Should Circumcision of Infant Males Be Routine?," *Medical Record and Annals*, vol. 48, Feb. 1954, p. 790.

75. W. F. Gee and J. S. Ansell, "Neonatal Circumcision: A Ten Year Overview," *Pediatrics*, vol. 58, no. 4, Dec. 1976, p. 827.

76. The women's figures are probably higher because in some cases the site is unspecified.

Unspecified Genital Cancer Sites, 1977		
	Deaths	New Cases
Male	31	200
Female	72	900

Source: Personal communication, American Cancer Society, July 27, 1977.

77. J. B. deKernion, et al., "Carcinoma of the Penis," *Proceedings of the National Conference on Urologic Cancer* (Washington, D.C.: American Cancer Society, 1973), pp. 1256-1262.

78. Ibid., p. 1256.

79. The derivation of the Indian rates, based on the 1977 male cancer data for the United States is as follows:

	Deaths	New Cases
Total United States Male Cancers:	210,500	347,000
If 12% were penile cancer, the penile cancer rate would be:	25,260	41,640
India's population is roughly 3 times that of the United States, therefore 25,260 and 41,640 were multiplied by 3:	75,780	124,920

80. J. T. Kuruvilla et al., "Results of Surgical Treatment of Carcinoma of the Penis," *Australian and New Zealand Journal of Surgery*, vol. 41, no. 2, Nov. 1971, p. 157.

81. S. K. Kyalwazi, "Carcinoma of the Penis," *East Africa Medical Journal*, vol. 43, no. 10, Oct. 1966, p. 415.

82. O. G. Dodge, "Carcinoma of the Penis in East Africans," *British Journal of Urology*, 1964, p. 224.

83. Editorial, "Circumcision Urged to Prevent Cancer," *Science Newsletter*, vol. 86, no. 18, Oct. 31, 1964, p. 281.

84. George W. Kaplan, "Circumcision—An Overview," *Current Problems in Pediatrics*, vol. 7, no. 5, March 1977, p. 10.

85. John Cairns, "The Cancer Problem," *Scientific American*, vol. 223, no. 5, Nov. 1975, p. 67.

86. Carl Sagan, *The Dragons of Eden* (New York: Random House, 1977), p. 184.

87. Denis P. Burkitt, "The Link Between Low-Fiber Diets and Disease," *Human Nature*, vol. 1, no. 12, Dec. 1978, p. 41.

88. David A. Grimes, "Routine Circumcision of the Newborn Infant: A Reappraisal," *American Journal of Obstetrics and Gynecology*, vol. 130, no. 2, Jan. 15, 1978, p. 128.
89. R. Schreck and H. Lenowitz, "Etiologic Factors in Carcinoma of the Penis," *Cancer Research*, vol. 7, 1947, p. 180.
90. deKernion, et al., "Carcinoma of the Penis," p. 1256.
91. Leiter and Lefkovits, "Circumcision and Carcinoma," p. 1521; S. Illingworth, *The Normal Child* (Boston: Little, Brown, 1968), p. 98. The author claims that the highest rate of penile cancer exists in Java, where the men are circumcised.
92. Preston, "Whither the Foreskin?," p. 1856.
93. R. Dagher, M. L. Selzer, and J. Lapides, "Carcinoma of the Penis and the Anticircumcision Crusade," *Journal of Urology*, vol. 110, no. 1, July 1973, p. 80.
94. Alex Comfort, *More Joy—A Lovemaking Companion to the Joy of Sex* (New York: Crown, 1974), p. 18.

11 Circumcision and Premature Ejaculation

1. Helen S. Kaplan, *The New Sex Therapy* (New York: Brunner/Mazel, 1974), p. 470.
2. David Reuben, *How to Get More Out of Sex* (New York: Bantam Books, 1974), p. 6.
3. A. G. M. Campbell, et al., "Circumcision: A Balanced Report Based on Facts, Not Conjecture," *Patient Care*, vol. 5, no. 13, July 15, 1971, pp. 60-62.
4. R. Burger and T. H. Guthrie, "Why Circumcision?," *Pediatrics*, vol. 54, no. 3, Sept. 1974, p. 363. This identical statement also appeared in the *Journal of the American Medical Association*, vol. 225, no. 10, Sept. 3, 1973, p. 1173.
5. L. J. Carbary, "Circumcision: Ancient Rite, Modern Operation," *Nursing Care*, vol. 8, no. 10, Oct. 1975, p. 27.
6. Nabors Muramoto, *Healing Ourselves* (New York: Avon, 1976), p. 132.
7. P. T. Knoepfler, "Duration of Intercourse," *Medical Aspects of Human Sexuality*, vol. 10, no. 9, Sept. 1976, p. 151.
8. Thomas N. Wise, Reply to Query, *Medical Aspects of Human Sexuality*, vol. 11, no. 10, Oct. 1977, pp. 6, 9.
9. Ibid.
10. J. R. David and E. M. Blight, Jr., "Interdisciplinary Treatment of Male Sexual Dysfunction in a Military Health Care Setting," *Journal of Sex and Marital Therapy*, vol. 4, no. 1, Spring 1978, p. 30.
11. Quoted by Lawrence Sharpe, Reply to Query, *Medical Aspects of Human Sexuality*, vol. 12, no. 3, March 1978, p. 77.
12. A. C. Kinsey, et al., *Sexual Behavior in the Human Male*, 1st ed. (Philadelphia: Saunders, 1948), p. 580.
13. Ibid.
14. L. Jerome Oziel, "Inconsistency of Coital Orgasm in Women," *Medical Aspects of Human Sexuality*, vol. 12, no. 9, Sept. 1978, p. 23.
15. Kinsey, et al., "Sexual Behavior in Male," p. 580.

16. Rabbi Samuel Glasner, "Judaism and Sex," in Albert Ellis and Albert Abarbanel (Eds). *The Encyclopedia of Sexual Behavior* (New York: Jason Aronson, 1973), p. 582.

17. Barry Farrell, "Running With Dick Gregory," *Ramparts*, vol. 13, no. 10, Aug.-Sept. 1975, p. 56.

18. B. H. Smith, Reply to a Query, *Medical Aspects of Human Sexuality*, vol. 10, no. 7, July 1976, p. 86.

19. M. A. LaRocque, Reply to a Query, *Medical Aspects of Human Sexuality*, vol. 10, no. 3, March 1976, p. 125.

20. M. R. Lansky, Reply to Query, *Medical Aspects of Human Sexuality*, vol. 10, no. 8, Aug. 1976, pp. 67, 68.

21. David and Blight, "Treatment of Male Sexual Dysfunction," p. 29.

22. Anthony Pietropinto and Jacqueline Simenauer, *Beyond the Male Myth* (New York: New York Times Books, 1977), p. 161.

23. David Jonas and Doris Jonas, "Ejaculation: Premature for Whom?," *Physician's World*, vol. 11, no. 7, July 1974, p. 92; P. J. Fink and S. Fink, "Current Concepts of Premature Ejaculation," *Medical Aspects of Human Sexuality*, vol. 10, no. 8, Aug. 1976, pp. 84-94.

24. Fink and Fink, "Premature Ejaculation," p. 89 (reporting on the experience of Masters and Johnson).

25. Robert J. Valentine (a pseudonymn), "Adult Circumcision: A Personal Report," *Medical Aspects of Human Sexuality*, vol. 8, no. 1, Jan. 1974, p. 33.

26. Lester Persky, Commentary, *Medical Aspects of Human Sexuality*, vol. 8, no. 1, Jan. 1974, p. 50.

27. L. King, R. Morris, and H. Pearson, "Circumcision: Rite, rational or both?," *Patient Care*, vol. 12, no. 5, March 15, 1978, p. 81.

28. W. H. Masters and V. E. Johnson, *Human Sexual Response*, 1st ed. (Boston: Little, Brown, 1966), p. 190.

29. Morton Friedman, Reply to Query, *Medical Aspects of Human Sexuality*, vol. 12, no. 1, Jan. 1978, p. 131.

30. James F. Glenn, Reply to Query, *Medical Aspects of Human Sexuality*, vol. 11, no. 9, Sept. 1977, p. 105.

31. M. C. Denholtz, Reply to Query, *Medical Aspects of Human Sexuality*, vol. 9, no. 7, July 1975, p. 25. See also James Leslie McCary, Reply to Query, *Medical Aspects of Human Sexuality*, vol. 12, no. 7, July 1978, pp. 61, 65. He reported that men age 19-30 have erections 5.8 times faster than men age 48-65.

32. Fink and Fink, "Premature Ejaculation," p. 87.

33. Ibid.

34. E. R. Adelson, "Premature Ejaculation," *Medical Aspects of Human Sexuality*, vol. 8, no. 9, Sept. 1974, p. 83.

35. "Study Finds Most Men Unaware Happy Wives Have Sex Problems," *New York Times*, July 21, 1978, p. A10.

36. Robert A. Hatcher, "Reasons to Recommend the Condom," *Medical Aspects of Human Sexuality*, vol. 12, no. 8, Aug. 1978, p. 91-92.

37. L. Salzman, "Premature Ejaculation In Young Married Men," *Medical Aspects of Human Sexuality*, vol. 9, no. 12, Dec. 1975, p. 66.

12 Circumcision and Masturbation

1. Peter Charles Remondino, *History of Circumcision from the Earliest Times to the Present* (New York: AMS Press, 1974), pp. 201, 224;originally published in 1891 by F.A. Davis Co., Philadelphia.
2. Rabbi Samuel Glasner, "Judaism and Sex," in Albert Ellis and Albert Abarbanel (Eds.), *The Encyclopedia of Sexual Behavior* (New York: Jason Aronson, 1973), p. 579.
3. Karen E. Paige, "The Ritual of Circumcision," *Human Nature*, vol. 1, no. 5, May 1978, p. 42.
4. René Spitz, "Authority and Masturbation," *Psychoanalytic Quarterly*, vol. 21, no. 4, 1952, p. 499.
5. J. L. McCary, *Sexual Myths and Fallacies* (New York: Van Nostrand, 1971); V. L. Bullough, "Sex and the Medical Model," *Journal of Sex Research*, vol. 4, 1975, p. 291 ff; regarding vasectomy, see Emil Steinberger, Reply to Query, *Medical Aspects of Human Sexuality*, vol. 11, no. 5, May 1977, p. 106.
6. L. E. Holt, *Diseases of Infancy and Childhood*, 1st ed. (New York: Appleton Century 1897.)
7. Ibid., pp. 696 ff.
8. Holt, *Diseases of Infancy*, 1936 ed., p. 780.
9. Gordon D. Jensen, Reply to Query, *Medical Aspects of Human Sexuality*, vol. 12, no. 8, Aug. 1978, p. 37.
10. L. E. Hinsie and R. J. Campbell (Eds.), *Psychiatric Dictionary* (New York: Oxford University Press, 1960), p. 444.
11. Ibid., p. 444.
12. William R. Reevy, "Adolescent Sexuality," in Albert Ellis and Albert Abarbanel (Eds.), *The Encyclopedia of Sexual Behavior* (New York: Jason Aronson, 1973), p. 62.
13. Ibid.
14. L. W. Dearborn, "Autoeroticism," in Albert Ellis and Albert Abarbanel (Eds.), *Encyclopedia of Sexual Behavior*, (New York: Jason Aronson, 1973), p. 206.
15. D. B. Marcotte et al., "Women's Misunderstandings About Male Sexuality," *Medical Aspects of Human Sexuality*, vol. 10, no. 12, Dec. 1976, p. 76.
16. M. S. Kennedy, "The Sexual Revolution Just Keeps On Coming," *Ramparts* magazine, vol. 1, no. 9, Dec. 1976, p. 29.
17. Dearborn, "Autoeroticism," p. 206.
18. Alan F. Guttmacher, *Pregnancy and Birth* (New York: Signet Books, 1962), pp. 239-241.
19. Benjamin Spock, "Notes On The Psychology of Circumcision, Masturbation and Enuresis," *The Urologic & Cutaneous Review*, vol. 46, Dec. 1942, p. 769.
20. Alan F. Guttmacher, "Should The Baby Be Circumcised?," *Parents' Magazine*, vol. 16, no. 9, Sept. 1941, p. 76.
21. Alan F. Guttmacher, *Pregnancy and Birth* (New York: Signet Books, 1962), p. 240. (Originally published in 1956.)
22. Gloria Whorton, "Should Your Child Be Circumcised?," *Life and Health*, vol. 74, no. 4, April 1959, p. 33.

Notes to Chapters

23. Morris Fishbein (Ed.), *The Modern Family Health Guide* (Garden City, N.Y.: Doubleday, 1959), p. 561.
24. Fred Rosner, "Circumcision: Attempt at Clearer Understanding," *New York State Journal Of Medicine*, vol. 66, no. 22, Nov. 15, 1966, p. 2920.
25. Roscoe L. Wall, Jr., "Routine Circumcision? Recent Trends and Concepts," *North Carolina Medical Journal*, vol. 29, no. 3, March 1968, p. 104.
26. Robert E. Gould, "What Distinguishes 'Healthy' From 'Sick' Sexual Behavior?," *Medical Aspects of Human Sexuality*, vol. 11, no. 10, Oct. 1977, p. 75.
27. L. J. Carbary, "Circumcision: Ancient Rite, Modern Operation," *Nursing Care*, vol. 8, no. 10, Oct. 1975, p. 27.
28. L. King, R. Morris, and H. Pearson, "Circumcision: Rite, rational or both?" *Patient Care*, vol. 12, no. 5, March 15, 1978, p. 81.

13 If Later, Why Not Now?

1. Dr. Dag Riis, Director of an Oslo well-baby clinic, Oslo, Norway. Telephone interview, August 1973.
2. Jacob Øster, "Further Fate of the Foreskin," *Archives of Diseases of Childhood*, vol. 43, no. 228, April 1968, pp. 200-203.
3. Dr. A. S. Härö, Private Communication, The National Board of Health, Helsinki, Finland, Oct. 24, 1973.
4. United States Department of Commerce, Bureau of the Census, Washington, D. C., World Population 1975, p. 185. The population of Finland in 1970 was 4,600,000, of whom 77% were age 15 and over: 3,542,000. Assuming that approximately half of this figure is male, that would mean a male population age 15 and over of 1,771,000. 409 cases among 1,791,000 males equal 0.023%.
5. David A. Grimes, "Routine Circumcision of the Newborn Infant: A Reappraisal," *American Journal of Obstetrics and Gynecology*, vol. 130, no. 2, Jan. 15, 1978, p. 127.
6.

Year	Circumcisions
1965	89,000[a]
1968	102,000[a]
1973	99,000[b]
1975	111,000[c]
1977	105,000[d]

(a) Private correspondence, Mrs. Grace K. White, Chief, Hospital Discharge Survey Branch, Feb. 8 and 24, 1972.
(b) *Surgical Operations in Short-Stay Hospitals, United States 1973* Series 13, No. 24, p. 26.
(c) *Surgical Operations in Short-Stay Hospitals, United States 1975* Series 13, No. 34, p. 29.
(d) Unpublished data, private correspondence Ms. Gloria J. Gardocki, Survey Statistician, Hospital Care Statistics Branch, Dec. 4, 1978.
Source: National Center for Health Statistics, Rockville, Md.

7. Ibid. The 1977 figures are not listed since they were unpublished and not broken out by age.

8. W. F. Gee and J. S. Ansell, "Neonatal Circumcision: A Ten Year Overview," *Pediatrics*, vol. 58, no. 4, Dec. 1976, p. 826. The most common defect is hypospadias, a condition in which the meatus opens on the underside of the penis rather than the tip of the glans. In this study of 5,882 live male births, the condition was found in 0.37% of the newborn.

9. There are no nationwide data on newborn illness; it would be reasonable to *guess* the figure to be a minimum of 1%. Based on data in Footnote 8, hypospadias alone may account for ⅓ of 1%. Low birthweight and prematurity data are from the National Center for Health Statistics, *Trends in "Prematurity" in the United States 1950-1967*, Washington, D.C., Dept. of Health, Education and Welfare, Series 3, No. 15, Jan. 1972 p. 2. (Of the total of 288,000 "low birth weight" infants, i.e., less than 2,500 grams, one-half were taken as males.) The home birth information is from the same source, p. 21. Also see: National Center for Health Statistics *Prenatal-Postnatal Health Needs and Medical Care of Children* Series 11, No. 125, (Washington, D.C., April 1973), Publication No. (HSM) 73-1607, p. 6.

10.

Estimated Pool of Uncircumcised Males in the United States

Age	Male Population	Estimated % Circumcised	Estimated % Uncircumcised	Approximate Number Uncircumcised
Under 5	8,119,000	85%	15%	1,218,000
5-13	17,056,000	80%	20%	3,411,000
14-17	8,626,000	75%	25%	2,150,000
18-21	8,191,000	70%	30%	2,450,000
22-24	5,474,000	70%	30%	1,830,000
25-34	15,206,000	60%	40%	6,090,000
35-44	11,088,000	55%	45%	5,000,000
45-54	11,484,000	55%	45%	5,150,000
55-64	9,345,000	50%	50%	4,650,000
65 and over	9,172,000	35%	65%	5,950,000
			Total	37,899,000

Sources: For data on number of males, by age group, see United States Dept. of Commerce, Bureau of the Census, *Statistical Abstract of the United States* (Washington, D.C.: 97th ed., 1976), p. 27. For derivation of estimated percent of males circumcised, see Appendix B of this book.

11. A. G. M. Campbell, et al., "Circumcision," *Patient Care*, vol. 5, no. 13, July 15, 1971, p. 59.

12. John L. Wirth, "Statistics on Circumcision in Canada and Australia," *American Journal of Obstetrics and Gynecology*, vol. 130, no. 2, Jan. 15, 1978, pp. 236-239. For the years 1972, 1973, and 1974, in four geographic areas, the nonweighted average was 1.6/1,000 males.

13. L. King, R. Morris and H. Pearson, "Circumcision: Rite, rational or both?" *Patient Care*, vol. 12, no. 5, March 15, 1978, p. 81.

14. Ibid.
15. A. G. M. Campbell, et al., "Circumcision," p. 71; also see Grimes, "Routine Circumcision," p. 126.
16. King, et al., "Circumcision: Rite, rational?" p. 72.
17. Kenneth A. Briggs, "Rabbis' Meeting Focuses on Proselytizing," *New York Times*, March 30, 1979, p. A16.
18. "How to Protect Yourself Against Needless Surgery," *Good Housekeeping Magazine*, vol. 185, no. 4, Oct. 1977, p. 245.
19. "National Health Service III," *Health Perspectives,* (New York: Consumer Commission on the Accreditation of Health Services, Inc.), vol. 4, no. 3, May–June 1977, p. 6.
20. "On The Need For Surgery," *New York Times*, Nov. 4, 1977, Sect. 4, p. 6.
21. "Needless Surgery," *Good Housekeeping*, p. 245. Ralph Nader puts the figure at 3.2 million operations at a cost of $5 billion, involving 16,000 deaths. See note 19.
22. "Needless Surgery," *Good Housekeeping*, p. 246; Edgar Berman, *The Solid Gold Stethoscope* (New York: Macmillan, 1976), p. 46.
23. "United States Seeks to Cut Amount of Unnecessary Surgery," *New York Times*, Nov. 2, 1977, p. A19.

14 Pain and Psychological Trauma

1. Virginia E. Pomerantz & Dodi Schultz, *The Mothers' Medical Encyclopedia* (New York: Signet Reference Books, 1972), p. 99.
2. Marvin S. Eiger, "The Case for Circumcision," *Today's Health*, vol. 50, no. 4, April 1972, p. 15.
3. L. J. Carbary, "Circumcision: Ancient Rite, Modern Operation," *Nursing Care*, vol. 8, no. 10, Oct. 1975, p. 27.
4. Edward T. Wilkes, "Should Your Son Be Circumcised?," *Parent's Magazine*, vol. 34, no. 2, Feb. 1959, p. 50; Frederick W. Rutherford, *You and Your Baby*, (New York: Signet Books, 1971), p. 100; Charles Schlosberg, "Thirty Years of Ritual Circumcision," *Clinical Pediatrics*, vol. 10, no. 4, April 1971, p. 205.
5. Boston Children's Medical Center, *Pregnancy, Birth and The Newborn Child* (Boston: Delacorte Press, 1972), p. 285.
6. Sharon Reeder et al., *Maternity Nursing,* 13th ed. (Philadelphia: Lippincott, 1976), p. 416.
7. Seymour Isenberg and L. M. Elting, *Consumer's Guide to Successful Surgery* (New York: St. Martin's Press, 1976), p. 271.
8. Joseph Katz, "The Question of Circumcision," *International Surgery*, vol. 62, no. 9, Sept. 1977, p. 491.
9. Charles Weiss, Reply to Query, *Journal of the American Medical Association*, vol. 214, no. 4, Oct. 26, 1970, p. 266.
10. Ronald S. Illingworth, *The Normal Child*, 4th ed. (Boston, Little, Brown, 1968), p. 98.

11. J. M. Howat, "Circumcision," *Nursing Times*, Sept. 16, 1976, vol. 72, no. 37, p. 1435.

12. C. Kirya and M. W. Werthmann, Jr., "Neonatal Circumcision and Penile Dorsal Nerve Block—A Painless Procedure," *Journal of Pediatrics*, vol. 92, no. 6, June 1978, p. 998.

13. David A. Grimes, "Routine Circumcision of the Newborn Infant; A Reappraisal" *American Journal of Obstetrics and Gynecology*, vol. 130, no. 2, Jan. 15, 1978, p. 127.

14. L. King, R. Morris, and H. Pearson, "Circumcision: Rite, rational or both?," *Patient Care*, vol. 12, no. 5, March 15, 1978, p. 90.

15. George Wald, "Circumcision," Unpublished manuscript, p. 23.

16. M. Calnan, J. W. B. Douglas, and H. Goldstein, "Tonsillectomy and Circumcision: Comparisons of Two Cohorts," *International Journal of Epidemiology*, vol. 7, no. 1, March 1978, p. 83.

17. Ibid.

18. Kirya and Werthmann, "Neonatal Circumcision," p. 1000.

19. Penelope Leach, *Babyhood* (New York: Knopf, 1976), p. 11.

20. Barbara Seaman, "Circumcision: The Pros and Cons," *Woman's Day*, Aug. 1976, p. 40.

21. Susan Heller Anderson, "A Plea For Gentleness to the Newborn," *New York Times*, Jan. 15, 1978, p. 48.

22. T. Berry Brazelton, *Doctor and Child* (New York: Delacorte Press/Seymour Lawrence, 1976), p. 31.

23. Peter F. Oswald and Philip Peltzman, "The Cry of the Human Infant," *Scientific American*, vol. 230, no. 3, March 1974, p. 89.

24. Lawrence K. Altman, "Fetal Brain Said To Live At 28 Weeks," *New York Times*, May 9, 1975, p. 36.

25. "Conference on Infants Studies the First Experience of Life," *New York Times*, March 14, 1978, p. 41. ©1978 by The New York Times Company. Reprinted by permission.

26. Ibid.

27. Ibid.

28. Joan Markessinis, *The First Week of Life* (Princeton, N.J.: Edcom Systems, 1971).

29. Ibid., p. 27. Earlier research techniques were less sophisticated than those of today. Physical skills were once used to indicate perception of objects—skills like visual tracking and reaching for an object, both of which the newborn does poorly. Then, too, assumptions that the newborn's eye and brain were too immature for anything as sophisticated as pattern recognition caused opposing data to be discarded or misinterpreted. Since perception of form was widely believed to follow more "basic" qualities like color and brightness, the possibility of its presence from birth was discounted out of hand.

30. Ibid., p. 27. Every newborn varies infinitely from another—in looks, feelings, movements, reactions to stimulation, and in his effect on his mother.

31. Ibid., p. 26. Newborns see. A newborn will alert, frown and gradually try to focus on a red or soft yellow object. Babies are also born hearing. Tests show that

newborns blink, jerk, and draw in their breaths sharply in response to sounds. They are also sensitive to touch and pressure.

32. Ibid., p. 24.
33. Ibid., p. 21.
34. Ibid.
35. Ibid., p. 25.
36. Ibid., p. 24.
37. Ibid., p. 23.
38. Oswald and Peltzman, "Cry of Infant," p. 85.
39. J. A. C. Brown (Ed.), *The Stein and Day International Medical Encyclopedia* (New York: Stein & Day, 1971), p. 92.
40. Frederick LeBoyer, *Birth Without Violence* (New York: Knopf, 1976).
41. Brazelton, *Doctor and Child*, p. 40.
42. Seymour Levine, "Stimulation In Infancy," *The Nature and Nurture of Behavior (Developmental Psychobiology)—Readings from Scientific American* (San Francisco: Freeman, 1972), p. 55. Originally published in May 1960. Levine noted: "Under stress, in response to prompting by the central nervous system, the pituitary releases larger quantities of various hormones, one of the principal ones being the adrenalcorticotrophic hormone (ACTH). . . . [This, in turn activates other endocrine reactions.]
43. Ibid., p. 56, 61. The researcher found that: Whereas the two groups (test and control) showed the same volume of steroids in circulation before shock, the animals that had been exposed to stress in infancy showed a much higher output of steroids in the first 15 minutes after shock.
44. M. P. M. Richards, J. F. Bernal, and Yvonne Brackbill, "Early Behavioral Differences: Gender or Circumcision?," *Developmental Psychobiology*, vol. 9, no. 1, Jan. 1976, p. 90.
45. Ibid., p. 92.
46. Ibid., p. 91. The NREM study (1971) found that circumcision was followed by prolonged non-rapid eye movement (NREM) sleep. Not only was the amount of NREM increased, but the latency to onset of NREM sleep decreased and both the total number of NREM sleep periods and the number of very long NREM sleep periods increased. The sleep study (1974) found prolonged wakefulness with fussing and crying during the hours immediately after circumcision. The researchers suggest that later NREM sleep shifts may be secondary to changes in wakefulness and also pointed out that the differing techniques used for circumcision may have differential effects on behavior.
47. Ibid., p. 91.
48. Ibid.
49. Luther M. Talbert et al., "Adrenal Cortical Response to Circumcision in the Neonate," *Obstetrics/Gynecology*, vol. 48, no. 2, Aug. 1976, pp. 208-210.
50. American Orthopsychiatric Association, *Newsletter*, Summer 1978, p. 11. In this study, boys were shown to be more awake and active than girls. Also see Diane McGuinness, "How Schools Discriminate Against Boys," *Human Nature*, vol. 2, no. 2, Feb. 1979, p. 83.
51. Muriel Sugarman, "Paranatal Influences on Maternal-Infant Attachment," *American Journal of Orthopsychiatry*, vol. 47, no. 3, July 1977, p. 415.

15   Circumcision Risk

1. Fred Rosner, "Circumcision—Attempt at Clearer Understanding," *New York State Journal of Medicine*, vol. 66, no. 22, Nov. 15, 1966, pp. 2920, 2921.

2. Harold Speert, "Circumcision of the Newborn," *Obstetrics/Gynecology*, vol. 2, no. 2, Aug. 1953, pp. 164–172.

3. Roscoe L. Wall, Jr., "Routine Circumcision? Recent Trends and Concepts," *North Carolina Medical Journal*, vol. 29, no. 3, March 1968, pp. 104, 105.

4. Karen E. Paige, "The Ritual of Circumcision," *Human Nature*, vol. 1, no. 5, May 1978, p. 46.

5. Marvin S. Eiger, "The Case For Circumcision," *Today's Health*, vol. 50, no. 4, April 1972, p. 15.

6. Wall, "Routine Circumcision," p. 105.

7. Edgar Berman, *The Solid Gold Stethoscope* (New York: Macmillan, 1976), p. 135; "Health Professionals Seek to Avert Risk of Hospital-Related Infections," *New York Times*, June 5, 1978, p. A14.

8. Mike Wallace, "Ghost Surgery," Columbia Broadcasting System, (CBS-TV), "*60 Minutes*," Feb. 27, 1977.

9. Boyce Rensberger, "Patients Unaware Surgeon May Be a Beginner," *New York Times*, Feb. 1, 1978, p. B5.

10. S. B. Levitt, et al., "Iatrogenic Microphallus Secondary to Circumcision," *Urology*, vol. 8, no. 5, Nov. 1976, p. 472.

11. W. F. Gee and J. S. Ansell, "Neonatal Circumcision: A Ten Year Overview," *Pediatrics*, vol. 58, no. 4, Dec. 1976, p. 824.

12. David A. Grimes, "Routine Circumcision of the Newborn Infant: A Reappraisal," *American Journal of Obstetrics and Gynecology*, vol. 130, no. 2, Jan. 15, 1978, p. 126.

13. Joseph Katz, "The Question of Circumcision," *International Surgery*, vol. 62, no. 9, Sept. 1977, p. 491.

14. E. J. Dionne, Jr., "A Medical Salesman Did Surgery For Doctors, A Legislator Told," *New York Times*, Oct. 29, 1977, p. 21. This is an extreme example of surgical negligence. A medical equipment salesman performed intricate surgical tasks on at least 12 patients in 3 hospitals. He assisted in surgery in many ways—"using surgical drills, reamed bones, held retractors, cut sutures, etc." Not only did the hospitals list this untrained person on the surgical records but put a "Dr." before his name. Granted, this is an *extreme* example, but if this can occur in complex surgery, there is no doubt that circumcision can be performed with little or no supervision. For a fuller description of these activities by the salesman himself, see William Mackay, *Salesman Surgeon* (New York: McGraw-Hill, 1978.

15. Wall, "Routine Circumcision," p. 106.

16. Gee and Ansell, "Neonatal Circumcision," p. 826.

17. Alan F. Guttmacher, "Should the Baby Be Circumcised?," *Parents' Magazine*, vol. 16, no. 9, Sept. 1941, p. 77; Speert, "Circumcision of Newborn," p. 171; Rosner, "Circumcision," p. 2921. The pro-circumcision physicians were R. Burger and T. H. Guthrie, "Why Circumcision?," *Pediatrics*, vol. 54, no. 3, Sept. 1974, p. 363; the anti-circumcision physician was G. E. Demetrakopoulos, "A Different View of the Facts," *Pediatrics*, vol. 56, no. 2, Aug. 1975, p. 340.

18. Ronald S. Illingworth, *The Normal Child* (Boston: Little, Brown, 1968), p. 98.

19. Editorial, "Should Your Child Be Circumcised?," *Family Health*, vol. 4, no. 2, Feb. 1972, p. 54.

20. Sydney S. Gellis, "Circumcision," *American Journal Diseases of Children*, vol. 132, no. 12, Dec. 1978, p. 1168.

21. John Denton, et al., "Circumcision Complication," *Clinical Pediatrics (Phila.)*, vol. 17, no. 3, March 1978, pp. 285–286.

22. Ibid; also see Rosner, "Circumcision," p. 2921.

23. Gee and Ansell, "Neonatal Circumcision," p. 825.

24. Ibid.

25. L. King, R. Morris, H. Pearson, "Circumcision: Rite, rational or both?," *Patient Care*, vol. 12, no. 5, March 15, 1978, p. 81.

26. John van Duyn and William S. Warr, "Excessive Penile Skin Loss from Circumcision," *Journal of the Medical Association of Georgia*, vol. 51, no. 8, Aug. 1962, p. 394.

27. A. G. M. Campbell, et al., "Circumcision," *Patient Care*, vol. 5, no. 13, July 15, 1971, pp. 67, 68.

28. Levitt, et al., "Iatrogenic Microphallus," pp. 472, 473.

29. M. M. Rubenstein, et. al., "Complications of Circumcision Done With A Plastic Bell Clamp," *American Journal of Diseases of Children*, vol. 116, no. 4, Oct. 1968, pp. 381–382.

30. Campbell, et al., "Circumcision," p. 68.

31. Ibid., p. 78.

32. Ibid., p. 72.

33. Ibid., p. 67.

34. Hawa Patel, "The Problem of Routine Circumcision," *Journal of the Canadian Medical Association*, vol. 95, no. 11, Sept. 10, 1966, pp. 577, 578.

35. E. Noel Preston, "Whither The Foreskin?," *Journal of the American Medical Association*, vol. 213, no. 11, Sept. 14, 1970, p. 1853–1854.

36. Campbell, et al., "Circumcision," p. 77.

37. Levitt, et al., "Iatrogenic Microphallus," p. 472.

38. J. T. Lackey, et al., Letter to Editor, *Journal of the American Medical Association*, vol. 206, no. 10, Dec. 2, 1968, p. 2318.

39. Grimes, "Routine Circumcision," p. 126.

40. Ibid., p. 127.

41. Barry V. Kirkpatric and Donald V. Eitzman, "Neonatal Septicemia After Circumcision," *Clinical Pediatrics*, vol. 13, no. 9, Sept. 1974, p. 768.

42. Gee and Ansell, "Neonatal Circumcision," p. 826.

43. "$733,000 Damage Awarded Boy in Faulty Circumcision," *New York Times*, May 8, 1974, p. 91; "Family Is Awarded $850,000 For Faulty Circumcision Accident." *New York Times* Nov. 2, 1975, p. 54.

44. John Money and Patricia Tucker, *Sexual Signatures* (Boston: Little, Brown, 1975), p. 91.

45. There are malpractice records of adult circumcisions. See *N.A.I.C. Malpractice Claims* (Milwaukee: National Association of Insurance Commissioners), vol. 1, no. 4, May 1977, pp. 10, 35, 67, 109, 127, 173.

46. W. H. Masters and V. E. Johnson, *Human Sexual Inadequacy*, 1st ed. (Boston: Little, Brown, 1970), p. 290.
47. Campbell, et al., "Circumcision," p. 68.
48. Ibid., p. 71.
49. Gee and Ansell, "Neonatal Circumcision," p. 827.

16 Jews and Circumcision

1. Erich Isaac, "The Enigma of Circumcision," *Commentary*, vol. 43, no. 1, Jan. 1967, p. 51.
2. Sigmund Freud, *Moses and Monotheism*, (New York: Vantage Books, 1959), p. 34.
3. Vern L. Bullough, *Sexual Variance in Society and History*, (New York: Wiley, 1976), p. 60.
4. "Women and Health: Female Circumcision—Ethiopia," *Women's International Network (WIN) News*, vol. 3, no. 1, Winter 1977, p. 26, quoting A. Huber, "Female Circumcision and Infibulation in Ethiopia," *Acta Tropica* (Basel), vol. 23, no. 1, pp. 87-91 ff.
5. Menahem Stern, "Strabo," *Encyclopedia Judaica* (Jerusalem, Israel: Macmillan, 1971), vol. 15, p. 418.
6. Fran Hosken, *The Hosken Report* (Lexington, Mass.: W.I.N. News, 1979), in the chapter, "History—Tales of History," p. 9; Elizabeth Gould Davis, *The First Sex* (New York: Penguin Books, 1972), p. 155.
7. Leonard V. Snowman, "Circumcision," *Encyclopedia Judaica*, (Jerusalem, Israel, Macmillan, 1971), vol. 5, pp. 567-572; Max Joseph, "Circumcision," *The Universal Jewish Encyclopedia* (New York: Universal Jewish Encyclopedia Co., 1948), vol. 3, pp. 211-216.
8. See Genesis 17:10-17 for God's ordination to Abraham; Leviticus 12:3 re: 8th day; and Exodus 4:25 and Joshua 5:2-3 regarding the use of a flint knife.
9. Leviticus 19:23.
10. Samuel: Book 1, 18:27.
11. Genesis 34:1-25.
12. Erich Isaac, "Enigma of Circumcision," p. 53.
13. Moses Maimonides, *The Guide for the Perplexed* (New York: Dover Publications, 1956), p. 378.
14. Exodus 4:25-26.
15. Peter Charles Remondino, *History of Circumcision from the Earliest Times to the Present*, 1st ed. (New York: AMS Press, 1974), p. 66. Originally published in 1891 by F.A. Davis, Philadelphia. Also see Charles Weiss, "Reply to Comments," *Jewish Social Studies*, July 1962, p. 188.
16. Amos Elon, *Herzl* (New York: Holt, Rinehart, & Winston, 1975), p. 93. Herzl's son was not circumcised at birth. As an adolescent, he was circumcised at the urging of his father's disciples. See also Hedrick Smith, *The Russians* (New York: Quadrangle/New York Times Books, 1976), p. 476. Russian U.N. Delegates had their sons circumcised on the 8th day at New York's Mount Sinai Hospital. Ronald Sullivan,

"Millions of Medicaid Overbillings Laid to N.Y.C. Hospitals," *New York Times*, Nov. 9, 1976, p. 1. Maimonides Hospital in Brooklyn offered free circumcision to Russian immigrant Jews.

17. Charles Weiss "A Worldwide Survey of the Current Practice of Milah (Ritual Circumcision)," *Jewish Social Studies*, Jan. 1962, p. 40.

18. Remondino, *History of Circumcision*, p. 68; Genesis 17:14.

19. L.V. Snowman, *The Surgery of Ritual Circumcision*, 3rd ed. (London: London Initiation Society, 1961), p. x.

20. Weiss, "Current Practice of Milah," p. 41.

21. Snowman, *Ritual Circumcision*, p. viii.

22. Nadine Brozan, "Despite Opposition, Jewish Ritual of the Mikvah is Revitalized," *New York Times*, Aug. 16, 1976, p. 36. Mentions symbolic circumcision on a New York City man who converted to Judaism. See also Irving Speigel, "Conversion Issue Disturbs A Rabbi," *New York Times*, June 25, 1974, p. 5. An uncircumcised Jew must be circumcised, according to Orthodox rabbis.

23. Kenneth A. Briggs, "Rabbis' Meeting Focuses on Proselytizing," *New York Times*, March 30, 1979, p. A16.

24. Eleanor Blau, "A Little This, A Little That—Poof! Jewish Magic," *New York Times*, May 31, 1975, p. 31.

25. Isaac, "Enigma of Circumcision," p. 52.

26. Ibid.

27. Quoted by Weiss, "Current Practice of Milah," p. 38.

28. Isaac, "Enigma of Circumcision," p. 52.

29. Ibid.

30. S. I. McMillen, *None of These Diseases* (Old Tappan, N.J.: F. H. Revell Co., 1970), p. 18. Remondino also accepted the divine origin of Jewish circumcision.

31. Abraham Ravich, Letter to Editor, *Commentary*, vol. 5, no. 43, May 1967, p. 20.

32. Isaac, "Enigma of Circumcision," p. 51.

33. Ibid.

34. Remondino, *History of Circumcision*, p. 32.

35. Weiss, "Current Practice of Milah," p. 31; "Circumcision," *The Universal Jewish Encyclopedia*, vol. 3, p. 211-216; "Circumcision," *Encyclopedia Judaica*, vol. 5, p. 567-577.

36. Weiss, "Current Practice of Milah," p. 31.

37. Ibid.

38. Aaron Friedenwald, "Circumcision," *Jewish Encyclopedia* (New York and London: Funk & Wagnalls, 1903), vol. 4, p. 99.

39. Weiss, "Current Practice of Milah," p. 47.

40. Eugene A. Hand, "History of Circumcision," *Journal Michigan State Medical Society*, vol. 49, no. 5, May 1950, p. 574.

41. Snowman, *Surgery of Ritual Circumcision*, pp. 30-31.

42. Weiss, "Current Practice of Milah," p. 47.

43. *Circumcision, A Guide to the Methods to be Employed by Mohalim* (New York: Dept. of Health, City of New York), Reprint Series No. 38, Jan. 1916, p. 6. (Seven pages in English, five pages in Yiddish.)

44. Snowman, "Ritual Circumcision," p. 28, Appendix p. vii.

45. "Circumcision," *Universal Jewish Encyclopedia*, vol. 3, pp. 211-216; "Circumcision," *Encyclopedia Judaica*, vol. 5, pp. 567-577.

46. Guido Majno, *The Healing Hand* (Cambridge: Harvard University Press, 1975), pp. 86-90, 247-248, 359-360.

47. A. G. M. Campbell, et al., "Circumcision," *Patient Care*, vol. 5, no. 13, July 15, 1971, p. 78.

48. Majno, *Healing Hand*, pp. 15, 53-54, 96-97, 106, 153, and 298.

49. H. Speert, "Circumcision of the Newborn," *Obstetrics/Gynecology*, vol. 2, no. 2, Aug. 1953, p. 169.

50. Lawrence K. Altman, "Genetic Help For the Layman," *New York Times*, Oct. 8, 1977, p. C21. A review of the book by Audrey Milunsky: *Know Your Genes* (New York: Houghton Mifflin, 1977).

51. Weiss, "Current Practice of Milah," p. 32.

52. Ibid., p. 32.

53. See note 43.

54. Weiss, "Current Practice of Milah," p. 33.

55. Ibid. Quoting *Jewish Communal Register* 2nd ed. (New York: 1918), pp. 321-328.

56. Speert, "Circumcision of Newborn," p. 171.

57. Weiss, "Current Practice of Milah," p. 36.

58. Ibid., p. 36.

59. Harry Apfel, "Ritual Circumcision," *Archives of Pediatrics*, vol. 68, no. 9, Sept. 1951, pp. 427-430.

60. Weiss, "Current Practice of Milah," pp. 30-47.

61. "Rating the Circumcisers," *Newsweek*, vol. 80, no. 10, Sept. 4, 1972, p. 67.

62. D. Annunziato and L. M. Goldblum, "Staphlococcal Scalded Skin Syndrome—A Complication of Circumcision," *American Journal Diseases of Children*, vol. 132, no. 12, Dec. 1978, p. 1187.

63. Weiss, "Current Practice of Milah," p. 43.

64. "A Training School For Circumcision Opens at Mount Sinai," *New York Times*, March 19, 1968, p. 53.

65. Weiss, "Current Practice of Milah," p. 33.

66. Ibid., pp. 46-47.

67. Ibid., p. 47.

68. M. Frand et al., Letter to Editor, *Pediatrics*, vol. 54, no. 4, Oct. 1974, p. 521.

69. Wilfred Berman, Letter to Editor, *Pediatrics*, vol. 56, no. 4, Oct. 1975, p. 621.

70. Weiss, "Current Practice of Milah," p. 47.

17 Female Circumcision

1. Dr. R. Cook, *Damage to Physical Health From Pharaonic Circumcision (Infibulation) of Females. A Review of the Medical Literature* (World Health Organization: Regional Office for the Eastern Mediterranean, 1976), p. 1.

2. Seymour Isenberg and L. Melvin Elting, "A Guide to Sexual Surgery,"

Cosmopolitan, vol. 181, no. 5, Nov. 1976, pp. 104-108. The readership estimate is from *Advertising Age*, Apr. 7, 1975.

    3. Fran P. Hosken, *The Hosken Report* (Lexington, Mass.: Women's International Network News), 1979. See chapter "Medical Facts and Summary," p. 2. *The Hosken Report* is the most comprehensive work on female genital surgery and contains a copious bibliography.

    4. Ibid., pp. 1, 2, 3.

    5. Fran P. Hosken, "Female Circumcision in Africa," *Victimology*, vol. 2, nos. 3/4, 1977-1978, p. 489; also J. A. Verzin, "Sequelae of Female Circumcision," *Tropical Doctor*, vol. 5, Oct. 1975, p. 163.

    6. Fran P. Hosken, "Female Circumcision and Fertility in Africa," *Women and Health*, vol. 1, no. 6, Dec. 1976, p. 3. This figure was updated in 1979 to 68 million. See "Excision/Infibulation in Africa" *W.I.N. News*, vol. 5, no. 4, Autumn 1979, p. 28. Since the precise figure is admittedly uncertain, I am using the 20-25 million figure in the text.

    7. Verzin, "Sequelae of Female Circumcision," p. 163.

    8. Hosken, *The Hosken Report*, "Personal View," p. 4.

    9. *WIN News* is available from 187 Grant St., Lexington, Mass., 02173.

    10. John Gunther, *Inside Africa* (New York: Harper & Bros., 1953), p. 298.

    11. Jomo Kenyatta, *Facing Mount Kenya* (New York: Vantage Books, 1962), p. 140.

    12. Colin Turnbull, *Man In Africa* (Garden City, N.Y.: Anchor Books/Doubleday, 1976), p. 221.

    13. Jacques Lantier, *La Cite Magique Et Magie En Afrique Noire*, (Paris: Librarie A. Fayand, 1972), p. 226. (Translated by Ms. F. Hosken.) From *Munger Africana Library Notes*, Issue No. 36, California Institute of Technology, Oct. 1976, p. 11.

    14. L. Hall, "Arthritis After Female Circumcision," *East African Medical Journal*, vol. 40, no. 2, Feb. 1963, pp. 50-57.

    15. Hosken, "Female Circumcision and Fertility," *Women and Health*, vol. 1, no. 6, p. 8.

    16. Hosken, "History: Tales of History," *The Hosken Report*, pp. 7, 8.

    17. "Genital Mutilation of African Girls Through Ritual Operations," *W.I.N. News*, vol. 3, no. 1, Winter 1977, p. 27.

    18. Hosken, "Kenya," *The Hosken Report*, p. 16.

    19. Hosken, "Female Circumcision in Africa," *Victimology*, p. 494.

    20. Hosken, "History: Tales of History," *The Hosken Report*, p. 5.

    21. Hosken, "Upper Volta," *The Hosken Report*, p. 2.

    22. Hosken, "Reasons Given," *The Hosken Report*, p. 7.

    23. Elizabeth Gould Davis, *The First Sex* (New York: Putnam's, 1971), p. 154.

    24. Fran P. Hosken, "Female Circumcision and Fertility," *Women and Health*, vol. 1, no. 6, p. 6.

    25. "Women and Health: Female Circumcision, Ghana: Accra," *Women's International Network News*, vol. 3, no. 2, Spring 1977, p. 38. Also see Kenyatta, *Facing Mount Kenya*, pp. 125-148.

    26. Hosken, "Female Circumcision and Fertility," *Women and Health*, vol. 1, no. 6, p. 8.

    27. This Freudian concept is still discussed in the psychiatric literature. See R. A.

Lattore, "Psychological Correlates in Clitoral/Vaginal Stimulation," *American Journal of Psychiatry*, 136 (2), Feb. 1979, pp. 225-226.

28. Hosken, "Female Circumcision in Africa," *Victimology*, p. 492.

29. Anthony Pietropinto and Jacqueline Simenauer, *Beyond the Male Myth* (New York: New York Times Books, 1977), p. 327.

30. Hosken, "History: Tales of History," p. 8, also "Case History—Ethiopia," p. 6, *The Hosken Report*.

31. "In Africa Moslems Thoroughly Mix Their Culture With Their Faith," *New York Times*, Sept. 17, 1974, p. 16.

32. John Darnton, "Somalia Tries to Live by Both the Koran and 'Das Kapital,'" *New York Times*, Oct. 11, 1977, p. 3.

33. Michael Langley, "A Barbaric Custom," *The Spectator*, Feb. 4, 1949, pp. 155-156; John Gunther, *Inside Africa* (New York: Harper & Bros., 1953), p. 298; Shirley MacLaine, *Don't Fall Off The Mountain* (New York: Bantam Books, 1971), p. 275.

34. "Children's Aid Movement Urges End to Circumcision of Females," *New York Times*, April 26, 1977, p. 9; Roger Chateauneu, "Millions of Little Girls Mutilated for Life," *Paris Match*, May 13, 1977, p. 88-94.

35. Hosken, "Preface," *Hosken Report*, p. 4.

36. "Feminist Parley Ends On Optimistic Note," *New York Times*, March 9, 1976, p. 2.

37. Hosken, "Preface," *The Hosken Report*, p. 3.

38. Hosken, "Case Histories—Upper Volta," *The Hosken Report*, p. 5.

39. Hosken, "Case Histories—Ethiopia," *The Hosken Report*, p. 1.

40. Hosken, "Reasons Given," *The Hosken Report*, p. 4.

41. Hosken, "Case Histories—Ethiopia," *The Hosken Report*, p. 5.

42. Hosken, "Case Histories—Nigeria," *The Hosken Report*, p. 1.

43. Ibid, p. 4.

44. Fran P. Hosken, "Special Report: Women and Health in Africa/A Personal View," *W.I.N. News*, vol. 5, no. 2, Spring 1979, pp. 1-13.

45. S. Fortunoff, J. K. Latimer, and M. Edson, "Skin Flap in Vaginoplasty," *Modern Medicine*, vol. 32, no. 4, July 6, 1964, p. 131. Also see B. S. Verkauf, "Acquired Clitoral Enlargement," *Medical Aspects of Human Sexuality*, vol. 9, no. 4, April 1975, pp. 134-151. (This article has 60 references.)

46. Robert Gross et al., "Clitorectomy for Sexual Abnormalities," *Surgery*, vol. 59, no. 2, Feb. 1966, pp. 300-308.

47. Ibid., p. 307.

48. Ibid., p. 300.

49. Ibid., p. 307.

50. Barbara Gelb, "A Journey to Israel and Egypt," *New York Times*, Nov. 26, 1978, Magazine Section, pp. 123-124.

51. Hosken, "History: Tales of History," *The Hosken Report*, pp. 5-6. Soramus (Soranus) c. 138 A.D., and Aetius (502-575 A.D.) recommended clitoridectomy for hypertrophy. The former practiced medicine in Alexandria, Egypt, and the latter stated that he was following the Egyptian practice.

52. Hosken, "Western World," *The Hosken Report*, p. 3.

53. Richard Burton, *Personal Narrative of a Pilgrimage to Al-Madinah and Mecca* (New York: Dover, 1964), 3 vols.

54. Peter Charles Remondino, *History of Circumcision from Earliest Times to the Present*, 1st ed. (New York: AMS Press, 1974), p. 270. Originally published by F.A. Davis, Philadelphia, in 1891.

55. J. G. Jisr, "Circumcision in the Female," *American Medicine* (Burlington, Vermont), vol. 26, no. 2, Feb. 1920, p. 106-107.

56. Stephen Kern, *Anatomy and Destiny* (Indianapolis: Bobbs-Merrill, 1975), p. 101.

57. J. B. Fleming, "Clitoridectomy—The Disastrous Downfall of Isaac Baker Brown, F.R.C.S. (1867)," *The Journal of Obstetrics and Gynecology of the British Empire*, vol. 67, no. 6, Dec. 1960, p. 1020.

58. René Spitz, "Authority and Masturbation," *Psychoanalytic Quarterly*, vol. 21, no. 4, 1952, p. 502. Also see H. E. Beebe, "The Clitoris," *Journal of Orificial Surgery*, vol. 6, no. 1, July 1897, p. 9.

59. Fleming "Clitoridectomy," pp. 1017-1018.

60. J. Duffy, "Masturbation and Clitoridectomy," *Journal American Medical Association*, vol. 186, no. 3, Oct. 19, 1963, p. 247.

61. Fleming, "Clitoridectomy," p. 1019.

62. Ibid., passim.

63. Duffy, "Masturbation," p. 247.

64. Ibid.

65. G. J. Barker-Benfield, *The Horrors of the Half Known Life: Male Attitudes Toward Women and Sexuality in Nineteenth Century America*, (New York: Harper and Row, 1976), pp. 88-89, 96-97.

66. Marie Bonaparte, *Female Sexuality* (New York: International Universities Press, 1973), pp. 156-157.

67. Wayland Young, *Eros Denied* (New York: Grove Press, 1964), p. 206.

68. Duffy, "Masturbation," p. 247.

69. Spitz, "Authority and Masturbation," p. 504.

70. Barker-Benfield, *Horrors of Half Known Life*, p. 132.

71. Isaac Harvey, *Eternal Eve* (Garden City, N.Y.: Doubleday, 1951), pp. 433-434.

72. Barker-Benfield, *Horrors of Half Known Life*, p. 120.

73. Duffy, "Masturbation," p. 248.

74. Barker-Benfield, *Horrors of Half Known Life*, p. 132.

75. S. L. Kistler, "Rapid Bloodless Circumcision," *Journal of the American Medical Association*, vol. 54, no. 22, May 28, 1910, p. 1782.

76. Alan F. Guttmacher, *Pregnancy and Birth* (New York: Signet Books, 1956), p. 241.

77. A. J. Wabrek and C. J. Wabrek, "Dyspareunia," *Journal of Sex and Marital Therapy*, vol. 1, no. 3, Spring 1975, pp. 238-239.

78. Mary J. Grey, "Clitoral Pain," *Medical Aspects of Human Sexuality*, vol. 10, no. 12, Dec 1976, pp. 105-106.

79. Robert B. Butler and Myrna I. Lewis, *Sex After 60* (New York: Harper & Row, 1976), p. 19.

80. "Working With Older People," *Clinical Aspects of Aging*, P.H.S., Washington, D.C., vol. 4, Publication #1459, July 1971, p. 150.

81. David Reuben, *How To Get More Out Of Sex* (New York: Bantam Books, 1974), p. 11.

82. See Hosken, "Female Circumcision in Africa," *Victimology*, p. 487, re: health benefits; see "Male Circumcision," *Hosken Report*, pp. 1, 2, re: orgasmic delay; see "Female Circumcision," *W.I.N. News*, vol. 3, no. 2, Spring 1977, p. 30, re: painlessness of circumcision.

83. Spitz, "Authority and Masturbation," p. 503.

84. Bonaparte, *Female Sexuality*, p. 150.

85. Ibid., pp. 151-152.

86. Jodi Lawrence, *The Search For The Perfect Orgasm* (Los Angeles: Nash Publishing, 1973), p. 162.

87. Kermit Krantz, Reply to Query, *Medical Aspects of Human Sexuality*, vol. 8, no. 11, Nov. 1974, pp. 107-110.

88. Morton Hunt, *Sexual Behavior in the 1970's* (Chicago: Playboy Press, 1975), p. 209.

89. Isenberg and Elting, "Sexual Surgery," p. 104.

90. Ibid.

91. Diane S. Fordney-Settlage, "Clitoral Abnormalities," *Medical Aspects of Human Sexuality*, vol. 9, no. 5, May 1975, p. 183.

92. Gene G. Abel, et al., "Women's Vaginal Response during REM Sleep," *Journal of Sex and Marital Therapy*, vol. 5, no. 1, Spring 1979, pp. 6, 14.

93. Thomas P. Lowry, Reply to Query, *Medical Aspects of Human Sexuality*, vol. 11, no. 12, Dec. 1977, p. 60.

94. Barbara Schneidman, Reply to Query, *Medical Aspects of Human Sexuality*, vol. 11, no. 8, Aug. 1977, p. 76.

95. Mary Jane Grey, "Women's Preferences Regarding Clitoral Stimulation," *Medical Aspects of Human Sexuality*, vol. 12, no. 1, Jan. 1978, p. 35.

96. Lonnie G. Barbach, Response to Query, *Medical Aspects of Human Sexuality*, vol. 12, no. 5, May 1978, p. 27.

97. Fred Seligman, Reply to Query, *Medical Aspects of Human Sexuality*, vol. 12, no. 3, March 1978, p. 9.

98. Marcia J. Coleman, Reply to Query, *Medical Aspects of Human Sexuality*, vol. 13, no. 2, Feb. 1979, p. 30.

99. Caroline Preston, Reply to Query, *Medical Aspects of Human Sexuality*, vol. 11, no. 12, Dec. 1977, p. 59.

100. Estelle Fuchs, *The Second Season* (Garden City, N.Y.: Doubleday, 1977), p. 130.

101. Shere Hite, *The Hite Report* (New York: Dell, 1977), p. 271.

102. Merle Sondra Kroop, "Are 'Frigid' Women Capable Of Love?," *Medical Aspects of Human Sexuality*, vol. 11, no. 12, Dec. 1977, p. 41.

103. Lawrence Sharpe, Reply to Query, *Medical Aspects of Human Sexuality*, vol. 11, no. 12, Dec. 1977, p. 29.

104. P. W. Toussieng, "Men's Fear of Having Too Small a Penis," *Medical Aspects of Human Sexuality*, vol. 11, no. 5, May 1977, p. 62.

105. Robert E. Rothenberg, *Understanding Surgery* (New York: Pocket Books, 1966), p. 498.

106. Verkauf, "Acquired Clitoral Enlargement," pp. 134-151, passim.

107. Lawrence, *Perfect Orgasm*, p. 163.

108. R. B. Greenblatt, Reply to Query, *Medical Aspects of Human Sexuality*, vol. 9, no. 11, Nov. 1975, p. 127.

109. Roger J. Williams, "Nutritional Individuality," *Human Nature*, vol. 1, no. 6, June 1978, p. 46.

110. M. J. Grey, Reply to Query, *Medical Aspects of Human Sexuality*, vol. 10, no. 11, Nov. 1976, p. 41.

111. National Center for Health Statistics, Washington, D.C., Private correspondence, Grace K. White, May 12, 1972, for 1968; Private correspondence, Gloria J. Gardocki, Dec. 4, 1978, for the years 1973 and 1977.

Year	Operations on External Female Genitalia
1968	5,000
1973	4,000
1977	7,000

112. Leo Wollman, "Female Circumcision," *Journal of the American Society of Psychosomatic Medicine and Dentistry*, vol. 20, no. 1, pp. 3, 4, and vol. 20, no. 4, 1973, pp. 130, 131.

113. B. Graber and G. M. Graber, "You and Your Sexuality," *Playgirl*, vol. 2, no. 4, Sept. 1974, p. 83.

114. Lawrence, *Perfect Orgasm*, p. 162.

115. A. H. Chapman, *The Strategy of Sex* (New York: Putnam's, 1970), p. 23.

116. Cathrine Kellison, "Circumcision for Women—The Kindest Cut Of All," *Playgirl*, vol. 1, no. 5, Oct. 1973, pp. 76, 124.

117. *Advertising Age*, April 7, 1975.

118. Cathrine Kellison, "$100 Surgery For A Million Dollar Sex Life," *Playgirl*, vol. 2, no. 12, May 1975, p. 52.

119. William D. Walden, Letter to the Editor, *Playgirl*, vol. 3, no. 5, Oct. 1975, p. 6.

120. See note 2.

121. James P. Semmens and F. Jane Semmens, Reply to Query, *Medical Aspects of Human Sexuality*, vol. 8, no. 7, July 1974, pp. 99-101.

122. Johanna F. Perlmutter, Reply to Query, *Medical Aspects of Human Sexuality*, vol. 10, no. 1, Jan. 1976, p. 143.

123. John W. Huffman, "Some Facts About the Clitoris," *Postgraduate Medicine*, vol. 60, no. 5, Nov. 1976, p. 245.

124. Lawrence S. Jackman, Reply to a Query, *Medical Aspects of Human Sexuality*, vol. 12, no. 3, March 1978, p. 13.

125. Takey Crist, Reply to Query, *Medical Aspects of Human Sexuality*, vol. 11, no. 8, Aug. 1977, p. 77.

126. Martin Shepard, *Ecstasy* (New York: Moneysworth, 1977), p. 125.

127. Karen E. Paige, "The Ritual of Circumcision," *Human Nature*, vol. 1, no. 5, May 1978, p. 45.

128. Press release, National Blue Shield Association, Chicago, May 18, 1977. Personal telephone communication, May 20, 1977, National Blue Shield Association.

129. Paige, "Ritual of Circumcision," p. 46.

130. Isenberg and Elting, "Sexual Surgery," p. 104.

131. Ibid.

132. Ibid.

133. Cook, *Pharaonic Circumcision*, p. 1.
134. W. G. Rathmann, "Female Circumcision, Indications and a New Technique," *General Practitioner*, vol. 20, no. 3, Sept. 1959, pp. 115-120. See note 112 for Wollman reference.
135. Rathmann's reference was Felix Bryk's *Circumcision in Man and Woman* (New York: AMS Press, 1974). Written in 1930, the first English translation was published by the American Ethnological Press, New York, 1934.
136. Rathmann, "Female Circumcision," p. 115.
137. Ibid.
138. Ibid., p. 116.
139. Ibid.
140. Ibid., p. 117.
141. Ibid.
142. Ibid.
143. Ibid., p. 116.
144. Ibid., p. 117.
145. See note 112 for Wollman reference. The Wollman article referred to on p. 189 is "Hooded Clitoris," *Journal of the American Society of Psychosomatic Dentistry and Medicine*, vol. 19, no. 1(3), 1973.
146. Fordney-Settlage, "Clitoral Abnormalities," p. 183.
147. James C. Burt, *Surgery of Love* (New York: Carlton Press, 1975).
148. Barbara Demick, "Love Surgery," *The Real Paper*, (Cambridge, Mass.: Aug. 26, 1978), pp. 6-12.
149. Ibid. p. 6.

18 An Appeal to Reason

1. David A. Grimes, "Routine Circumcision of the Newborn Infant: A Reappraisal," *American Journal of Obstetrics and Gynecology*, vol. 130, no. 2, Jan. 15, 1978, p. 128.
2. Lendon Smith, *The Children's Doctor* (Englewood Cliffs, N.J.: Prentice Hall, 1969), p. 195.
3. Bruno Bettelheim, *Symbolic Wounds*, 1st ed. (New York: Collier Books, 1962), p. 147. This book provides a copious bibliography.
4. Ibid.
5. Ibid.
6. R. A. Shaw and W. O. Robertson, "Routine Circumcision," *American Journal Diseases of Children*, vol. 106, no. 2, Aug. 1963, p. 217.
7. Sylvia Topp, "The Argument Over Circumcision; The Case Against," *The Village Voice*, June 16, 1975, pp. 8 and 9.
8. Ibid.
9. Grimes, "Routine Circumcision," p. 127.
10. Ibid.
11. Edward B. Feehan, Letter to the Editor, *Pediatrics*, vol. 60, no. 4, Oct. 1977, p. 566.
12. Grimes, "Routine Circumcision," p. 128.
13. Ibid., pp. 128-129. Also see Karen E. Paige, "The Ritual of Circumcision,"

Human Nature, vol. 1, no. 5, May 1978, p. 46. Dr. Paige estimates the cost at $200 million annually.

14. Jane E. Brody, "House Panel Calls For More U.S. Control of Surgery," *New York Times*, Dec. 27, 1978, p. 1.

15. Daniel S. Greenberg, Book review of *Doing Better and Feeling Worse*, by John H. Knowles (New York: W. W. Norton & Co., 1977), *New York Times* Book Review Section, July 24, 1977, p. 10.

16. H. H. Hiatt, "Protecting the Medical Commons: Who Is Responsible?," *New England Journal of Medicine*, vol. 293, 1975, p. 235.

17. Grimes, "Routine Circumcision," p. 128.

18. Ibid., p. 129.

19. Ibid.

20. Ibid.

21. *Health Facts* (New York: Center for Medical Consumers and Health Care Information), vol. 1, no. 6, Dec. 1977, p. 1.

22. Doris Jonas and David Jonas, "Ejaculation: Premature for Whom?," *Physicians World*, vol. 11, no. 7, July 1974, p. 92.

23. Mary Jane Sherfey, "Some Biology of Sexuality," *Journal of Sex and Marital Therapy*, vol. 1, no. 2, Winter 1974, p. 100.

24. James Reston, "Silly Season Samples," *New York Times*, Aug. 12, 1977, p. A21.

25. "Circumcision Test in '61 Disclosed in C.I.A. Data," *New York Times*, Oct. 2, 1977, p. 35. (Reuters Dispatch, datelined Washington, D.C., Sept. 30, 1977.)

26. Richard Cohen, "C.I.A. Circumcision Study Secretly Circumscribed," *Washington Post*, Oct. 20, 1977, p. C1.

27. Paige, "Ritual of Circumcision," pp. 46-47.

28. Sydney S. Gellis, "Circumcision," *American Journal Diseases of Children*, vol. 132, no. 12, Dec. 1978, p. 1169.

Appendix A   What Is Circumcision?

1. W. G. Rathmann, "Female Circumcision, Indications and a New Technique," General Practitioner, vol. 20, no. 3, Sept. 1959, pp. 115-120.

Appendix B   The Circumcision Frequency Rate

1. Roscoe L. Wall, Jr., "Routine Circumcision? Recent Trends and Concepts," *North Carolina Medical Journal*, vol. 29, no. 3, March 1968, p. 106.

2. *Surgical Operations in Short-Stay Hospitals for Discharged Patients United States 1965*, (United States Department of Health, Education and Welfare, Public Health Service, Rockville, Md.), Public. #1000, Series 13, No. 7.

3. Hawa Patel, "The Problem of Routine Circumcision," *Canadian Medical Journal*, vol. 95, no. 11, Sept. 10, 1966, p. 576.

4. D. Gairdner, "The Fate of the Foreskin," *British Medical Journal*, vol. 2, Dec. 24, 1949, p. 1436.

5. M. P. M. Richards, J. F. Bernal, and Yvonne Brackbill, "Early Behavioral Differences: Gender or Circumcision?," *Developmental Psychobiology*, vol. 9, no. 1, Jan. 1976, pp. 90-91.

6. C. H. Garvin and L. Persky, "Circumcision: Is It Justified in Infancy?," *Journal National Medical Association*, vol. 58, no. 4, July 1966, p. 234.

7. Donald Kariher, Reply to Query, *Journal American Medical Association*, vol. 194, no. 3, Oct. 18, 1965, p. 319.

8. Richards, et al., "Early Behavioral Differences," p. 90.

9. Deron Hovsepian, "The Pros and Cons of Routine Circumcision," *California Medicine*, vol, 75, no. 5, Nov. 1951, p. 361.

10. Patel, "Routine Circumcision," p. 579.

11. Karen E. Paige, "The Ritual of Circumcision," *Human Nature*, vol. 1, no. 5, May 1978, p. 43.

12. A. Guttmacher, "Should the Baby Be Circumcised?," *Parents Magazine*, vol. 16, no. 9, Sept. 1941, p. 76.

13. Hovsepian, "Routine Circumcision," p. 361.

14. Garvin and Persky, "Circumcision," p. 234.

15. "Circumcision and Cancer," *Time* magazine, vol. 63, no. 14, Apr. 5, 1954, p. 96.

16. L. Emmet Holt, Jr., "The Children's Corner," *Good Housekeeping Magazine*, vol. 139, Aug. 1954, p. 128.

17. Kariher, "Reply to Query," p. 319.

18. W. E. Masters and V. E. Johnson, *Human Sexual Response*, 1st ed. (Boston: Little, Brown, 1966), p. 190.

19. "The Medical Controversy Over Circumcision," *Good Housekeeping Magazine*, vol. 167, Sept. 1968, p. 179.

20. "The Case Against Circumcision," *Time* magazine, vol. 96, no. 16, Oct. 19, 1970, p. 58.

21. L. P. Williams, *How To Avoid Unnecessary Surgery* (Los Angeles: Nash, 1971), p. 106.

22. W. F. Gee and J. S. Ansell, "Neonatal Circumcision: A Ten-Year Overview," *Pediatrics*, vol. 58, no. 4, Dec. 1976, p. 824.

23. "Rating the Circumcisers," *Newsweek Magazine*, vol. 80, no. 10, Sept. 4, 1972, p. 67.

24. Desmond Morris, *Intimate Behavior* (New York: Bantam, 1973), p. 241.

25. G. T. Klauber, "Circumcision and Phallic Fallacies, Or the Case Against Routine Circumcision," *Connecticut Medicine*, vol. 37, no. 9, Sept. 1973, p. 447.

26. David A. Grimes, "Routine Circumcision of the Newborn Infant: A Reappraisal," *American Journal of Obstetrics and Gynecology*, vol. 130, no. 2, Jan. 15, 1978, p. 128.

27. T. E. Schwark, Letter to Editor, *Pediatrics*, vol. 60, no. 4, Oct. 1977, p. 563.

28. John L. Wirth, "Statistics on Circumcision in Canada and Australia," *American Journal Obstetrics and Gynecology*, vol. 130, no. 2, Jan. 15, 1978, p. 236.

Glossary

Balanitis—inflammation of the penis.
Benign—non-cancerous.
Brith Milah Board—group supervising Jewish ritual circumcision.
Carcinogen—cancer-causing agent.
Castration (male)—removal of the testes.
Cauterization—burning.
Chancroid—a venereal disease.
Clitoris—female sexual organ corresponding to the penis.
Coitus—sexual intercourse.
Clitoridectomy—removal of the clitoris.
Congenital—defect or disease transmitted via heredity, or prenatal or birth environment.
Cunnilingus—oral sex applied to a female.
Cyanotic—bluish coloration.
Dilation—to make wider or larger (for example, separation of the foreskin from the glans).
Electroencephalograph—device to record brain waves.
Enuresis—bed wetting.
Episiotomy—incision made during labor from the lower part of the vagina toward the anus to enlarge the vaginal opening to ease the passage of the fetus.
Etiology—cause.
Fellatio—oral sex applied to a male.
Foreskin—tissue covering the head (glans) of the penis or the clitoris. Also called prepuce. In the female the tissue is sometimes referred to as the hood.
Frenum—ridge on the underside of the glans where the inner foreskin lining is attached to the penis.

Glans—rounded head at the end of the penis or clitoris.
Hood—tissue covering the clitoris. See also *Foreskin*.
Hydrocephaly—an abnormal condition in which an excess of fluid enlarges the cranium (skull).
Hypertrophy—abnormal enlargement.
Impotence—the inability to have an erection.
Infibulation—sewing together (of the labia or foreskin). In ancient Rome accomplished by means of a clasp (fibula).
Labia—literally, lips. There are two folds of tissue: the larger, labia majora, covers the vulva; the smaller, labia minora, lies within the labia majora.
Laceration—tear.
Malignant—cancerous.
Meatus—a passage or an opening. The urinary meatus in the male is located at the tip of the penis; in the female, it is located between the clitoris and the vagina.
Mohel—Jewish ritual circumciser (pronounced moyel; plural mohelim).
Morbidity—illness.
Mortality—death.
Neonate—newborn.
Onanism—coitus interruptus (withdrawal). More frequently used as a euphemism for masturbation.
Orifice—a mouth or opening. The preputial orifice is located at the tip of the prepuce.
Paraphimosis—a condition in which the foreskin is forcibly retracted, exposing the glans, but too tight to permit the foreskin to return to its normal position.
Paresis—a severe mental disorder caused by untreated syphilis.
Pathology—a branch of medicine dealing with the nature of disease.
Pathological—involving disease.
Pederasty—sexual intercourse with a boy.
Phimosis—a condition in which the foreskin cannot be retracted.
Plethoric—swollen. An excess of blood in any part of the body.
Prepuce—see *Foreskin*.
Prophylactic—disease preventative.
Pubococcygeal muscle—located at the floor of the pelvis.
Quartile—a frequency distribution divided into four parts.
Redundant—excessively long (referring to the foreskin).
Sequela—a diseased condition resulting from a previous disease or medical procedure.
Sulcus—circular groove located between the glans and the shaft of the penis.
Therapy—treatment.
Therapeutic—curative.

Glossary

Urethra—canal through which urine is discharged from the bladder. Male: the urethra passes through the penis to the opening at the tip of the glans (the meatus). Seminal fluid also passes through the urethra. Female: much shorter than the male. Opening at the meatus located between the clitoris and the vagina.
Utero—uterus (womb).
Venereal disease—any disease transmitted by sexual contact.
Vulva—the external female genitalia.

Subject Index

Ablation of clitoral foreskin, 165
Abraham, 7, 8
Ad Hoc Task Force on Circumcision, 3, 23, 46, 116
   report on neonatal circumcision (1975), 64–65, 77–78
Adult male circumcision, 127–128, 129
   in Canada, 131
   in Finland, 128, 132, 133, 134
   need for, 134
   nonmedical reasons for, 132–133
   penile hygiene and, 134
   in U.S., 131, 132
Africa, 68, 111–112, 171, 172
   See also names of countries
Agnes of Blannbekin, Saint, 10
Albert Einstein Medical School, 139
Algeria, 163
American Academy of Pediatrics, 3, 23, 46, 64, 66, 77, 150
American Board of Obstetrics and Gynecology, 193
American Cancer Society, 88, 91, 99, 100, 102
American College of Obstetricians and Gynecologists (ACOG), statement on neonatal circumcision, 218

ACOG *Journal*, 218
ACOG *Newsletter*, 218
American Indians, 8
American Journal Diseases of Children, 148, 196
American Journal of Orthopsychiatry, The, 144
American Medical Association, 20, 55, 118
American Psychiatric Association, 117, 118, 181
Amish, 99
Anesthesia, 36
   newborns and, 138–139
Animal circumcision, 60–61
Anthropological writings about circumcision, 10–13
Anti-circumcision literature, 4, 221–222
Apostles, The, 9
Appendectomy, 134
Arabs, 7, 11, 171, 172
Athabascan Indians, 68
Australia, 1, 7, 8, 27–28
   circumcision rate in, 29
Australian Health Service, 30
Australian Journal of Medicine, 29, 194
Aztecs, 8

265

Baby and Child Care (Spock), 47–48
Bangladesh, 68
Barbarity of Circumcision, The, 17
Battle Creek Sanitorium, 33
Bearstead Memorial Hospital, 162
Bed-wetting, 14, 126
Beth Israel Hospital, 96
Bible, The, 8, 17, 50
   references to circumcision in, 155
Blacks, 7, 20, 34, 69, 133
   myths about penis size, 11–12
   venereal disease and, 81–84
Blue Shield, 30, 185
Body hygiene, 72–74
Body secretions, 59–60
Boston Children's Hospital, 135, 170
Boy Scout Handbook, The, 124
Breast cancer, 89
Brenneman's ulcers, 63
Brigitta, Saint, 9
British Department of Health and Social Security, 215
British Medical Journal, 63, 148
British National Health Service, 22, 28, 30, 70
Brown University, 139, 140
Burns, 55

Calymmato bacterium granuloma, 99
Cambodia, 68
Canada, 1, 27–28, 76, 131, 150–151
   adult male circumcision in, 131
   circumcision frequency study (1966), 69
   circumcision rate in, 29
Canadian Health Service, 30
Canadian Medical Journal, 29
Cancer, 2, 88–114
   alleged benefits of circumcision, 89
   estimates for women (1978), 92
   frequency of new cases, 88
   Jewish women and, 89
   national data provided on, 96–97
   selected occurrences of (1977), 109
   smegma and, 89–90, 91, 95, 96–99, 105, 106, 108, 113

   of the tongue, 20–21, 39
   See also Breast cancer; Cervical cancer; Genital cancer; Penile cancer; Prostatic cancer; Scrotal cancer; Uterine cancer
Carcinogens, 88, 105, 106
"Carcinoma of the Penis and the Anti-Circumcision Crusade," 24–25
Case Western Reserve School of Medicine, 110, 112, 140
Castration, 7, 37
Central Intelligence Agency (C.I.A.), 195–196
Cervical cancer, 50, 67, 89, 91–99, 133
   circumcision and, 95, 96
   development of, 91
   Indian women and, 94
   Jewish women and, 92, 99
   rate of (1977), 105
   sexual intercourse and, 99
   Terris study of, 94–95
   in U.S., 95
   viruses as cause of, 98
   Wynder study of, 92–93
Charles V, King, 9
Charlemagne, 9
Chinese people, 11
Circumcision clamp, 39, *see also* Gomco clamp
Circumcision frequency rate, 214–217
"Circumcision for Women—The Kindest Cut of All," 183
Clitoral foreskin, 5, 213
   ablation of, 165
Clitoral surgery
   in the Third World, 165–169
   in the U.S., 170
Clitoridectomy, 13, 14, 68, 165
   in England, 172–173
   masturbation and, 171–172
   in the U.S., 173–175
Clitoridotomy, 165
Clitoris, 72, 210–212
   hypertrophied, 171
   orgasm and, 179–182
   removal of, 38–39

Coital anorgasmia, 181
Columbia Presbyterian Medical Center, 170
Columbia University College of Physicians and Surgeons, 19, 96
Condoms, 86
Cornification, 115
Cosmopolitan, 164, 178, 183, 185
Cradle of Erotica, 11
Cruex, 74
Curability of Certain Forms of Insanity, Epilepsy, Catalepsy and Hysteria in Females, The (Brown), 173

Denmark, 31, 86, 106, 107
　circumcision frequency, 127
Dental hygiene, 70–71, 73, 78
Dervishes, 7
Diagnostic Manual, 181
Diethylstilbesterol (DES), 105, 113
Diseases, germ theory of, 37
Diseases of Infancy and Childhood, 123
"Drapetomania," 34
Dyspareunia, 176
Dysplasia, 94

East Africa Medical Journal, 111
Ecstasy (Shephard), 184
Egypt, 7, 8, 68, 171, 172
Ejaculation, premature, *see* Premature ejaculation
Ejaculatory control, 59
El Salvador, 101
Electron microscope, 58
Encyclopedia Britannica, 7
Encyclopedia Judaica, 7, 8, 9
Encyclopedia of Religion and Ethics, 10
Encyclopedia of Sexual Behavior, The, 56
England, 1, 13, 22, 27–28
　circumcision rate in, 28, 29–30, 49
　clitoridectomy in, 172–173
　Jewish ritual circumcision in, 162
　newborn circumcision in, 68, 114
　Victorianism in, 34–35
Enuresis, 14, 126
Eros Denied (Young), 11–12

Eternal Eve (Harvey), 174–175
Ethiopia, 8, 9, 167, 168, 169

Family Health, 148
Feast of the Circumcision, 9
Fellashas, 9
Female circumcision, 5, 8, 164–190, 212–213
　definitions, 164–165
　direct surgery for, 212
　genital hygiene and, 72, 176
　masturbation and, 175–177
　research conducted on, 185–189
　sexual enhancement and, 164, 190
　squeeze technique for, 212
　in the U.S., 182–185
Female genital hygiene, 71–72, 74–75
Female genital surgery, 177–179, 257
Female masturbation, 74–75
Female smegma, 90
Finland, 31, 86, 106, 107, 128, 133, 134
　adult male circumcision in, 128, 132, 133, 134
Finnish National Board of Health, 32, 128
First International Conference on Child Studies (1978), 139–140
Flexner report (1910), 36
Foreskin, 2, 3, 12, 13, 52–61, 201, 213
　clitoral, 5, 213
　ejaculatory control and, 59
　lack of hygiene and, 54
　lack of information about function of, 52–53, 63, 65
　mystique surrounding, 9–10
　prevailing medical view of, 52, 54, 64–65
　redundant, 49
　sexual function of, 56–58
　smegma and, 59, 60, 64
　tight, 2, 62–66, 128, 132
　usefulness of, 53, 55, 56
　　in experimental biology, 60
　　in plastic surgery, 60
Fournier's syndrome, 196
France, 95, 106, 107

Gall bladder removal, 134
Genital cancer sites, unspecified (1977), 239
Genital cancer in Sweden (1977), 110
Germ theory of disease, 37
Glossary, 262
God, 8
Gomco clamp, 207, 208
Gonorrhea, 81-87
　new cases reported (1945-1977), 82
Good Housekeeping, 45, 46, 216
Great Britain, *see* England
Greece, ancient, 68

Harvard Medical School, 44, 170
Harvard University, 137
Hatafath dam berith, 156
Health care, 70-71
Health education, 70, 71
Heart rate responses, effect of circumcision on, 144
Hemorrhage, 149
Herodotus, 8, 154
Herpes Simplex Virus, 87
Herpes II Virus, 50, 82-87, 98
Highland Park Hospital, 215
Hindus, 11, 68, 74
History of Circumcision From the Earliest Times to the Present (Remondino), 17-18
Honduras, 100, 101
How to Get More Out of Sex (Reuben), 85
Human Nature, 87
Huntington Memorial Hospital, 146
Hygeia, 45, 81
Hypersexuality, 37
Hypertrophied clitoris, 171
Hypospadias, 152
Hysterectomy, 77, 134

In the Name of Humanity (Lewis), 18
Incas, 8
Index Medicus, 145, 218
India, 68, 74, 95, 111, 112

Infibulation, 8, 12-14, 38, 68, 165, 166, 168, 177
Initiation Society of London, 159
International Agency for Research on Cancer, 88
Iraq, 163
Israel, 68, 96, 100, 101
　circumcision practices in, 163

Jesus Christ, 8, 9-10
Jewish Circumcision Society, 162
Jews, 154-163
　ancient references to health benefits of circumcision, 154-155
　cancer and, 89, 92, 99, 102, 103, 108
　immigration to U.S. of, 36-37
　masturbation and, 123
　modern-day challenges to health benefits of circumcision, 157, 161, 162-163
　the mohel, 147, 157-163
　mystical powers attributed to circumcision, 10, 12-13
　nonmedical status of circumcision, 156
　Philistines and, 68
　ritual circumcision, 7, 8, 9, 20, 155-163
　　in England, 162
　　folklore concerning, 9
　　in Israel, 163
　　U.S. problems with, 160-162
　　unsanitary conditions of, 158-160
　venereal disease rate of (1885), 18, 37, 80
John, Saint, 9
Johns Hopkins Medical Center, 92, 96, 99, 117, 174
Journal of the American Medical Society, 22-23, 25, 39, 46, 55, 57, 125, 136, 176
Journal of the Orificial Surgical Society, 39
Journal of Urology, 24

Kenya, 166, 167

Index

Keratinization, 115
Knesset, 163
Koran, The, 8

Laos, 68
London *Spectator*, 168
London Surgical Home, 172, 173

McCall's, 46
Major Medical (health insurance), 30
Malaysia, 8
Male circumcision procedures, 204–210
  direct surgery, 205
  presurgery preparations, 205
  squeeze techniques, 205–210
Male circumcision rates, estimated, in the U.S., 217
Malpractice, 152, 162
Man in Africa (Turnbull), 166
Mary, 9
Mary Magdalen, 9
Mastectomy, 77
Masturbation, 2, 13, 14, 32–33, 49–50, 122–126
  clitoridectomy and, 171–172
  false claims about circumcision and, 122–123, 125–126
  female, 74–75
  female circumcision and, 175–177
  guilt feelings arising from, 124, 126
  history of, 123–124
  illnesses attributed to, 36, 37, 124
  Jews and, 123
  medical profession's changing attitude toward, 123–126
  medical treatments to prevent, 36, 37–38, 125
  Victorian attitude toward, 37, 40
Maternity Nursing, 136
Mayans, 7, 8
Meatal stenosis, 55
Meatitis, 55
Meatus (urinary opening), 55, 63, 85, 98, 151, 152, 178
Medicaid, 30

Medical Aspects of Human Sexuality, 184
Medical profession (U.S.)
  bias of professional literature about circumcision, 16–25
  changing attitude toward masturbation, 123–126
  controversy over neonatal circumcision, 3, 16–25
  dilemma between theory and practice of circumcision, 5
  early acceptance of operation as "cure" for variety of ailments, 2, 14, 17
  health reasons given for operation, 2–3, 44, 79
  influence of Jewish immigration on, 36–37
  mystique surrounding circumcision, 15–16
  need to encourage health education, 79
  in 19th century, 32–33, 36–39
  present-day doubts about validity of operation, 3, 23–24
  prevailing views about foreskin, 53, 54, 64–65
  reasons opposing circumcision, 44
  sexist attitude of, 75–77, 79, 173–175
  unnecessary surgery charges against, 22, 39, 133–134
Medical risks, 145–153
  absence of hospital reports of operation, 146
  complications, 147, 150–151
  deaths from, 148–149
  electrocautery danger, 152
  hemorrhage, 149
  infant selection errors, 152
  infections, 147, 149
  lack of medical information about circumcision, 145, 148, 153
  lack of well-trained personnel performing operation, 147–148
  loss of penile skin, 150
  mutilation, 152
  problems in later life, 163

Medical Society of London, 172, 173
Memorial Hospital for Cancer and Allied Diseases, 109
Mental disorders, 37
Messisa, 158, 159
Metropolitan Free Hospital (London), 13
Metropolitan Hospital (New York City), 80
Mikvah, 73, 92
Milah, 158, 162
Milah Board, 159, 161
Modern Family Health Guide, The, 125
Mohammed, 8
Mohel, the, 147, 157–163
Moneysworth, 46
Moses, 156, 157
Moslems, 7, 8, 68, 74, 94, 169
Mothers' Medical Encyclopedia, The, 135
Mutilations to the body, 3

National Cancer Registry, 102
National Center for Health Statistics, 128–130
National Conference on Urologic Cancer (1973), 110–111
Natural childbirth, 142
Netherlands, 100, 101
New England Journal of Medicine, The, 21
New Guinea, 8
New Orleans Medical and Surgical Journal, The, 34, 36
New York City Department of Health, 161
New York Times, 16, 46, 47, 66, 71, 72, 82, 85, 147, 152, 168, 169, 193, 195
New Zealand, 27–28
Newborns
 anesthesia and, 138–139
 psychological trauma of circumcision, 141–142
 studies of gender behavioral differences in, 143–144
Newsweek, 20–21, 45, 81, 162, 216
Nigeria, 169
Non Rapid Eye Movement (NREM), 143

Norway, 31–32, 86, 95, 106, 107, 128
 circumcision rate in, 127
 penile cancer in, 107–108
Nursing Care, 89

Obstetrical Society of London, 172
Oceania, 7
"$100 Surgery for a Million Dollar Sex Life," 183
Oophorectomy, 174
Oral hygiene, 73, 78
"Orgasm, Anatomy of the Female" (Masters and Johnson), 56
Orgasms, 32, 57–58
 clitoris and, 179–182
Orificial Surgical Society, 38–39, 176
Orthodox Jews, ritual circumcision and, 159, 160
Othello (Shakespeare), 10
Our Bodies Ourselves, 50

Pain of circumcision, 135–144
Pakistan, 68
Pap Test, 19–20, 99
Paraphimosis, 128, 132
Parents' Magazine, 44, 45, 81
Paresis, 36
Paris Match, 168
Parsis, 74, 94
Paul, 8
Pediatric Urologist Association, 3, 24, 114
Pediatrics, 46, 163, 218
Penile blood, 7
Penile cancer, 24, 44, 45, 67, 90, 104–114
 age and, 104, 112
 deaths from (1978), 148
 Jews and, 108
 in Norway, 107–108
 prevalency in poor countries, 113–114
 problems of, 114
 rate of (1977), 105, 106
 in Third World, 111–112
 in U.S., 106, 107, 114
Penile hygiene, 2, 67–79
 adult male circumcision and, 134

alleged advantages of circumcision and, 67
coitus and, 76
as an educational problem, 77–78
matter of social and economic status, 69–70
role of mothers in practicing, 75–76
uncircumcised males and, 67–68, 77
Penile identification, 48–49
"Penile Plunder," 29
Penile size, 11–12
Penile strangulation, 55
Penile structures, 198–204
Penis tourniquet syndrome, 55
People's Republic of China, 95, 111, 112
Periah, 158
Phallic worship, 10
Pharaonic circumcision, *see* Infibulation
Pheremones, 60
Philistines, 10, 68
Philo of Alexandria, 154
Phimosis, *see* Tight foreskin
Plastic bell, 207, 209
Plastic surgery, 60, 151, 152
Playgirl, 183
Practice of Circumcision, The: A Reevaluation (Foley), 18–19
Pregnancy and Birth (Guttmacher), 125
Premature ejaculation, 57, 67, 115–121
alleged effects of circumcision on, 115–116, 118–119
causes of, 117–118
conflicting theses concerning, 116–117, 118
as an emotional problem, 120–121
as major sexual dysfunction in U.S. males, 120–121
sex researchers on, 117
Preputial dilation, 64
Preputial opening, 62
Preventing V.D. and Cancer by Circumcision (Ravich), 19–20, 85
Preventive medicine, 71
Proceedings of the National Conference on Urologic Cancer, 112
Prophylactic circumcision, 62

Prostatic cancer, 67, 90, 100–104
circumcision and, 100–104
death rate from (1972–1973), 100
Jews and, 102, 103
rate of (1977), 105
in U.S., 100–101
Psychiatric Dictionary, 124
Psychological aspects of circumcision, 135–144
contradictory views of medical profession, 135–139
effects on future life, 142–143
as stress factor, 143, 144
trauma of remembered pain, 137–138, 141, 142
Ptolemy, 9
Pure Food and Drug Act (1906), 36
Pythagorus, 8

Radioisotopes, 58
"Rape of the Phallus, The" (Morgan), 23
Readers Guide to Periodical Literature, 44
Reform Jews, ritual circumcision and, 159
"Ritual of Circumcision, The" (Paige), 25
"Ritualistic Surgery: Circumcision and Tonsillectomy" (Bolande), 21
Rochester School of Medicine, 194
Roman Catholic Manual for Confessors, 174
Rome, ancient, 68
"Routine Circumcision," 22–23
Royal College of Surgeons, 172

Scandinavian countries, 31–32
opposition to circumcision, 57
See also Denmark; Finland; Norway; Sweden
Science Newsletter, 45–46, 112
Scientific American, 46, 112
Scotland, 32
Scrotal cancer, 88
Search for the Perfect Orgasm, The (Lawrence), 178

Sexist attitude of U.S. medical profession, 75–77, 79, 173–175
Sexual Behavior in the 1970's (Hunt), 178
Sexual overindulgence, 35–36
Sexual Variance in Society and History (Bullough), 35
Sexuality, improved, 2, 13, 14
Skopts, 7
Sloane Hospital, 69, 146
Smegma, 55, 67, 72, 80, 176
    cancer and, 89–90, 91, 95, 96–99, 105, 106, 108, 113
    carcinogenic study of, 96–98
    female, 90
    foreskin and, 59, 60, 64
Somalia, 166, 168
South America, 8, 68
Strabo, 8–9, 154
Subincision, 7
Surgeons to the Poor (Maynard), 38
Surgery, 170
Surgery of Love (Burt), 190
Surgery of Ritual Circumcision, The (Snowman), 158
Surgical Diseases of Women (Brown), 172
Sweden, 31, 95–96, 100, 101, 106, 107, 128
    genital cancer in, 110
Switzerland, 100, 101
Symbolic Wounds (Bettelheim), 192
Syphilis, 21, 81–87, 113
    new cases reported (1945–1977), 83

Taking Care of Your Children, 49
Tamils, 7
Thailand, 68, 101
Therapeutic circumcision, 62–66
Third World
    clitoral surgery in, 165–169
    penile cancer in, 111–112
Tight foreskin, 2, 62–66, 128, 132
Time, 45, 46, 93, 216
Timothy, 8
Today's Health, 85, 92
Toilet seat syndrome, 55

Tongue cancer, 20, 21
Tonsillectomy, 5, 134
Total body care, 78
"Traditional Practices Affecting the Health of Women," 169
Trepanning, 6–7
Turkey, 171

Uganda, 111
Uncircumcised males
    age 50 and over (1975), 238
    in U.S., 244–245
Union of Chassidic Rabbis of the United States and Canada, 157
Union of Soviet Socialist Republics, 95
United States
    adult male circumcision in, 131, 132
    attitudes toward body hygiene, 73–74
    body modifications practiced in, 6
    cervical cancer in, 95
    child health and care in, 30–31
    clitoral surgery in, 170
    clitoridectomy in, 173–175
    delayed newborn circumcision in, 130–131
    female circumcision in, 182–185
    health care in, 69–71
    health problems in, 71
    health reasons for circumcision, 2–3, 44
    introduction of circumcision in, 2, 13
    Jewish immigration (19th century), 36–37
    Jewish ritual circumcision problems in, 160–162
    lack of available unbiased literature about circumcision in, 4, 41–51
    male circumcision rates (estimated) in, 217
    masturbation, attitudes toward, 33–34, 74–75
    neonatal circumcisions performed in, 1, 4
    non–newborn circumcision in, 129
    penile cancer in, 106, 107, 114
    personal reasons for circumcision, 2
    postnewborn circumcision in, 128–129

poverty in, 71
premature ejaculation as major male sexual dysfunction in, 120–121
prostatic cancer in, 100–101
uncircumcised males in, 131, 244–245
Victorianism in, 34–35
widespread practice of nonreligious circumcision in, 26–27, 37
United States Army, 131
University of Michigan Medical Center, 24
Upper Volta, 169
Urinary tract infections (U.T.I.), 72
Uterine cancer, 91–92

Vaginal surgery, 190
Vasectomy, 123
Vassar, 140
Venereal disease, 2, 44, 45, 71, 80–87, 176
 alleged protection provided by circumcision, 81, 84
 blacks and, 81
 condoms and, 86
 female genitalia and, 87
 increase in, 81–83, 98
 Jews and, 18, 37, 80
 male genitalia and, 87
Victoria, Queen, 34
Victorianism, 34–35
Vietnam, 68
Village Voice, The, 192
Vulvectomy, 165

Washington Post, 195–196
Wasserman test, 84
West Germany, 77
"Whither the Foreskin?" (Preston), 46
"Why Circumcision?" (Burger and Guthrie), 103
Woman's Day, 46
Women
 cancer estimates for (1978), 92
 sexist attitude of U.S. medical profession toward, 75–77, 79, 173–175
Women's International Network (WIN) News, The, 166

World Health Organization (W.H.O.), 52, 88, 95, 164, 169, 185
World War II
 circumcision frequency of draftees in, 69
 total health status of draftees in, 70–71

X-rays, 113

Yale University, 140
Yemen, 163

Zipper injuries, 55

Author Index

Abel, Gene G., 180, 256
Adelson, E. R., 242
Aitken-Swan, J., 236, 237
Altman, Lawrence K., 235, 246, 252
Amstey, M. S., 234
Anderson, Susan Heller, 246
Annunziato, D., 253
Ansell, J. S., 109, 147, 148, 149, 152, 153, 216, 239, 244, 248, 249, 250, 261
Apfel, Harry, 161–162, 252
Apt, A., 101, 237

Baird, D., 236, 237
Barbach, Lonnie G., 180, 257
Barber, M. K., 86
Barker-Benfield, G. J., 255, 256
Barrett-Connor, Elizabeth, 235
Beard, George M., 35
Berman, Edgar, 248
Berman, Wilfred, 253
Bernal, J. F., 28, 143, 224, 230, 247, 260
Bettelheim, Bruno, 192, 259
Blau, Eleanor, 251
Blight, E. M., Jr., 117, 118, 241
Block, A. J., 36, 175

Bolande, Robert P., 21, 219, 222
Bonaparte, Marie, 177–178, 256
Botts, Emma R., 227
Brackbill, Yvonne, 28, 143–144, 224, 230, 247, 260
Braun, Gustav, 172
Brazelton, T. Berry, 138, 140–141, 142, 246, 247
Briffault, Robert, 8, 220
Briggs, Kenneth A., 245, 251
Brody, Jane E., 46, 47, 69, 72, 85, 223, 228, 231, 232, 234, 236, 237, 259
Brown, Isaac Baker, 172–173, 174
Brown, J. A. C., 247
Brozan, Nadine, 251
Bryk, Felix, 12, 186, 219, 220, 221, 258
Bullough, Vern L., 33, 35–36, 220, 225, 226, 242, 250
Burger, Robert, 30, 103–104, 108, 116, 224, 238, 239, 240, 249
Burkitt, Denis P., 113, 240
Burt, James C., 190, 259
Burton, Sir Richard, 11, 154, 172, 219, 255
Butler, Robert B., 256

275

Cairns, John, 112, 113, 240
Calnan, M., 231, 246
Campbell, A. G. M., 132, 150, 151, 153, 223, 227, 240, 245, 249, 250, 252
Campbell, Barbara, 225
Campbell, Meredith F., 223, 229, 235
Campbell, R. J., 242
Carbary, Lorraine J., 116, 135, 236, 240, 243, 246
Carpenter, G. G., 238
Carter, Nicholas, 221–222
Cartwright, Samuel, 34
Chapman, A. H., 258
Chateauneu, Roger, 254
Claiborne, Robert, 232
Clifford, M., 222
Cohen, Richard, 195–196, 260
Coleman, Lee, 225
Coleman, Marcia J., 181, 257
Colp, O. S., 230
Comfort, Alex, 60, 114, 230, 240
Cook, R., 185–186, 253, 258
Costain, T. E., 39, 226
Cox, C. D., 86
Crist, Takey, 184, 258
Cunningham, Nicholas, xv

Dagher, R., 24–25, 223, 233, 240
Darnton, John, 254
David, J. R., 117, 118, 241
Davis, Elizabeth Gould, 154, 250, 254
De Witt, Karen, 231
Dearborn, Lester W., 124–125, 242, 243
DeKernion, J. R., 110–111, 240
Demetrakopoulos, G. E., 238
Demick, Barbara, 190, 259
Denholtz, M. C., 241
Denton, John, 149, 249
Dionne, E. J., Jr., 249
Dodge, O. G., 231, 239
Douglas, J. W. B., 231, 246
Duffy, John, 225, 226, 255, 256

Duyn, John van, 249

Eaton, Cora Smith, 39, 226
Edson, M., 255
Edwards, Allen, 220
Eiger, Marvin S., 85, 92, 100, 101, 135, 146–147, 234, 236, 237, 245, 248
Eitzman, Donald V., 152, 250
Ellis, Junius, 233
Elon, Amos, 251
Elting, L. Melvin, 138, 178, 185, 246, 253, 256, 258
Ephron, Nora, 37, 226

Falkin, Stanley, 83
Falliers, C. J., 230
Farrell, Barry, 241
Feehan, Edward B., 193, 227, 259
Fiedler, Doris E., 75, 233
Fink, P. J., 118, 120, 241, 242
Fink, S., 118, 120, 241, 242
Fishbein, Morris, 125, 243
Fiumara, N. J., 235
Fleming, J. B., 255
Flock, M. H., 231
Foley, John M., 18, 76, 222, 233
Fordney-Settlage, Diane S., 256, 259
Forel, August, 220
Fortunoff, S., 255
Frand, M., 253
Franks, L. M., 102, 112, 237
Frazer, J. C., 220
Freud, Sigmund, 124, 168, 177, 192, 195, 219, 250
Friedenwald, Aaron, 252
Friedman, Morton, 119, 241
Fries, J. F., 228
Fuchs, Estelle, 257

Gadpaille, W. J., 232
Gairdner, Douglas, x, 28–29, 45, 53, 63–64, 65, 66, 78, 229, 230, 233, 260
Ganelin, R. S., 21–22, 223

Index

Gardocki, Gloria, 257
Garvin, C. H., 85, 216, 233, 234, 260, 261
Gee, W. F., 109, 147, 148, 149, 152, 153, 216, 239, 244, 248, 249, 250, 261
Gelb, Barbara, 255
Gelles, Richard J., 225
Gellis, Syndey S., 148, 196, 249, 260
Gilmore, Michael, 140
Glaser, William, 161
Glasner, Rabbi Samuel, 117, 234, 241, 242
Glenn, James F., 241
Goldblum, L. M., 253
Goldstein, H., 231, 246
Goodwin, Willard E., 223
Gould, Richard A., 219, 220
Gould, Robert E., 126, 243
Graber, B., 258
Graber, G. M., 258
Graham, Saxon, 94, 227, 236
Graham, Sylvester, 33, 35, 225
Gray, L. H., 220
Green, R. L., 234
Greenberg, Daniel S., 259
Greenblatt, R. B., 257
Greensher, J., 55, 229, 233
Gregory, Dick, 117
Grey, Mary Jane, 180, 256, 257
Grimes, David A., 113, 128, 137, 147, 151, 191, 193, 194, 216, 240, 243, 246, 248, 250, 259, 261
Gross, Robert, 255
Gunther, John, 166, 168, 253, 254
Guthrie, Thomas H., 30, 108, 116, 130, 224, 238, 239, 240, 249
Guttmacher, Alan F., 44–45, 81, 125, 148, 176, 216, 227, 231, 234, 243, 249, 256, 261

Haire, Doris, xix
Halban, Joseph, 178

Hall, G. Stanley, 39
Hall, L., 254
Hand, Eugene A., 20–21, 69, 81, 158, 220, 252
Harnes, Jack R., 223
Härö, A. S., 225, 243
Harvey, Isaac, 174–175, 232, 256
Hatcher, Robert A., 242
Hennessy, William J., 237
Hervada, A. R., 238
Hiatt, H. H., 194, 259
Hinsie, L. E., 242
Hite, Shere, 257
Hoke, A. W., 235
Holt, L. Emmet, Jr., 43, 123, 216, 227, 242, 261
Hosken, Fran P., 166, 167, 168, 171, 172, 177, 250, 253, 254, 255, 256
Hovsepian, Deron, 53, 108, 215, 216, 227, 229, 238, 260, 261
Howat, J. M., 136, 246
Howell, Mary, 43–44
Huffman, John W., 184, 258
Hunt, Morton, 178, 256
Hutchinson, Jonathan, 80
Hyamson, Rabbi Moses, 161

Illingworth, R. S., 53, 136, 223, 224, 229, 246, 249
Isaac, Erich, 155, 157, 250, 251, 252
Isenberg, S., 136, 178, 185, 246, 253, 256, 258

Jackman, Lawrence S., 184, 258
Jacobi, Abraham, 36
Jakobovitz, Immanuel, 157
Jensen, Gordon D., 124, 242
Jisr, J. G., 255
Johnson, Robert L., 235
Johnson, Virginia, 13, 52, 56–57, 59, 117, 119, 216, 221, 228, 229, 230, 241, 250, 261
Jonas, David, 118, 241, 260

Jonas, Doris, 118, 241, 260
Jones, Joseph, 33

Kampmeier, R. H., 235
Kaplan, George W., xiv-xv, 16, 23, 55, 66, 112, 221, 223, 227, 229, 231, 235, 237, 238, 240
Kaplan, Helen S., 115, 117, 118, 240
Kapuciunas, Andrew, 228
Kariher, Donald, 216, 260, 261
Katchandourian, H. A., 231
Katz, Joseph, 136, 246, 249
Kaviti, J. N., 231
Kellison, Cathrine, 258
Kellogg, Harvey, 33-34, 35
Kelly, Howard, 174
Kennedy, Edward, 223
Kennedy, M. S., 233, 243
Kenyatta, Jomo, 166, 167, 253
Kern, Stephen, 226, 255
Keynes, Richard D., 230
King, L., 131, 149, 233, 241, 243, 245, 246, 249
King, Wayne, 232
Kinsey, Alfred C., 117, 119, 120, 241
Kirkland, Valdemar, 31, 225
Kirkpatric, Barry V., 152, 250
Kirya, C., 136-137, 246
Kistler, S. L., 226, 256
Klauber, George T., 27, 216, 226, 261
Knaus, William A., 98, 237
Knoepfler, P. T., 240
Kohn-Speyer, Alice C., 237
Krantz, Kermit, 229, 256
Kreider, M. K., 39, 226
Kroop, Merle Sondra, 181, 257
Kurovilla, J. I., 239
Kyalwazi, S. K., 239

Lackey, J. T., 250
Laing, R. D., 138
Lake, Alice, 228
Landesburg, M., 36
Langley, Michael, 254
Lansky, M. R., 118, 241
Lantier, Jacques, 254

Lapides, J., 24-25, 223, 233, 240
LaPlace, John, 228
LaRocque, Michael L., 229, 241
Latimer, J. K., 255
Lawrence, Jodi, 178, 256, 257, 258
Leach, Penelope, 137, 246
Leaf, Alexander, 232
LeBoyer, Frederick, 142, 247
Lefkovits, Albert M., 239, 240
Leiter, Elliot, 239, 240
Lenowitz, H., 240
Levine, Milton I., 231
Levine, Seymour, 247
Levitt, S. B., 147, 151, 248, 249, 250
Lewis, Joseph, 18, 222
Lewis, Myrna I., 256
Licklider, Samuel, 109, 110, 239
Lilienfeld, Abraham M., 94, 99, 227, 236
Linde, Shirley Mitter, 228
Little, J. A., 223
Lobitz, W. Charles, 229
Lochner, Jon C., 234
Loeb, Edwin M., 231
Lowry, Thomas P., 180, 257
Lunde, Donald T., 231
Lyons, Richard D., 223

McCary, J. L., 242
McGuire, Thomas, 232
MacKay, William 249
MacLaine, Shirley, 168, 254
McMillen, S. I., 91, 98-99, 157, 236, 237, 252
Maimonides, Moses, 58, 59, 155, 160, 251
Majno, Guido, 252
Malinowski, Bronislav, 166
Marcotte, D. B., 243
Markessinis, Joan, 247
Marshall, Victor F., 109, 239
Martin, Daniel S., 232
Masters, R. E. L., 220
Masters, William H., 13, 52, 56-57, 59, 117, 119, 216, 221, 228, 229, 230, 241, 250, 261

Index

Maynard, Aubre de L., xi, 38, 226
Mello, A. de Silva, 12
Merzbach, Charles, 157
Meyer, Jon, 117
Miller, Joseph, 156–157
Miller, R. L., 146
Mofenson, Howard C., 55, 229, 233
Money, John, 250
Montague, Ashley, 219
Morgan, W. K. C., 23, 223, 224
Morris, Desmond, 26, 216, 224, 261
Morris, R., 233, 241, 243, 245, 246, 249
Moss, John, 193
Muramoto, Nabors, 240
Murphy, P. I., 232
Murphy, R. C., 232
Mustard, John K., 235

Nelson, J. H., 43, 227
Nelson, Vaughn, and McCay, 223
Norsigian, Judy, xix
Now, Herbert, 222

O'Connor, Vincent J., 237, 238
Osborne, B. M., 233
Oster, Gerald, 219
Øster, Jacob, x, 64–65, 66, 78, 230, 233, 243
Oswald, Peter F., 138, 141, 246, 247
Oziel, L. Jerome, 241

Paige, Karen E., 25, 123, 146, 153, 185, 196, 216, 224, 235, 242, 248, 258, 260, 261
Panter, Gideon G., 228
Pariser, H., 234
Patel, Hawa, 28, 29, 42, 75, 150–151, 216, 224, 227, 231, 233, 250, 260, 261
Pearson, H., 233, 241, 243, 245, 246, 249
Peltzman, Philip, 138, 141, 246, 247
Perlmutter, Johanna F., 184, 258
Persky, Lester, 59, 85, 86, 216, 222, 223, 226, 230, 233, 234, 235, 241, 260, 261

Philip, A. G. S., 238
Pietropinto, Anthony, 241, 254
Planck, Max, 195
Plaut, Alfred, 237
Pomerantz, Virginia E., 228, 245
Pontell, R. H., 228
Pott, Percival, 88
Pratt, E. H., 38
Preston, Caroline, 181, 257
Preston, E. Noel, 23, 46, 47, 69, 78, 101, 114, 151, 223, 226, 228, 231, 233, 237, 240, 250
Purpura, Dominick P., 139

Rafferty, Keen A., Jr., 237
Rathmann, W. G., 186–187, 212, 258, 260
Ravich, Abraham, 19–20, 85, 92, 98, 104, 157, 220, 222, 234, 236, 237, 238, 252
Reeder, Sharon, 246
Reevy, William R., 242
Remondino, Peter Charles, 13, 17–18, 53–54, 75, 122–123, 158, 220, 221, 222, 229, 233, 242, 251, 252, 255
Rensberger, Boyce, 221, 223, 248
Reston, James, 260
Reuben, David, 85, 93, 115–116, 177, 181, 234, 236, 240, 256
Richards, Catherine V., 225
Richards, M. P. M., 28, 143, 224, 230, 247, 260
Riis, Dag, 31–32, 225, 243
Risa, N. B., 12
Robertson, William, 57, 223, 227, 230, 259
Rodin, P., 235
Rosner, Fred, 103, 126, 145–146, 148, 153, 238, 243, 248
Rothenberg, Robert E., 257
Rubenstein, M. M., 249
Rush, Benjamin, 32–33, 225
Russel, Charles P., 160–161
Russell, Bertrand, 195
Rutherford, F. W., 135

Sachs, Bernard, 37
Sagan, Carl, 113, 240
Salzman, L., 242
Saward, Ernest W., 194
Schlosberg, Charles, 66, 135, 231
Schmeck, Harold M., Jr., 232, 234, 235, 236
Schneidman, Barbara, 180, 257
Schreck, R., 240
Schultz, Dodi, 245
Schwark, T. E., 216, 261
Schwartz, June V., 227
Seaman, Barbara, 46, 138, 227, 228, 246
Sebastian, James A., 237
Secondi, John J., 85, 234
Seligman, Fred, 180, 257
Seligmann, Jean H., 231
Selzer, M. L., 24–25, 223, 233, 240
Semmelweis, Ignaz Philipp, 195
Semmens, F. Jane, 258
Semmens, James P., 258
Shakespeare, William, 10
Sharpe, Lawrence, 241, 257
Shaw, Robert A., 223, 227, 259
Shepard, Martin, 184, 258
Shepherd, Gordon M., 230
Sherfey, Mary Jane, 195, 229, 260
Sherman, Charles C., 221
Shiller, Jack G., 233
Shiller, T. G., 79
Ship, A. G., 147, 151
Shultz, Dodi, 228
Silvert, Mark A., 103, 238
Simenauer, Jacqueline, 241, 254
Sims, J. Marion, 174
Smith, Bernard H., 229, 241
Smith, R. B., 147, 151
Smith, Hedrick, 251
Smith, Lendon, 192, 259
Snowman, Leonard V., 158, 219, 220, 250, 251, 252
Snyder, D. C., 146
Speert, H., 58–59, 60, 69, 108, 146, 148, 160, 161, 230, 231, 239, 248, 252

Spence, Sir James, xv
Spitz, René, 37–38, 123, 138, 226, 242, 255, 256
Spock, Benjamin, 24, 47–48, 75, 125, 223, 228, 233, 243
Steinberger, Emil, 242
Stekel, Wilhelm, 124
Stern, Menahem, 250
Stoll, Otto, 219
Stone, L. Joseph, 140
Storer, Horatio, 174
Strax, Philip, 236
Subak-Sharpe, Gennell, 234
Sugarman, Muriel, 144, 248
Sullivan, Ronald, 251
Sutor, Jacobus, 10–11, 220
Swenson, O., 223, 239

Takla, Laila, 170
Talbert, Luther M., 248
Taylor, P. K., 235
Terris, M., 43, 94–95, 227, 236
Thomas, A. J., 55, 229
Topp, Sylvia, 192–193, 259
Toussieng, P. W., 257
Tucker, Patricia, 250
Turnbull, Colin, 166, 253

Ubell, Earl, 82, 234

Valentine, Robert (pseudonym), 118–119, 222, 229, 230, 233, 241
Valinoti, Joseph R., 235
Verkauf, B. S., 257
Vermooten, Vincent, 85
Verzin, J. A., 253
Vickey, D. M., 228
Vinocur, John, 233

Wabrek, A. J., 225, 256
Wabrek, C. J., 225, 256
Wald, George, 137, 246
Walden, William D., 258
Wall, Roscoe L., Jr., 27, 126, 146–147, 148, 224, 243, 248, 249, 260

Index

Wallace, Mike, 248
Walls, C. B., 39, 226
Warr, William S., 249
Weiss, Charles, 28, 136, 156, 162,
　　224, 246, 251, 252, 253
Wendel, R. G., 235
Werthmann, M. W., 136–137, 246
Whorton, Gloria, 125, 233, 243
Wiesner, P. J., 234
Wilcox, Herbert, xiv
Wilkes, Edward T., 135, 227, 246
Williams, L. P., 216, 261
Williams, Roger J., 182, 257
Wilson, F., 43, 227
Wirth, John L., 216, 224, 245, 261
Wise, Thomas N., 240
Witte, John J., 225
Wolbarst, A. L., 108, 238
Wollman, Leo, 186, 188–189, 257
Wooten, James T., 232
Wright, J. E., 53, 227, 229
Wynder, E. L., 93–94, 236

Young, Alexander, W., Jr., 234
Young, Wayland, 11–12, 174, 221,
　　256
Yunker, Barbara, 228

DATE DUE